AF334367

Values of the University in a Time of Uncertainty

Paul Gibbs • Jill Jameson • Alex Elwick
Editors

Values of the University in a Time of Uncertainty

 Springer

Editors
Paul Gibbs
CERS, Middlesex University
London, UK

Jill Jameson
University of Greenwich
London, UK

Alex Elwick
CERS, Middlesex University
London, UK

ISBN 978-3-030-15969-6   ISBN 978-3-030-15970-2   (eBook)
https://doi.org/10.1007/978-3-030-15970-2

This Springer imprint is published by the registered company Springer Nature Switzerland AG.
The registered company address is: Gewerbestrasse 11, 6330 Cham, Switzerland

To Leo, Zoe, Maggie and Sonny, hoping your values fit you well, Grandpa
For Phyllis, Peter, Celia, Kevin and Imogen, with all my love, from Jill
For Catriona, from Alex

Foreword

The essays in this collection originated from a symposium held at Oxford's New College in the autumn of 2017. Dr Paul Gibbs, sponsor and organiser of the symposium, made a call for papers to a preselected panel of colleagues and concordant-minded academics on the subject of "values in higher education" positing the question "what do we value in higher education and what values should those in higher education have about their work?", the overarching theme of the symposium being "the nature of grace". In addition to the mixture of globally renowned academic authors on the subject matter, there were also a few nonacademic individuals whose professional and personal praxis reflected an interest and understanding of the subject matter "in thought and action". I was one of those fortunate professionals, who also happened to be a doctoral candidate in the Professional Doctorate (DProf) programme at Middlesex University.

I feel obliged, in introducing these works, to speak incidentally of myself and how I came to have the undeserved honour of introducing this collection to the world. Undeserved in that I am without the usual acclaim (I have none) that frequently accompanies the writer of a Foreword of such a prodigious and prestigious author's work. I have been given an honour that I do not deserve by an unobligated giver. That makes the gift an act of grace. An act of grace has very little to do with the receiver and everything to do with the giver. "The cause of grace dwells outside man, but its condition is within him".[1]

> Grace is irrational in the sense that it has nothing to do with weights and measures. It has nothing to do with intrinsic qualities or so-called 'gifts' (whatever they may be.) It reflects a decision on the part of the giver…in relation to the receiver…that negates any qualifications the receiver may personally hold. Grace is one way love.[2]

Grace is a platonic love. Platonic love here is not meant as it is perceived in the world today, a romantic love, but a love born of wisdom where "the beauty of people's souls is more valuable than the beauty of their bodies, so that if someone is

---

[1] Weil, S. (1997). *Gravity and grace*. Lincoln, Neb.: University of Nebraska Press.

[2] Zahl, P. (2007) p. 36. *Grace in practice*. Grand Rapids, Mich.: William B. Eerdmans Pub.

decent in his soul…he will be forced to gaze at the beauty of activities and laws… and gives birth to many gloriously beautiful ideas…in unstinting love of wisdom".[3] Platonic love proceeds from the soul and "gives birth" to what is "fitting for a soul to bear and bring to birth…wisdom and the rest of virtue".[4] Grace, the mother of virtues that gives birth to love, compassion, mercy, empathy and kindness, is wise love in action. The original meaning of the word "philosophy" comes from the Greek roots "philo-" meaning "loving" and "-sophia" meaning "wisdom".

Plato places wisdom as the lead virtue: then all the rest follow. Thomas Aquinas refers to wisdom as "the very act of reason", also placing it first among four cardinal virtues, with justice, temperance and fortitude following.[5] These cardinal virtues are also referred to as intellectual virtues. A cardinal virtue "is the disposition of a perfect thing to that which is best…that which is disposed according to nature".[6] Grace (charity), faith and hope are divine virtues, those that are "above nature… distinct from that which is according to his nature".[7] Einstein refers to this disposition of divine virtues as a "cosmic religious experience…the strongest and the noblest driving force behind scientific research",[8] suggesting that science by its very nature implies a relationship to some particular good seeking the ultimate good, that of grace, grace (divine love) as the cosmological origin of the "noblest driving force". Aquinas puts grace in this same position hundreds of years before by naming it "the mother and the root of all virtues".[9] Only two of all of these virtues of the intellectual and divine are both a state of being and a way of being: grace and hope. The amalgamation of the preceding concepts of grace is that it justifies the soul and unites with it through love: the efficacy of the form of grace, intellectual or divine (grace being the "root", the "mother", of all virtues), depends on the power of the agent who instils it, gives it, and receives it. *There but for the grace of God, go I.* I have never heard "there but for the grace of man, go I". The concept of grace and its two different natures, that of humankind and that of the divine, is also witnessed as a metaphor in Simone Weil's *Gravity and Grace* (1952): "Gravity makes things come down…wings make them rise".[10] Grace is both the principal of and the principle of the movement of the forces that comprise "grace".

---

[3] Plato (1997) loc. 13009. *Plato - Complete Works*. Indianapolis: Hackett Publishing Company, Inc.

[4] Ibid.

[5] Aquinas, T. (2018) loc. 33596. *The Complete Works of St. Thomas Aquinas (ebook)*. umma Theologiae (1265–1274) Summa contra Gentiles (1259–1265) A Patristic Commentary on Matthew A Patristic Commentary on Mark A Patristic Commentary on Luke A Patristic Commentary on John. Omaha, Nebraska.

[6] Ibid, loc. 33781.

[7] Ibid.

[8] Einstein, A. (1930). *Religion and Science*. The New York Times Sunday. November 9,1930 p. 136. [Article] https://nyti.ms/2RByn3h.

[9] Aquinas, T. (2018) loc. 33846. *The Complete Works of St. Thomas Aquinas (ebook)*. umma Theologiae (1265–1274) Summa contra Gentiles (1259–1265) A Patristic Commentary on Matthew A Patristic Commentary on Mark A Patristic Commentary on Luke A Patristic Commentary on John. Omaha, Nebraska.

[10] Weil, S. (1997) p. 48. *Gravity and grace*. Lincoln, Neb.: University of Nebraska Press.

Today's world, including the world of universities, appears to suffer from the conflation of virtues and values: virtues as the "character" of individuals and values as the "character" of the university.

> There are people with the most extraordinary ability to transform everything into a business operation, whose whole life is a business operation, who fall in love and are married, hear a joke, and admire a work of art with the same business-like zeal with which they work at the office. (Kierkegaard, Either/Or, p. 289)

Thank you for making it this far into the musings of a neophyte, thank you for your grace. I will now leave you to wander through the following ideations of virtues and values, where the passions of the mind and heart are indistinguishable; where leadership blindly creates cultural values with the well-being of others nowhere in sight; where kindness prevails in both words and deeds; where justice is not disinterestedly cemented in artefacts but hopefully and carefully discerning, being neither distributive nor contributive but cooperative; where wisdom is embedded in humanity's collective memory, sharing itself reflectively across cultures through song, poetry, humour and story-telling; and where values are linguistic forms depicted as "things" or "promises" in mission statements with none of them being reducible to, or measurable as, a real obligation.

Enjoy the book.

Connie Klepper

Contents

Part I
Systems of Values

Chapter 1
Introduction

Paul Gibbs, Jill Jameson, and Alex Elwick

Abstract Higher education, and especially universities, is undergoing tremendous change. Many directly affect the lives of the academics and student whose presence defines the university. In this short introduction to the book we explore the context in which values in higher education are being questioned, defended and ignored. We then offer an outline of the content of the book.

Keywords Values · Higher education · Contributions · Truth · Common good · Private good

Values in and of Higher Education

What do we value in higher education and what values should those in higher education have about their work? When we first considered this issue our thoughts fell upon the ideas which might best be considered as moral values: values of compassion, tolerance, care and respect, integrity, truthfulness and prudence. These are transformative values which might bring about changes in a person's attitudes or positionality with respect to personal happiness and/or social justice. These values can be contrasted with 'performative values' which a colleague of ours, Professor Bruce Macfarlane, considers in the context of education to be those that can help to facilitate career success and/or economic growth for the benefit of a wider society. These two sets of values form a nexus for higher education: adding value to the host communities in which it contributes to infrastructure and economic worth (as well as to the earning potential of its students) in addition to bringing a tolerance and

---

P. Gibbs (✉) · A. Elwick
CERS, Middlesex University, London, UK
e-mail: p.gibbs@mdx.ac.uk; A.Elwick@mdx.ac.uk

J. Jameson
University of Greenwich, London, UK
e-mail: j.jameson@gre.ac.uk

P. Gibbs et al. (eds.), *Values of the University in a Time of Uncertainty*,
https://doi.org/10.1007/978-3-030-15970-2_1

respect through its community engagement with others outside the university. This helps, we hope, to enrich students' ways of being: to enable them to flourish and transform their being through the experience of higher education. In a very true sense it is hard to demarcate these two interactive notions of values which weave the tapestry of higher education institutions.

One of the consequences of the massive changes in contemporary higher education is the shift in the power relationship between teachers and students, due to the marketisation of higher education and the shift in role for institutions to reflect, rather than critically to comment upon, society. This has led to the assimilation of market values in universities' practices, away from a Socratic questioning as a pedagogy of critical reasoning and speaking out; but this is not new. The essence of Socrates' Apology to the Athenians can be seen to have resonance today if we take the liberty of substituting students and academics for the polis of Athens:

> [*Students and Academics*] from the city that is greatest and best reputed for wisdom and strength: are you not ashamed that you care for having as much money as possible, the reputation, and the honour, but that you neither care for not give thought to prudence, and truth, and how your soul will be the best possible? (Plato 29d [*italics* are our addition])

However, a lack of originality is no reason to accept self-serving and self-deceptive behaviours which excuse the academy and its members as manifestations of neo-liberal, politically motivated directives.

We must guard against deception and self-deception, both of which may be identified in the policy and practice of higher education. They can be seen in education's drift from being an end in itself towards an imperative of supply economics; or in the practice of scholars seeking favourable student evaluations rather than stretching their capabilities, fuelled by managerial performativity or NSS emotional labour and needing to stand out for their own careers by creating personal brands. Although such practices seem counter to principles of liberal, transformative education, they present a dilemma. Should we facilitate students and staff to speak the truth to each other when this might not be in their best interests in a world that encourages compliance rather than free thinking; a world where we are under constant surveillance and are often herded by industrial and commercial global powers? Without addressing such issues, any notion of an education as an authentic freedom to think and act becomes superficial, leaving scholars and students always boxed in a context of others. How, morally, should we prepare them to help them to flourish? What is at stake is much more important than economic satisfaction or the consumption of knowledge spat out in the form of first class honours degrees but the values that ought to sustain an institution worthy of public trust and how these values are manifest in the institutions' interaction with their community.

Values have been at the core of higher education whether they be those embedded in religious doctrine, professional practice or common decency. Higher education has been expected to provide an environment for study where knowledge creation can be undertaken in the assurance of non-interference. Clearly, this has not always been the case and nor is it now in a number of prominent regimes where truth, and the freedom to speak it to the powerful, is under threat as 'fake news'.

Among the most important of the values which have been articulated by a number of well-respected scholars such as Barnett (1990), is the pursuit of truth and objective knowledge. This underpins the specific values associated with higher education such as academic freedom, open discussion based on critical reasoning, institutional and personal autonomy and freedom of speech. Yet the contemporary public discourse about higher education has questioned these privileges, questioned if higher education institutions should be sites of free speech, respectful debate and the unfettered search for knowledge. It has done so with the blunt instrument of value for money assessed by the ignorant and propagated by those desiring control. We need to reassert basic academic values and set them in a moral context of care and tolerance, pushing back hard at the pervading values of individualism, consumerism and self-interest. This book tries to go some way towards that.

Truth is, and has been, at the heart of what universities do. They seek truth, teach truthfully and construct a community which enables all to flourish under a compassionate, sincere ethos – or at least a university which reflects the notion of Bildung does. Whether the same applies to neoliberal concepts of the university, concerned with measurement and metrics and condensed in terms of time and space, is a matter which can be contested.

Although broadly still relevant in the contemporary era, the stability implied by Foucault's regimes of truth have become susceptible to change as post-modernism and relativism become the intellectual rhizomatic stems lurking in the background of a post-truth era. The dynamics between apparatus and discourse that now form these regimes of truth have shifted and it could be argued that contemporary forms of truth are wider than Foucault recognised, their relations to power more various, and their historicity more complex. Indeed, the regimes of post-truth are a confluence of cultural production, journalism, political communication, speed and affect, plus marketing and algorithms of big data.

Fuelled by the press, social media and political cynicism, we have the risk of imminent nihilistic conflagrations but don't have time to dampen them with the extinguishers of rationality, for it is the moment that counts and rebuttal in the form of an assembled evidence base simply takes too long. So, alongside these new regimes of truth is an acceptance that there is no way to ultimately verify truth and this fans the flames of these fires with vigorous counterclaiming and discrediting and, importantly, belief in their own arbiters of what is worthy. However, as Giroux suggests, informed citizens are critical for democracy and "the university must play a vital role in creating the formative cultures that make such citizens possible" (2014: 210).

Much has been written about the common or public good of higher education, and we do not want to rehearse the arguments here or comment on the shifts in focus that have occurred in educational policy, as this has been done well by others (see Jonathan 1997; Nixon 2012; Marginson 2011; Williams 2016). Each of these authors develops the idea that there has been a shift from a good that has distinctive values intended for the society in which the institutions of higher education are located, to that which is focused on the personal and private gain of the individual. But we need to assert that higher education in and of itself should be a good, it should facilitate flourishing and in doing so it has to embrace values which are wider than the intrinsic. Certainly, truth is central to the ideal of a university but so are other values such as integrity and respect, along with values of compassion, love, tolerance, freedom and duty. Practise of these values may lead to significant challenge to the personal values of paying customers. Should we be concerned if they reject these values that have previously guided an individual's actions? This can lead to moments, or perhaps longer periods, of frailty as an individual either adapts or finds appropriate compromises. In this sense Weil's (1953) essay 'On the needs of the Soul' provides a grounding, for it declares that obligations come before rights which are then subordinate and relative to the former. Surely this is correct in institutions where (not exclusively) young people offer up their vulnerability to a new future and academics risk ridicule by expressing new ideas which are in the process of formation?

Such an approach moves towards acting ethically toward each other but also has implications or obligations for the promotion of a process of higher education which propagates the values that it upholds. This becomes trickier. There is a clear moral issue in itself as to whether students sign up to be taught how to behave beyond the formalities of collaboration within the policies of the university; should universities assume such moral responsibilities? Should the university be the place where one is taught how to behave towards others as well as oneself? Should passing on the values of the university be a goal for the pedagogical practice and the curriculum design of the university? Should students sign up to and participate in the spirit/spirituality of the university as well as in the space to learn and teach? (Indeed, certain faith-based universities would say 'yes' and address their response to students in ways that reflect that position). The same applies to faculty and staff: how does morality of the institution coalesce with the faculty beyond their academic duties? Why should they care, show compassion and be sincere? How should we expect staff to respond when the performative values conflict with the transformative values? Should we provide tuition in value judgment making? Should we expect only 'good' people to be teachers? These issues are implicit in considering the role of moral values in and of the universities.

This deliberately wide-ranging book addresses issues related to trust, compassion, well-being, grace, dignity and integrity. The book explores these within the context of higher education, giving existential and empirical accounts of how these moral duties can be expressed within the academy and why they ought to be. The chapters range from values used in the marketing of institutions to their realisation in therapeutic and teacher training spaces. The book encompasses a wide range of issues from multi-disciplinary and geo-political regions. Our authors are a mixture of world-leading authorities on values in higher education and earlier career researchers, who are nonetheless equally passionate contributors.

The neoliberal context woven into the post-truth media has placed the self-interested economic purpose at the fore and with it the personal good of education rather than the moral common good that universities can and do provide. This collection of chapters takes a different view. The revelation of the worthiness of moral values in higher education alongside value for money is clear from the collection and offers an interesting context for the creation of an obligations-led university of the future at a time when spurious 'rights' claims seem to dominate the agendas for higher education.

How the Book Works

The contributions here are the development of many of the papers which were presented at a symposium at New College, Oxford and hosted by the editors and David Palfreyman, OBE. The papers developed into chapters over a year-long period and form distinctive approaches to the study of moral values in higher education. The book explores the question of values of and within higher education from a number of different perspectives across the UK and internationally, including theoretical and practical approaches, evidenced by reflective engagement with differing conceptual and cultural understandings of values and of meaning-making, as well as prior literature and empirical findings. The four sections into which they are grouped are: Systems of Values; the University as a Values Organisation; Caring for Others; and Making a Difference.

In the first section we briefly talk of systems of values, of virtues, and duties and how they apply in higher education. In the second section we consider how the organisation of the institution of the university might be conceived in terms of values, in the third we look at specific forms of values and how they might manifest themselves and in the final section we look at the practical implications of some of these moral values in the structure and practice of higher education. The book is designed to be read either in its entirety, as chapters, or sections – each has its own internal integrity.

In the First Section the two chapters lay the philosophical groundwork for what follows in terms of the book's discussion around values in higher education institutions in the UK and globally.

David Scott's opening chapter, Chap. 2, takes the concept of virtue ethics and applies this to the university, to questions of how we learn and to the divergence between different forms of knowledge (knowing-that and knowing-how). He explores virtue ethics as different from deontological and consequentialist ethical forms. They are related to dispositions. Dispositions, as inner states, precede, condition and have some influence over actions. A disposition is a character type, an habituation, a state of preparation or readiness and a tendency to act in a specified way. Two further issues are relevant to his conception of virtue ethics: notions of causality and free will. The deontological perspective is taken.

Paul Gibbs, in Chap. 3, draws on Simon Weil's belief in human goodness to investigate the tension between rights and obligations within higher education that he argues arose from the 1948 Declaration of Human Rights. Since a policy-driven discourse of rights dominates student engagement, the benefit of higher education shifts from being a public good to a private good, a right rather than an obligation.

Putting duties before rights, Gibbs critiques the one-way overemphasis on, and enactment of, rights within higher education that has insufficiently recognised the importance of duties, given that higher education is neither a right nor an obligation on humanity in general to provide. He proposes that, as a core duty of their role as truth-tellers, 'good' higher education institutions need to be trustworthy, accurate and sincere in that truthfulness, exposing deceit and confronting obscurity. Academics have a responsibility of trustworthy care in practising their transcendent moral duty to help students make authentic, personal decisions that prepare them to take up a significant, worthy place in the world.

The Second Section considers the way in which the institutions of higher education can embed their use of moral value in their vision of how they ought to work both internally and with the externalities of their publics.

Ronald Barnett's chapter, Chap. 4, advocates a re-valuing of the university and of higher education, noting that the reluctance to discuss 'values' in higher education may arise from instrumentalist imperatives drawing universities into the value framework of economic and market rationality and state managerialism. Values pessimism therefore avoids unworldly academic sentimentality that yearns for an earlier – if imagined – age, while still enabling debate around the term 'value' and the wider notion of 'public good' in recognising that higher education offers valuable ends beyond itself. Barnett argues for an ecological approach to the revaluing of higher education that repositions its value in relation to its interconnectedness with the major ecosystems of the world. He reminds us of the responsibilities of universities within these ecosystems to help restore impairments in which it has been involved, even if unwittingly. He highlights the role and value of the university as an ecosystem itself in a fluid set of relationships that reach out to global ecosystems of knowledge, social institutions, the economy, learning, persons, culture and the natural environment.

In Chap. 5, Alex Elwick looks at universities' own promotion of their values as a starting point, through the value statements advertised on university websites and in their prospectuses and promotional material. Based upon an empirical study of English universities the chapter proposes explanations as to why the trend has developed and what function these statements serve. Overarching themes which are evident across the corpus of value statements suggest that there are similarities between universities' positions; while other patterns can also be identified amongst groupings of institution-type. As well as exploring which values are most common across UK institutions and touching upon key institutional differences, the chapter asks what role such explicit value statements play in the sector.

In Chap. 6, Kate Maguire discusses the nature of relationality and its relationship with these values it proclaims in higher education, observing the interconnectedness of positive relationality with the 'shadow' side or *skia* of dissonance and pain within organisations in higher education. She uses the concept of relationality to capture multi-layered aspects of interconnectedness and complexity. Informed by clinical practice with survivors of extreme experiences, Maguire explores human relations between self, others and the world in higher education, what we talk about and with whom; what we hide or silence. She discusses the ways in which pain occurs and is silenced in unseen ways at many levels, providing a detailed case study of a patient from NHS clinical practice. Both pain and people are 'disappeared' when trust is eroded in organisations in which authority dynamics suppress and exploit employees. There is a need therefore to be conscious of the skia, the shadow sides of organisational cultures, to recognise and heal the dynamics of pain, in order to create healthy values-infused environments in higher education.

The theme of institutional leadership is featured in Ian McNay's Chap. 7. He considers the effect of institutional and sector-wide values on university academics and staff, as well as the community stoicism evident amongst university staff, including 'a role as critic and conscience of society'. He contends that universities in the UK, at corporate and senior manager level, have lost the moral high ground necessary to fulfil such a role. The Code of Practice of the Committee of University Chairs (of governors) sets the Nolan Principles of conduct in public life as a benchmark for recognised standards of good practice, but states that members must act in line with the accepted standards of behaviour in public life. McNay's chapter provides something of a counterpoint to Elwick's discussion in Chap. 4 by contrasting the words of institutions with the sector's portrayal in the media. The chapter combines an authoritative presentation of the historical development of values in UK higher education with a critique of their current status.

Some of the themes identified by McNay finds a new reading in the work of Simon Robinson who focuses in Chap. 8 on integrity in higher education, including governance and institutional identity, to examine recent debates about the meaning of integrity, both personal and organisational. He links integrity to identity and the interconnected meanings of responsibility, involving: critical agency which acknowledges and engages a plural identity (focused in narrative); accountability which engages the narratives of others (focused in dialogue which enable mutual support and challenge); and positive responsibility (focusing on creative practice and shared responsibility rather than negative blaming). In considering how this concept of integrity applies to the university and to its governance, he reflects on the importance of clarity about purpose and worth, and of engaging dialogue inside and outside the institution to develop identities. He reminds us that integrity is focused in responsibility, so that the key signs of good governance then become: narrative, dialogue and the ongoing negotiation of responsibility in practice; the practice of associated virtues, intellectual, moral and psychological; as well as integrated thinking and communication. Robinson offers a vision of the university which is primarily about the quality of thinking and the quality of relationships inside and outside the university.

The next chapter by Sabina Siebert, Chap. 9, focuses on students and the impact on students of particular approaches to employability and work experience examines the practice of student work experience as a route into employment through the theoretical lens of Louis Althusser's ideological state apparatuses. In particular, she focuses on unpaid work experience which is compulsory or highly recommended, but not formally facilitated by the university. Work experience such as this raises a concern about the exploitative nature of unpaid work. She investigates to what extent such consideration is evident in the universities' discourse of employability. She poses the question whether the universities' approach to employability, based on the values of individualism, can be held responsible for legitimising unpaid labour as a method of gaining access to paid employment.

Finally in this section and by way of contrast, in her chapter on values and international collaborative research, Chap. 10, Carolina Guzmán-Valenzuela takes a global view of values in higher education – drawing her comparisons not historically but geographically – by contrasting the Global North and the Global South. She focuses on problematising and deconstructing international collaboration. In doing so she explores the weight of different cultural contexts, language issues, power relationships and values in shaping such collaboration. The chapter suggests that international academic collaboration and the construction of knowledge in the social sciences require spaces to think critically. In particular, Guzmán-Valenzuela concentrates on the role of academic partnership and collaboration across country barriers. The chapter suggests that international academic collaboration and the construction of knowledge in the social sciences require spaces to think critically but highlights the competition amongst institutions as a result of ranking exercises and the profound effect that this has on university values. I AM HERE

Section Three considers the core of moral behaviour that of looking after others. It opens with the obvious notion of love. The values discussed here are those humanity might ascribe to as the core of a caring social agency, one we ascribe to individual and corporate bodies.

In Chap. 11 Victoria de Rijke explores the role of love within higher education from a revolutionary point of view. Critiquing the 'coldness' of logical scientific scholarship within market-driven fear-based economic materialism, she pits the values of the 'military-industrial-academic complex' against philosophical, spiritual, political and literary understandings of love as an other-focused commitment to the humanitarian values of courage, freedom, truth and authenticity. De Rijke observes that in post-truth discourse, accountable evidence-based research has eroded the freedom and fluidity of academic life, while anti-elite populist sentiments have challenged the expertise and confidence of professional scholars and teachers. Arguing for an epistemology of love, she advocates a hopeful development of self-love and authenticity in recognition of the value of playful affiliation to the practice of freedom and the revolutionary call for the radical equality-consciousness of the moral force of universal love in higher education.

In Chap. 12, Martin G. Erikson explores both everyday and academic definitions of kindness, identifying its functions within social practices guided by values in higher education. He defines kindness as a quality in teacher-student and student-student social interactions within a framework of values that shapes such interactions. While it is problematic to include kindness in academic discourse because of its 'everyday' quality, it has particular value at the core of all work in higher education in relation to the academic responsibility of both teachers and students to achieve clarity and quality of communication. Both kindness and proficiency in communication are necessary, as clear ideas and arguments are essential to the practice of academic freedom. Kindness is not about limiting discourse but about ensuring how communication ought to take place to enable the best outcome in relation to academic values. Erikson considers how, in the practice of kindness, communication and academic freedom are influenced by whether students are viewed as customers, as victims, or as free adults who are academic partners in constructing knowledge.

In his Chap. 13, Jon Nixon draws on the Aristotelian notion of virtuous friendship to characterise ideal collegial relationships as relationships of virtue enacting a reciprocity of trust between 'educational professionals' across a wide range of occupational groupings. He argues that, in an increasingly professionalised society, professionals from different walks of life and institutional settings define both their professionalism and their practice in increasingly pedagogical terms, being now expected to explain, persuade, mediate, consult, negotiate, and learn from, and with, their clients. Therefore, new forms of collegiality and public-professional engagement are developing across professional boundaries. Nixon identifies the emergence of a renewed sense of intellectual solidarity between 'scholar-teachers' carrying forward a radical tradition of 'critical humanism' to form 'the next intellectuals' who value mutually respectful recognition of the virtues of truthfulness, trust and justice. In taking responsibility mutually for a shared capability of justice and friendship towards others, such affiliative reasoning together enables the making and remaking of democratic systems of education and the institutions that sustain it.

We widen our cultural base for the next chapter, Chap. 14, where Abdullah Sahin critically examines changing values in higher education in the context of culturally, ethnically and religiously plural modern European societies, focusing on emerging European Islamic higher education institutions. Sahin's study adopts a phenomenologically-informed critical, comparative thematic analysis framework to compare Islamic and western values of higher education. He develops this conceptual framework to facilitate a contemporary pedagogic dialogue among communities of learners and teachers from these educational cultures, who increasingly share the same social space. He deconstructs the logic of binary literalism that argues Islamic and western values of education are incompatible, drawing on evidence for a shared reflective, critical educational heritage. He argues that there is a need to rethink the core values in both traditions to facilitate a new creative engagement between these two distinctive perspectives, given that they share an intertwined intellectual legacy. He investigates whether the central educational values of Islam and western secular higher education remain in conflict, and how far a critical dialogue of convergence can be facilitated. Such a critical engagement could be based on a shared relational ethics of respecting the dignity of difference and recognition of mutual interdependence.

Closing this section, Alison Scott-Baumann's Chap. 15 draws on the philosophy of Ricoeur to interrogate dominant discourses and attempt a better world for higher education. She reflects on the May 1968 mass student movements in France in which the left-wing collaborative shared agency between university students and workers' unions stimulated protests against de Gaulle's government. These protests did not take place in 1968 in Britain, nor would they currently: Scott-Baumann argues that in Britain young adults comfortably assume values of freedom of expression, equality and fraternal relations, since the appearance of these occurs in the digital world. She highlights, by contrast, urgent uncontrolled issues regarding ethical behaviour in which online and offline use of language is sharply racialised and gendered, hate speech against women and minority ethnic people is poorly controlled and legal restraints lag behind global digital empires. Government-driven intervention in campuses has accelerated to make some students less free, less equal and less fraternal than others. While free speech is constrained, populism is on the rise, framed by political alienation, and precarity affects young students' responses to university.

The Fourth Section considers how we might actually understand and then change institutional cultures.

In the first two chapters of this fourth section we consider compassion. First, Manuel Lillo-Crespo and Cristina Sierras-Davó, Chap. 16, focus on healthcare education (using their own context in Spain as an exemplar). They point to the espoused notion that patient-centred care should be the golden thread that runs through all healthcare education and continuing professional development nowadays but suggest that the values and attitudes supposed to be part of healthcare professions, such as compassion, address an important gap in training today. As compassion is a complex culturally-based value, the challenge for healthcare educators consists of providing and evaluating compassionate care practice in a global society within contexts with different social and cultural value systems. They illustrate how this might be approached as a core value within the health education programmes and connecting compassion as the baseline was the purpose of the ISTEW Project (Improvement Science Training for European Healthcare Professionals) funded by the European Commission.

The second chapter relates to compassion but now especially within the university. Kathryn Waddington, in Chap. 17, identifies and explores the values and assumptions underpinning compassionate institutional cultures and practices. It presents, and further develops, a conceptual framework for creating conditions for compassion which is theoretically informed by insights and evidence from psychodynamic psychology, work and organisational psychology. It also draws lightly upon empirical material and findings from a small-scale mixed methods study exploring Human Resource Management (HRM) strategies and academic engagement in six universities in the UK. A key finding from this study was that HRM strategies and practices were often viewed in a negative light, described in language that implied a sense of conflict. The chapter includes activities that encourage readers to question and critically reflect on the organisational dynamics, issues and challenges they have experienced and/or are facing in their work, signposted as 'Slowdown and Think'.

We draw towards the close of the book with the importance of wellbeing in higher education. Frances Maratos, Paul Gilbert and Theo Gilbert explore in Chap. 18 the role of direct compassion training across the education system and focus on the links between the value of compassion and mental health and wellbeing.

Compassion-based initiatives are beginning to be utilised within a wide range of organisations, including educational settings. They show that a large and established body of evidence is now well established that demonstrates that focusing on the cultivation of compassion-based motives and affiliative emotions has important effects on mental states and well-being. Indeed, compassion training is now known to have a range of physiological effects, to improve both moral and prosocial behaviour and to enhance connections between people that are rescuing, sustaining and rational. In universities and schools, the call for compassion training is set against a growing concern with the pressure for individual success. In doing so they consider the metricisation of UK higher education in particular, and the potential discrepancies between values of compassion advertised by universities and their actual practice.

Jill Jameson closes the book in Chap. 19, providing a reflective model of 'critical corridor talk' to exemplify the role of informal collegial leadership in facilitating kindness in higher education, given the performative values of academic capitalism promoted through economic rationalism. Echoing a recurring theme from the book, the chapter highlights mismatches between values often inherent within individual higher education institutions. Drawing from interview, survey and autoethnographic data in her analysis of the interrelationship of trust and leadership in higher education institutions, Jameson reflects on the complex role of negative capability and stoic virtue in enabling reflective space for contemplation and moral resistance at a time of uncertainty in higher education. The chapter should be seen as a source of optimism: the resistance shown by university staff represents a challenge to the manufactured performativity of higher education environments – and represents a blueprint to embed values of kindness whatever the values espoused or practised by universities as institutions and their managers.

In this book we have worked with colleagues from across the world and we are grateful to them. We hope that the result of this collaboration is a book which is an enjoyable and helpful contribution to the literature. We have brought together different cultures, nationalities and insights which will enhance our understanding of values and encourage readers to act on what they believe to be right.

References

Barnett, R. A. (1990). *The idea of higher education*. Buckingham: SRHE and Open University Press.

Giroux, H. A. (2014). *Neoliberalism's war on higher education*. Chicago: Haymarket Books.

Jonathan, R. (1997). Educational 'goods': Value and benefit. *Journal of Philosophy of Education, 31*(1), 59–82.

Marginson, S. (2011). Higher education and public good. *Higher Education Quarterly, 65*(4), 411–433.

Nixon, J. (2012). *Higher education and the public good*. London: Continuum International.

Weil, S. (1953). *The need for roots: A prelude to a declaration of duties toward mankind*. London: Routledge.

Williams, J. (2016). A critical exploration of changing definitions of public good in relation to higher education. *Studies in Higher Education, 41*(4), 619–630.

Chapter 2
Virtues and Dispositions as Learning Theory in Universities

David Scott

Abstract Virtue ethics is one of the three normative approaches to ethics. It foregrounds the virtues or moral character of the individual and can be contrasted with approaches that focus on duties or rules, as in deontological ethics, or on the consequences of actions, as in consequentialism. Virtue Ethics are different from deontological and consequentialist ethical forms. They are related to dispositions. Dispositions, as inner states, precede, condition and have some influence over actions. A disposition is a character type, an habituation, a state of preparation or readiness and a tendency to act in a specified way. Two further issues are relevant to the conception of virtue ethics: notions of causality and free will. The reason why these two notions are important is that in the first case the identification and conceptualisation of the virtues requires a theory of knowledge (i.e. epistemology) and of being (i.e. ontology) and the identification of a relationship between the two, including a notion of causation; and in the second case, any ethical theory (deontological, consequentialist or virtue-based) requires a theory of intention.

Keywords Dispositions · Learning · Virtue ethics · Causation · Ethical theory

Introduction

Virtue ethics is one of the three approaches to ethics that have a normative dimension. It foregrounds the virtues or moral character of the individual and can be contrasted with approaches that focus on duties or rules, as in deontological ethics, or on the consequences of actions, as in consequentialism. The first of these alternatives is a deontological framework, where a judgement is made in terms of a set of absolutely right actions or a set of universal rule-bound precepts. A second alternative is consequentialism. This suggests that a judgement is made in relation to the

D. Scott (✉)
Institute of Education, University College London, London, UK
e-mail: d.scott@ucl.ac.uk

P. Gibbs et al. (eds.), *Values of the University in a Time of Uncertainty*,
https://doi.org/10.1007/978-3-030-15970-2_2

consequences of the actions of participants in society. Different versions of consequentialism have been developed. One version is actual consequentialism, where an act is judged to be correct or morally right in relation to those consequences that actually resulted from the actions of the individual. Another is direct consequentialism, which suggests that an act is morally right only in relation to the consequences that directly flow from the act itself, as opposed to consequences relating to the agent's motives, or acts of a similar kind.

Virtue Ethics are different from deontological and consequentialist ethical forms for a number of reasons. They are related to dispositions, and what this means is that the ethical act comprises an inner state, which is already there (in some form or another), having been learnt, seeking to express itself in the world in relation to a problem in the world that requires some action. Dispositions, as inner states, precede, condition and have some influence over actions. A disposition is a character type, an habituation, a state of preparation or readiness and a tendency to act in a specified way. For Pierre Bourdieu (1986), dispositions have the power to allow an individual to take a specific position in a field. The habitus is the choice of the individual in taking up a position in that field according to their dispositions; but it cannot determine in any absolute sense what the person does. Dispositions then have this persistent quality although, because they are acquired, they can in time be modified. They have a strong affinity with a person's chosen identity.

The virtues also operate at the cultural or discursive level. In this form, they are dependent on membership of a practice, and this includes how they are instantiated in that practice. They are practice-based insofar as being excellent in the practice requires a judgement to be made as to what is considered to have value in the practice. This therefore implies a relation (a type of progression) between a novice and an expert within the practice. Alastair MacIntyre's (1981) notion of a practice in which virtue resides in the pursuit of excellence within that practice would also embrace witchcraft, iniquity, autocracy and the like, and thus there needs to be some notion of deontology or consequentialism attached to the particular goods that are being sought in the practice and which the practice is about. The crucial issue is that any designation of an ethical virtue is always, and can only be, understood in terms of some conception of how the society is organised or even perhaps about excellence within the practice. Ethical judgements always supervene on epistemological judgements.

Dispositions are learnt in a particular way. In other words, they cannot be learnt through instructional or disquisitional methods. What they are may be determined through these methods, but they require practice in simulated or real-life environments. Furthermore, acquiring a virtue requires being able to perform in the spaces associated with that virtue. Dispositional learning is a prerequisite of skill- and knowledge-based learning. In other words, how that person acquires a skill or item of knowledge is dependent on the dispositions they have and on progressive manifestations of particular dispositions that have already been learnt or acquired.

Learning

A university curriculum in essence is a planned programme of learning, or series of learning programmes (in the UK these operate within a wide variety of institutions since there is no national higher education curriculum), and therefore if we are to understand what it is, we also have to develop a theory of learning. As a concept, learning (i.e. learning the virtues and in the process creating dispositions internally) is fundamentally related to knowledge, and therefore if we are thinking about learning and the practices of learning, we also need to make reference to what is to be and how it is learned, and typically what we are aiming at in such considerations is some form of knowledge. Philosophers usually divide knowledge into two principal categories, knowing-that and knowing-how. (They sometimes also add a third category, knowing-by-acquaintance, but this is not central to the argument that is being made). The suggestion here is that these forms of knowledge are fundamentally different; in other words, there are strong and impermeable boundaries between them. I want to suggest that this is misleading, and that consequently some of the problems that these strong insulations have created can be resolved. In society these different forms of knowledge are given different statuses or have different attachments of importance, so, for example, vocational knowledge (broadly thought of as being about processes) is considered to be less important than academic knowledge (broadly understood as being about propositions), but these ascriptions of importance do not lie in the intrinsic nature of each knowledge form but in the way these knowledge forms are realised in particular societies or social units.

Knowledge then, is fundamental to the three types of learning that can be identified: cognitive (relating to propositions), skill-based (relating to processes) and dispositional (relating to embodied virtues). This after all is where the virtues come in. Cognition comprises the manipulation of those symbolic resources (words, numbers, pictures etc.), which points to (though not necessarily in a mirroring or isomorphic sense) something outside itself, though the referent might also be construed as internally-related, or more specifically, as a part of an already established network of concepts. Skill-based knowledge is different from cognition because it is procedural and not propositional. Dispositional knowledge refers to relatively stable habits of mind and body, sensitivities to occasion and participation repertoires. Distinguishing between knowledge of how to do something (or process forms of knowledge), knowledge of something (or judging that claim in terms of its relations within and to a network of concepts) and embodied or dispositional forms of knowledge (assimilating an action and being able to perform in the spaces associated with that action) is important; however, they are in essence all knowledge-making activities, and furthermore as we will see can be formulated generically as acts of learning.

Knowledge is transformed at the pedagogic site, so it is possible to suggest that qualities such as: the simulation of the learning object, the representational mode of the object, its degree and type of amplification, control in the pedagogic relationship, progression or its relations with other learning objects (i.e. degrees of curriculum integration), the type of pedagogic text, relations with other people in the learning process, the organisation of time (temporal relations) and types of feedback mechanism are fundamental components of this pedagogic transformation. What this means is that in the learning process, the learning object takes a new form as a result of changes to its properties: simulation, representation, amplification, control, integration, textual form, relations with other people, time and feedback.

This suggests that acting in the world requires the use of, and is underpinned by, conceptual frameworks of one type or another. Propositional knowledge or making a claim that this or that is the case is, in common with the other two forms of knowledge, a process of doing and thus of knowing how to do something or other. And this results in all three types of knowledge having the same general form, and this allows them, in this form, to be understood as learning actions or acts of learning. What this means is that notions of asserting, claiming, judging and believing can be understood as having active features, such that when we assert something, or claim something, or judge something or believe something, we are engaged in processes of asserting, claiming, judging and believing.

This means that propositional knowledge cannot be thought of as fundamentally different from procedural and embodied forms of knowledge since assertings, claimings, judgings and believings are of the same order as riding (a horse, for example), being kind (to another person, for example), teaching (a class, for example) or reflecting on the self. Note the way these four activities are typically thought of as knowing-how processes, whereas the first four activities are usually thought of as knowing-that processes. However, what I am suggesting is that in order to make a claim of knowing, we are not, as commonly thought, providing a description of an experience (i.e. constructing propositional knowledge) but making a claim about it in what Sellars (1997) has described as 'a space of reasons', and that what follows from this is that we can and should understand and use concepts specifically in relation to networks of meanings. Brandom (2000: 48) has described this as playing a role in the inferential game of making claims and giving and asking for reasons, with the notion of giving a reason being understood in terms of making an inference, so that if one makes a claim of knowledge, the contents of that claim consist of inferential commitments made in applying it in the world and further to this, these commitments refer to both the circumstances surrounding its content and its consequences.

The Determination of the Virtues

How does one determine what these virtues are? It should be noted that an answer to this question is not a requirement for acquiring these virtues. These virtues are in essence valued expressions of the good life; in other words, they offer an ethic about living and are a corrective to other ways of living in and understanding the world. Margaret Archer (2007) in determining what these might be argues against three individualistic versions of the human being. The first is what she calls homo economicus and she means by this that the person does not and cannot contribute to the common good unless they do so inadvertently. The wellspring for their actions is not derived from the betterment of society or the maintenance of social bonds, because the desire is always to maximise preferences and their utility. A second version of this individualistic ethic is what Archer calls bureaucratic man (*sic.*) and for her this signifies a contractual social bond, rather than a universal one, so that society is organised in opposition to genuine co-operation. The third version of individualism is libertarian in orientation. With the breakdown of familial, communitarian and other types of social bonding structures, there is a compulsion to reinvent oneself at every opportunity. We can add a fourth type and this is where the individual's actions are habitual, with the person acting in a non-reflexive manner. And a fifth, perhaps, is normative, so that the person chooses to behave in terms of a norm or standard, rather than ipsatively. In its place she would like to substitute three virtues. The first of these is practices that always refer to the inalienable dignity of all human beings. The second, solidarity, is that of shared values within communities, and thus, as Archer (ibid.) describes it, the provision of 'social cement'. The third virtue is subsidiarity where the principle is that a higher authority should not usurp control of activities and functions that are the province of the lower order, with this understood in an agential context.

The identification of the virtues is the hardest part of the argument to sustain because it opens up a series of unresolved issues, expressed perhaps as a series of questions: What is their (i.e. the virtues) provenance? Why is one set of virtues to be preferred over another? Why should one prefer a teleological account (of society and it has to be extra-individual or broadly social, such as rationality) to a social/political value-impregnated utopian view?

Aristotelian Virtue Ethics

Aristotle's view of the virtues is encapsulated in the doctrine of the mean. For example, in any sphere of action or domain of feeling such as strength and health, there is both an excess and a deficiency:

> First, then, let us consider this, that it is the nature of things to be destroyed by defect and excess as we see in the case of strength and of health (for to gain light on things imperceptible we must use the evidence of sensible things); both excessive and defective exercise destroys the strength, and similarly drink or food which is above or below a certain amount destroys the health, while that which is proportionate both produces and increases and preserves it. (location 33689 in the on-line ShandonPress edition of Aristotle's Nicomachean Ethics 2018b)

Another example concerns the sphere of action or feeling associated with fear and confidence. In relation to this there is a mean virtue of courage. For Aristotle an excess of courage is rashness and a deficiency of courage is cowardice:

> So too is it, then, in the case of temperance and courage and the other virtues. For the man who flies from and fears everything and does not stand his ground against anything becomes

a coward, and the man who fears nothing at all but goes to meet every danger becomes rash; and similarly the man who indulges in every pleasure and abstains from none becomes self-indulgent, while the man who shuns every pleasure, as boors do, becomes in a way insensible; temperance and courage, then, are destroyed by excess and defect, and preserved by the mean. (location 33689 in the ShandonPress on-line edition of Aristotle's Nicomachean Ethics 2018b)

Other spheres of action or feeling discussed by Aristotle in the Nicomachean Ethics are: pleasure and pain (the mean is temperance, an excess of this is licentiousness and a deficiency is insensibility); getting and spending in a minor way (the mean is liberality, an excess of this is prodigality and a deficiency is illiberality); getting and spending in a major way (the mean is magnificence, an excess of this is vulgarity and a deficiency is pettiness); anger (the mean is patience, an excess of this is irascibility and a deficiency is a lack of spirit); self-expression (the mean is truthfulness, an excess of this is boastfulness and a deficiency is understatement); conversation (the mean is wittiness, an excess of this is buffoonery and a deficiency is boorishness); social conduct (the mean is friendliness, an excess of this is obsequiousness or flattery and a deficiency is cantankerousness); shame (the mean is modesty, an excess of this is shyness and a deficiency is shamelessness); and indignation (the mean is righteous indignation, an excess of this is envy and a deficiency is malicious enjoyment). A number of questions need to be asked about this list. The most important of these is whether this list of virtues is universal (that is, it applies equally to people across time and place) or specifically to a particular social formation, i.e. ancient Greek society.

Aristotle's notion of a mean or middle point between two extremes has the effect of restricting the possible number of the virtues. It also acts to create a hierarchy amongst the virtues, with some of what might be considered virtues now understood as extremes of some principal virtues. So, for example, prodigality and illiberality are understood as extreme versions of liberality and are thus deficient in some sense or another, and relative to a virtue that is considered sufficient. So, they are understood both in a negative sense and as inferior in virtue of some other ethical position. What it does is identify a list of virtues with some being considered to be more important than others (this of course can be achieved by inclusions and omissions) and some being parasitic on others. Further to this it constructs sets of relations between the primary virtues and particular strengths attached to those virtues. We have already suggested that Aristotle's primary virtues are choices made from a list of all the possible virtues that could be envisaged. (This list might include past, but now archaic, virtues, currently fashionable virtues or virtues that reflect the current arrangements in society and even virtues yet to be instantiated, though imagined). Furthermore, this choice depends on the semantic content of the virtue.

Evaluating these virtues is difficult because their acquisition can only be determined by the actions of individuals in the world and even then one doesn't know if the ethical behaviour is deontological, consequentialist or virtue-based. Some people possess the virtues; others do not. Thus, this can act as a means of differentiating between people: some have the virtues, others do not; or at least, some possess particular virtues in greater measure than others. This raises the issue of concept development or at least how we learn the virtues. The practising of the virtues is not the same as the internal development of the virtues, which are in conformity with a practice, where *in conformity* means that they have social and extra-embodied characteristics, and also emergent characteristics. The interesting question then is whether the good life consists of an endless practicing of the virtues or living a life which is informed by an individual's acquisition of the virtues, in full or incomplete form.

A number of well-known objections have been made to Aristotle's doctrine of the mean, not least Bernard Williams' (1985: 36) well-known characterisation of it as unhelpful and depressing:

> Aristotle's views on [virtue] are bound up with one of the most celebrated and least useful parts of his system, the doctrine of the mean, according to which every virtue of character lies between two correlative faults or vices…, which consist respectively of the excess and the deficiency of something of which the virtue represents the right amount. The theory oscillates between an unhelpful analytical model (which Aristotle himself does not consistently follow) and a substantively depressing doctrine in favour of moderation. The doctrine of the mean is better forgotten.

The first of these objections then is that though this rule-based ethical schema is considered to be deontological, in fact it doesn't always follow the rules and on occasions is arbitrary. Aristotle is clear in the Nicomachean Ethics that 'the mean is not of the thing itself, but relative to us' (location 33692 in the on-line ShandonPress edition of Aristotle's Nicomachean Ethics 2018b). However, he qualifies this with regards to some of the virtues or vices or he suggests that at least some emotions or acts are wrong per se regardless of circumstance. He gives a number of examples: malice, shamelessness and envy (these are emotions) and adultery, theft and murder (these are acts). In other words, there cannot be praiseworthy exercises of malice, shamelessness, envy, adultery, theft or murder. However, this in itself can be challenged especially from a consequentialist ethical framework; for example, if Claus Von Stauffenberg had succeeded in murdering Adolf Hitler in 1944, this would have saved many lives and foreshortened the war.

However, for Aristotle to sustain the argument of the virtuous mean, he needs to develop a notion of difference between human beings because as he makes clear, in determining the right action for an individual human being it is not just that this person should follow the implicit rules of the already identified and learnt virtuous mean but also judge the right action in relation to the details of the case, which includes above all else the actual set of dispositions that person has acquired at a particular point in time. These character traits comprise tendencies towards excesses and deficiencies, and towards committing certain types of errors: logical, epistemological, biases of viewpoint and the like. Thus the virtuous act requires a prior disposition of self-regulation or self-observation that is sufficient to identify these character flaws and allow for some type of compensation. This in itself is a deontological judgement; however, regardless of this, what this means is that both the identification of the mean and the identification of its excesses and deficiencies requires a judgement to be made about whether those dispositions qualify as virtues and furthermore about whether they can produce excesses and deficiencies that fit with the virtue and with the overall and desired ethic of living. In short, the question needs to be asked: why these and not others? The doctrine of the mean cannot provide a satisfactory answer to this question. A further unanswered question, to which Aristotle provides only a partial answer, is that the mean (whether the process is from the mean to the identification of excesses and deficiencies or from those excesses and deficiencies to the mean) is differently calculated for each of the virtues; thus they are not exclusively rule-bound in the sense that there is no rule that covers the determination of the excesses and deficiencies for all the possible virtues.

However, difference can be understood in a number of ways. There is the common use given to the term, where difference is understood as not being or as being opposite to something else. Then there is the meaning given to the term by Jacques Derrida (1982). In his essay 'Différance', he suggests that the term points to a number of ways that textual meaning can be produced. The first of these relates to the idea that words and signs only have meaning within other arrangements of words and concepts, from which they differ. Meanings are thus forever deferred. The second way that Derrida uses the term is to refer to a notion of espacement or spacing, so that what should concern us is the force that differentiates social elements from other social elements, and in the process, as we have suggested, engenders binary oppositions and endlessly reiterated hierarchies of meaning.

The most important issue, however, lies with the initial determination of the virtues, and this in turn requires some other over-arching determining factor, to which the virtues, their excesses and deficiencies, and the relations between the virtues and their excesses and deficiencies, are subject. There are a number of candidates for this. Aristotle is clear that this is not to maximise pleasure and to diminish pain, in other words, not for utilitarian reasons, but because it might impair judgement about how to act (good judgement is being treated here as of primary concern and as requiring no further justification).

The doctrine of the mean does not amount to the idea that emotions should always be of moderate intensity, or that strong emotions are in some sense pathologies, or that in acting the human being should always express their emotions moderately, or that human beings should seek everything in moderation, or that every virtue has correlative faults and vices, or that the relations between the virtues and their corresponding excesses and deficiencies are rule-based. Rather, excellence is observed by following the mean as far as this is possible.

The Telos

The telos or end point of a virtuous action is important for Aristotle. Goals are purposive and they are future orientated; that is, the goal is by definition something that seeks fulfilment in a state of affairs (i.e. a future arrangement of material and discursive objects) that hasn't yet happened. Furthermore goals require intentional activity; that is, they require a sentient human being to have an intention to do some thing or other. Thus a virtue-directed activity, such as being courageous, requires both the envisaging of an end point, i.e. a better arrangement of material and discursive objects in the world, not least in the capacity of the individual to be in a relationship with the world, and an intention, i.e. some notion of a self-directing person and that person having a desire or intention to do something in the world.

The ethical value of the intention and the action resides in the particular virtue being instantiated. A purposive goal then can refer to a self-ordered setting of goals where the goal is essentially arbitrary, or it can refer to intentional behaviour, or it can refer to some notion of completeness as in a rational design process. This last is important because it adds a further dimension to the development of virtue ethics. Goals may be related to other goals, as in a goal such as justice being subservient but a necessary stepping stone to eudaimonia.

Eudaimonia has been translated as happiness or welfare. Etymologically, it derives from two ancient Greek words meaning good and spirit and it is central to Aristotle's ethical theory, along with notions of virtue or excellence or practical wisdom as in phronesis. For Aristotle, eudaimonia is the highest possible good and all other goods, such as justice or friendship are subservient to it. This means that Aristotle is arguing that there is a hierarchy of values, which in their achievement through individual actions of for example being just or friendly will lead inevitably to a higher state, which is achievable. This higher state is in the first instance individualistic, though we will see he added an important condition or proviso relating to chance.

In the Nicomachean Ethics (2018b), Aristotle suggests that eudaimonia involves virtuous activity in accordance with reason. A view of knowledge as intrinsically worthwhile has persisted for a long time; for example, Aristotle presents his readers with the following argument. The purpose of life is predetermined, as is the individual's nature, though it is not always clear to the individual what this natural purpose is. However, this lack of clarity can be corrected through rational deliberation and reflection on the self; and it is the possession of reason that distinguishes human beings from other animals. If this is accepted, then the end-point of human life is to pursue this aim; and therefore from this set of premises can be deduced the aim of an education in a university as the pursuit of rational activities that develop the mind. It is fairly easy to see how this syllogism rests on false or at least disputed premises, so that predetermination and a fixed nature are concepts that are not readily accepted in the modern era. Thus the fullest or most perfect life is the exercise of reason; eudaimonia is achieved by the proper development of reason (the pedagogical element) and is understood as the attainment of excellence in reason. It is not sufficient for that person to have a strong sense of good character, where this is understood as the acquisition of the virtues, but also and in addition that person is required to live a life in pursuit of excellence in the virtues. From this it follows that the state of eudaimonia comprises activities, which have as their principal function the exercising of individual rational capability or excellence in reason. However, Aristotle does suggest that it is extremely difficult to achieve a eudaimonistic state of being unless one has a birthright, or social arrangements allow it or one is fortunate.

Causation

Two further issues are relevant to the conceptualisation of virtue ethics: the notions of causality and indeterminacy. The reason why these two notions are important is that in the first case the identification and conception of the virtues requires a theory of knowledge (i.e. epistemology) and of being (i.e. ontology) and the identification of a relationship between the two, including a notion of causation; and in the second case, any ethical theory (deontological, consequentialist or virtue-based) requires a theory of intention. The first issue then is causality. Aristotle's causal explanatory framework comprises the following: (i) material causation – an object such as a statue is generated from something else, e.g. a base metal; (ii) formal causation – an object such as a statue represents something else and thus this something else can be said to have caused the object; (iii) efficient causation – an object can be said to have been intended so we can say that it has been caused by the intention of the person and the work of that person in fulfilling his or her intention as in a sculptor making a statue; then there are (iv) final causes (and this is the area of concern for us) where we are dealing with ends or purposes – the statue has some purpose such as satisfying an aesthetic need or honouring an important public figure (cf. Aristotle (2018a) *Physics, or, Natural Hearing*, Book II, Chap. 3). However, in order to provide a satisfactory account of causality, the philosopher must also develop a satisfactory account of epistemology, the latter supervenes on the former. Critical realism offers one possibility.

Roy Bhaskar (2010) makes three claims about the world, and thus also about knowledge of it: there are important differences between the transitive realm of knowing and the intransitive realm of being; the social world is an open system; and reality has ontological depth. The first of these then, is a distinction between the intransitive world of being and the transitive world of knowing, with the consequence that if they are conflated, either upwards, resulting in the epistemic fallacy, or downwards, resulting in the ontic fallacy, some meaning is lost. There are two implications. Social objects, and the relations between them (i.e. networks, confluences and conjunctions), though real, are constantly changing, and it is therefore the changing object which endures, even if that object has been so utterly transformed that it is barely recognisable in relation to its former self. The second implication is that, in certain circumstances and within certain conditions, social objects from the transitive realm can penetrate the intransitive realm and be objectified.

The second claim he makes is that the social world is an open system. Closed systems are characterised by two conditions: objects operate in consistent ways, and they do not change their essential nature. Neither of these conditions pertains to open systems. In closed systems measured regularities are synonymous with causal mechanisms. Experimentation is therefore unnecessary because experimental characteristics are naturally present. There are two alternatives: artificial closure and the use of methods and strategies that fit with systemic openness, including, but not exclusively, inferential judgements from the analysis of evidence. The first of these alternatives, artificial closure, makes a number of unsubstantiated assumptions:

transferences can be made even if the original knowledge is constructed in artificial conditions; and this original knowledge is correctly related to the constitution of the object. The second alternative is that we adopt methods and strategies that conform to the principle of systemic openness. This would seem to be the more appropriate option.

The third claim he makes is that social reality has ontological depth. Social objects are the real manifestations of the idealised types used in discourse and are the focus for any enquiry. They are structured in various ways, and because of this, they possess powers. The powers that these structures (or mechanisms) exert can be one of three types. Powers can be possessed, exercised or actualised. Powers possessed are powers that objects have whether they are triggered by the circumstances or not. Their effect may not be evident in any observable phenomena. Powers exercised have been triggered and are having an effect in an open system, and as a result they are interacting with other powers of other mechanisms within their sphere of influence. These exercised powers may still not give rise to any observable phenomena as these other powers may be acting against them. Powers that have been actualised are generating their effects; within the open system they are working together with other powers but, in this case, they have not been suppressed or counteracted. Embodied, institutional or discursive structures can be possessed and not exercised or actualised, possessed and exercised, or possessed and actualised. As a result, a causal model based on constant conjunctions is rejected and replaced by a generative-productive one, and objects and relations between objects have emergent properties. This is an example of a knowledge tradition that is extra-disciplinary, holistic, emergent and transformational.

Those subscribing to empiricist and positivist philosophies claim that it is possible to predict events, and this is founded on the idea that both the original account (at the first time point – T_1) and the predicted account (at the second time point – T_2) are adequate in all essential respects. Critical realists, on the other hand, do not accept that it is possible to make law-like predictions about social and educational matters. What this means is that laws should not be thought of as constant conjunctions, or even as determinate causal sequences, but as tendencies of powerful objects (cf. Bhaskar 2010), and these are understood as the properties of those objects, and not as predictive accounts of behaviours yet to be performed.

Critical realists advance a particular view of causality, that is, generative-productive. Here causality is understood as a property of objects, which may or may not be realised, and this has implications for how social and educational researchers should act, and whether it is possible and appropriate to use descriptions of current educational settings as a basis for predictions about future ones. Scientific realists and statistical positivists generally subscribe to a Humean theory of causality as spatio-temporal contiguity, succession and constant conjunction, and this is founded on the idea that though it is not possible to observe a relation between cause and effect, it is possible to identify a persistent association between two or more events, and then infer a causal relation.

Objections to this point of view have been frequently made. It cannot account for spurious associations or order cause and effect, and there is no guarantee that all the possible interacting variables have been identified. Furthermore, it is reductionist because it treats these variables as real, and therefore elides epistemology with ontology. A concept is always embedded in a framework of other concepts, and that when we refer to the detheorisation of research what we are talking about here is that traditional and reductionist forms of research separate out the concept from the framework, in order for it to have the properties of a variable. Having detheorised the concept relations are then identified between these different variables, even if the variable itself does not enter into a meaningful relationship with the world. So, for example, race as a concept is always positioned in a complicated network of other terms, such as innateness, trait theory, genetics, phenotypicality, biology, historical origin, evolutionary theory and many more, and if we are to use this concept then we have to give due consideration to this network of other ideas.

An opposing view of causality is that researchers cannot observe such relations, and in addition, they do not exist in nature since events are not caused. There are only apparent regularities, and therefore what is understood as a causal relationship, that is, E_a has led to E_b on every occasion that E_a and E_b have interacted (where E refers to an event), is a product of chance, and is thus randomly produced. Regardless of whether any investigation of those supposed causal relations has taken, or is taking, place, no work is ever performed by a phenomenon on another, causing changes in the latter. There is nothing in nature that causes anything to happen; in short, there is an ontological void. This is an extreme version of causality; effectively, a denial of causality as ontologically real. A further argument, in opposition to this, is that in nature, again regardless of any act of knowing, causal work can take, and has taken, place; however, the observer or researcher is not able to either know that it has taken place or what the precise causal sequence is that has occurred, and thus a reasonable response to this would be a belief in the randomness of nature. Social researchers and observers may be wrong about the world, but they have no means of knowing that they are wrong, and, thus for all practical purposes, they have to carry on in their lives as if they were right. On the other hand, if they genuinely believe that they cannot know what reality is like, then they may decide, and have good grounds for making such a decision, that there are causal mechanisms in the world. In this case, they are literally imposing a set of causal conditions on the world, which are not replications, reproductions or simulations of what exists in nature, but constructions or inventions by groups of social actors. And given the looping nature of the relationship between ideation and reality, then these inventions or constructions may become ontologically real.

The first of these two arguments suggests that causality is an ontological fiction, and the second suggests that causality is an epistemological construct and nothing more. However, despite the apparent impasse here, there is another way of looking at the problem, and this is to question the starkness of the distinction that is being made between causality and randomness. For example, researchers can say that some things are caused, but these coexist with a number of random events; or they can suggest that the only two alternatives on offer (randomness and causality) do not cover all the possible descriptions that could be made of objects and appropriate knowledge of them.

A more radical solution is to argue that there are different types of causes and they are different in kind because they operate in different ways; a person having a reason for doing something which also causes her to do it, such as keeping an appointment, is different from that person not being able to leave a room because the door is locked. If asked what caused her to do it, she might provide a different reason for her action than the one that motivated her in the first place or conditioned her action. This, however, is not a refutation of the belief that reasons can in certain circumstances be causes, but only an observation that an investigator may be misled about the actual reasons that caused another person's actions, or even that the person herself may have been confused about what actually caused her to do something. This type of causal sequence is different from a causal sequence in which an object with its potential powers and liabilities comes into contact with another object, which both triggers a change in these objects and creates a new object with new powers and liabilities, though this needs to be qualified in so far as interacting effects may be offset by the workings of other mechanisms and other transfactual occurrences. In the latter case, there is no human intervention; in the former case there is human intention. Second, in order to determine whether an event is caused or is merely random, one has to have an a priori theory about what constitutes a cause and underpinning this is a set of beliefs about how causes work. So, causes operate differently and are understood differently in a deterministic universe than they do in one with both random and caused events and happenings. Events can be caused even if the results are not as intended by any individual or group of individuals; in other words, predicting the future cannot be achieved by investigating what people intended should happen, though this might be a starting point.

Let us now imagine that the default mechanism is set up so that the world is not random but caused. Again, there are a number of possible models. The first of these (let us call it M_1) is that everything is caused: the universe is a closed system of objects, including individual human beings (the individual as both causal object and causal effect); these objects have causal powers which may or may not be activated; and if they are activated they behave mechanically, so that when object (O_a) comes into contact with object (O_b) then a new object is formed (O_c) and this is what constitutes a causal sequence. All events are caused whether observers are fully able to understand them or not. Incomplete or deficient understandings occur because an observer or researcher does not know enough about the world, or because she does not know how she could investigate the event in a reliable way, or even because she could never be in a position to conduct a reliable investigation. Indeed, she might think that she knows the cause of something, especially if the cause–effect–cause sequence involves an intentional act; however, she could be mistaken even if she is the intentional being. This process takes place in the ontological realm and it takes place regardless of whether it can be or is described or theorised about; thus, notions of probability do not come into the equation at this level of explanation. The important point to note about this model is that intentionality is treated as of the same type as any other material or ideational causal substance. Thus, one substance in conjunction with another substance necessarily causes a new substance to be formed. This inevitably implies determinism and necessity.

The second model (M_2) is different and is predicated on the idea that reasons can be and are causes; however, this needs to be qualified by the adoption of a further premise, which is that reasons are not causes in the same way that events have antecedent conditions which necessarily have to be present for that event to take place. If they are not the same as necessary antecedent conditions, then what are they? Again, we need to distinguish here between actual reasons for an action and rationalisations of those reasons after the event or activity. However, even if we distinguish between the two, we are not identifying a new argument, because we are not ruling out the possibility that a reason has caused something to happen, even if subsequently, that causal mechanism of which the action is the central component has been incorrectly described.

A reason has to relate to the action it seeks to explain; it has to, in other words, be relevant. It takes the form of a justification for an action yet to be performed, and thus this implies that there are competing actions between which a human being has to choose. (This would include all the possible ways of behaving relevant to the proposed course of action). It is valued in relation to other possible reasons for action, and these values are embedded in those structures of agency that act as conditions for the agent. What this means is that certain actions and therefore the reasons for those actions are privileged over other actions and their reasons, and this forms the backdrop to the choosing of a reason for an action and ultimately the performance of the action itself. A reason has a justificatory form; thus, it precedes an action (the reason refers to the action and to nothing else), provides the antecedent conditions for that action (thus it is necessary in the sense that it could not and would not have been performed without the reason), and the sequence may not be repeatable.

There is a further model, which in essence is epistemological. This is that any causal model we want to adopt is probabilistic rather than deterministic in structure. We may be unable to determine whether this model was a viable one because the world is essentially deterministic or because the world is too complicated to allow us to give a full account of it. However, it works (the model allows us to successfully predict within certain parameters of error), but we don't know why it works. Does it work because it is an accurate reflection of the way the world works or because in predicting the future researchers are activating mechanisms that will bring it about? Second, probabilistic reasoning does not account for every case being considered, but only a majority of cases; outliers are confined to the realm of either the unknowable (error at the case level) or theoretical inadequacy (the theory that is being used and which allows prediction is not sophisticated enough to account for every single case, but, though flawed, is the best there is). Third, the empirical indicators used to construct the causal narrative are inadequate for the task, and thus the post hoc theory that is developed is at fault.

A final model is that events are caused but can only be retrospectively known. Events that have taken place are caused, that is, by an intention of a human being or by a group of human beings or by the conjunction of two or more mechanisms; but to say that this causal sequence can be known only after the event has taken place is to say virtually nothing at all; and this is because it tells us nothing about whether events are caused or not, but only whether and at what point we can identify a particular causal sequence. However, we can take this model one stage further and suggest a generative/productive view of causation. We can hypothesise a relationship and then try to work out what the mechanism might be. By mechanism I mean literally that an object has causal powers to effect change in another object, these powers may or may not be exercised, and, even if they are, there is no guarantee that change will occur in the targeted object. Because we are dealing here with objects that are in part formed by our conceptualisations of them, that is, we can only know an object and its workings through a conceptual framework, and that choice of conceptual framework may influence the nature of the object, then generative causal sequences cannot safely be extended into the future.

Free Will

The second issue that relates to the identification and instantiation of virtue ethics is the notion of free will, i.e. volition. John Searle's (1984) position on the issue is confused. He accepts a physicalist position, i.e. that all forms of conscious life involve the interaction of molecules and thus implicitly accepts a mechanical causal view of the mind-body relationship, and from this he concludes that free will is merely an illusion. This means that for Searle the mental is also physical (and therefore has to abide by the laws of physics), and if it is any notion of intentionality influencing our actions or even causing further mental actions could be and is likely to be simply the operation of prior molecular processes, with their commitment to a notion of cause and effect. However, again for Searle, we have a strong sense that in life we subscribe to a notion of having a mental state, which in some way causes (not in a Humean sense) other mental states or physical actions. However, this cannot, if we subscribe to the notion of the operation of the mind being in no fundamental sense different from the operation of physical objects outside the mind, be anything other than an illusion. There is no such thing as free will, only a thought in our heads that we freely choose some action or some other thought from a range of possible thoughts and actions. This is of course not just a criticism of anti-physicalism but also a sceptical position per se. Unless we can establish some certain point outside of the particular case that we are considering, by which we can then judge our original claim to knowledge, then we are forced to withhold assent to it being a valid claim of knowledge. Further to this, if we cannot find good grounds for suggesting that the basis for having any mental function at all is not illusory, then we are forced to accept a sceptical position with regards to knowledge of anything, if and only if we construe all mental processes as conforming to the principles of physicalism. What this means is that everything is literally physical or at least everything supervenes on the physical, and further to this that these principles of physicalism (i.e. all events, including mental events in individual minds, are the product of the play of molecules at a lower level) cannot save us in this regard.

Scepticism, further, is necessarily false. For if we support a notion of scepticism, then we additionally have to show why it is true. If we do this, and we are, I think, committed to doing this, then at least one item of true knowledge exists, i.e. that we should be sceptical about knowledge, and this of course contradicts the original premise. We cannot be sceptical about knowledge in its entirety. For any theory of learning there needs to be some reconciliation of the persistent problem of the relationship between mind and matter. The reason for this is that one element of the learning process may be conceived as a transfer of a material object, an entity, to, what some think of as a non-material object, a mind.

Thomas Nagel (2012), coming from a dualist position, suggests that mental substances and processes cannot be directly subsumed into physical substances and processes, i.e. there are significant differences between the two; however, we do not have at present and possibly ever, a language for describing mental states, even if we can provide good grounds for suggesting they are different; and what this means is that we cannot provide a convincing account of the relationship between the two, although we can acknowledge that differences exist between them. Causal explanations in science are necessary. Given the theory, the observed effects must follow. For example, we can deduce from the molecular composition of H_2O certain properties or features, such as solidity, liquidity, etc. But no necessary connection exists between the physical and the mental. No matter how much we know about the brain, we could never deduce a single mental predicate. It is logically impossible to deduce any mental statement from any non-mental statement.

Some Brief Conclusions

Determinism would imply in its strongest form that our thoughts, feelings and subsequent behaviours do not deviate from the impulsions laid down in our genetic make-up or in customised knowledge within our bodies or in the social arrangements (i.e. embodied, discursive, agential, institutional and systemic) that constitute our lives. However, if we want to build in notions of agency and therefore virtuous behaviour, then we have to believe that our cognitive and volitional capacities can operate without recourse to, and outside of, those causal impulses that come from these determining impulses. Furthermore, if we hold to a belief that our cognitive and volitional capacities are inextricably tied to our genetically-determined, embodied or socially-determined impulses, then it follows that our capacity to determine whether or not we are being deceived, i.e. our capacity to tell the truth or not about our fundamental belief in determinism, is thoroughly compromised. Agency therefore involves a set of activities that are not caused or influenced by those impulses that emanate from our genetic, embodied or social beings; that is, they do not involve an affirmation or a negation of them or even a reaction against them. Any coherent notion of virtue ethics, besides much else, requires a theory of causality and a theory of intention or agency.

Virtue ethics is one of the three approaches to ethics that have a normative dimension. It foregrounds the virtues or moral character of the individual and can be contrasted with approaches that focus on duties or rules, as in deontological ethics, or on the consequences of actions, as in consequentialism. Virtue Ethics are different from deontological and consequentialist ethical forms. They are related to dispositions, and what this means is that the ethical act comprises an inner state, which is already there (in some form or another), having been learnt, seeking to express itself in the world in relation to a problem in the world that requires some action. Dispositions, as inner states, precede, condition and have some influence over actions. A disposition is a character type, an habituation, a state of preparation or readiness and a tendency to act in a specified way. I have examined two further issues, both of which are relevant to the instantiation of virtue ethics: the notions of causality and indeterminacy. The reason why these two notions are important is that in the first case the identification and instantiation of the virtues requires a theory of knowledge (i.e. epistemology) and of being (i.e. ontology) and the identification of a relationship between the two, including a notion of causation; and in the second case, any ethical theory (deontological, consequentialist or virtue-based) requires a theory of intention.

References

Archer, M. (2007). *Making our way through the world*. Cambridge: Cambridge University Press.

Aristotle. (2018a). *The complete Aristotle, part 2: Physics or natural hearing* (8 books) (R. P. Hardie, & R. K. Gaye, Trans.). ShandonPress Kindle Edition.

Aristotle. (2018b). *The complete Aristotle, part 6: The Nicomachean ethics* (10 books) (R. D. Ross, Trans.). ShandonPress Kindle Edition.

Bhaskar, R. (2010). *Reclaiming reality* (New ed.). London: Routledge.

Bourdieu, P. (1986). The forms of capital. In J. G. Richardson (Ed.), *Handbook of theory and research for the sociology of capital*. New York: Greenwood Press.

Brandom, R. (2000). *Articulating reasons: An introduction to inferentialism*. Cambridge, MA: Harvard University Press.

Derrida, J. (1982). Différance. In *Margins of philosophy*. Chicago: University of Chicago Press.

MacIntyre, A. (1981). *After virtue*. Notre Dame: University of Notre Dame Press.

Nagel, T. (2012). *Mind and Cosmos: Why the materialist Neo-Darwinian conception of nature is almost certainly false*. Oxford: Oxford University Press.

Searle, J. (1984). *Minds, brains and science*. Cambridge, MA: Harvard University Press.

Sellars, W. (1997). *Empiricism and the philosophy of mind*. Cambridge: Cambridge University Press.

Williams, B. (1985). *Ethics and the limits of philosophy*. London: Fontana Press.

Chapter 3
Duties Before Rights: A Notion of the University of the Future

Paul Gibbs

Abstract The 1948 Universal Declaration of Human Rights states:

> Everyone has the right to education. Education shall be free, at least in the elementary and fundamental stages. Elementary education shall be compulsory. Technical and professional education shall be made generally available and higher education shall be equally accessible to all on the basis of merit. (United Nations 1948: Article 26)

It is from this declaration that the tension between rights and obligations has arisen, for a right is an entitlement and not an obligation (McCowan T, Theory Res Educ 9(3):291, 2011). However, education (and we will discuss what this means as higher education) is assumed to be an intrinsic good for individuals, so education became an obligation, and was no longer an entitlement that all human beings have in order to fulfil their humanity. The discourse of rights dominates discussions of student engagement in the UK higher education system, and the obligation to use the secured benefits of these rights shifts from being a public good to a private good, confirming the shift to rights from obligations. Indeed, with regard to higher education, a system of rights seems to be forced by those in power on the youth of the country. Indeed, is this not the discourse of social mobility and access? It is the central platform of government policy, albeit often interpreted as consumer rights, and it is also evident in the growing literature on the rights of students: values for money; good teaching; facilities; well-being; and a good job. Less is said about whose function it is to provide these 'rights' and the obligation that they owe to, and are owed in their role as, academics, administrators and support staff. A recent display of unruly student behaviour by members of our most prestigious universities indicates a rather one-way enactment of rights. Indeed, in a more subtle and reflective discussion of student rights in his book Freedom to Learn (Freedom to Learn. Routledge, London, 2017), Macfarlane uses the word rights 85 times, obligations seven times and duty/duties eight times. I recognise the crudity of these measurements, but they do offer an insight into the emphasis on the notion of rights. In a

P. Gibbs (✉)
CERS, Middlesex University, London, UK
e-mail: P.Gibbs@mdx.ac.uk

© Springer Nature Switzerland AG 2019
P. Gibbs et al. (eds.), *Values of the University in a Time of Uncertainty,*
https://doi.org/10.1007/978-3-030-15970-2_3

manner similar to Guilherme (Power Educ 8(1):3–18, 2016), I will argue that higher education, if not education itself, is not a right but an obligation. However, unlike his reliance on Fichte's notion of human evil for the emergence of right entitlements, I will argue from Simone Weil's belief in human goodness.

Keywords Duties · Rights · Obligations · Kant · Weil. O'Neill

Introduction

Rights are not the way in which I will develop this discussion on values in higher education and, by extension, beyond the institution. I will be considering the idea of Weil, amongst others, that obligations precede rights and how these might impact on how we conceive our higher education. I will proceed with a discussion of Weil's argument for obligations over rights, consider this in the context of an obligation of truth telling within the institution and then compare such an institution, based on obligation, to the model of education commonly experienced today.

Simone Weil, Personalities, People and Universal Rights

At the core of Weil's ideas on rights, obligations and justice is the notion that justice or right is conceptually disassociated from obligation. This is predicated (and most compellingly written about in her essays Human Personality and the Needs of the Soul, both written in 1943) on the idea that the human personality is an act, a social construct to engage with the world, and that rights are attributable to this false notion of our being. Indeed, this duty, as Weil (1953) advocated in the first sentence of her book The Needs for Roots, 'comes before that of rights, which is subordinate and relative to the former' (1953: 3). This is a view support by O'Neill, who suggests:

To put matters broadly, before turning to some more specific issues, if we focus on obligations we see the primary question of ethics as 'What ought each of us do?', whereas if we treat rights as fundamental, we see the primary question as 'What ought each of us get?'

The perspective of rights serves to privilege recipience and claiming; the perspective of obligations privileges acting and providing (2010: 164). From such reasoning I suggest that: rights for academic freedoms are subordinate to our obligations of truth-telling; students' obligations to engage in learning supersede their rights for value for money; and institutional obligations to the common good surpass their right to make profit. I acknowledge the simplicity of this argument but, should we accept it, it might require us to consider a reorientation of the contemporary notion of a rights-based university in future as the duty university (O'Neill, 2002).

Weil opens Human Personality by distinguishing between being and personality, suggesting that:

> 'You do not interest me' cannot be said to another without cruelty and offending against justice. 'Your person does not interest me.' These words can be used in an affectionate conversation between close friends, without jarring upon even the tenderest nerve of their friendship. (2015a, b: 9)

In this we might identify that, for Weil, a human being is more than the sum total of the particular roles that she adopts or the personae that she assumes. As such, she understands rights as the claims of possessive individuals against others, rather than moral community members' entitlement to things that function to secure choices – rather than welfare rights or entitlements that prescribe standards of conduct and care. Her position is not that there are real needs that ought to be agreed, but that these are better conceptualised as an obligation upon other to resolve them. Her argument is captured in The Needs of the Soul:

> A man, considered in isolation, only has duties, amongst which are certain duties towards himself. Others, seen from his point of view, only have rights. He, in his turn, has rights when seen from the point of view of others who recognise that they have obligations towards him. A man who was alone in the universe would not have any rights, but he would have obligations. (1953: 3)

From this, we can conclude that the notion of rights is relative and subordinate to the notion of obligation. Weil argues that the 'notion of rights, by its very mediocrity, leads on naturally to the person, for rights are related to personal things' (2015a, b: 21), and these personal rather than collective rights reflect and are inflated by social prestige. In this sense, rights are justified claims that individuals (and sometimes groups) can make on others, and one can choose not to exercise that right at a particular moment – but this is not true of obligations. Weil seeks to find what is common to humanity, and it is this which ought not to be violated and for which we have an obligation to prevent or ameliorate. In The Needs of the Soul she explores the nature of these obligations and states that all 'human beings are bound by identical obligations although these are performed in different ways according to particular circumstance' (2002: 4). She claims that no human being is exempt from these obligations, and to resist them is to be guilty of a crime other than where two obligations lead to incompatible obligations. Further, she states that obligations, 'whether unconditional or relative, eternal of changing, direct or indirect with regards to human affair, all stem, without exception, from the vital needs of human beings' (2002: 6). Obligations, rather than rights, remain independent of conditions for how the rights are imposed by the will of those who have power and authority so to do. Indeed, Weil suggests that that rights talk can trivialise the injustice that some people suffer and, reifying the notion, indiscriminately cover unrelated conditions. She does this by comparing the right of a farmer who evokes his right not to sell eggs and a woman evoking her right not to fall into prostitution (see 2015a, b: 21). Again, Weil sees that obligation can be converted into rights. She sees that the notion hides the realism of exploitation. For example, the right of workers to be respected in their labour is subordinated to market efficacies and the hours of work or rates of pay, not the indignities of soul-destroying monotony. For Weil and the author, it seems a question of realising the essential issue, identifying the obligation to be exercised and then to consider how these may be actualised in a defined context.

Rights and/or Obligations?

Rights are considered as an entitlement given by the powerful to the less so, and thus to allow the powerful to dictate the form and benefits of these rights. In a neo-liberal system, this means that education is not for the common good but for the self. Indeed, as Foucault points out in his study of prison, rights (law) are not equally applied to all and that it would be 'more prudent to recognise that it was made for the few and that it was brought to bear upon others' (Foucault 1979: 276). A duty-based notion of education seeks to reveal the good, beauty and justice in us all. In doing so, it forms a duty upon us to improve the nature and action of humanity through a 'certain contact with the reality, the truth, and the beauty of this universe and with the eternal wisdom which is the order of it' (Weil 2015a, b: 17).

The evidence that higher education is an obligation upon us is very thin. But that does not mean that there is an argument for it to be a right, at least in principle. Given that, for this to be sustained, higher education needs to be accessible to all and that this access is not constrained by barriers such as unacceptable debt, it is hard to see that higher education is, in itself, so conceived in many countries of the world, and it is certainly not in the United Kingdom. In a more general sense, the literature does support, and the evidence reinforce, that elementary education is supported as a right that is acted upon but, according to McCowan, there is 'surprisingly little discussion of the nature of education that might correspond to the right' (2010: 510). McCowan goes further and suggests a notion where rights are separated into a positional aspect that has emerged, which sees education as both an intrinsic and as a positional good (McCowan 2012). This two-pronged expression of right involves access both to meaningful learning and to institutions that confer positional advantage. As would Weil, he acknowledges that by recognising a positional aspect one accepts a universal entitlement to positional advantage in relation to others. In this respect, it is hard to disaggregate it from the notion of access, especially if that access is designed to provide selective benefits, secured by society for several beneficiaries to function. Indeed, as Macfarlane points out, it is a contradiction for a positional right to need to retain a distinction that confers prestige and the benefits that accrue, much in the same way as Weil criticises rights themselves. Indeed, Macfarlane goes so far as to confirm that 'although rights may be associated with duties they do not carry direct obligations' (2017: 20).

It seems that that higher education is neither an obligation on humanity nor a right of citizens. So, what are the implications of a system that rests on social position, which has no implicit justification? Clearly, its function can be other than this and has several instrumental benefits, underpinning a broad range of human functions, such as work, political participation and health. Moreover, it can have 'positional' benefits, which refer to the opportunities that one has in relation to the opportunities of others. That is, in the context of scarce goods, if my opportunities increase then the opportunities of others are diminished, and vice versa. It is hard in this case to envision it as a right for all rather than a privilege for a few.

However, given that higher education is neither a right nor an obligation upon us all to provide, do the notions of right and obligation apply to those who engage in it?

Duties and Obligations – Demonstrating Worthiness as an Academic

Duty, I propose, in this existential sense is not the Kantian imperative of following given universals (although we might choose to act as if they did) or the liberal balance of rights, but is an accountability to oneself to have the courage and skill to interpret one's individuality within our world as a dialectic between oneself and humanity. In this, it is an ethical exercise and is built through trust as an implicit obligation – voluntarily accepted, in the case of the academic – to pursue worthy activities and not just the mechanisms of performance. It is implicit in what Infinito (2003: 157) voices: 'one cannot be entirely detached from one own actions and possibilities nor inconsiderate for others and still be free'. To be aware of one's duty is not equivalent to performing it. The discussion of duties ranges from the rather rigorous, such as of those of Fichte's Divine Idea (2017), which drives academics in search of, and requires them to live by, a way of life of inquiry for an ultimate unifying truth within the learned culture of their age, to the more pragmatic. Fichte's notion of being a scholar is much more robust and isolating than our current idea, whose function of good may well not fully extend to a duty of public good and education for the sole purpose of knowing, especially given the self-interest model of neo-liberal higher education, although it does not explicitly encourage the endorsement of evil. One contemporary example might be entrepreneurial activities that are in addition to scholars' traditional roles of teaching and research yet which improve their traditional academic duties (De Silva 2016).

For Kennedy, academics within higher education also have associated obligations and privileges. Kennedy suggests that 'If we can clarify our perception of duty and gain public acceptance of it, we will have fulfilled an important obligation to the society that nurtures us. These obligations constitute the highest institutional form of academic duty' (1997: 22). By placing duty centrally to the notion of academics in higher education institutions, Kennedy identifies a moral responsibility for academics that offers a way of re-establishing the trust that there had been between the university sector and the general public. He sees the contemporary university in a time of challenge: 'Higher education today is challenged to fulfill a new and staggering burden.' Always expected to make young people more skilled, more cultured, and more thoughtful, it is now seen as the motive power for regional economic improvement and even international competitiveness (1997: 3). Within this epoch, Kennedy envisions academic duties in the area of academic life as ranging from academic freedom, to service to the university, to reaching beyond the university and public duty, including telling the truth.

So, what might be the duties that the university should build itself upon? They might be on several levels: a duty to see tolerance in those taking positions of authority on world stages (an academic role, according to Barnett (2017), is to be always on duty); a duty of care for our environment; speaking truth to power; enhancing host communities; and a duty of care to those who work in their domain. Perhaps, as institutions of transformation and vulnerability, one of the core duties is that of care. Three 'duties of care', internalised as integrity, are pertinent here: the quality of teaching and research; the organisation of adequate staff and student participation; and good governance. These might be operationalised, as de Boer and Goedegebuure (2007: 52) suggest, as:

- carefulness: preciseness and dedication; increased workloads and pressures may not lead to sloppy work;
- reliability: honesty; no selectivity or manipulation of data and results;
- verifiability: openness and public scrutiny of results;
- impartiality: priority to academic interests and readiness to account for it; and
- independence: academic freedom.

These duties have at their core a notion of integrity, or at least implicit good in the functions of university. In addition, as Collini advocates, there 'is an obligation on scholars in universities to try to hand on to their successors an intellectual and institutional inheritance that will enable enquiry to be carried out at the highest level' (2012: 148).

I am cautious here, for the ideology of the market and of a government that sees its duty toward universities is, primarily, to promote competition. This so underscores what higher education does now that, in and of itself, it throws into ambiguity the duty of care in the sense of equality, diversity and inclusion. However, many of these duties apply equally well to other public and private institutions. What sets higher education apart is our duty to tell the truth to power.

The Obligation to Seek and Tell the Truth

If higher education institutions, like any institutions in society, are to sustain themselves, then I propose that as truth-tellers (academic and students have a duty to seek to be trusted and practise the virtues of truth), as Williams (2002: 93) suggests, they are connected with trust and that truthfulness is a form of trustworthiness (ibid.: 94). To do that, they must confront the notion of self-deception that allows for the seeking of truth to be turned into blind faith in, and appeasement towards, others. We must hold ourselves and others to account for being trustworthy and sincere in our truthfulness. This disposition, as Williams (2002) proclaims, is based on our assertions being both accurate and sincere. Moreover, such truthfulness is in the words, intentions and actions of the one deemed trustworthy. It is a value-laden notion that transcends mere instructional contractualism and word games of deception; it is about being intrinsically comfortable with one's truthfulness in the assertions that one makes and the implications that can be reasonably assumed to follow such assertions. It is not about self-interest. Williams illustrates this with the example of a woman proclaiming that 'someone had opened' the post of the other person in her conversation. The assertion was accurate yet far from sincere if, indeed, it was she herself who had opened the post. The phrasing implies that it was not her, although the sentence does not deny this possibility.

As O'Neill proposes, we need ways to distinguish trustworthy from untrustworthy informants. However, a university carelessly embracing league tables when it suits and critically objecting to them when it doesn't – or arguing for an income benefit from education that applies only to certain groups; or not making clear that fees from poorer students subsidise those on more prestigious yet more expensive courses; or academics lending their authority to populist media programmes – does nothing to build confidence in it as a site of truth-tellers.

Amongst the things that we can do is to help students to make authentic, personal decisions based on what we have offered them for their futures and to ensure that they are aware of what that is, rather than what they want or it might be. This is a duty, I believe, for academics that transcends their discipline in the preparation of students for a world in which their contribution can be both significant and worthy. I find an inspirational source in the Socratic notion of the harmony of truth-telling and behaviour, as revealed in laches as 'care for the soul'; a caring for the morality of oneself through knowing, trusting and being the stance that one takes for oneself. This requires a sense of courage to grasp freedom to be for oneself amongst others. This ancient example can be matched by many others from various regimes of truth, for instance a Confucian model that embeds a familial relational model nested in one of cultivation of self, family and state. In this context, a medical deception of patients is acceptable, at the family's wish. It is not a decision taken through medical paternalism so much as personal and professional ethics.

As universities become more instrumental, extended and digital, they are less conducive to such freedom and tend to encourage a fiction of the 'good' future – paradoxically, one built upon a lack of hope, oppression and super-surveillance. At the policy level, in the United Kingdom such deception is illustrated by the implementation of our Counter-Terrorism and Security Act 2015. This requires universities to give 'due regard' to the risk of 'radicalisation' among students –sensible enough, but its implementation guidelines have been considered to be discriminatory or even racist by leading legal counsel. However, they are followed to the letter by most institutions, for fear of reprisals under the terms of the Higher Education and Research Act 2017.

But lack of originality is no reason to accept the self-serving and self-deceptive, politically motivated directives imposed on educational institutions, ostensibly to enable greater transparency and accountability yet whose function is more to do with control. In the United Kingdom, this can be seen in the confusion and inaccuracies of the excellence framework for research, teaching and knowledge, in terms of what they do and what they are meant to measure. Ironically, the salary hikes of those whose have led the implementation of these policies on behalf of the government have led to their own rewards being questioned: a betrayal of those betraying liberal education?

In this sense, I am reminded of Foucault's Paris lectures (2010) on parrhesia, of truth-speaking and of Peters' (2003) discussion of truth-telling as an educational practice. To speak out when the consequences may be unfavourable to oneself requires courage and a reconstitution of what higher education has become; a return to an ethos of personal growth, both moral and intellectual, that represents what humanity might become better than through offering a service of blinkered higher skill training. For Pickup, academics could demonstrate their preparedness for personal loss when speaking 'ethically laden truths' (2016: 19). To do so requires a form of self-trust that avoids any deception of society and of oneself, a deception that was prevalent even before a post-trust era yet is more acute and acceptable within it. Foucault suggests that in ancient texts there are ways in which we can develop and maintain our ability for telling the truth to ourselves, and that these include: solitary self-examination; self-diagnosis; and self-testing.

So, given that we might accept that deception and self-deception can be identified in its policy and practice, what does higher education look like? It can be seen in how education has drifted from being an end towards being a supply economics imperative, in scholars seeking favourable evaluations from students rather than stretching their capabilities, fuelled by emotional labour, and in creating personal brands! Although such practices seem counter to the principles of liberal, transformative education, they present a dilemma: should we facilitate students and staff speaking truth to each other, when this might not be in their best interests in a world that encourages compliance rather than free thinking? A world in which we are under constant surveillance and are often herded along by industrial and commercial global powers? How, morally, should we prepare them to help them flourish?

A Duty of Truth at the Core of Higher Education

One way that a contemporary higher education system can help itself out of the moral dilemma created by post-truth more generally is by confronting self-deception through encouraging living an examined life. The deceptions already mentioned, and many more examples could be given, may be hidden for a while if a university education predominantly gives value, in terms of money and personal profit, for both students and academics – that is, until the market itself normalises the situation.

We can manifest this change in our discourse, our curriculum and our reason for being. Nixon (2004) suggests that the intrinsic dispositions of academic practice should not concentrate on citations so much as dispositions of truthfulness, respect and authenticity: virtues that are intrinsic to being a good academic practitioner. This is achieved through reflection, evaluation and monitoring, which are acts of autonomous thinkers of the type that liberal education and, indeed, industry claim to want. These reflective practices also contribute to self-belief, knowledge and prudence. To believe in one's own ability to make decisions on one's own preferences is central to liberal ideals of autonomous, free action. To be able to accept the responsibility that this implies, of constituting a reasoned world reality, facilitates the ontological integration of self with others. It encourages creativity, confidence and community through the negotiation of shared realities.

Higher education should encourage self-trust through reasoned argument and debate as free speech and reject, rather than ignore, discourses of dogma and hate. For students to be prepared to risk their socially-constructed self in a process of authentic discovery of worth demands mutual and empathetic trust. Students need to trust that, if they stray too far from the commonality of experience, they will not be expelled or vilified as eccentrics or charlatans but will be critiqued and supported. Such behaviours facilitate sincerity, empathy and resilience, which can be manifested in the praxis of critical being (Barnett 1997). The recognition of the existence of the potential for such mutuality is held in the collective goodwill of all the stakeholders of the institution and is (or, perhaps, ought to be) the basis of public trust in higher education institutions. I have a view that this requires the academic to be a truth-teller. This view is not shared by all: Fish (2014), for instance, sees the academic role as 'just a job', where only the contractual terms of employment determine one's activities. Indeed, this is an example of higher education employers enacting their rights within a contract, forgoing the obligations to truth and the flourishing of students.

As, Ball (2017) suggests, these ideas might be facilitated by an educational practice of self-formation, each one raising questions of agency, truth and subjectivity. They are:

- Developing an environment of experimentation, spaces for ongoing ethical construction
- An awareness of one's current conditions, as defined by culture and history – genealogy as curriculum; and
- An attitude or disposition to critique or Socratic interrogation, leading to the resilience of self-trust.

The emphasis here should be on taking a dialogical, rather than didactic, approach, ensuring reciprocity between students and teachers. Through such dialogue, deliberative thoughtfulness can be facilitated and followed, wherever it goes.

Concluding Remarks: Truth-Telling as an Obligation of Higher Education

Briefly, in concluding, the trustworthiness of educational truth-tellers is a virtue of 'good' higher education. Within it, there are opportunities to question the importance of self and one's contribution to society, which deserve public affirmation.

Certainly, in an educational framework where the self has to expose its vulnerability to another, anything other than a moral duty of trusting care would make the offer of education potentially loaded and exploitative. Indeed, a failure to respect others is a violation of the duty placed on us, as academics, by those to whom we are responsible.

To close, two of the most important problems for the future of higher education are, I think, to:

1. Construct an entity where duties precede rights of all its members, and
2. Construct an entity where those who speak on behalf of, and within, higher education are truth-tellers.

In both, we need to question in order to seek clarity and confront obscurity in both our institutions and the wider public space and, through such questioning, reveal deception in others and ourselves. To hold someone accountable for their use of state-sponsored education, in the sense of value, requires a clear statement of the expected responsibility and output. The cultivation of teaching and researching as phronesis, phantasia and parrhesia orients inquirers toward moral and intentional truth-telling practices that resist a simplistic rendering of 'criticality and overly technical understandings of research' (Pickup 2016: 178).

Finally, we return to Foucault. He speaks of the general significance that we might find in society as a battle, not on behalf of truth but 'about the status of truth and the economic and political role it plays' (1980: 132). As academics, if we should fail to speak out against the self-deception encouraged in our engagements with students and policy, and for our institutions likewise to speak out to policy, we can easily end up with the objectification of the others within and outside academia. The issue has to be addressed through an assessment of what we can expect from our higher education institutions and ourselves: a Socratic examination that can be put quite simply: in whom can we trust to be the truth-tellers, if not ourselves?

References

Ball, S. (2017). *Foucault as educator*. Cham: Springer Briefs.

Barnett, R. A. (1997). *Higher education: A critical business*. Buckingham: SRHE and Open University Press.

Barnett, R. (2017). Constructing the university: Towards a social philosophy of higher education. *Educational Philosophy and Theory, 49*(1), 78–88.

Collini, S. (2012). *What are universities for?* London: Penguin Press.

de Boer, H., & Goedegebuure, L. (2007). 'Modern' governance and codes of conduct in Dutch higher education. *Higher Education Research & Development, 26*(1), 45–55.

De Silva, M. (2016). Academic entrepreneurship and traditional academic duties: Synergy or rivalry? *Studies in Higher Education, 41*(12), 2169–2183.

Fichte, J. G. (2017). *On the nature of the scholar*. Dumfries/Galloway: Anodos Books.

Fish, S. (2014). *Versions of academic freedom*. Chicago: University of Chicago Press.

Foucault, M. (1979). *Discipline and punish: The birth of the prison*. New York: Vintage Books.

Foucault, M. (1980). Knowledge and power. In M. Foucault & C. Gordon (Eds.), *Power/ Knowledge: Selected interviews and other writings 1972–1977* (pp. 108–133). Hertfordshire: Harvester Wheatsheaf.

Foucault, P. (2010). *The government of self and others*. Basingstoke: Palgrave Macmillan.

Guilherme, A. (2016). Do we have a right to education or a duty to educate ourselves? An enquiry based on Fichte's views on education. *Power and Education, 8*(1), 3–18.

Infinito, J. (2003). Ethical self-formation: A look at the later Foucault. *Education Theory, 53*(2), 155–117.

Kennedy, D. (1997). *Academic duty*. Cambridge: Harvard University Press.

Macfarlane, B. (2017). *Freedom to learn*. London: Routledge.

McCowan, Y. (2010). Reframing the universal right to education. *Comparative Education, 46*(4), 509–525.

McCowan, T. (2011). Human rights, capabilities and the normative basis of 'Education for All'. *Theory and Research in Education, 9*(3), 283–298.

McCowan, T. (2012). Is there a universal right to higher education? *British Journal of Educational Studies, 60*(2), 111–128.

Nixon, J. (2004). A profession in crisis? In D. Hayes (Ed.), *Key debates in education* (pp. 165–169). London/New York: RoutledgeFalmer/Taylor and Francis Group.

O'Neill, O. (2002). *A question of trust. BBC Reith lectures* (p. XXX). Cambridge: Cambridge University Press.

O'Neill, O. (2010). Rights, obligations, priorities. *Studies in Christian Ethics, 23*(2), 163–171.

Peters, M. A. (2003). Truth-telling as an educational practice of the self: Foucault, parrhesia and the ethics of subjectivity. *Oxford Review of Education, 29*(2), 207–223.

Pickup, A. (2016). Critical inquiry as virtuous truth-telling: Implications of phronesis and parrhesia. *Critical Questions in Education (special issue), 7*(3), 177–196.

United Nations, 1948: Article 26. http://www.claiminghumanrights.org/udhr_article_26.html. Accessed 1 Mar 2018.

Weil, S. (1953). *The need for roots: A prelude to a declaration of duties toward mankind*. London: Routledge.

Weil, S. (2015a). Human personality. In R. Rees (Ed.), *Selected essays, 1934–1943* (pp. 19–34). Eugene: Wipf and Stock Publishers.

Weil, S. (2015b). Draft of a declaration of human obligations. In R. Rees (Ed.), *Selected essays 1934–43* (pp. 219–227). Eugene: Wipf and Stock.

Williams, B. (2002). *Truth and truthfulness*. New York: Princeton University Press.

Part II
The University as Values Organisation

Chapter 4
Re-valuing the University: An Ecological Approach

Ronald Barnett

Keywords Ecological · Hierarchy of values · Universities · Choices · Responsibilities

Introduction

Universities and the values that they embody are on a cusp. Over the past half century or more, they have been drawn into, if not corralled into, a value framework of economic and market rationality and state managerialism and have, in turn, been obliged at least to ventriloquise the values of those powerful forces, if not actually to take on those attendant values. Some see the university as occupying a values desert, being devoid of values. For them, the university has fallen in with an age of nihilism (Blake et al. 2012).

However, such a values pessimism may be underestimating the space available to universities and so may be unwittingly helping to surrender the university to malign forces, the values of which privilege the economic sphere and which are diminishing the university. A heightened realism may, perhaps surprisingly, serve to draw out a wider worldly framework, in which universities may be seen as possessing a degree of value agency. The values of the university are neither necessarily those of half a century ago, still less of the nineteenth century; but then neither are they necessarily those of either the entrepreneurial university or the corporate university. Now, for the first time, the university has opening to it value options and so it now has the responsibility of *re-valuing its values* and of working out possibilities for realising its chosen values. And those values may be quite new values, appropriate to the situation of the university in the twenty-first century, diligently and adroitly fostered and worked at.

R. Barnett (✉)
University College London, Institute of Education, London, UK
e-mail: ron.barnett@ucl.ac.uk

P. Gibbs et al. (eds.), *Values of the University in a Time of Uncertainty*,
https://doi.org/10.1007/978-3-030-15970-2_4

In unravelling this thesis, an ecological approach may be helpful. At the heart of the ecological perspective, after all, is not only that human-kind is entangled with many ecosystems but that it is partly responsible for any impairments that those ecosystems may be facing. Accordingly, the matter of the university's values in the twenty-first century becomes now a matter of the university's responsibilities in putting its resources into play, in improving and developing all the many ecosystems of the world with which it is entwined.

A Hierarchy of Values

The value of anything can only become a matter of sensible consideration within certain boundaries. And the boundaries are themselves layered. At the first level, value is engendered through prior criteria. The criteria supply a set of means or considerations that allow a value to be imputed to the entity in question. For example, the worth of a student essay is established through the application of some set of criteria, which may differ across disciplines, or across the assignment tasks within a programme of studies. For one assignment, soundness of argumentation and an understanding of key concepts in the field might be important; for another, originality and risk-taking might be what is sought; and in yet another, practical deftness and judgement *in situ* might provide the relevant criteria. The criteria, by which the value or worth of the assignment is to be judged, can legitimately vary, therefore.

However, all such sets of judgements and their associated criteria, would still – for many across the world – constitute legitimate examples of practices within the field of higher education. So the criteria are nested within an overarching understanding of higher education. This means, in turn, that there are tacit boundaries as to what is to count as higher education. And that, in turn, suggests that values attach to higher education itself, in order that those particular practices – those assignments and their connected teaching and learning processes – can be felt to be worthwhile and to warrant judgemental activities being applied to them. There is at work here a broad value framework, seldom spelt out, that helps to carve out a sense as to the general character of higher education.

This value framework does not and cannot have firm borders. It has fuzzy edges that allow for differences of view. Some will consider that the university is essentially a space for sustaining and developing reasoned inquiry. Others will see the university as an institution that has a responsibility to advance practical knowledge. And yet others, for example, will hold to the university as an institution concerned to promote human being. Such value frameworks indicate that the university is a space in which values clash and yet overlap sufficiently to allow matters to progress without too much violent dispute at any one time. This orderliness certainly breaks down at occasional flashpoints, for example where states see the university as a harbinger of unsettling dissensus or even radicalism, or where students seek collectively to advance a programme of political reform; and which then intervene on the campus, even with military force. Power (or powerlessness) resides in value positions.

But a yet further level of value now emerges. For value can only attach to a complex and worldly institution such as the university against some kind of framework. What is important in the world? Against what transversal set of priorities or considerations is the university to be understood – and evaluations to be made of it? Is it, for example, that a high priority is to be awarded knowledge as such or to social justice or a well-functioning economy or national identity or human understanding or the wellbeing of the entire world? In short, on this understanding, the value of the university would be set against a fundamental set of values as to what is important – in relation to life, or to the world. This value background would have the status as to that which is held to be of foundational significance. (cf Taylor 1992, Part I).

There is, then, a hierarchy of values that potentially, at least, comes into play when the matter arises concerning the value of the university. And at each level, nice semi-empirical questions would arise as to the extent to which the university in practice could be judged to be fulfilling the sets of value. With the value position of the university being understood in this way as situated in a hierarchy of values, it is hardly surprising if the university is a site of value conflict, for dispute can and does break out at every level. Different people, disciplines, groups, societies and nations express different values at each level. The value position of the university is, as a result, extremely fragile.

Value Dissensus

Is that it, then? Simply to observe that the university is both a site and an object of value conflict; indeed, a set of value conflicts that goes all the way to what is held to be fundamental in life? There is, inevitably, more to be said.

A first tack is to note that the discussion so far has consisted in noting that value frameworks can and are brought to bear upon the university. Even at the first level, in the example of student assignments and marking criteria, the matter was posed as that of bringing evaluative frameworks to bear upon those activities. All of that may be accepted as a legitimate way of looking at the relationship between values and the university but yet it might be wondered as to whether the activities of the university hold or bequeath values within themselves.

Just this was the line taken by Alistair MacIntyre in his (1985) suggestion that the practices characteristic of the university held within themselves their own 'internal goods', and that the practising of those practices therefore acted as a carrier for certain kinds of virtue. I am not sure that MacIntyre spelt out this argument but it isn't difficult to supply examples of the kind of thing he might have had in mind. The giving of reasons requires an allegiance to truthfulness, the pedagogical relationship calls for a respect and even a concern for persons, the making of truth claims relies on a measure of integrity, the continuous pursuit of the activities of learning or teaching or research or scholarship demands both self-discipline and persistence, and maintaining the community within such activities might be sustained calls in turn for reticence and considerateness. On this approach to values, therefore – what has come to be known as a virtue ethic in relation to the university – what counts is not values that are brought to bear upon the university but rather values that are held to be naturally embedded within the activities characteristic of the university.

This virtue perspective can be pressed even further in the idea of 'epistemic virtues' (Brady and Pritchard 2003), namely the idea that the very pursuit of knowledge at any level requires and helps to develop certain kinds of virtues – as intimated of carefulness, diligence, courage, concern for the other, truthfulness, and so on and so forth. Just such a way of thinking about the values internally sustained within the university provides a way of filling out the further idea that a higher education naturally provides an institutional and an educational vehicle for character formation.

There are two additional points to note about this approach that help to mark out its strength; and there is a link that may be made between them. The first is that it embodies a distinction between the university qua institution and the university as a set of practices; and this distinction MacIntyre himself was at pains to make. This distinction allows evaluations to be made of the extent to which the university qua institution is sustaining the values identified as inherent in the practices characteristically held to be constitutive of it. It can be asked: is this university x really upholding the values of respect for persons or truthfulness or respect or integrity (and so on)? (cf Nixon 2008).

The second point is that this conception of values not only signals virtues held within a form of life but also implies a spirit that is immanent in such a form of life (cf Jaspers 1965: 44–45). This is a particular form of life, this academic life. It is carried forward by the collective ethos that the virtues constitute. It is particularly particular in that it is bound up with thought. It embodies a 'unity of life and thought'. The phrase is that of Deleuze, in drawing out Nietzsche's view of the philosopher, and it has point here. Deleuze (2012: 66) goes on: 'Modes of life inspire ways of thinking; modes of thinking create ways of living. Life activates thought, and thought in turn affirms life.' Such sentiments have direct application to the academic life: its thinking creates and sustains its particular form of life, the virtues embodied in its collective processes containing value and so imparting value to the whole enterprise.

Putting these two points together – the distinction between the university qua institution and the university qua processes of human engagement on the one hand, and the academic life as a certain kind of spirit generated by and itself sustaining certain kinds of value or virtue on the other hand – we can press the earlier question: is this university x really embodying the spirit of the academic life and helping to sustain its inner virtues or, to the contrary, is it even diminishing that life, and so diminishing its value?

How does this set of reflections – building on MacIntyre's thesis – connect with the earlier observation about the university as a site of dissensus, as a site that refuses to countenance consensus? (Readings 1997). There is a twofold set of connections.

In the first place, the virtue ethic as just teased out – the particular virtues that attach characteristically to particular acts in the academic life – is itself embattled, both within the university and in the wider society. To steal the title of that book of Deleuze, there is no 'pure immanence' to be found any longer in the university, anywhere in the world. The virtues exhibited by the academic way of life – of care, thoughtfulness, reasonableness, reticence, considerateness, even-handedness, respect for persons, integrity and truthfulness – are now no longer accepted uncritically as expressions of a valuable form of life and, in some quarters, are maligned and even downright repudiated. This wariness towards the academic life and its inner values is of course to be found in both strong and weaker forms, in political statements and in policy papers that urge universities to become more innovative, and to move at a faster pace, and to be more competitive, quite apart from directly hostile voices coming the way of the university.

In the second place, these values are now frequently undermined within the university itself. This is not just to make the obvious point that many managerial practices not infrequently – if inadvertently – have the effect of undermining the virtues traditionally held to be characteristic of academic life. It is also to observe that academics themselves are sometimes complicit in practices that run against the values hitherto held to be characteristic of the academic life. Pressures to publish in 'world-class' journals, to pass examinations, to win research grants and to gain demonstrable external impact are contributory factors in the growth of the manipulation of data, plagiarism (by both academics and students), unduly hostile reviews by academics of papers submitted to journals (not to mention suggestions in such reviews – under the cloak of anonymity – that the author cite publications of the reviewer), a falling away of care in the compilation of academic texts and a disregard for persons (that is leading even to suicide, again among both staff and students): responsibility for all of these phenomena and more can be laid at the door both of managerial policies and practices and of the unfolding behaviours of academics themselves (doubtless partly in response to the oppressive and competitive environment in which they find themselves).

The university has become, therefore, as well as a site of value carelessness, a site of value dissensus, in which it cannot be not assumed that consensus is possible (Readings,). It may be indeed that rival sets of values are and can be hardly on speaking terms. The value dispositions pass each other by, their adherents evincing incomprehension of each other's positions. Just how can the university align itself so as to underpin 'cognitive capitalism' (Boutang 2011; Roggero 2011)? Just how can the university live in the past? Just how can the university seek to hold to tropes of critical reason and freedom? Just how might the university be transformed into an engine of innovation? Just how is the university to develop an ethos of care towards its members? The questions are directly about the values that the university might sustain and yet they run against each other, with much antagonistic force.

The Matter of Responsibility: Chicken and Egg

The matter of responsibility is highly pertinent in this context although, so far as I know, it has not been treated to much serious attention in the philosophy of higher education. However, it quickly brings into view a panoply of relevant issues (and on which we can only lightly touch here).

It is not irrelevant, although telling, that Derrida himself (1992) raised the matter of the responsibility of the university but then backed away from the difficulties that were eschewing. For the idea of responsibility implies that there are values at stake in a situation to which actors should be sympathetic. Given Derrida's deconstructionist approach to philosophy, with its excavation of concepts such that they frequently lost their power to sustain clear practices and institutions, it was hardly surprising that Derrida found difficulty with the concept of responsibility. In parallel, it is worth noting, too, that the idea of responsibility is seldom if ever to be seen in university web-sites. It is as if, in the twenty-first century at least, the very idea of responsibility causes a certain frisson among institutional leaders. Prima facie, then, while at first blush, it may seem a way forward into university values, there are warning signs that it may not readily provide firm ground on which to progress.

There is, in fact, a long literature on the idea of responsibility. A key distinction in that literature, and which is relevant here, is that between retrospective responsibility and prospective responsibility. Retrospective responsibility characteristically poses a causal link: x is responsible for event y. x might be a physical entity – a disease, say – or a human being; and in this latter case, the responsibility takes on a moral aspect. Person x caused y, and is held responsible for it. Prospective responsibility, on the other hand, comes into play in a situation where x is held to have a duty to act, and possibly in a certain way. There is an oughtness here: in this situation y, x ought to do such and such. Linked here is a form of responsibility that has perhaps not received much attention in the philosophical literature, that kind of responsibility that issues from someone's office or position. People in certain positions in organisations have responsibilities thrust upon them, as it were, in virtue of particular responsibilities attaching to certain roles. In the UK, vice-chancellors of university are accounting officers, with responsibilities literally to account for the financial well-being of the institution.

A further distinction relevant here is that between responsibilities that attach to individuals and responsibilities that attach to collectives. With regard to collective responsibilities, it is a moot point whether, for example, universities can be held to have responsibilities. My view is clear, namely that universities can be considered to constitute 'corporate agents' (List and Pettit 2011). As such, they can be said to have responsibilities qua universities.

The responsibilities, therefore, that come into play in relation to universities are several – of individual members of universities and of universities as collectives, of individuals as human beings and of individuals as office holders, and of both retrospective responsibility (had the tutor not acted in that way, the student would have gained her diploma) and of prospective responsibility (each student has responsibilities toward their participation in their programme of studies if they are to succeed). It is self-evidently the case that in all these instances, the fulfilment of responsibilities calls for certain qualities or virtues, both in individual members and as characteristics of the ethos of a university as a whole.

I want to press further at certain points in this set of considerations. The identification of prospective responsibilities can only take place against the background of a definite value-background. A university has a responsibility to constitute itself as a space of truthfulness only insofar as truthfulness is held to be a value worth upholding. However, and this is crucial, the overall situation in which an institution such as the university finds itself is always changing. It then becomes an issue as to whether the responsibilities of the university are fixed or are changing. I would want to say that the situation in front of universities in the twenty-first century is that not only is it changing (and with remarkable rapidity) but that it is opening possibilities for the university to form new kinds of relationships with the wider society. It then becomes a further issue as to whether the responsibilities of the university are changing or whether, rather, that the university's responsibilities hold constant but may now be filled in different and perhaps larger ways, and now on a global stage.

In turn, the following becomes a nice question: is it that a university's responsibilities flow from its opportunities or do its opportunities emerge from its values as they might be worked out in a changing world? Its collective responsibilities must flow in part from the opportunities that present themselves; and these opportunities may be arising anew all the time (to draw in students from wider segments of society, to put its research into the public domain and so forth). But then the perception of those opportunities will be coloured by the values that our university keeps and comes to be known for. (An explicitly entrepreneurial university will have and be perceived to have a different set of values from a specialist university, perhaps with a religious foundation.) The university's opportunities and its responsibilities play into each other in a chicken-and-egg relationship. The one helps to produce the other and so on and so forth.

Choices, What Choices?

The identification and the holding of values has meaning only in a situation that offers choices. It is therefore an open situation, although what form that openness takes is a further matter. So far as universities are concerned, a number of kinds of potential openness can be identified: discursive, financial, pedagogical, research topics, and the range and manner of engagement with the wider society. It is an empirical matter as to the extent of the openness that characterises each of these spheres but that empirical setting is relevant here.

Many speak and apparently believe – in the first quarter of the twenty-first century – that the university has limited degrees of openness. Indeed, many consider that the university's room for manoeuvre is diminishing, in the wake of a tightening of the audit environment, a lessening of state monies and yet a heightening of societal and even global expectations. And the further observation may be added that in many regimes around the world, the autonomy available to the university is deliberately being diminished as the state intervenes in it, even to the extent of imprisoning its academics. But it just may be that, while all of this curtailment of the university's freedoms is now happening, still pari passu in many jurisdictions at least, the possibilities available to the university are actually widening.

These observations cut two ways. The values of universities and their institutional leaders, as well as those of their members more generally, are especially exposed at times of great travails that befall them. A sudden and dramatic lessening of state funding, the emergence of a populist government for whom universities represent an awkward source of critique, and a heightened level of public attention such that quite minor matters on campus are treated disproportionately will all severely test and, indeed, expose the core values that the university holds. Just this situation arose in Germany in the 1930s and we see it too today in certain countries in the world. Much less obviously, a university's values come – or should come – to the fore in a situation in which options are opening. But this is surely the situation facing most universities across the world.

The university is now entangled with the world and this is a new situation. Whereas until very recently, the university occupied a minor place in the nether reaches of society, now it sits on the high ground in the centre of society. The forces at work and the features that it now possesses that help to explain this situation are not our main interest here (they include such phenomena as the coming of 'cognitive capitalism', its impact on both research and teaching, and the consequent heightened interest taken by the state in its higher education sector and enlargement of the sector). What is to the point here is that this change, in which higher education has both enlarged and come into the centre of society, has brought with it an entanglement in many segments of society.

That word 'entanglement' is deliberately used. It is increasingly in vogue in social theory but perhaps a key aspect of its original use is underplayed. Originally established in quantum mechanics, the concept refers to a situation in which there is a strong reciprocity between entities. Here, it is not just that, for instance, that the economy and society affect universities and vice versa but that we can no longer understand one of the entities without bringing the other entity into view. We can no longer understand the university without having recourse to the economy; that much is obvious. But also we can no longer fully understand the economy of advanced societies unless we embrace the way that research and the skilled labour emerging from universities is part of the economy.

It follows that the university, in turn, can only be understood in virtue of the way it is now entangled with many facets of the world. But then, if this is the case, we have to say that the plane of choices opening to the university is widening. And therefore the spaces in which it expresses its values and the ways in which it expresses those values are all the time widening too.

But this set of observations should be pressed a little further and tellingly so. If the plane of choices in front of the university is widening and if the university is moving in messy and even dark waters, the university is all the time faced with value conflicts. To which sets of values does it hold as it engages with the political sphere, the wider society, the economy and the natural environment, and with which values does it unfold its research strategy, its teaching strategy and its 'human resource' strategy, still less the way it works at its relationships with its students? In short, a value plane now opens to the university on which the university will and must make value choices and in many directions of the world. That 'must' is not prescriptive but empirical in the sense that the university is now placed in a position in which it is compelled to make value choices, whether it recognises it or not.

An Ecological Vista

I have been suggesting that the identification and the upholding of a set of values makes sense only within a particular context. The idea of a context is itself multi-stranded. It will involve a value background, extending into a hierarchy of values. But it will also involve considerations of the social and wider context at play. This is not to rule out the notion of duties but it is to say that they do not present themselves as binding or as absolute but take on contours in particular circumstances. And circumstances may be such that duties may clash and so value preferences have to come into play. Furthermore, situations may present with possibilities for values to have expression and, moreover, those situations may change, so presenting new possibilities for the expression of values. All this may be seen with regard to universities.

I have intimated something of the changing context of universities in which values attaching to the university may find expression. In particular, I have observed that the university is now entangled in the wider world in a number of ways, but that observation must now be radicalised. The university, across the world, is entangled with seven ecosystems, those of the economy, social institutions, persons, knowledge, learning, culture, and the natural environment (Barnett 2018). Simply to set these down in this way indicates that the economy is not to be privileged in any understanding of the context within which the university is situated. (We may note that Guattari (2005) considered that there were 'three ecologies' – of social institutions, subjectivities and knowledge – but this depiction severely underestimates the ecological context within which an institution such as the university finds itself.)

Why the term 'ecology'? An ecology has certain features: it has an array of elements loosely held together; self-sustaining powers, not least in competitive situations; self-reproducing capacities; an inherent value; and a fragility such that it can be impaired, not least by human actions. All of these attributes are exhibited by each of the seven ecosystems just identified.

Why identify these seven ecosystems? I identify these seven ecosystems here because they are particularly germane to the university as an institution: the university is necessarily bound up with the economy, social institutions, knowledge, learning, persons, culture and the natural environment. Why not other clusterings that might be suggested as other candidates as ecosystems of the university, such as the polity, the internet, the law or the built environment? I do not regard such other clusterings as necessarily bound up with the university but note: even if it could be shown that there are other ecosystems of the university that fulfil the criteria just set out, that would in no way dent my argument. To the contrary, it would only indicate that the ecological situation of the university is even more complicated than my seven ecosystems would imply.

This, then, is the context in which the university is placed, and is therefore the context in which its values will and must find expression. The university is caught up in a panoply of ecosystems, whether it wishes it or not (cf Bhaskar 2012). To say this is to invoke a realist dimension into our explorations. It is to say that the relationships between the university and the wider world are of this kind. This set of relationships configures the ontological situation in which the university finds itself. This ontological situation is real and is independent of any explicit stance that the university may adopt. The university may wish to be silent about much of this, and may prefer to give preference to certain features of this complex situation – say to the economy and to knowledge transfer (and so boost its own 'academic capitalism') – but it is entangled in a web of relationships with a wider range of ecosystems whether it wishes it or not.

(Re)Valuing the University

It follows from these explorations that the matter of values and the university has to be re-thought. In the process, the values of the university need to be re-thought; re-valued indeed.

The first point arises from the notion of entanglement. It will be recalled that the notion of entanglement cuts two-ways. If x is entangled with y, then y is entangled with x. If the university is entangled with a number of ecosystems, then each of those ecosystems has influence on the university but so too does the university have influence on each of those ecosystems. Such considerations open the way to a relational view of the university. Questions can be asked about the character of the relationship between each of the ecosystems and the university; and they will differ, across the ecosystems and across universities, and across disciplines and programmes of study even within a single university. Each university will have its own imprint in each of the seven ecosystems and vice versa. It follows that each university possesses its own possibilities in developing and extending its relationships with each ecosystem. It will possess its own ecological footprint.

If this set of reflections holds water, it follows, too, that the *value territory* in front of the university is dynamic as its relationships with its ecosystems change. The developing ecological landscape in front of any university all the time presents with new opportunities to realise its values. A university may be well placed to reach into the cultural sphere, or engage anew with particular social institutions, or use new technologies to advance societal learning and so on. And to reiterate the point, these possibilities will differ across disciplines and across programmes of study within the same university.

But now a crucial matter arises. As well as opening possibilities for the university to realise its already-held values, does this ecological vista not open the possibility of *new values* coming the university's way?

Let us back-track for a moment. Some, especially some concerned with education, consider that values have been discarded by the university. That there is often a squeamishness in speaking openly of values is testimony to the point. Some go even further and – as noted – claim that we are now in an age of nihilism, so far as values in education are concerned. This is not, I suggest, a helpful way of understanding the matter. It is both more helpful and more accurate to say, for example, that one set of values, largely internal to the university, have – over the past 50 years or so – come to be supplanted by a different and externally-framed set of values. The key concepts that marked out the value territory of the university were those such as truth, understanding, personal development, inquiry, learning, critical thought and reason. Now the key concepts that mark out the present value territory of the university are those such as profit, innovation, economy, competition, knowledge transfer, markets, student-as-customer, value-for-money and so on. In short, the value landscape of the university has shifted. It is not that the university is devoid of values but that it has come to place itself against the horizon of a particular set of values. And it is a horizon in which the economy is accorded a privileged position.

But then, if this is the case, there is no a priori reason to believe that this is the end of the matter. The values landscape of the university can continue to change; and, indeed, they are already continuing to evolve. As those ecological entanglements of the university increase, so new opportunities open to the university for new relationships with the wider world. But then, and more especially, it cannot be discounted that the value territory will so change that the opportunity will present itself – and maybe is already presenting itself – for the university to associate with a new set of values. Such values might be marked out by concepts such as societal collaboration, societal learning, public sphere, public reason, public goods, community, social justice, wellbeing, democracy, care, concern and so on and so forth. And if we look carefully enough, we see many instances across the world of universities and their members exploring possibilities that are emerging that allow the realisation of such a new kind of value framework.

What is in prospect, then, is not that the values of the university are in ruins or that the values which universities now represent have to be resisted but that, understood ecologically, there are now emerging multiple spaces in which the values of the university may be re-valued. There can be no return in the twenty-first century to the values of the 1950s (as some seem to be hoping for) but neither should the present values – built around cognitive capitalism and state managerialism – be assumed to constitute the end-game. Understood ecologically, universities possess a widening panoply of terrains on which to work out their value positions and, indeed, some degree of agency so to do.

There is a final point to be made here. As intimated, bringing such an ecological perspective into play opens the matter of responsibilities befalling universities. *If* it is the case that a university has certain values – say, to promote learning in the fullest way, or to advance human understanding, or to widen public reason – and *if* the intertwinedness of the university in multiple ecosystems is opening spaces anew and *if* those ecosystems are impaired in any way (say, the level of public understanding of complex issues is unduly limited), then any university that possesses values of that kind has new responsibilities falling on it imaginatively to bring its resources into play such that it seizes new possibilities for realizing its values.

For example, a heightened concern for and respect towards all matter, organic and inert, appears to be emerging (Bennett 2010) and that new sensitivity opens new considerations as to the features of the Earth towards which the university might become sensitive. In short, therefore (and to pick up earlier points), an ecological vista opens to new collective prospective responsibilities coming the way of universities *and* their members.

Conclusions

The values of the university are not given. To speak of a value framework being imposed upon the university is not without point. In every jurisdiction of the world, universities work out their situations under the imprint of powerful forces – of the state, of cross-national agencies and of the economy (both locally and globally) acting upon them. But characteristically universities have some room for their own corporate agency. The values of the university, accordingly, have continually to be worked at and eked out, practically, laboriously, and with some political astuteness.

Moreover, an ecological perspective – as proposed here – opens the possibility that new spaces may be emerging in which the university may imaginatively work out and live out its values anew. The university now finds itself entangled with multiple ecosystems which present not just dynamic relationships and new spaces but, thereby, open to the university – each university – the chance to glimpse new values for itself as it probes the possibilities of those new spaces; possibilities with society, culture, persons, learning, knowledge and the natural environment and even with the economy. A revaluing of the university's values is on the cards.

It follows that it is no longer open to the university to excuse itself that 'there is no alternative' but to fall in with the dominant values and ideologies of the age. Such a TINA stance is an indication of institutional bad-faith. Now, for the first time, the university has value options before it. Some universities around the world are beginning to seize the opportunities of these new spaces and relationships to explore quite new activities both within the university and with their members and with the wider world. Collective imaginings are being developed to form new imaginaries of the university, in some universities at least. Will other universities follow?

References

Barnett, R. (2018). *The ecological university: A feasible Utopia*. London: Routledge.

Bennett, J. (2010). *Vibrant matter: A political economy of things*. Durham: Duke University.

Bhaskar, R. (2012). Critical realism in resonance with Nordic ecophilosophy. In R. Bhaskar, K. G. Hoyer, & P. Naess (Eds.), *Ecophilosophy in a world of crisis*. London/New York: Routledge.

Blake, N., Smeyers, P., Smith, R., & Standish, P. (2012). *Education in an age of nihilism: Education and moral standards*. London: Routledge.

Boutang, Y.-M. (2011). *Cognitive capitalism*. Cambridge: Polity.

Brady, M., & Pritchard, D. (Eds.). (2003). *Moral and epistemic virtues*. Malden/Oxford: Blackwell.

Deleuze, G. (2012/1995). *Pure immanence: Essays on a life*. New York: Zone Books.

Derrida, J. (1992). Mochlos; or, the conflict of the faculties. In R. Rand (Ed.), *Logomachia: The conflict of the faculties*. London: University of Nebraska.

Guattari, F. (2005). *The three ecologies*. London/New York: Athlone.

Jaspers, K. (1965/1946). *The idea of the university*. London: Peter Owen.

List, C., & Pettit, P. (2011). *Group agency: The possibility, design and status of corporate agents*. Oxford: Oxford University Press.

MacIntyre, A. (1985). *After virtue*. London: Duckworth.

Nixon, J. (2008). *The virtuous university*. London: Routledge.

Readings, B. (1997). *The university in ruins*. Cambridge, MA: Harvard.

Roggero, G. (2011). *The production of living knowledge: The crisis of the university and the transformation of labour in Europe and North America*. Philadelphia: Temple University Press.

Taylor, C. (1992). *Sources of the self: The making of the modern identity*. Cambridge: Cambridge University Press.

Chapter 5
The Purpose of University Value Statements

Alex Elwick

Abstract In light of the growing promotion of value statements by universities, this chapter sets out to explore why such institutions explicitly and publically set out their values. Based upon an empirical study of English universities it will propose explanations as to why the trend has developed and what function these statements serve. Overarching themes which are evident across the corpus of value statements suggest that there are similarities between universities' positions; while other patterns can also be identified amongst groupings of institution-type (e.g. Russell Group universities). These themes and patterns are used to exemplify broad sector-wide and alternately more specific explanations as to the adoption and proliferation of value statements in England.

Keywords Value statements · Positioning · Branding · Missions

Introduction

Universities now routinely promote their own mission and value statements in order to express their purpose, strategy, values and behaviours – adopting the behaviour of many commercial organisations in a practice derived from management studies (e.g. Drucker 1973; Campbell 1996). In light of such growing promotion of, specifically, value statements by universities, this chapter sets out to explore why such institutions explicitly and publically set out their values. At the heart of the chapter are the results of an empirical study of English universities – 77 sets of current value statements were collated (from all those that make them publically available online) and thematically analysed in order to propose explanations as to why the trend has developed and what function these statements serve. Overarching themes which are evident across the corpus of value statements suggest that there are similarities

A. Elwick (✉)
CERS, Middlesex University, London, UK
e-mail: a.elwick@mdx.ac.uk

© Springer Nature Switzerland AG 2019
P. Gibbs et al. (eds.), *Values of the University in a Time of Uncertainty*,
https://doi.org/10.1007/978-3-030-15970-2_5

between universities' positions; while other patterns can also be identified amongst groupings of institution-type (e.g. between pre- and post-1992 universities).

This chapter will begin by outlining the context and, briefly, how value positions have developed in higher education, before proposing (partly as a result of the marketisation of the English system) that there has been a loss of trust in university values (both externally and internally). There then follows a synopsis of the results of the analysis of current university value statements and a discussion around what such results can tell us about the role and purpose of these statements.

A History of Value Statements and Values in Higher Education

The term 'values' is a contested and complex phenomenon, as is explored elsewhere in this volume, and indeed – when considering the role played by universities' value statements – such contestation is inherent in any discussion. Nonetheless, Kleijnen et al.'s definition of them as 'desirable, motivational goals' (2009: 234) and as 'one of the most powerful and stable forces that influence an organisation's performance and strategic success' (ibid.: 235) is useful as a starting point. Value statements can be thought of as related to mission and vision statements, the adoption of which is relatively common practice across all organisations, and which were widely employed by higher education institutions from the 1980s onwards (Cortés-Sánchez 2017). While there has been much research into such mission statements (e.g. Morphew and Hartley 2006; Sauntson and Morrish 2010) there remains a lack of proper empirical investigation into their value-related counterparts in higher education, although Altinas and Kavurmaci conducted one such exercise working with Turkish universities (2018). In particular, following Dey and Steyaert, I am interested in the performative aspect of value statements (2007), e.g. HEFCE (the Higher Education Funding Council for England – a non-departmental government body which was responsible for the distribution of funding to universities in England until April 2018) takes a view that mission and value statements can act as an accountability tool – allowing universities 'to demonstrate more broadly the value they provide' (HEFCE 2017a: 34).

Macfarlane has proposed that university values could be grouped into 'Christian', 'liberal', 'market' and 'socialist' forms (2017) – each with different purposes, and each (to a greater or lesser extent) a product of a particular time period and environment (e.g. Christian values reflecting the connections many earlier universities had with the Church). Such a typology is useful in highlighting the shifts between these distinct value sets and in particular in terms of characterising the current zeitgeist. It is worth, at this point, remembering Collini's advice that we should beware mythologizing previous eras of higher education and that there has never been a 'golden age' for universities (2012). What follows is not intended to suggest that universities were perfect, or even necessarily better, when liberal/academic values held more weight than market values, but rather to point out the changes that are inherent in each mode: making plain the values of a university allows one to 'decipher the ideologies that permeate the work of higher education institutions' (Skelton 2012: 257).

There is a long tradition of reverence for academic or liberal values in higher education (see Barnett 1990) which are often held to be central to the whole concept of academia, e.g.: 'there are values shared throughout higher education and without which higher education, as we understand it, could not exist' (McNay 2007: 44). The Dearing report quotes John Masefield when noting the importance of values which characterise and are fundamental to an understanding of higher education, and it is worth repeating his words which were deemed of such importance to the 1997 committee:

> It is a place where those who hate ignorance may strive to know, where those who perceive truth may strive to make others see; where seekers and learners alike, banded together in the search for knowledge, will honour thought in all its finer ways, will welcome thinkers in distress or in exile, will uphold ever the dignity of thought and learning and will exact standards in these things (Masefield 1946, in National Committee of Inquiry into Higher Education 1997).

It is interesting that this report placed considerable emphasis on such values (listing 'respect for evidence, rational argument, debate and tolerance of alternative viewpoints' as characteristics of higher education (ibid.: 64) despite also being credited as one of the key steps in the marketisation of the sector (Palfreyman and Tapper 2016). Although there has been a gradual and lengthy (Brown 2015) move towards the introduction of 'market' or 'business' values (Macfarlane 1998), Jameson's 2012 work found that 'staff continued to adhere to the enduring values and purposes of higher education' (410). Nonetheless:

> Given the unequal distribution of power, there is a danger that the operational values embedded through bureaucratic processes in a corporate culture will dominate over the normative values of the academic staff (McNay 2007: 49).

As Evans noted, such values are at least partly imposed upon universities as an expectation they should fulfil, as opposed to the liberal values of their past (2004). Similarly Pring, although talking largely about school-based education, noted that there was a tension, a clash of values, between 'liberal values, protected within an independent academic tradition, and … a shift from producer dominated control of what should be learnt to that of the consumer, or, indeed, of government' (1996: 105). Such a clash was vividly described by Geppert and Hollinshead as the opposition between collegiate collaboration and 'cut throat competition' – the former representing the 'lifeblood of the system in the past' which has been eroded 'through draconian managerial interventions predicated upon idealised conceptions of rationalist organisation in which market- driven and 'performative' imperatives are transcendent and regarded by the power elite as sacrosanct' (2017: 14).

As well as the dichotomy between liberal and market values, it is worth noting that there still appears to be room for the final conception of values in Macfarlane's typology (2017): 'socialist' values are reflected in the 'third mission' of universities that has become more prominent according to Seeber et al., and which 'urges universities to be guided by utilitarian values in their activities' (2017: 3). Scott noted that universities cannot simply be reduced to the aggregation of transactions as per an entirely quasi-economic view of their value, and instead noted the importance of civic values and the role of universities as civic institutions (2005), which Nixon, amongst others, has also spoken about at length (2012).

It should be remembered that a university is not a homogenous organism which is able to operate independently of its members, and as such its values (and value statements) are the products of human interaction and decision-making within the organisation. However, often such decisions are made managerially – academic staff withdraw from such roles (Macfarlane 2005) 'either because of pressure of other work or because of a view that participation [does] not influence those with power' (McNay 2007: 46). Nonetheless, the variety of constituents of a university infuse their institutions with different values (Kraatz 2009) and Seeber et al. believed that 'organisations will prioritise and conform to those expectations that are consistent with those values that are heavily represented among its members' (2017: 5).

A Loss of Trust in University Values?

The nature of a higher education sector in England in which students pay for their tuition has fundamentally changed the relationship students, academics and the wider public have with the system, which has been extensively explored in debates around consumerisation, marketisation and neo-liberalism (see Olssen and Peters 2005) – leading to a 'gradual erosion of trust in the values, collegial ethos and civic role of universities' (Jameson 2012: 391). As Ball neatly surmises: 'value replaces values – commitment and service are of dubious worth within the new policy regime' (2003: 217).

Although the concept of trust is hugely complicated, I use it here to explain the perceived value of universities to society more widely – and as such the loss of trust in university values can be thought of as a faltering in the esteem held for our higher education institutions more widely. As higher education is understood 'in terms of its contribution to human capital and economic growth in a global knowledge economy' (Holmwood 2016: 63) so those other roles and values are dismissed, forgotten about or ignored. In particular this reflects a dominance of the 'knowledge economy' over the 'knowledge society' – a function of policy, e.g. Olsen and Maassen's suggestion that 'the role of Academia and Democracy is primarily defined as serving economic purposes and the growth of competitive markets' according to reform documents from the European Commission (2007: 9). Such systemic practice becomes manifest on an individual level – once again we can turn to Ball for a lucid summation – where 'a kind of values schizophrenia is experienced by individual teachers where commitment, judgement and authenticity within practice are sacrificed for impression and performance' (Ball 2003: 122) – an inevitable result of 'a more market-focused, utilitarian system' (Jameson 2012: 404).

As has already been alluded to in the previous section of this chapter, there is often animosity between academics and management implicit, or at times explicit, in the definition of a university's values. Within this is the tension, or even the contradiction, of 'institutional' values when an institution is comprised of (often) thousands of people. It could be argued that such tension can be resolved if one thinks of the university as a community: Donaldson and Dunfee describe a community as a 'self-defined, self-circumscribed group of people who interact in the context of shared tasks, values, or goals and who are capable of establishing norms of ethical behaviour for themselves' (1999: 39). Such a definition allows for values to be shared, although does not preclude some forms of conflict: 'the university is itself a community in which communitarian values jostle with individualistic values' (Scott 2005). Govoni et al. talk about a 'values-infused model' which 'recognises that it is a fusion of the entire community that provides for an effective college life experience where students, faculty, and staff can become more aware of their own values and begin to examine and live these values' (2005: 1). The European Universities Association (EUA) describe this marriage as characterised by two elements: 'a cultural/psychological element of shared values, beliefs and expectations as well as a structural/managerial element with defined processes that enhance quality and aim at coordinating individual efforts' (2006).

To scrutinise the community-model, however, is to make plain its flaws. As Skelton noted, values operate at the micro, meso and macro levels of the system (2012) and within a university, although there may be multiple smaller communities (e.g. at departmental or school level) it is not obvious that these might be able to come together in one shared community – as Kleijnen et al. have noted: 'current values, however, vary substantially over departments and might be susceptible of structural/managerial influences' (2009: 245). Indeed, it is these smaller communities that might allow for resistance to high-level messaging or branding: 'the requirement to uphold the University's corporate brand runs in tension with strong traditions of outspoken critical thinking, which nevertheless remain integral to the brand' (Geppert and Hollinshead 2017: 12). Nonetheless, my choice of language is not accidental, and as per Kogan and Hanney, the move towards marketisation in higher education has led to a 'shift in power from senior academics and their departments to the central institution and the dominance of systems over academic values' (2000: 186). While there are limits to the metaphors of conflict and oppression within the university and we should be careful not to take this too far, the idea that consensus can be found across a whole institution (from managers and centralised bureaucracy, through academic schools and departments and ultimately to students) in order to settle upon a set of shared values within one community is, I would argue, farfetched. As such, the value statements purported by a university should be regarded with at least a certain degree of suspicion and should be interrogated as a form of discourse and not, necessarily, as a set of practices – as McNay puts it: 'the gap between espoused policy and policy in practice' (2007: 51). Similarly, Ahmed, in discussing university diversity statements, make a related point – 'the politics of diversity has become what we could call "image management"' (2007: 605), where such statements tell us more about the projection of values universities wish to demonstrate than the values they actually embody (although in this remains the issue of collectivity discussed above).

What Current English University Value Statements Tell Us

In order to understand the role and purpose of current university value statements it holds that we must first assess what exactly it is that such statements say, and also ascertain whether there are similarities or differences across what is a diverse body of institutions. As such there follows a summary of an empirical investigation into this topic. At the point of data collection (summer 2017) according to HEFCE there were 109 English universities and university colleges (HEFCE 2017b) which represented the population for this study. A search of the websites of all 109 universities identified 77 which had explicit values or principles listed (normally on their own webpage, but in some cases within annual reports or strategic plans). The focal point for collecting data was on what universities declared their current values to be – and hence was not concerned with missions, visions, aims or priorities: the research was about what universities state their values to be and not what they intend to do in the future. In case of doubt, universities' own definitions were always used (i.e. when there were multiple lists or statements under different headings, those that the university in question described as 'values' were used). All relevant statements (in some cases up to 19 different statements) were imported into NVivo 11 and inductively coded in order to identify common themes.

In general there were considerable overlaps between institutions, with five particularly prevalent themes appearing in the statements of (almost) half the sample and above – these have been characterised as per Table 5.1.

The most prevalent theme was related to the idea of achieving excellence and impact. Fifty-five of the universities in the sample included values related to this concept, often expressed simply as aiming to be excellent:

We strive for excellence.

Some institutions specified the areas in which they believed they excelled, citing both more traditional academic concerns and also referencing the concept of 'service delivery':

Table 5.1 Main emergent themes from university value statements

Theme	Number of universities (n = 77)
Excellence and impact	55
Diversity and equal opportunities	51
Community and support	46
Collaboration and partnership	39
Innovation and creativity	37

Excellence: We take pride in ensuring the highest quality standards of academic achievement and professional service delivery.
We create world-class research and teaching.

It was also common for universities to cite wider forms of impact that they valued:

Engaging actively to change the world, through our teaching and research and also by leading on economic and social improvement.

The second most common theme across universities related to issues of diversity, inclusion and equality. Again, around two thirds of institutions referred to these principles of EDI:

Respect each other and celebrate our diversity.
Valuing the rights, responsibilities and dignity of individuals through our commitment to equality and diversity.
Celebrating diversity and being committed to equality of opportunity and treatment in our staff and student community.

The third most common theme generally referred to universities valuing the creation and development of a community amongst their own staff and students. In the majority of cases references to community did not speak to wider communities and groups (which was instead captured under the below theme of collaboration and partnership). Around three fifths of universities expressed this value, often along with the explicit provision of support:

We support people: Together, we create a nurturing environment for our students and employees.
Our friendly, inclusive and professional community of students and staff.
All our staff work to create a supportive community that is built upon relationships.
Community: We support and inspire each other to be the best that we can be.

Alongside the internal development of a community, when referencing the range of stakeholders involved in higher education, many universities cited collaboration and partnership as one of their values: often with business and employers, and often located within the region in which the university was located:

We work collaboratively. In partnership with our students, communities and business we innovate in tackling shared challenges.
Partnership is at the core of who we are. Through partnership we create distinctive educational programmes, we share and disseminate our research and enterprise and we create mutual benefit to our city, our region and globally.
We will work in partnership with our collaborators to ensure their interests and aspirations inform our activities.

The final significant theme, present in around half of the sample, was that of innovation and creativity. The two terms were commonly used together:

Innovation: We will apply our collective and individual creativity to conceive and develop new ideas, implementing them for the benefit of the communities we serve.
Nurturing creativity is key to ensuring we continue to grow and develop our activities. We're committed to creating new, radical and exciting opportunities for our students, staff and community. We recognise the scale of the challenges we face as an institution, society and world and place value on tackling these in creative and innovative ways.

Table 5.2 Different themes between Pre- and Post–1992 universities

Theme	Pre-1992 universities (n = 28)	Post-1992 universities (n = 49)
Academic freedom	11	8
	39%	16%
Research	10	6
	36%	12%
Global	12	4
	43%	8%

> Our strongest roots lie in being innovative and creative. By applying these principles across all that we do, we enable our staff, students and graduates to succeed in a dynamic and turbulent environment.

Although these five themes were present across the majority of the sample and so reflect the broader values expressed by universities in England – and will be explored as such in the following section – it should be noted that there were some significant differences between institution types. In particular, as can be seen from Table 5.2, in some areas there were pronounced differences between post-1992 universities (largely former polytechnics that gained university status upon the introduction of the Further and Higher Education Act 1992) and older institutions.

In particular, the older universities tended to promote values that centred on academic freedom, research and maintaining a global outlook – whereas these were far less common amongst the more modern institutions. This illustrates the lack of homogeneity across the whole sample and is included at least partly as a reminder that although there were many similarities in value statements, we must nonetheless be mindful of key differentials between not just individual institutions, but also between groupings, such as above.

What Role Do Value Statements Play in English Higher Education?

This brings me to the central point of the chapter – questioning what role and purpose value statements play for English universities. Necessarily this will involve at least a degree of hypothesising as – without investigating more fully individual statements in terms of their creation, intention and impact on practice – there is only so much inference that can be drawn from a 'raw' look at universities' own projections of their values. However, based upon the themes that are prevalent in such a large proportion of university statements it is possible to make some assumptions around the role they might be playing.

The most prevalent theme, that of excellence and impact, speaks to ideas of setting high standards and equally, high expectations. Such values suggest a focus on either meeting external such standards, or outdoing competitors in relative terms. It is not a hugely surprising value for universities to adopt as, when projecting an image, it makes sense to project one of success, of high ambitions and achievements. As such, values which align with this theme might suggest a focus on attracting the best students, the best staff etc. via projecting an 'excellent' image of themselves, or might, more simply, suggest a belief that one of the fundamental purposes of being for a university is to be excellent (and that this should drive what is done across the organisation).

The second theme discussed above, and which also appears within over two-thirds of the universities' sets of statements, related to diversity, inclusion and the promotion of equal opportunities. Again, there are multiple possible explanations for the prominence of this theme, and as above it may simply be related to a fundamental belief that this is something that universities should value – that promotion of equal opportunities is in the lifeblood of the sector (harking back to the Robbins Report of 1963 which assumed as an axiom 'that courses of higher education should be available for all those who are qualified by ability and attainment to pursue them and who wish to do so'). However, somewhat more cynically, it could be argued that given some of the regulations universities face, such a value might actually serve to show adherence to such regulations (including the Equality Act 2010). As Kimura noted – by making public claims in the form of statements and policy documents it may be that institutions feel they are achieving something without actually having to do much more:

> The question is whether by just claiming their commitment to equality and diversity in institutional policy documents, universities actually do promote (racial) equality and diversity. Has the existence of these documents made institutions free from racism and more socially inclusive? (Kimura 2014: 529).

Since the mid-2000s universities in England have been required to submit an access agreement to OFFA (the Office for Fair Access) subsequently published – setting out the access arrangements they intended to put in place – in order to charge higher tuition fees; from April 2018 these were renamed 'access and participation plans' and regulated by the Office for Students (OfS 2018). Although these agreements/plans contain quantitative measures, there is also a qualitative, more subjective aspect to them and as such value statements provide a form of evidence which can be drawn upon. Statements which, therefore, directly speak to the equality, diversity or inclusion of an institution arguably feed into the projection institutions make in order to comply with such regulatory frameworks.

Finally, with regards this theme, there is also often public pressure on universities – illustrated by the media attention generated by criticism from David Lammy MP towards Oxford and Cambridge Universities throughout 2017–2018 (e.g. Horton 2018) – specifically relating to the lack of diversity in their intakes. Again, while a relatively weak form of evidence, value statements of this type contribute to an institution's public profile and attempt to counter such criticism (although when other evidence is so strongly weighted against you, Cambridge University's core value of 'the widest possible student access to the University' (as one example) does seem somewhat contradictory).

The dual themes of community and support, and collaboration and partnerships referred, as above, to slightly different focuses: the internal community building amongst staff and students in the case of the former, and the external relationships with (often local) businesses and employers in the case of the latter. Adhering, or promoting, such values could be seen as an opportunity to strengthen work in both areas, a relatively instrumentalist approach to develop by highlighting them (particularly in the case of external partnerships). Equally, as above, it could also be a marketing/self-promotion tool to improve an institution's public image and then subsequently attract (primarily, as the largest source of income) students. These themes do, however, highlight some of the complexity around the issue of the purpose that such values serve – with multiple explanations potentially seeming as likely as others.

To think holistically about these themes and the universities in England, there is arguably a tension within these value statements (or perhaps that should be, a tension within this analysis of them) between their use as a form of marketing, a way to attract students, lecturers, research and funding; and more deep-rooted beliefs in what a university should be for, what fundamental aspects should be valued over others. In the marketised system of higher education in England there is, undeniably, a need to recruit students in order to generate funding and as such all public statements by an institution have to be viewed through the lens of those potential students. However, that is not to say that this tension results in a zero-sum outcome, and instead I would argue that actually these value statements could be conceived of as fulfilling multiple roles at once. Furthermore, it is not clear that the distinctions drawn by Macfarlane in terms of distinct types of values have to be so clearly delineated: instead perhaps universities can combine liberal/academic, market and socialist values within their remit – doing what might be necessary to survive within the quasi-marketplace of higher education while maintaining a commitment to traditional liberal/academic ideals and (slightly) more modern socialist ones.

Conclusions

Based around an analysis of current university value statements in England, this chapter has suggested some of the potential roles and purposes that such statements might fulfil. However, such a task is fraught with difficulty and in the absence of research which engages more fully with these statements as products of their time – treating them more individually in order to study them in situ (i.e. in relation to their current context, and the context of their creation) – such propositions can only be, at this stage, hypothetical.

Research which focuses on statements more individually, and which engages in qualitative research, directly involving stakeholders, would be a productive way to further explore this topic. In addition, evidence such as the access agreements/access and participation plans that universities are required to produce would allow for these statements to be better tested against the actual practice of universities –

which itself would provide explanatory power in terms of the role played by value statements. As such, whether universities actually live their values could be explored, in keeping with the Kantian notion that there is virtue in actions as opposed to discussion, this would address a version of Kimura's argument that perhaps by having value statements organisations do not feel they need to do any more in terms of demonstrating (acting on) their values (2014).

Nonetheless, by identifying themes across the corpus of statements available it has been possible to suggest that value statements for universities might play a role in terms of their marketing and appeal to (primarily) students, while recognising that they might also represent the facets of higher education which individual institutions genuinely believe to be the most important. By setting out their own institutional values an organisation might be better placed to inculcate those values in their students, to take an example from the USA:

> At Saint Leo University, educating students means giving them the tools to awaken their highest potential, to recognisethe importance of values in their lives, and to empower them with the knowledge that they need not 'to take the world as it comes' but to use a values-defined education to change the world-and themselves-for the better (Govoni et al. 2005: 1).

Clarity over one's own values would seem a pre-requisite to provide a 'values-defined education' and though not all institutions would necessarily subscribe to the outlook of Saint Leo University, such a position does provide a potential rationale for value statements which is perhaps less cynical than the instrumentalist position that their purpose might only be, ultimately, economic.

References

Ahmed, S. (2007). 'You end up doing the document rather than doing the doing': Diversity, race equality and the politics of documentation. *Ethnic and Racial Studies, 30*(4), 590–609.

Altıntaş, F. Ç., & Kavurmacı, C. (2018). Value statements in web pages of Turkish state universities: A basic classification. In *Advocacy in academia and the role of teacher preparation programs* (pp. 302–316). Hershey: IGI Global.

Ball, S. (2003). The teacher's soul and the terrors of performativity. *Journal of Education Policy, 18*(2), 215–228. https://doi.org/10.1080/0268093022000043065.

Barnett, R. (1990). *The idea of higher education.* Buckingham: SRHE and Open University Press.

Brown, R. (2015). *The marketisation of higher education: Issues and ironies.* http://repository.uwl.ac.uk/id/eprint/3065/1/The%20marketisation%20of%20Higher%20education.pdf

Campbell, A. (1996). *Mission and management commitment.* http://tools.ashridge.org.uk/Website/Content.nsf/FileLibrary/3F75A6C68227EDE980257911003158FA/$file/Mission%20%26%20Management%20Commitment%20article%20-%20mar96.pdf

Collini, S. (2012). *What are universities for?* London: Penguin.

Cortés-Sánchez, J. (2017). *Mission and vision statements of universities worldwide – A content analysis.* Bogotá: Universidad del Rosario.

Dey, P., & Steyaert, C. (2007). The troubadours of knowledge: Passion and invention in management education. *Organisation, 14*(3), 437–461.

Donaldson, T., & Dunfee, T. (1999). *Ties that bind: A social approach to business ethics.* Boston: Harvard Business School Press.

Drucker, P. (1973). *Management: Tasks, responsibilities and practices*. New York: Harper and Row.

European University Association (EUA). (2006). *Quality culture in European universities: A bottom-up approach. Report on the three rounds of the Quality Culture project 2002–2006.* Brussels: EUA.

Evans, M. (2004). *Killing thinking. The death of universities*. London: Continuum.

Geppert, M., & Hollinshead, G. (2017). Signs of dystopia and demoralisation in global academia: Reflections on the precarious and destructive effects of the colonisation of the Lebenswelt. *Critical Perspectives on International Business, 13*(2), 136–150.

Govoni, J., Wright, V., & Wubbenhorst, P. (2005). Fusions: Integrating values in higher education. *Journal of College and Character, 6*(5). https://doi.org/10.2202/1940-1639.1456.

HEFCE. (2017a). *Guide to funding 2017–18.* http://www.hefce.ac.uk/media/HEFCE,2014/Content/Pubs/2017/201704/HEFCE_Funding_Guide_2017-18_.pdf

HEFCE. (2017b). *Register of HE providers.* http://www.hefce.ac.uk/reg/register/search/Home/ByProperty?uni=1

Holmwood, J. (2016). 'The turn of the screw'; Marketisation and higher education in England. *Prometheus, 34*(1), 63–72.

Horton, H. (2018). Oxford University in spat with David Lammy over diversity figures, as official account retweets post calling MP "bitter". *The Telegraph*, 23rd May.

Jameson, J. (2012). Leadership values, trust and negative capability: Managing the uncertainties of future English higher education. *Higher Education Quarterly, 66*(4), 391–414.

Kimura, M. (2014). Non-performativity of university and subjectification of students: The question of equality and diversity in UK universities. *British Journal of Sociology of Education, 35*(4), 523–540.

Kleijnen, J., Dolmans, D., Muijtjens, A., Willems, J., & Van Hout, H. (2009). Organisational values in higher education: Perceptions and preferences of staff. *Quality in Higher Education, 15*(3), 233–249. https://doi.org/10.1080/13538320903343123.

Kogan, M., & Hanney, S. (2000). *Reforming higher education* (Vol. 50). London: Jessica Kingsley Publishers.

Kraatz, M. (2009). Leadership as institutional work: A bridge to the other side. In T. Lawrence, R. Suddaby, & B. Leca (Eds.), *Institutional work: Actors and agency in institutional studies of organisations* (pp. 59–91). Cambridge: Cambridge University Press.

Macfarlane, B. (1998). *Business lecturers in higher education: Outsider reputations, insider values*. Paper presented at higher education close up, an international conference from 6–8 July 1998 at University of Central Lancashire, Preston [online] available from: http://www.leeds.ac.uk/educol/documents/000000678.htm

Macfarlane, B. (2005). The disengaged academic: The retreat from citizenship. *Higher Education Quarterly, 59*(4), 296–312.

Macfarlane, B. (2017). *Values in higher education: An introduction*. Paper presented at symposium on values in higher education. Oxford, September 11–14.

Masefield, J. (1946). *A university splendid, beautiful and enduring*. Speech at the installation of the Chancellor of the University of Sheffield, June 25.

McNay, I. (2007). Values, principles and integrity: Academic and professional standards in UK higher education. *Higher Education Management and Policy, 19*(3), 43–64.

Morphew, C., & Hartley, M. (2006). Mission statements: A thematic analysis of rhetoric across institutional type. *The Journal of Higher Education, 77*(3), 456–471.

National Committee of Inquiry into Higher Education ('The Dearing Report'). (1997). *Higher education in the learning society: Report of the National Committee.*

Nixon, J. (2012). *Higher education and the public good: Imaging the university*. London: Bloomsbury.

Office for Students (OfS). (2018). *Access and participation plans*. https://www.officeforstudents.org.uk/advice-and-guidance/promoting-equal-opportunities/access-and-participation-plans/

Olsen, J., & Maassen, P. (2007). European debates on the knowledge institution: The modernisation of the university at the European level. In P. Maassen & J. Olsen (Eds.), *University dynamics and European integration*. Dordrecht: Springer.

Olssen, M., & Peters, M. (2005). Neoliberalism, higher education and the knowledge economy: From the free market to knowledge capitalism. *Journal of Education Policy, 20*(3), 313–345.

Palfreyman, D., & Tapper, T. (2016). The marketisation of English higher education and the financing of tuition fees. *London Review of Education, 14*(1), 47–55.

Pring, R. (1996). Values and education policy. In M. Halstead & M. Taylor (Eds.), *Values in education and education in values* (pp. 104–118). London: The Falmer Press.

Robbins, L. (1963). *Higher education: Report of the committee appointed by the Prime Minister under the chairmanship of Lord Robbins 1961–63*. London: Her Majesty's Stationery Office.

Sauntson, H., & Morrish, L. (2010). Vision, values and international excellence: The 'products' that university mission statements sell to students. In M. Molesworth, R. Scullion, & E. Nixon (Eds.), *The marketisation of higher education and the student as consumer* (pp. 73–85). Abingdon/New York: Routledge.

Scott, P. (2005). The University and civic values. In S. Robinson & C. Katulushi (Eds.), *Values in higher education*. Leeds: University of Leeds.

Seeber, M., Barberio, V., Huisman, J., & Mampaey, J. (2017). Factors affecting the content of universities' mission statements: an analysis of the United Kingdom higher education system. *Studies in Higher Education*, 1–15.

Skelton, A. (2012). Value conflicts in higher education teaching. *Teaching in Higher Education, 17*(30), 257–268. https://doi.org/10.1080/13562517.2011.611875.

Chapter 6
Relationality: Deconstructive, Reparative, Generative: Relating Through Valuing Pain

Kate Maguire

Abstract It is the nature of relationality and its relationship to values with which I am most occupied. For the purposes of this chapter, relationality is used to capture something of the multilayers of interconnectedness and complexity when we begin to explore our relations with 'things' (Morton, Hyperobjects: philosophy and ecology after the end of the world (Posthumanities). University of Minnesota Press, 2013): what we talk about and with whom and what we hide or silence. In exploring the philosophy of relationality and relational ontology, Wildman (An introduction to relational ontology, Wesley J. Wildman, Boston University, May 15, 2006 Open Source http://people.bu.edu/wwildman/media/docs/Wildman_2009_Relational_ Ontology, 2006) proposes four layers of complexity in the study of relations. In the context of higher education, I am informed by his third category: allegiance to a flag. There is a shadow in values of allegiance.

Keywords Pain · Relationality · Allegiance · Silence · Guilt

Overview

> One man is a king only because other men stand in the relation of subjects to him. They on the contrary, imagine that they are the subjects because he is the king. Karl Marx (1967)

The nature of the world, what it is made up of and how things connect, what is unchanging (substance) and what is mutable (dynamic energies), are questions which have occupied philosophers from Aristotle to Kant to Hegel. Kant was among the first to include in his categories of 'things' the dynamic relational. Contemporary thinkers are understandably even more occupied with ways of confronting, under-

K. Maguire (✉)
Middlesex University, London, UK
e-mail: k.maguire@mdx.ac.uk

© Springer Nature Switzerland AG 2019
P. Gibbs et al. (eds.), *Values of the University in a Time of Uncertainty*,
https://doi.org/10.1007/978-3-030-15970-2_6

standing, articulating and responding to the implications of the interconnectedness of things for us as individuals and members of societies portending the demise of the notion of autonomy in identity and action. We are, as Whitehead (1920) points out, a *relatum* in the complexity of nature, which is the past participle of to relate. We can no longer peddle the myth of 'I', as relatedness is the nature of the world.

> …Whitehead [1938] argued that the fundamental concepts by which we understand the world are activity and process (LeRon Shults 2003: 29).

In his chapter on "The philosophical turn to relationality" LeRon Shults continues

> The philosophical turn to relationality has shaped not only the way we think about knowing and being, but also our understanding of human acting …Instead of autonomous subjects that stand over against the natural world and other subjects, today human self consciousness is understood as always and already embedded in relations between self, other and the world…Today human acting is rarely described in terms of substantial soul with abstract faculties (or powers) to influence the material world, but more often in terms of dynamic self community (2003: 31).

Almost symbiotically related to this search for the implications of interconnectedness is the frenetic one for values, the likes of which have not been seen since the anthropologist Kluckhohn's substantial Rimrock project to recover the credibility of anthropology by establishing a theory of values. After a lifetime's work with considerable resources, financial and human, he found that it could not be done. Graeber (2001) offers another perspective on values which he calls the phenomenon of social power in the face of social theory 'now largely unable to imagine people being able to change society purposefully'.

> I have argued that one way to overcome this problem is to look at social systems as structures of creative action, and value, as how people measure the importance of their own actions within such structures. (Graeber 2001: 230)

Graeber (2001) allots only the last few words of his engaging work with what I believe to be a neglected area in the rush to prove the value of values as a weapon against depersonalised collectivisation, and relationality as a one-sided coin of cohesion and social good. I believe it is something we are all complicit in denying or avoiding, to greater and lesser degrees. He states, in relation to the pursuit of pleasure, that pleasure and the phenomenon of social power '… if one is entirely unaware of the larger social context in which it takes place, also produce unparalleled misery' (p. 261).

Burkitt (2016) steers clear of commenting on values and on such potential negative impacts of relationality, seeing the concept as more one of network in which we are all interactants, challenging both Giddens (1979, 1984) and Archer (2003) on their beliefs about individual agency and reflexivity. However, through his skilled conceptualisation of relationality, he does provide a thinking frame for possibilities of addressing the other, more perplexing sides of the form of relationality expected in organisations and institutions which will be explored in more detail later.

It is the nature of relationality and its relationship to values with which I am most occupied. For the purposes of this chapter, relationality is used to capture something of the multilayers of interconnectedness and complexity when we begin to explore our relations with 'things' (Morton 2013): what we talk about and with whom and what we hide or silence. In exploring the philosophy of relationality and relational ontology, Wildman (2006) proposes four layers of complexity in the study of relations. In the context of higher education, I am informed by his third category.

> Relations commonly convey or encode or express value, especially in personal contexts, but also in aesthetic and moral contexts. For example, the relation between a nation and its flag confers dignity on the flag and identity on the nation (p. 1).

Embedded in such relations is also the *skia* (shadow) of positive relationality, that is, the exploitation and manipulation of such relations when the system is already, or becomes, divorced or dissociated from the individuals who make up the collective. Individuals experience the 'awe' of collective identity and swear allegiance to it, often at the expense of personal integrity, causing anxiety-provoking dissonance. The recognition of the *skia* in any organisation, I would suggest, has a role in understanding and improving relations between the individuals in the organisation and between the guardians of the culture and its members. Milgram (1974) carried out experiments in the early 1960s on the human capacity for obedience to authority influenced by events in the Second World War, particularly the Holocaust and against the backdrop of the trial of Adolf Eichmann as a Nazi war criminal. Although retrospectively castigated for his challenging exploration of our willingness as ordinary people to be obedient to an authority for a noble cause, even if that means inflicting pain on a fellow human being, even if that noble cause is education, he did hit on an observation of *skia* which has not been resolved: the willingness of ordinary people through plausibility, fear or collective coercion, who, in private life love their children and their pets, to do extraordinarily cruel things in the 'workworld.' We most often conceive of the workworld as some busy, well organised entity with a moral compass of sorts, but for many the workworld is a coercive institution of varying degrees from military to politics, from climate polluting multinationals to neo-colonial exploiters of resources in the poorest countries, from local authorities to prisons, from places of worship to institutions of education. In Goffman's classic work, Asylums, he talks about how characteristics of 'total institutions' like prisons, orphanages and asylums can be shared in different intensities in other institutions.

> A basic social arrangement in modern society is that the individual tends to sleep, play and work in different places, with different co-participants, under different authorities, and without an overall rational plan. The central feature of total institutions can be described as a breakdown of the barriers ordinarily separating these three spheres of life…the various enforced activities are brought together into a single rational plan purportedly designed to fulfil the official aims of the institution. (1970: 17)

'Asylums' was first published in 1961, the same year that Foucault published his intensive work, 'Madness and Civilisation'. These are two powerful, diffracted lenses on what lies behind the institutional veneer of virtue and righteousness which are indicators of civilisation, or at least civilised behaviours, to comply with justified expectations of its members to keep it civilised lest it fall into madness.

> Everything was organised so that the madman would recognise himself in a world of judge-
> ment which enveloped him on all sides; he must know that he is watched, judged and con-
> demned; from transgression to punishment, the connection must be evident, as guilt is
> recognised by all. (Foucault 2006: 253)

Foucault sees the attempts of civilisation's guardians to instil norms as a process of objectifying. In a contemporary context this could be seen as keeping everyone too busy and compliant to complain, too fearful of being considered odd or 'mad', the consequences of which are alienation from self and others by self and others.

> The asylum no longer punished the madman's guilt, it is true; but it did more; it organised
> the guilt, it organised it for the madman as a consciousness of himself, and as a non-
> reciprocal relation to the keeper. (2006: 235)

In such climates, not only does the dissolving of work life balance become endemic, dissonance also emerges between collective and individual values and the inability to reconcile these can lead to withdrawal, lack of engagement and loss of creativity. In some cases, it can lead to aggression as the result of misplaced frustration and tension. Proclaimed enlightened industry leaders and leadership in higher education often talk about creating cultural value shifts without a deep understanding of what values are, their function in context (one person's or society's values are another person's or society's antithesis) and how to achieve such an environment without a critique of the function in context. Therefore there cannot be a realistic assessment of the gap between vision and reality, what a values culture might look like, what if anything can be achieved by such an environment and what lies beneath, remaining concealed, which inhibit and subvert values driven culture formation and endurance. More seriously, the general conception of the issue, which informs the approach to be taken to shifting the culture, is one that assumes the absence of positive values (in service to the common good) and the need for the institution to take the moral high ground. The declared intention then is a mission to somehow insert or enforce values, rather than engage in a self exposé of what it is in the institution's practices which inhibit the expression of the positive values which are so evidently already there at individual and group levels but to which the institution has become blind or myopic.

Millions of lives have been sacrificed and unparallelled misery has been caused by human beings' desire for identity, belonging and meaning, manifested in allegiance to flags, brands, words and other unifying forms of identity. According to Graeber (2007: 64), desire

(a) is always rooted in imagination
(b) tends to direct itself towards some kind of social relation, real or imaginary
(c) that social relation generally entails a desire for some kind of recognition and, hence, an imaginative reconstruction of the self; a process fraught with dangers of destroying that social relation or turning it into some terrible conflict.

But what is the price in everyday life? While relationality would not be viewed as an unusual approach to explore values in education, pain and suffering cannot make this claim and therein lies the possibility of its positive disruptiveness. I would propose that values cannot be explored without starting from a position of their presence, not absence, then considering the inhibition of them and the symptoms of their inhibition in certain institutional structures. I will also use the Greek word *pistis* for to bind/be faithful.

Pain

> You think your pain and your heartbreak are unprecedented in the history of the world, but then you read. It was books that taught me that the things that tormented me most were the very things that connected me with all the people who were alive, who had ever been alive. (Baldwin 1999).

Here Baldwin indicates another form of relationality, that which binds people to each other and to things through universal experiences, mostly of pain and its state of undergoing pain which is suffering. Perhaps C.S. Lewis (2012) would be not be so surprised that today it is higher education of all places that has joined the deaf world which has to be roused with a megaphone of shouts of pain. What higher education can do, should do, is to create the conditions for a relationality of creative engagement not a relationality of pain or deficit.

Of course pain is not a word one hears much in academia except in reference to medical and health issues but there are plenty of manifestations of the experience of it using other words: discomfort; stress; tiredness; overwhelming; anxious; worried. Pain is, for many people, deconstructive of who they perceive themselves to be and this is why it is important in higher education today that for both staff and students it is addressed in its raw form rather than hidden behind descriptions which are euphemistic of what is actually going on. Current trends such as 'well being' can be no more than a plaster on a gaping wound manifested in suicides among talented young students and sick leave by staff. The Health and Safety (UK) Executive Report of 2016/17 states that 526,000 employees were suffering from work related stress, anxiety or depression and 12.5millions days of work were lost in 2016/17 due to these factors. The Institute for Public Policy Research published a report in 2017 on the suicide rate among UK students: suicides among students in the UK have risen above the general youth population for the first time and the rate has increased by 56% in the last 10 years. While the accuracy of figures has been challenged, it is agreed by all current reports that student suicide is very much on the rise and incidents under-reported. Is it our subconscious recognition of this that is moving the current trend in research and discourse towards positive values? The kind of pain I am talking about is that experienced at many levels, not just physical pain which is what we immediately think of when we hear the word, but a kind of pain that pervades who we are and how we relate to each other and our workworlds, and to notions of expectation and hope. Exploring this pain as a symptom of 'lack' in the environment where we spend most of our time, makes visible the *skia* in our contexts and the prevention of cultures of health.

> Though there is ordinarily no language for pain, under the pressure of the desire to eliminate pain, an at least fragmentary means of verbalisation is available both to those who are themselves in pain and to those who wish to speak on behalf of others…pain enters into our midst, as at once something that cannot be denied and something that cannot be confirmed…to have pain is to have certainty; to hear about pain is to have doubt (Scarry 1987: 13).

Pain can be due to unintended psychological, emotional and physiological experiences (sometimes described as acts of God or misinformed good intentions), or the sequelae of the intentional infliction of pain by another for exploitative purposes or a wilful violation of another vulnerable human being or the by-product of self-referenced, narcissistic personas or of objectifying structures and beliefs. At the core of our experience of the world, and indeed what keeps us alive, is the human ability to feel, endure, and seek to recover from pain. However, fear of it is also exploited to instil fear, to perpetuate unjust beliefs and practices, to monopolise resources and to marginalise and demonise, in order to ensure compliance to the structure and practices of the entity. We all have a relationship to pain and engage with both its alleviation and its perpetuation.

It may seem an unusual lens to take, but as higher education involves itself much more with professional knowledge and a belief or a marketing brief that it has a role to play in instilling professional practitioners of tomorrow with social responsibility and a moral compass, many of us are turning to values to provide the counterpoint to managerialism, instrumentalisation and freezer packed compliant employees. We are collecting the ingredients and do not yet fully comprehend why and who for and what difference it will make. Why have compassion, trust, grace and other 'virtues' become so important that we should seek them out and write lengthy discourses on them or recover discourses from the past? What has filled the space where they should be, or have been, or have never been? How do we recognise the *skia*, that which is concealed behind the beautiful shop frontage? Perhaps we recognise it but do not speak about it in case it awakens, like some Kraken, and creates havoc in our individual lives, such as taking our jobs away which will, in turn, negatively impact those connected to us. They will be the collateral damage of speaking out about what lies beneath. Collateral damage has itself become a phrase that normalises negative by products as somehow being inevitable and therefore acceptable. Such fear is a recognition that the structure and systems, in denying the interconnectedness of things, have no mercy. We have all witnessed acts in our institutions which appear to lack grace, compassion, empathy, trust. We cannot fail to notice the increasing gaps between espoused values and what happens in everyday practice, precisely because writers and commentators are providing the language to speak about values but not how they can operate in practice in a way that addresses our desirability of what ought to be or the creative action Graeber speaks of (2001) in his theory of value.

In addition to these observations, my ideas are informed by clinical practice with survivors of extreme experiences; the role of the state structure which allows these practices to take place; the role of silence; the notion of disappearedness; the impact of pain on the concept of creative consciousness and the possibilities of reparative and generative relations if we pay attention to it. Extreme experiences imposed on an individual or group are no more than the substantial amplification of what happens in everyday life. We can learn from the knowledge that has emerged from this specialist practice, the sense making that survivors and witnesses have been driven to make in order to understand the level of inhumanity an 'ordinary' human being can reach in the right circumstances where every actor – the captor, captive, witness; the employer, employee, consumer; the university, staff, student – is caught up in the same relational dynamic of negative *pistis* but with different scripts of greater or lesser pain.

What higher education can offer during this liminal period of identity formation for students between the end of adolescence and the beginning of adulthood is an environment that leans more towards relations which inspire a positive, aware *pistis* rather than one of blind faith and following; not that which embeds the deficit that has often preceded entry into higher education; nor that which keeps staff and students in a state of replicating stasis. We need, for ourselves and our students, to be more aware of what flag is being offered, to what is allegiance being expected and what goals are to be achieved. We need to ask whether the higher education institution is an organisation driven by the exploitation of the fear of the pain of failure, unworthiness, marginalisation, unfulfilled promise, being invisible, pointless, jobless and – I am talking about staff and students here – an exploitation which inhibits freedom of speech and expression among its students and staff. Silence, as Shakespeare so eloquently put it in 'Much Ado about Nothing', is the 'perfectist herault' of joy. In certain circumstances it is also the indicator of a climate of fear, fear of deep feelings of discomfort which are painful and alter behaviour.

Can we see the value of thinking differently about what we witness, or what we have stopped seeing and what we accept as the norm when we should not? Can we find the courage and indeed the patience to listen, patience usually requiring a suspension of belief that you can do anything about another's pain other than listen, other than be a witness?

Pain and the Individual

We have an intolerance to hear about the pain of others perhaps because in the face of all kinds of pain of the other, we feel powerless, beyond *I have some painkillers in my bag*, or because memory of our own pain is notoriously elusive, which can lower the empathy with another, or because at some level we are not sure what to believe about what is being said. We may have time for the questions *How are things? How are you?* but not for the answer, as the answer may be too complex and so we miss what the story is really about. Take this true account of Mary which captures both these issues as well as the pain of shame:

> Mary came in to see the doctor with severe pain in her shoulder. She had been coming to his clinic for years and before him to the previous consultant. She was possibly in her mid 70s but her dress and make-up were more those of a teenager of another time down to the short

skirt and bows in her shoes and hair, even younger – a kind of Shirley Temple. She was charming and disappeared behind a curtain with the consultant whom I could hear saying that he really couldn't give her any more cortisone. She was flirting beautifully with him, confident that she would eventually get her way. I sat with her husband, a dapper man who was obviously still very much in love with his wife. They had never had children. I asked him how he was and how he was coping. He was very surprised at my enquiry saying no one had ever asked him this before. He said it wasn't easy because sometimes his wife was fine and at others time the pain was shocking. Did he know what caused it? No. It had just come upon her when she was about 24 and no one could find a source. He hoped the doctor would be kind enough to give her something as they had a wedding to go to. Had they been coming to this hospital for long? Oh yes, they had lost a baby here after the war and had been coming back ever since. He thought it was her way to be close to the baby she never got to take home, the pain relief was like her taking her baby home instead of leaving the baby here and taking her pain home. Had he ever mentioned this to his wife, to the doctors. No never. No one ever asked and they would think him mad anyway (Maguire 2000).

I was reminded of this observation I had made as a clinician in the NHS when I was in a large sharing department at a previous university and could not help overhearing in the kitchen and the washroom talented professional women having conversations about their weekend working, looking after children, elderly parents and cleaning; how they had migraines, sore backs, trouble with their hearts but they did not complain or take time off for fear of redundancy and could not speak out for fear of 'hanging a target board round my neck.'

Morris (1991) challenges this notion that physical pain and mental pain are different calling it the Myth of Two Pains. Referring to Wittgenstein's metaphor of language which is 'a maze of little streets and, of old and new houses, and of houses with additions from various periods; and this surrounded by a multitude of new boroughs with straight regular streets and uniform houses' (Morris 1991: 15), he states from a medical practitioner perspective that:

> Scientists and philosophers seek to make pain into an orderly citizen of the new suburbs of knowledge but at some point it invariably darts back into the maze of ancient city streets where maps prove almost useless and where you know your way around, if at all, by feel.

He brings to attention another fundamental concept in understanding pain and that is meaning making.

> …human kind –across cultures and across time – has persistently understood pain as an event that demands interpretation. Pain not only hurts but more often than not frustrates, baffles and resists us. It seems we cannot simply suffer pain but are almost always compelled to make sense of it (18).

This meaning making is paradoxically challenged by pain and suffering often being beyond expression in verbal terms and those words or phrases used are often euphemistic or devoid of the conveyance of the experience except through the language and metaphors used to describe physical pain (Scarry 1987). This enforced severing of the depth of experience and the utterance of it to communicate to others, is either a self- imposed silence or a silencing brought about by socio/political factors in the contexts in which pain takes place. Silence should never be assumed as the absence of pain but as a possible indicator of its presence.

For survivors of extreme suffering, words or communication are found in metaphors. Brian Keenan (1993: 297), held hostage for several years in Lebanon, describes the darkness of isolation which words can never really capture.

I know that nightmares have their source
Like the abstract has some social sense
Time fluxes in the dark
Night Stalking mind, closer than blood.
Dreams, worsen things felt – not said,
Spaces on every side:
Bat's wings beat like heart
Or drum
Translating silence into insanity

Sometimes, there are too many words, as the speaker struggles to explain the pain and we stop listening or wish to get away. Hearing of pain is often perceived as whingeing or an excuse. *People should just get on with it, we all hurt*, might be one reaction, or it is distracting, requiring us to change our behaviour. Sophocles captures something of both the physical and symbolic dimension of pain with the tale of Philoctetes who was abandoned by Odysseus and his companions during the Trojan war to a barren rock so that they would no longer hear his pain from a rotting wound. What was it the Greeks could not hear? Philoctetes abandoned on his rock of pain is visited once again by Odysseus on his way home at the end of the war and only then, when Odysseus was, after all, only passing through, can something humanising be said but there is still no recognition of the responsibility of those who put him there, nor the recognition that the physical pain is the symbolic scream of the waste of all the lives that have been lost because of the vagaries of vain men. His pain had gone beyond expression in language so all he could do was wail. Odysseus had this to say of Philoctetes while waving goodbye and abandoning him once again as he was a busy man and needed to get on with things. He was not moved to change his behaviour. He was too important:

Alone on this inhospitable shore,
Where waves forever beat and tempests roar,
How could he e'er hope or comfort know,
Or painful life support beneath such weight of woe.

Then there is the silence which arises from the fear of being shamed or of drawing attention to oneself, or of risking everything to speak truth to power.

Compared to the incessant dialogue of reason and madness during the Renaissance, classical internment had been a silencing. But it was not total: language was engaged in things rather than really suppressed. Confinement, prisons, dungeons, engaged in a mute dialogue between reason and unreason – the dialogue of struggle. This dialogue itself was now disengaged; silence was absolute; there was no longer any common language between madness and reason; the language of delirium can be answered only by the absence of language, for delirium is not language at all. (Foucault 2006: 249).

On this latter point I disagree, the delirium, the 'madness' is a language of pain in itself. In my clinical practice, prior to the setting up of my new trauma unit, separating survivors of extreme experiences from those who were mentally ill, expressions of pain were seen as indicators of mental illness such as self- harming. When seen as an attempt at communicating internal ravaging pain from which there seems little release, a kind of possession, greater possibilities are then opened up for more appropriate interventions. There is often both shame in expressing weakness and fear of contaminating those one tells, and of contaminating the everyday relationship as if the possession could be passed on. This was the concern of a young man who had been held in Khmer Rouge camps at the age of 12 and escaped with two friends, one who died on the way:

> …pain has separated us from you. Part of us is already dead to this world … I want to swallow my children, both of them, keep them inside me and carry them everywhere I go, … so they both won't lose the love they want to have… The beautiful dream has gone, hope has become meaningless. Love has more pain… the world has become too small to walk … I have no more love to give to anyone. (From the unpublished diaries of L. who committed suicide in 1997). (Maguire 2001: 128)

Disappearing People

> Disappearances, apparitions; few clues, or none at all. Mostly it isn't murder, a punishable crime – the people just vanish. They go away, in sorrow, in pain, in mute astonishment, as of something decided forever. But sometimes you can't be sure, and a thing will happen that remains so unresolved, so strange, that someone will think about it years later; and he will sit there in the dusk and silence, staring out the window at another world (Haines 2003).

The accounts in the previous section highlight the destructive nature of being disappeared by a person, by society or by systems. It is perhaps only from going to the far end of the scale of inhumanity that the everyday routines of disappearing can be brought into awareness. Every day people and systems disappear humans. We say we are busy when someone wants to tell us something; we do not respond to emails because the person is not a priority; at home we can disappear children by not engaging them in chatter or by sending them to their rooms or disappear a partner by not looking at them because we are angry about something. *I am busy, I don't have time* have become the two most common responses to calls from communities who need our values to support cohesiveness and healthy community environments. We are so busy doing, that we do not have time to be. We disappear that which is most resonant with our values in order to be occupied with 'things' dissonant with them.

This term 'disappeared' is well known in the field of torture dynamics studies and refers to the authorities 'disappearing' people by imprisoning them and/or brutally killing them but all the time denying their existence so no investigation can be carried out. It also refers to a form of torture in which the victim is hooded often for long periods of time and also during torture. This separates the individual from his or her world and denies the person their survival skill of anticipation. It also dehumanises the person in the eyes of the torturer. If they do not look into the victim's face, they cannot be confronted by their own cruelty reflected there. When a person has been hooded for a long time, there is an adaptive response. The torturer cannot see the victim's face, their tears, their anger, their expression. It can become a private, withdrawal place or the only means the individual can have of reacting against the torturer, as the torturer cannot read the face. Even if a person has not been hooded during imprisonment, imprisonment itself is a form of being disappeared. The world goes on outside as normal and nobody and nothing is making this horror stop. People who have been tortured, abused and severely deprived have been disappeared by the rest of society, a society which is often justly perceived as having failed to prevent these terrible things from happening – the law, justice, other people, authorities, governments, international bodies. For others, physical pain is the acceptable face of an emotional pain which is often too shaming, too complex, too annihilating to be brought into the staff room. I am not saying people are tortured in our higher education institutions or indeed in most other workworlds. What I am saying is that what happens at the micro level can be a diluted version of what is acted out at the macro level, with terrible consequences, which are explicit and therefore have much to say about what is happening in a 'milder' form at the micro level. All collectives are made up of people, human behaviour is manifest positively and negatively, not differently, at all levels. Staff stop speaking openly to the executive and are losing solidarity with colleagues because trust has been eroded. In turn, staff who are disappeared into substantial workloads start to disappear their students and their families because there is no work life balance. People are made redundant at a distance, made to disappear quietly, preferably, or the package might be reduced. People disappear themselves from institiutions seeking a better flag. In a compliance culture students and staff can be assessed against compliance not against quality and creativity, integrity and respect in what they actually do which is disappeared. After all, an institution or organisation has no need to be appreciative of that which, through a culture of disappearing, now is not seen to exist. These are complex interconnected systems and, as it is in the workworlds where most time is spent, it is there that issues of disappearing need to be addressed even if they are believed not to be frequent.

The Dynamics of Pain

What has emerged from clinical practice may begin, firstly, to enable us to conceptualise what is going on in our own organisations to better understand what we can do to address them. Authority dynamics are fundamentally an abnegation of responsibility and accountability. The authority or decision makers, the guardians of the 'culture' of the organisation, have a host of people under them who are both the instigators of practices and the monitors of compliance to them. These monitors for the flag are usually the ones blamed by staff for exploitation or unfairness relating to staff, and for being silenced or not heard in the name of customer satisfaction. However, customers are increasingly blaming organisational management rather than the organisation's non-management employees, as they begin to see such staff as being exploited by guardians of the flag, unless of course the organisation is a big social media company with a host of trust-inducing formulae, such as reviews and money back guarantees and endless perks for employees to maintain the façade of a great organisation to work for. Research shows that trust is, on the whole, attributed to the front liners who anthropomorphise the organisation. Why then should an organisation create conditions for the negative *skia* of pain rather than a positive creative environment of trust?

> Our system is one of detachment: to keep silenced people from asking questions, to keep the judged from judging, to keep solitary people from joining together, and the soul from putting together its pieces. (Galeano 1993)

Conclusion: The Importance of Consciousness

Seeing the well-known Maslow's hierarchy of needs (2013) as a deprivation scale is more unusual than it is normally perceived. However, exploring what it is that has been deprived and can be repaired raises issues in ourselves as well as our students as to whether we feel we can impact our environment and how. Do we check on the safety and security needs of our students in terms of their living conditions, their economic status, their sense of love and belonging, their fears of family members being deported, their freedom to choose, their aspirations, their cultural dissonances, imposed or elected? Do we check if our students believe they can impact their environment to respond positively to their situation (locus of control)? Do we check whether they are being or feeling disappeared? Do we offer creative channels for them to express their thoughts and feelings in ways which are culturally appropriate or personally appropriate so they are not shamed in the face of the other, not made to feel they are unstable or feel that speaking out will cost them the price of good marks (silenced and shamed) or even their university place or future.

The role pain plays in the consciousness we have of ourselves and others can be best understood when we look at what happens when we experience pain. It causes a major disruption with perception which is beyond the physiological understanding of pain. This is the phenomenology of pain. If we are to look at pain as a disrupter of our sense of self, which is actually what the Maslow deprivation scale is used to achieve, then instead of a shutting down, a dissociation, we can focus on the right prompts, creating the right conditions for understanding to take place (Gadamer 1992: 12). We can explore different ways of expressing self, a more creative, emotional and insightful translation of self into the world. Humphrey (1999) sees this as the brain's conjuring trick, that consciousness is the introspective access to mental states. Therefore when pain, or fear of pain, which is also pain, disrupts perceptions of self and engagement with others and objects, in other words disrupts relations, the brain can restore that which constitutes self as a mind wide forum for planning and decision making with the right tools of interventions.

If HEIs are interested in identity, allegiance, bonding and having a role in creating a better future for all its participants, a positive *pistis*, it could do well to pay attention to the organisational dynamics which replicate systems which can be dehumanising and painful, which can disappear, marginalise and misunderstand its members. HEIs, despite supposedly claiming knowledge and enlightenment, with the mandate to enlighten others, are notoriously hierarchical, aurally challenged, exploitative, instrumental and whimsically trend following. Higher education sells relationality, allegiance to the brand, a sense of belonging and pride, but until it addresses the *skia* which causes pain, it cannot hope to be fully commercially or educationally successful. Healthy identity formation, guides through liminal space, healing of preceded deconstruction are being addressed by many teachers and individuals working creatively with students to develop their potential within HE cultures which do not encourage-in-action the creation of integrity environments. HEIs need to offer better conditions for such an approach to thrive. Perhaps it could start by not silencing its members and adopting a mandate that upholds its own espoused principle of do no harm and, in true hermeneutic tradition, if you take care of the conditions for understanding, understanding will take place. If HEIs recognise that their institutions are made up of many individuals brimming with values and begin to understand the institution's role in inhibiting them, then we do have a chance of unconcealing a values-infused culture of higher education. A way to recognise when our positive values are being forced into silent abeyance by the negative values – the self-ish desires of others for power, status, wealth and exclusion – is captured in the words of Bruno Bettelheim (1991), a survivor of the World War II concentration camps,who said that the most difficult thing to live with is to know that you behaved in a way you did not approve of in yourself (Preface:xii). That is the shadown cost of allegiance to a flag.

It would seem appropriate to reach the closure of this chapter with the voice of a student and the voice of a clinician who have found their own ways to bring attention to the problem of pain in our small and large cultures.

> Letter to the Academy
>
> I need to commend you, for you have been astute at giving me attention through all your cognitive capacities. …I have now managed to find myself in a wide variety of discourses …I am now even being discussed at the tables of some of the finest institutions in the world… Yet in this presence there are absences, ones that have implications for the health of developing the scope of full body intellectuals, scholars and educators…I am a gift for you, far more than you know…that guides you towards what can unfold within you including the depths of pain and beauty. (Snowber 2011)
>
> We certainly cannot succeed as a culture by continuing to deny and ignore pain, as if we could silence it beneath a mountain of pills. That clearly does not work. Nor can we help each other by continuing to place unblinking faith in an outworn organic model as limited in its way as the theory that attributes pain to the arrows of the gods. We are more than bundles of neurons. We must recover a sense of the importance of minds and cultures in the construction of pain… (Morris 1991: 289)

To end with where I began, it is not that there are no positive values in higher education, there are, a considerable number. It is that the intended and unintended suppression of them by the culture will lead to a dangerous stasis; the release of them through recognising the *skia* and attending to it will move the entity towards a generative state of positive relationality where allegiance will be freely and gladly given and identity and belonging a fulfilled desire.

References

Archer, M. S. (2003). *Structure, agency and the internal conversation*. Cambridge: Cambridge University Press.

Bettelheim, B. (1991). *The informed heart*. London: Penguin Books Ltd.

Baldwin, J. (1999). *The price of the ticket*. New York: St Martin's Press.

Burkitt, I. (2016). Relational agency: Relational sociology, agency and interaction. *European Journal of Social Theory, 19*(3), 322–339. Sage.

Foucault, M. (2006). *Madness and civilisation*. Oxon: Routledge Classics.

Gadamer, H. (1992). In: G. Bruns (Ed.), *Hermeneutics ancient and modern*. New Haven: Yale University Press.

Galeano, E. (1993). *Divorces in the book of embraces*. London: W.W. Norton and Company Ltd.

Giddens, A. (1979). *Central problems in social theory: Action, structure and contradiction in social analysis*. Basingstoke: Macmillan.

Giddens, A. (1984). *The constitution of society: Outline of the theory of structuration*. Cambridge: Cambridge University Press.

Goffman, I. (1970). *Asylums: Essays on the social situation of mental patients and other inmates*. Harmondsworth: Pelican Books.

Graeber, D. (2001). *Toward and anthropological theory of value*. New York: Palgrave.

Graeber, D. (2007). *Possibilities: Essays on hierarchy, rebellion and desire*. Oakland: AK Press.

Haines, J. (2003). *Lost in the stars, the snow the fire: Twenty-five years in the Alaska wilderness*. Minneapolis: Graywolf Press.

Health and Safety Executive (HSE). (2016/17). *Annual report*. http://www.hse.gov.uk/statistics/causdis/stress/

Humphrey, N. (1999). *A history of the mind: Evolution and the history of consciousness*. New York: Springer.

Keenan, B. (1993). *An evil cradling*. London: Vintage.

LeRon Shults, F. (2003). *Reforming theological anthropology : After the philosophical turn to relationality*. Grand Rapids: Eerdmans Publishing Company.

Lewis, C. S. (2012). *The problem of pain*. London: Collins.

Maguire, K. (2000). *Clinical notes* (contact author for more information).

Maguire, K. (2001). Working with survivors of torture and extreme experiences. In S. King-Spooner & C. Newes (Eds.), *Spirituality and psychotherapy* (pp. 122–136). Ross-on Wye: PCCS Books.

Marx, K. (1967). *Capital* (3 volumes). New York: New World Paperback.

Maslow, A. H. (2013). *A theory of human motivation*. Virginia: Wilder Publications.

Milgram, S. (1974). *Obedience to authority*. New York: HarperCollins.

Morris, D. B. (1991). *The culture of pain*. Berkeley: University of California Press.

Morton, T. (2013). *Hyperobjects: Philosophy and ecology after the end of the world* (Posthumanities): University of Minnesota Press.

Scarry, E. (1987). *The body in pain*. Oxford: Oxford University Press.

Snowber, C. (2011). Let the body out: A love letter to the academy from the BODY. In E. Malewski & N. Jaramillo (Eds.), *Epistemologies of ignorance in education*. Charlotte: Information Age Publishing Inc.

Sophocles. *Philoctetes*. 409 BCE. (T. Francklin, Trans.). www.ancientgreektexts.com/library/Soph/Phil/eng/index.html. p. 14 Strophe1 [5].

Whitehead, A. N. (1920). *Nature and thought in the concept of nature*. Cambridge: Cambridge University Press.

Whitehead, A. N. (1938). *Modes of thought*. New York: Capricorn Books.

Wildman, W. (2006). *An introduction to relational ontology*, Wesley J. Wildman, Boston University, May 15, 2006 Open Source. http://people.bu.edu/wwildman/media/docs/Wildman_2009_Relational_Ontology.

Chapter 7
Governance, Leadership and University Cultures: Do Universities Critique Social Norms and Values, or Copy Them?

Ian McNay

Abstract The New Zealand Education Act of 1989 lists characteristics of universities, including 'a role as critic and conscience of society'. My contention here is that universities in the UK, at corporate and senior manager level, have lost the moral high ground necessary to fulfil such a role. The Code of Practice of the Committee of University Chairs (of governors) sets the Nolan Principles of conduct in public life as a benchmark for recognised standards of good practice, but states that members must act in line with the accepted standards of behaviour in public life. I demonstrate that what is accepted in action – operational values and standards – falls well below espoused values and principles. With mass participation, universities have become part of mainstream society, not separate, monastic communities in the reflective Newman tradition. They, therefore, receive attention from a press acting as their 'critic and conscience'. I examine some of the discourse used in this context, straddling the campus boundary in scope and style. The values essential to academic autonomy operate throughout a university, so enacted values will be examined within the context of organisation culture to draw out lessons from contemporary events to show how they mirror campus norms, as well as to emphasise to leaders the ethics and behavioural standards essential within a higher education context in defending the exceptionality of universities.

Keywords Governance · Leadership · Culture · Social norms · Accountability

Introduction

In New Zealand, the 1989 Education Act lists characteristics of, and criteria for, universities, including (section 162/4) 'they accept a role as critic and conscience of society'. This is not only an institutional role: it implies that university academic

---

I. McNay (✉)
University of Greenwich, London, UK
e-mail: I.McNay@greenwich.ac.uk

© Springer Nature Switzerland AG 2019
P. Gibbs et al. (eds.), *Values of the University in a Time of Uncertainty*,
https://doi.org/10.1007/978-3-030-15970-2_7

staff have a legitimate role as public intellectuals operating critically, not only in reviewing research *within* the university sector, where criticism is intrinsic to rational enquiry (Russell 2015) but in the political public sphere. Opinions expressed must be based on reason/research, conform to the law, set high ethical standards, and be themselves subject to criticism, without which, as Kant (1998) said, they must risk a damaging suspicion. They should be principled, but also practical, developmental, not simply destructive (Gledhill n.d., online). That public role is recognised by universities in New Zealand. For instance, the University of Auckland builds it in to performance appraisal under the heading of 'contributions to the community' (Gledhill n.d.).

In the UK, the protection of such academic freedom has had to be fought for with successive education Acts, and, on a broader base, individual academic freedom is constantly subject to erosion, just as is institutional academic autonomy. The Committee of University Chairs (CUC), in its *Code of Governance* (CUC 2014), expects governing bodies to commit to 'autonomy as the best guarantee of quality and…reputation' and 'academic freedom and high quality research, scholarship and teaching'. It also endorses and builds on the 'Nolan Principles of Public Life', listed as selflessness, integrity, objectivity, accountability, openness, honesty, leadership (CSPL 2015). The *Code* sets these as a reference point for *recognised* standards of good practice, but later states that 'members must act… in line with the *accepted* standards of behaviour in public life' (my emphasis). One contention here is that what is accepted in action falls well below what should operate in principle, and that it is the enacted standards that lose UK universities, as organisations, the moral ground for acting as credible critics and consciences of the communities within which they are located.

Universities espouse values through governance codes, but governors and senior staff seem to be not fully aware of such values in operation. With mass involvement, universities have become part of mainstream society, not separate, reflective communities in the monastic Newman tradition. As such, they receive attention for their failings from a press acting as their 'critic and conscience'. Less pleasant aspects of their behaviour are uncovered as they pursue their mission of turning gilded youth into society's leaders. Journalistic language is, at times, replicated in this essay. I suggest that the debased values of nationalistic neo-liberalism have infiltrated their boundaries. Press headline are used to illustrate the increasingly imitative culture within universities and to relate this to wider socio-economic norms. So this essay straddles campus and community/country, using both academic practices of citation of research and scholarly study and enquiry-based journalism.

As John Harris reported on the 50th anniversary of the 'events' of 1968, one graffito in Paris said: 'to call in question the society you live in, you must first be capable of calling yourself into question' (Harris 2018: 34). It was the students who were the critics, and their targets included their universities. Not only in France: in the USA Columbia University was exposed as doing research in support of the Vietnam war and of demolishing homes in Harlem to expand its campus. Harris claims that, at the time, there was 'a widespread conviction that traditional power structures were so problematic as to be almost useless' (p. 33). That is true now in the UK, where students are campaigning about the chaos and incompetence of the Brexit process, according to one front page headline,

13 May 2018 **One million students join calls for vote on Brexit deal**, *The Observer*

It is worth remembering that de Gaulle won a landslide victory soon after the 'events'. French students are now protesting more parochially about exams and entry levels, but this time do not have working class support from the trade unions. UK students never have had – the elitism gap is too wide; values are not shared.

A survey by the Leadership Foundation for HE (LFHE 2016) included questions on values and found, among governor respondents, 'little mention of ethics…sustainable development, corporate social responsibility…partnerships…equality and diversity' (p. 14). Yet those governors are the voice of what Dearing (1997) called a university's 'constituencies'; they determine the educational character of an institution, which must rest on underpinning values, and monitor its performance against that vision. Successive surveys by PA Consulting Group have shown that vice-chancellors are dismissive of governing bodies, as were my respondents in interviews with current and former senior staff about changes after fees were trebled in England. They were neither effective nor supportive, and imported their values from the private sector, embraced the 'market' and were 'hardline' on issues of staff management and finance. Yet 45% of mainly those same vice-chancellors did not think they themselves had effective leadership capabilities (PACG 2010, 2011).

Academic autonomy and professionalism involve considerable leadership activities and self-governance below senior management, where the *Code of Practice* implies that governance stops. So enacted values at both levels will be considered within a context of organisational culture, first in looking at the active expression of standards in society and their reflection in universities, through news reports, and, second, in drawing out some lessons from contemporary events to inform institutional leaders about ethics and behavioural standards essential within a higher education context.

In the midst of war, F.R. Leavis (1943: 30) encapsulated his view of a university:

> … amid the material pressures and dehumanising complications of the modern world, a focus of humane consciousness, a centre where, faced with the specialisations and distractions in which human ends lose themselves, intelligence, bringing to bear a mature set of values, should apply itself to the problems of civilisation.

That may convey an ivory tower image to some but 'the problems of civilisation', scrutinised on the basis of a 'mature set of values', may be not far from being a 'critic and conscience'. Leavis prefaces his first essay, on 'The Idea of a University', with a quote from Meiklejohn's (1932) *The Experimental College*, reporting on a project at the University of Wisconsin, which claims:

> Closeness of connection between the character of a society and the character of its education cannot be too strongly stressed. Schools and colleges are not something apart from the social order to which they belong. They are that order trying to prepare its youth for participation in its own activities.

My concern is that the character of our contemporary society is not one I wish to stress as a model for universities. Others have had concerns (Hutton 1995; Neuberger 2005). They continue: a Chartered Institute for Personnel and Development UK workforce survey revealed that only 8% of leaders rated themselves highly on the 'moral self' component of purposeful leadership (CIPD 2017). That may be higher in universities, which still retain a high rating for public trust, but universities bear some responsibility. Garcia (2009, 2010) in his doctoral study straddling France and Britain, found little evidence of values being treated in the curriculum of MBA programmes. Parker (2018) was also critical: he reported a study comparing MBA students in the USA and people held in low-security prisons: he found that the latter were more ethical.

> Graduates are taught that greed is good…they almost never systematically address the simple idea that since current and economic relations produce the problems that ethics and corporate social responsibility courses treat as subjects to be studied, it is those social and economic relations that need to be changed. (p. 11)

The higher education world of Leavis and Meiklejohn changed. Twenty years after Leavis wrote, the Robbins Committee (Robbins 1963) reported. Its sense of values was expressed in one of its aims for HE: inculcation of a 'common culture', of 'providing influences that…compensate for any inequalities of home background', sending out graduates to lead society, with the university also having 'an important role to play in the general cultural life of the communities in which they are situated'. So, university values would be imbued in society, from the top, through training good members of society which Newman (1873) set as a practical end, and through graduates' leadership and example: a somewhat elitist, condescending approach. That continues. It was seen in the approaches from both sides in the Brexit referendum debate: one dismissing 'experts' and exploiting lack of knowledge and ill-based xenophobia, the other displaying a lack of knowledge beyond their own bubble, disconnected from the reality of people's lives: in public scandals over politicians' behaviour, not least over bullying and wide spread abuse of expense claims; over the priesthood in sexual abuse and exploitation, concealed by senior post-holders; over press abuse and criminality in seeking a story; over police corruption and racism, again denied or concealed over Hillsborough, the Stephen Lawrence murder, deaths in custody. It is worth noting the high number of graduates involved, dominantly from self-proclaimed excellent (and elitist) universities. Not, I hope, representing the 'common culture' that Robbins may have aimed at, but when the vice-chancellor of Oxford University cited bankers and footballers as benchmarks for salaries, it raised questions about how far their values, not costs, were also invoked. The vice-chancellor of Bolton parades with his Bentley as a role model of success, despite the record of the university he leads.

The massification of higher education brought a shift in values. Adelman's (1973) 'Holiversity' for Ontario had two forms – a Mission University offered society Leavis's mature set of values but a detached intelligence; the Mirror University entailed an engaged intelligence and a reflection of the current, and changing, values of society. Trow (1989) believed that the Robbins values were incompatible with mass provision with a separation of the elite institutions shaping the mind and character of the ruling class, and mass institutions developing skills for technical and economic (p)roles. Both he and Scott (1995) foresaw more freedom in the elite group and more regulation, government control and managerialism for the rest. And so it came to pass, though both have adapted to the dissonance between normative, espoused values, threatened by moral decline (Neuberger 2005) and operational values, expressed in deeds, not words. Ignatieff (2018) described this as a counter-majoritarian mission and message, in examining the role of the Central European University and its Budapest base, with a hostile government leader. Operational imperatives for the sector have seen a succession of 'E-factors': economy, efficiency, effectiveness (taken as a trio); equity, expansion, excellence (often seen as competing, not complementary); enterprise, employability, engagement (opening up the university and emphasising its role in serving the economy and re-building the nation). Strategic selection from among this list will be based on the identity of a university with differing values relating to this self-concept (McNay 2018).

There have been two important statements on values since Robbins. The Dearing Report articulated a set of values…

> …shared throughout higher education and without which higher education, as we understand it *could not exist* [my emphasis]. Such values include:
> A commitment to the pursuit of truth (see 1 below)
> A responsibility to share knowledge (2)
> Freedom of thought and expression (3)
> Analysing evidence rigorously and using reasoned arguments to reach a conclusion (4)
> A willingness to listen to alternative views and judge them on their merits (3)
> Taking account of how one's own arguments will be perceived by others (5)
> A commitment to consider the ethical implications of different findings and practices.
> (Dearing, 1997: 5.39)

A case can be made that there are pressures within HE which put some of them under threat:

1. Selective publication of data, particularly when commercially funded and not finding the 'right' result. Compare Volkswagen on vehicle emissions.
2. Competition among researchers (and their managers) for kudos of winning by first publication. Compare non-publication of evidence by police and the DPP to opposing/competing legal teams
3. Student pressure to 'no platform' those with whom they disagree and the bullying aggression of social media
4. Evidence that experiments reported in journals cannot be replicated with the same outcomes (Pells 2018; Mansell and Huddy 2018)
5. Universities UK consent to the appointment of Toby Young as a student representative to the Office for Students Board, allegedly out of fear of speaking out.

If we take the Nolan principles for activity in public life, developed within parliament and advocated by the CUC as indicated above, again there are examples within higher education of many of these not being observed:

- *Selflessness and objectivity*: nepotistic appointment of relatives and former colleagues to key roles
- *Integrity*: acceptance of funding from questionable sources – Ghaddafi and LSE was a prominent example, but Russian oligarchs have their names on a variety of units, and funding is taken from tobacco firms, oppressive Middle East regimes and the arms industry (Ramiro 2016)
- *Objectivity and accountability.* One senior management team was deciding to improve the quality of the student experience (good) by restructuring the university's organisation and provision (bad). When I asked if they had read the research on student experience – no. Were they intending to? No. A major decision was to be taken with less research underpinning than an undergraduate project. They asked me to summarise the research – I had just organised a conference on the issue – and they would take account of that when deciding what to do. I did; they did not, and the result was… not positive.
- *Openness and accountability.* A recent example is a student appeal against the decision of a viva panel I chaired that, after two fails at PhD level, an exceptional third submission be considered for MPhil, but only, among other things, after extra field work, which was needed to give sufficiently rigorous underpinning to the findings, even for an MPhil. The external examiners were not officially notified of the student's appeal, and, when the outcome overturned their decision, and awarded an MPhil without any further work, they were given no information about its basis, and no chance to comment. The recommendation for the third submission had already taken account of any factors that might have formed that basis.
- *Leadership and Integrity.* I have observed a governing body meeting being given false financial data by a member of a senior management team when deciding on an investment in a new site/campus for course provision. I did then brief the chair of governors, and the initiative was short-lived.

I did struggle to match some of those examples, since there is no principle about rigorous evidence to underpin decisions nor about basic competences, both of which, it can be argued, are also currently absent from UK government.

I am not arguing that the examples represent a norm. Open data on performance deters some excesses, and journalists seek out 'bad' news which makes for a 'good' story. I am concerned about the osmosis between society and academia, which I accept is no Arcadia, and the slow erosion of levels at which unacceptable behaviour within universities is identified, when one of their key roles is in setting and assessing standards for students.

In the News

With mass higher education meaning that about 50% of younger people, plus another 10% later in life, now enter universities and other degree awarding institutions, they have become of widespread public interest, and therefore newsworthy.

This section looks at how universities are treated by the press, and the image conveyed about their values and integrity. I will not cover everything here, but concentrate on Robbins' expectation, quoted above, that they will 'compensate for any inequalities of… background'; my focus is on performance on issues of equity in an increasingly inequitable society.

I start with money, since it is the dominant value driving government policy. High graduate salaries are used as a criterion of quality teaching in the Teaching Excellence Framework (TEF), despite evidence that family background and private school attendance are much more significant influences on salary levels, and that racism in employment means that the salary gap between black and white is wider for graduates than for school leavers. HE funding reflects a general government policy of reducing taxes for the rich and reducing support for the poor and disadvantaged. In this decade, most staff in HE have had a salary freeze, with an effective reduction in income because of inflation. Numbers of academic staff on part-time and casual, 'zero-hour' contracts have increased; those with a contract for both teaching and research have decreased, and two institutions have used public funds on legal processes to resist better conditions for those on basic wage levels. They lost (NCAFC 2017; Nicoll 2017; Chakrabortty 2017). Ironically, these were LSE, where staff were conducting research for the Low Pay Commission (Lordan 2017), and SOAS, where Lady Amos, its head, is cited below on staff inequalities.

Senior staff, not subject to national agreements, have had substantial increases approved by remuneration committees, of which vice-chancellors are usually members or are in attendance. The average VC salary, plus bonuses and benefits, in 2016–7 was over £268,000, up 3.9% year-on-year, when sector income rose only 2.9% and greater expenditure meant reserves fell (HEFCE 2018), and when rank and file staff got a 1.1% increase. One VC received over £800,000 in her final year and others received supplements when leaving their post, with four getting nearly £1 million in total.

Vice-chancellors pocket almost £1 million in exit payments *THE*, 22 February 2018

Revealed: the huge pay rises feathering vice-chancellors' cosy retirement nests, *The Guardian*, 26 April, 2018

Huge gulf in earnings across UK universities, study finds, *The Telegraph*, 18 July, 2017

Chakrabortty (2017), is scathing in a review of links between vice-chancellors and governors, and governors' backgrounds – Manchester has two from the VC's former employer, Astra Zeneca, where two other university senior managers also worked previously. At Bath, many are from finance: there are more governors representing that sector than representing students, and two members of the (small) remuneration committee are from PwC, unlikely to find excessive a salary and benefits total of over £500,000. Elsewhere, he points to Bolton where the VC was given a loan of nearly £1 million to buy a house, at a time when student recruitment was falling badly. Many universities provide 'grace and favour' houses. He compares that with academics exploited on casual contracts, and redundancies being announced. His conclusion?

> Ten years ago, British finance was held up to the world as a joke – full of flyboys paying themselves truckloads of money and running some fine old institutions into the ground…
> Yet the people running our universities are now importing that failed model.

The sums are small, in comparison with some in the private sector, where the boss of WPP took a salary cut to 'only' £42 million in 2016–7 (Sweeney 2018), and three Persimmon bosses collected over £100 million despite doing little to help the shortage of houses affordable for much of the population (Neate 2018). In both cases, non-executive directors are failing in their role and responsibilities. The issue is not just salaries, but ethics, as exemplified by one front page headline.

Millions spied on by greedy top universities, *Daily Mail*, 20 November, 2017

Wealth screening firms were used to trawl for information on their alumni, to target them for fundraising. Compare the use of Facebook data by Cambridge Analytics. Such behaviour brings consequences:

Embattled universities face limits on powers, *The Times*, 26 February, 2018

Another front page headline, as the new regulator, the Office for Students [sic], tested its new muscles. The pay gap is not only vertical. Nationally, across all employment, there is a gender gap of 9.7%; in HE, it is 15.6%, though at least one university, Essex, is doing something about it.

The gender pay gap is clear to see. Now we need decisive action to address it, *THE*, 3 May, 2018

That action included a one-off uplift in salaries for female professors. But the issue is structural: there are fewer women in senior posts, and many more women than men in low paid jobs. Richardson (2018) reports that universities in the main have been 'woefully slow to change' and points to paucity of childcare provision with 2-year waiting lists. He cites views of Jocelyn Bell Burnell, who discovered radio pulsars, who believes that the gender imbalance in a major learned society – women in the International Astronomical Union are only 17% of members – is in part because senior members, dominantly male, of course, nominate new members, perpetuating history into the future. University governing bodies do the same; it will require disruptive effort to change that.

#U's too: universities also reflect the consequent climate of sexual harassment in wider society, particularly by the privileged elite over the less powerful: staff and students. The problem was exposed before the Harvey Weinstein affair gave it prominence; it endures, and is denied and covered up:

Sexual harassment of students by university staff hidden by non-disclosure agreements, *The Guardian*, 26 August, 2016
London university professor quits over 'sexual harassment of female students by staff', *The Independent*, 9 June, 2016

Scale of sexual abuse in UK universities likened to Savile and Catholic scandals, *The Guardian*, 7 October 2016

UK universities accused of complacency over sexual misconduct, *The Guardian*, 8 December, 2017

That complacency about 'inequality' also applies to race, to students and staff (Bhopal 2016).

University racism 'complacency' warning, BBC News, 16 May, 2018

The BBC reported a speech by Baroness Amos, one of the very few BAME heads of an institution (but see above) and listing some of the 'gaps':

- Of more than 18,000 professors, only just over 100 are black
- Only 3.2% of senior staff are from ethnic minorities
- The race pay gap within that same group is 16%
- There is a 15 percentage point gap between ethnic minority and white students getting 'good' degrees

The discrimination starts early, is systemic and, in some institutions, embedded:

Black people in UK 21 times more likely to have university applications investigated, figures show, *The Independent*, 23 April, 2018

This can be compared to the imbalances among those chosen by police to stop and search, where the figure is 'only' four times more. Of British applicants through UCAS for 2017 entry, 419 out of 42,580 black applicants (1 in 102) were 'highlighted as a cause for concern'; the ratio for white British applicants was 1 in 2146.

Oxford and Cambridge universities accused of 'social apartheid' over failure to offer places to black students, *The Independent*, 20 October, 2017

The Independent recorded the campaign by David Lammy, MP, who identified that between 2010 and 2015 only three Oxford colleges, out of 32, made an offer to a black British A level student. Elite universities have blamed schools for not encouraging students to apply, and students for not getting the necessary grades, or applying for the 'wrong' courses where competition is strong. Yet work by Tariq Modood (2010), by Vicki Boliver (2015, 2017) and the hard facts of UCAS statistics show that, even when allowance is made for all other factors, BAME applicants require higher grades than white applicants to gain entry to Russell Group universities. The issue is not new, but Lammy's campaign is welcome. Cambridge claims the situation is changing. It needs to, but

Oxbridge universities fail to enrol ethnic minority students, *The Guardian*, 12 March 2009

The Guardian recorded five UK students of black Caribbean origin starting at Oxford in 2008, with eight at Cambridge. Ten years later the figures are comparable. Nothing has changed. As I finalise this contribution, Oxford produced its own figures, confirming the bias, with white British students twice as likely – 24% – to get in as Black British students – 12%. In 3 years to 2017 not a single black British student was admitted to theology, biomedical sciences, earth sciences, computer science, psychology, and a quarter of colleges admitted none. The head of admissions and outreach claimed, 'our admissions process here does work' and extended the blame for the university's record to over-ambitious parents. It led to another front page headline:

Oxford faces anger over failure to improve diversity among students, The Guardian, 23 May, 2018

As noted above, black students get lower degree awards, even when controlling for entry qualifications, their satisfaction in the annual survey is lower than for white students, and their graduate prospects are poorer because of the racism in employment practices. There has also been a surge in racism among students on campus, part of a wider bullying culture, also related to suppression of free speech for both staff and students.

Culture of cruelty: why bullying thrives in higher education, *The Guardian*, 3 November, 2014

All of this reflects the 'hostile environment' towards immigrants introduced by Theresa May as Home Secretary – and adopted by the public – 'society' (Malik 2018), the rise of UKIP and the xenophobia encouraged by the Leave campaign over the EU referendum. One would expect universities to be more serious about their deficiencies and pursue solutions with some urgency. That does not appear to be happening. Indeed, they are now agents of the state in pursuit of potential terrorists and illegal immigrants, checking on their students and staff: I have to give evidence of my British citizenship whenever invited to be an external examiner, or to give a guest lecture. Universities are, then, falling short of espoused values that should make them different from the enacted values of many from the society in which they are set.

They also now operate in a market, which has its own values, and regulators of operations. The 2018 annual report of the Office of the Independent Arbitrator for HE records the continuing failure of internal processes to treat students fairly as clients, or even people with legitimate complaints, with compensatory costs approaching £1 million. Students are also demanding refunds:

Students in legal bid against unis over lost strike days, *Morning Star*, 30 April, 2018, p. 3

External watchdogs include the Competition and Market Authority and the Advertising Standards Authority:

Students facing 'unlawful' small print at almost 30 universities, *Times Higher Education*, 5 February, 2015
Universities warned over breaching consumer law, *Times Higher Education*, 12 March, 2015

Universities to be warned over misleading adverts, BBC News, 10 November, 2017

Six universities break advertising rules with pitches to students, *The Guardian*, 15 November, 2017

Not, then, 'a commitment to the pursuit of truth, [and]… to consider the ethical implications…of practices'. More a mirroring of the 'mis-selling' of payment protection insurance (PPI).

Universities also fall below acceptable standards as landlords. UCL, not a lone example, is experiencing its third rent strike in 3 years by those in student residences.

UCL students begin rent strike over conditions, *Morning Star*, 9 May, 2018

The average cost of purpose built student accommodation went up by 23% in the 5 years after the last increase in fees in England, and in 2016 averaged £147 a week, which works out at more than the student living costs loan for some students, with some using food banks. It is a profitable enterprise for the private sector, as well as universities, with the value of contracts awarded to build student housing in February, 2017, totalling more than the deals to build care homes, sheltered housing, housing association accommodation, and local authority housing put together (Cannes 2017).

Leadership

Those headlines reflect operating values. Leaders set those values within universities and that is my third topic. Leadership at government and corporate level has been a recurrent theme in news and opinion pieces in the quality UK press over recent years. Macron in France set a new model, as did Trump in the USA, one provoking more shock and horror than the other. Angela Merkel's welcome to Trump after his election was conditioned by her emphasis on the need for 'common values' that bind countries (and universities?) together: democracy, freedom, as well as respect for the rule of law (bureaucracy has some purpose) and the dignity of *all* people. Theresa May claimed to be a 'strong and stable' leader, when evidence from other countries suggest that strong leaders often head, even create, unstable situations – Erdogan in Turkey, Orban in Hungary, among others – or retain a surface stability through strong controls. Many are hostile to universities in varying degrees: their independence of thought and academic autonomy, and would not welcome them as critics and conscience prickers. Erdogan arrested thousands of academics, and effectively closed Istanbul University and reshaped a dozen others because they were not in line with 'Turkish values' (*Morning Star*, 5 May 2018, p. 7); Orban changed the rules for recognition of international universities, which has forced the Central European University out of the country (Ignatieff 2018); Trump threatened to cut UC Berkeley's funding (beyond his power to do); May's ministers derided academic 'experts', included international students as 'immigrants' subject to a 'hostile environment' and tried to influence curriculum on European topics to follow the 'right' line.

I have worked in several Eastern European countries over the past 20 years and encountered a yearning for a return to previous strong leaders. When I asked a class of young students in Ukraine to give examples of role models of a good leader, their suggestions were Stalin, Hitler and Thatcher, which led to a debate differentiating 'strong' from 'good'. Civic compliance through fear, as with Putin in Russia and Xi in China again risks becoming normative, even at the level of sport, in this case Rugby Union:

Farrell can captain England with rule of fear, says Jones, *The Guardian*, 28 May 2018, p. 44

Jones, the head coach, was looking for strong leadership to repair the north-south divide in the England squad. It has not worked for May, and fear is not good for team spirit, nor for performance in teaching and research (Franco-Santos et al. 2014; Kallio and Kallio 2014). I do not expect a six nations triumph in the coming year. Gareth Southgate may be a better model (Saner 2018). The 2018 leadership summit for higher education, organised by Advance HE heard several vice-chancellors reject charismatic and 'heroic' leadership (Grove 2018).

In a poll of 13 former Soviet countries, cited in Brown (2014: 3), when asked 'would it be worthwhile to support a leader who could solve the problems facing [your country] today, even if he [sic] overthrew democracy?' a majority of Ukrainians preferred autocratic dictatorship. I have worked there on leadership development for the past 5 years, and can attest that such attitudes still exist, demanding sensitive approaches to getting participants to examine values and their consequences. When I joined the University of Greenwich, I met all of my staff individually to seek their views on planning the future of the School: their ideas and suggestions for innovations and change. From several I got the view that they had no view: that was my job. 'You are the boss', said one, 'tell me what to do and I will do it'. A sad comment on academic professionalism. The culture changed somewhat when innovators got personal promotion: a central panel judged them to be excellent and exceptional teachers. 'Exceptional' had a sad irony in this context.

So, a first message for university leaders is to re-inforce the importance of values. Brown's study, on the myth of the strong leader, chosen by Bill Gates as his book of the year, and endorsed by Barack Obama (now there's a pair of endorsements!) says:

> There are many qualities desirable in a… leader that should matter more than strength, one better suited to judging weightlifters or long-distance runners. They include integrity, intelligence, articulateness, collegiality, shrewd judgement, a questioning mind, willingness to seek disparate views, ability to absorb information, flexibility, good memory, courage, vision, empathy and boundless energy. (Brown 2014: 1–2)

So, this paragon of an HE leader should reflect the Dearing values of the sector given earlier.

A second message is embraced by Brown in that list, when he emphasises the importance of collective leadership and of checks and balances. There needs to be scepticism about policy pronouncements as there would be about claimed academic discoveries such as cold fusion. That does need people prepared to speak truth to power, and that, too, has diminished as people fear the consequences: whistle blowers and dissenters seem to feature disproportionately among those made redundant. But, such freedom is vital to universities; vital to creativity, which emerges enriched from the crucible of collegial academic disputation and collective, collaborative work. This is a contrast to the autocrat strong man or woman. Sir John Chilcot, chair of the inquiry into the Iraq war, speaking to the Liaison Committee of the House of Commons, said that the 'personal and political dominance' by Tony Blair of his party and government led to 'sofa governance', with what one of my interviewees called 'sycophantic parasites' in a university context, who failed to test the flawed evidence offered or to query Blair's unreflective conviction of his own self-righteous rectitude (Harding 2016).

The frequent justification for autocratic corporatism is crisis. Higher education seems to have been in such a state continuously, but the crisis discourse is often an excuse for control, when my work leads me to believe that it is the self-confessed lack of competence among leaders (PACG 2011) that leads to control models because of the lack of confidence to allow dissent, dialogue and disputation in policy fora as in academic networks, with time pressures added to the resistance argument. An open forum for expression helps, in that many dissenters accept democracy if outvoted, having had the chance to expound their views. Xu Liu (forthcoming) identified another model in her doctoral study of governance in private universities in China. One was a family run business: father and son plus three other relatives made up the board of governors; they were also the total membership of the University Communist Party Committee (UCPC), and five-sixths of the executive committee – they had had to appoint an outsider as president because none were qualified for the post under Chinese regulations. This arrangement was justified on grounds of efficiency – it reduced time spent on debate and ensured consistency in decisions.

There is a similar argument for suppressing collegiality in Marginson and Considine's book on the enterprise university in Australia (Marginson and Considine 2000):

> The Enterprise University is less cumbersome than previous forms, less open to veto and inertia within, and generally more capable of articulating a single defining strategy for its own 're-invention' during times of extreme turbulence in its environment. The logic of corporate decision-making is more freely embraced than before and collegial values are more frequently subordinated to central purposes… In response to outside imperatives, management has sought to re-focus [a euphemism] the representative role of [academic] councils and to define, and sometimes confine, their roles to that of supporters of a single corporate mission… Academic Board has had its role narrowed to procedural and curriculum matters which have little proactive impact. (p. 96)

I agree with Rowlands (2017) who, having examined the role of Senates in England, Australia and the USA, concludes that Australian universities have become corporatised and marketised, not entrepreneurial. That is true of modern universities in the UK where government legislation made academic boards simply advisory to the chief executive officer – the VC or Principal – and a majority of members must hold management roles, on an *academic* board. My model of university cultures makes a distinction between a corporate enterprise and a collegial enterprise (McNay 1995, 2002, 2005), the latter building on the best of what academics do, more than what top managers decide. Even fundamental academic activities are caught in the net, with a quality criterion for research in the UK Research Excellence Framework (REF) now being the 'fit' of research topics with corporate strategy.

The resistance to democracy reached farcical levels after the Brexit vote, when Theresa May had to be taken to court to get her to recognise that Parliament had a right to a decision-making role in the biggest constitutional change in the country in most people's memory, and used tax-payers' money in an attempt to stop taxpayers' representatives having a voice.

That links to a further lesson: listen to those you lead, or they will leave you. That was seen in the Brexit vote, and in universities in the fate of the vice-chancellor of the Open University, who insulted his academic staff after ignoring warnings about the consequences of his strategy for re-structuring, and then after a vote of no confidence by staff also lost the confidence of the university governors.

The risk of centralisation is summarised by W.B. Yeats in *The Second Coming*: 'things fall apart; the centre cannot hold; mere anarchy is loosed upon the world'. There needs to be collective leadership within a collegial culture, with the principle of subsidiarity operating: decisions are taken closest to the level at which they will be made operational. Most of today's universities are too big to be run from the centre as monoliths, especially when discipline cultures make them intrinsically diverse. Such devolution and bottom-up development would enhance enterprise because of proximity to clients, enhancing the relevance of decisions taken to the diverse markets being served. Relations across the border of the university, and partnerships to enhance co-operative networks, recognised by Rowlands (2017) as a rising feature of contemporary HE, would be enhanced if the centre could learn to let go and let others share in the destiny of their community.

That brings me to a final value for leaders of universities, linked to managing borders, another Brexit theme. Defend your borders against governmental bureaucratic, micro-management incursions into legitimate autonomy, but otherwise open them up. Theresa May claimed that citizens of the world were citizens of nowhere and is condemning many UK citizens to be citizens of nowhere through government border management. Universities have to fight that perverse value set in the shrinking, globalised world that is evolving. One role they have is to help students develop a strong mature sense of personal identity. That means care in challenging them to change: I have an abiding memory of working in Hackney, where students had a strong community identity and wanted to keep it: 'I don't want to be different; I want to be better'. However, they also had a world view, different from many whose forebears were immigrants longer ago, a view conditioned by living among a diverse cultural mix of people, different from many emerging from elite universities. Universities and their leaders need to develop an empathy for these 'others'. Access is not just about letting them in to a different world of higher education but, as one of my students defined enterprise: 'being open to the world and going out to greet it', valuing the experience and knowledge that they bring, not expecting one-sided assimilation of student 'immigrants' to 'our' way of being and thinking, but a reciprocal adaptation, a developmental mission, not a 'we know better' transformational one. Harder, when some institutional leaders have that as a style in dealing with strategic change. That outreach and adaptation needs exemplifying in action. One simple proposal I have failed to get accepted in my work base: establish a resource of books and course material in public libraries in the London boroughs from which we draw many of our students so that student journey time and cost can be kept low when they have no classes but wish to do course work outside a crowded, noisy home.

Government leaders give the impression of contempt for those on life paths outside Westminster, Kensington, Islington: note the glacial speed of operational response to the Grenfell disaster and the Windrush scandal, in contrast to espoused intent. The less advantaged are blamed for their plight in an Ayn Rand world. Universities should be a voice to criticise this, a means of stirring the consciences of those in power, and across the nation. But, I regret, in England (and I am deliberately specific) they have lost moral authority and therefore credibility and acceptability in performing such a role.

References

Adelman, H. (1973). *The holiversity*. Toronto: New Press.

Bhopal, K. (2016). *The experiences of Black and minority ethnic academics: A comparative study of the unequal academy*. London: Routledge.

Boliver, V. (2015). Exploring ethnic inequalities in admission to Russell Group universities. *Sociology, 50*(2), 247–266.

Boliver, V. (2017). Misplaced optimism: How higher education reproduces rather than reduces social inequality. *British Journal of Sociology, 30*(3), 423–492.

Brown, A. (2014). *The myth of the strong leader*. London: Vintage Books.

Cannes, R. N. (2017, March 17). Student digs give first class returns for investors. *The Guardian*, p. 33.

Chakrabortty, A. (2017, November 28). The fat cats have got their claws into our universities, and will eat them up. *The Guardian*.

CIPD. (2017, June 13). *CIPD research leads the way on purposeful leadership*. Chartered Institute of Personnel and Development. www.cipd.co.uk/news-views/news-articles/purposeful-leadership

Committee of University Chairs. (2014). *The higher education code of governance*. www.universitychairs.ac.uk. Accessed 5 Apr 2018.

Committee on Standards in Public Life. (2015). *Ethical standards for providers of public services – Guidance*. www.gov.uk/government/publications/ethical-standards-for-providers-of-public-services

Dearing, R. (1997) (chair) *Higher education in the learning society*. Report of the National Committee of Inquiry. Norwich: HMSO.

Franco-Santos, M., Rivera, P., & Bourne, M. (2014). *Performance management in UK higher education institutions*. London: Leadership Foundation for Higher Education.

Garcia, E. J. (2009). Raising leadership criticality in MBAs. *Higher Education, 58*, 113–130. https://doi.org/10.1007/s10734-008-9185-6.

Garcia, E. J. (2010). MBA lecturers' curriculum interests in leadership. *Management Learning, 41*(1), 21–36.

Gledhill, K. (online). *Critic and conscience – A legal right.* www.criticandconscience.org.nz/the-law.html. Accessed 14 Apr 2018.

Grove, J. (2018, July 5). Heroic leadership 'will fail' in higher education. *Times Higher Education*, p. 11.

Harding, L. (2016, November 3). Strength of Blair's will drove UK towards Iraq war, Chilcot tells MPs. *The Guardian*, p. 2.

Harris, J. (2018, May 12). Revolution in the air. *The Guardian Review*, pp. 32–34.

HEFCE. (2018, March 20). *Financial health of the higher education sector: 2016–17 financial results.* Press release.

Hutton, W. (1995). *The state we're in.* London: Jonathan Cape.

Ignatieff, M. (2018, April 11). *Academic freedom and the future of Europe.* Keynote lecture, annual conference of the Centre for Global HE, London.

Kallio, K.-M., & Kallio, T. J. (2014). Management-by-results and performance management in universities – Implications for work motivation. *Studies in Higher Education, 39*(4), 417–424.

Kant, I. (1998). *Critique of pure reason* (P. Guyer & A. W. Wood, Trans.). Cambridge: Cambridge University Press.

Leavis, F. R. (1943). *Education and the university.* London: Chatto and Windus.

LFHE. (2016). *Higher education leadership and management survey (HELMS): The results in brief.* London: Leadership Foundation for Higher Education.

Liu, X. (forthcoming). *Institutional governance in the development of Chinese private universities: The role of the Communist Party.*

Lordan, G. (2017). *Minimum wage and the propensity to automate or off-shore, LSE for the Low Pay Commission.*

Malik, N. (2018, May 14). Our hostile environment only exists with public consent. *The Guardian.*

Mansell, W., & Huddy, V. (2018, May 21). There's a crisis in psychology – Here's how technology could provide a solution. *The Conversation.*

Marginson, S., & Considine, M. (2000). *The enterprise university: Power, governance and reinvention in Australia.* Cambridge: Cambridge University Press.

McNay, I. (1995). From the collegial academy to corporate enterprise: The changing cultures of universities. In T. Schuller (Ed.), *The changing university.* Buckingham: SRHE/Open University Press.

McNay, I. (2002). The E factors and organisational culture. In G. Williams (Ed.), *The enterprising university: Reform, excellence and equity.* Buckingham: SRHE/Open University Press.

McNay, I. (2005). Managing institutions in a mass HE system. In I. McNay (Ed.), *Beyond mass higher education: Building on experience.* Maidenhead: SRHE/Open University Press.

McNay, I. (2018, July 5). *Current challenges for universities: some competing/conflicting pressures.* Plenary address, World Education Fellowship.

Meiklejohn, A. (1932). *The experimental college.* New York: Harper and Brothers.

Modood, T. (2010). *Still not easy being British.* Stoke-on-Trent: Trentham Books.

NCAFC. (2017). *Victories for workers at SOAS and LSE.* National campaign against fees and cuts. http://anticuts.com/2017/09/14/

Neate, R. (2018, April 25). Investor outrage fails to halt Persimmon's £75m payday. *The Guardian*, p. 35.

Neuberger, J. (2005). *The moral state we're in. A manifesto for a 21ˢᵗ century society.* London: Harper Collins.

Newman, J. H. (1873). *The idea of a university.* Oxford: Clarendon Press.

Nicoll, S. (2017, August 9). Low paid workers provide a lesson for the whole labour movement. *Socialist Worker.* https://socialistworker.co.uk/art/45127/

PACG. (2010). *A passing storm or permanent climate change? Vice-chancellors' views on the outlook for universities*. London: PA Consulting Group.

PACG. (2011). *Escaping the red queen effect: Succeeding in the new economics of higher education*. London: PA Consulting Group.

Parker, M. (2018, April 27). Bulldoze the business school! *The Guardian Journal*, pp. 9–11.

Pells, R. (2018, March 29). Is the reproducibility crisis an overblown distraction? *Times Higher Education*, p. 6.

Ramiro, J. (2016, June 7). Arms traders fund 'ethical' university. *Morning Star*, p. 3.

Richardson, S. (2018, April 18). You, too?. *Research Professional*.

Robbins, L. (1963). *Higher education: Report of the Committee appointed by the Prime Minister under the Chairmanship of Lord Robbins 1961–63*, Cmnd 2154, HMSO.

Rowlands, J. (2017). *Academic governance in the contemporary university*. Singapore: Springer.

Russell, M. (2015, February 10). *What does it mean to accept a role as 'critic and conscience of society'?* Paper presented to Universities and the Knowledge Economy conference, Auckland.

Saner, E. (2018). Get your head in the game. *The Guardian, G2*, 8.

Scott, P. (1995). *The meaning of mass higher education*. Buckingham: SRHE/Open University Press.

Sweeney, M. (2018, April 5). WPP hires top law firms for Sorrell misconduct enquiry. *The Guardian*, p. 5.

Trow, M. (1989). The Robbins trap: British attitudes and the limits of expansion. *Higher Education Quarterly, 43*(1), 55–75.

Chapter 8
University, Integrity and Responsibility

Simon Robinson

Abstract In this chapter I will explore the idea of the integrity of Higher Education. This is not integrity in the narrow sense of academic integrity, that is, honesty and responsibility in scholarship and research; though this, of course, is connected. I will focus on a wider sense of integrity, which includes governance and institutional identity.

In the first part, I will examine recent debates about the meaning of integrity, personal and organisational. I will suggest that integrity is tied to identity and this in turn in focused in the threefold, and interconnected, meaning of responsibility, involving: critical agency which acknowledges and engages a plural identity (focused in narrative); accountability which engages the narratives of others (focused in dialogue which enable mutual support and challenge); and positive responsibility (focusing on creative practice and shared responsibility rather than negative blaming).

The second part of the chapter considers how such a view of integrity applies to the university and its governance. This notes the importance of clarity about purpose and worth, and the importance of engaging dialogue inside and outside the institution to enable the development of identity. The key signs of good governance then become: narrative, dialogue and the ongoing negotiation of responsibility in practice; the practice of associated virtues, intellectual, moral and psychological; and integrated thinking and communication.

Keywords Integrity · Responsibility · Moral purpose · Dialogue · University

S. Robinson (✉)
Leeds Beckett University, Leeds, UK
e-mail: S.J.Robinson@leedsbeckett.ac.uk

© Springer Nature Switzerland AG 2019

P. Gibbs et al. (eds.), *Values of the University in a Time of Uncertainty*,
https://doi.org/10.1007/978-3-030-15970-2_8

Introduction: Integrity – Philosophical Perspectives

Four different major philosophical approaches to integrity have attempted to offer some clarity (cf. Palanski and Yammarino 2007): self-integration; identity; moral purpose and commitment.

Self-integration: This account (Frankfurt 1971) focuses on the integration of higher and lower order volitions. The first involve long-term desires, the second immediate desires. The higher order volition of the drug addict, for instance, may be to be a drug-free person and the lower order volition to take drugs. Integrity, and with that free will, argues Frankfurt, is achieved when both sets of volitions cohere, bringing together volition and action.

Identity: Williams (1973) argues that integrity is based in the identity of the person. Arguing against a simple utilitarian approach he suggests that simple calculation of consequences is not sufficient. Moral decisions tell us something about the core moral beliefs that make up the identity of the person.

Moral purpose: Rawls (1972) and Halfon (1989) argue that integrity must include an acceptable moral purpose at the base. For Rawls this would involve a conception of justice, defined in terms of fairness. Halfon argues that the person of integrity will give a clear account of moral purpose as part of following a rigorous moral decision-making process.

Commitment: Calhoun (1995) argues for a sense of commitment which is about 'standing for something'. She argues that this involves more than simply standing for an individual moral purpose, but rather one recognised by some community. Integrity here is associated explicitly with something worth striving for, and it assumes a degree of agency, courage and perseverance that will enable the person or group to stand up against internal and societal pressures that impose obstacles to the purpose. Mason (2001) argues for the importance of respect for human dignity as a core community principle. In all this integrity becomes more a social value than an individual one.

All of these views have problems; recognised by Halfon (1989). All, for instance, presume some moral good that will act as the basis for integrity. However, the moral good and any identity based upon it may be flawed. It is possible, for instance, to see the SS guard basing a view of integrity on a set of principles and an underlying world view which excludes different races. This demands a view of moral principles which is both critical and beyond one's narrow community. In terms of identity this then looks to group and self-identity which is plural and therefore always being tested. Calhoun partly recognises this with her stress on agency, courage and so on. However, even she rests on what 'the community' recognises as of value.

Some have tried to bring these together in integrity as a mega-virtue (Solomon 2007), one which connects different virtues or values (Wolf 2009). Others express this as in several categories (ICAEW 2009), involving:

Integration: of the different parts of the person: affective, cognitive, social and so on (Solomon 1992, 2007). Such holistic thinking involves an awareness and appreciation of the self, alongside awareness and appreciation of external relations.

Consistency: between the self, values and practice; past present and future; and different relationships, situations and contexts. The response may not be exactly the same in every context but will remain consistent to the identity and purpose of the person or the organisation. Central to this is the idea of being true to purpose and identity.

Honesty and transparency: involving an openness to the self and others.

Independence. Key to this is disinterestedness, such that the person or organisation can stand apart from competing interests, and more effectively focus on the core purpose.

Commitment: to purpose, project and people over time, and to the common good. The narrow view of integrity within a closed system has to be tested against fundamental principles such as justice. Such principles have in turn to be tested.

The sense of a mega-virtue grows, involving an epistemic element (Scherkoske 2013), and a learning idea; integrity does not reflect perfection. All this takes place in the context of the authentic re-presentation of the self or organisation, something akin to Aristotle's virtue of truthfulness (Curzer 2014). The self here is seen as one's history, current character, and future projects expressed in one's commitments (to ideals, values, goals and projects), especially about those that are important to one's reputation. The stress is on being true to the self, one's identity. However, even such an apparently simple notion of integrity involves greater complexity. Curzer (2014) notes that identity, individual and institutional, is not discrete or univocal but made of many different, often conflicting relationships and related value narratives. He argues that integrity does not demand compatibility between all these narratives, or an attempt to integrate all of the meanings. It does demand engaging the different narratives, conceptually and relationally. Psychological theory also suggests that there is no simple sense of the self, but rather that there are very different narratives which constitute the self (Burkitt 2008; Cooper-White 2007; Beebe and Rosen 2005; Haste and Abrahams 2008). In this light integrity is not about wholeness as homogeneity, with everything fitting together, but about an honest and open engagement with the different narratives. The different narratives are related to different formative relationships, which have a strong affective content and often create dissonance which challenge the sense of self. In this light, integrity involves hard work and even suffering (Cottingham 2010; Pianalto 2012; Noelliste 2003; Callender 2010); recognizing contradictions and inconsistencies in the self as well as in others (Cooper-White 2007). The self is then constituted through deliberation and dialogue (Burkitt 2008; Cottingham 2010; Greenblatt 2012; Taylor 1989). Integrity then begins to focus on taking responsibility both for the ideas and values and for plural relationships.

Responsibility

The term responsibility suggests three interconnected modes, the first two of which are found in Aristotle (Schweiker 2010; Robinson 2009):

Imputability, critical agency which determines meaning and action (in contrast to thinking and behaviour determined by others).
Accountability, the capacity to give an account of meaning and practice to the self and others.
Positive or responsive responsibility, taking responsibility for creative response to the social and physical environment.

The first mode involves taking responsibility for core values (and related affect), purpose (and related pre-moral good such as health or justice), related sense of worth (individual and organisational), and practice, and its effect on the social and cultural environment. This is core to personal or organisational identity (Taylor 1989), and thus to autonomous agency. The second mode demands taking responsibility for giving an account of this identity to the self/organisation and others. Such accountability is often viewed as one way, focused in hierarchy. This precisely ignores the complex social context of responsibility and accountability which is both plural and mutual (Robinson 2013a, b). The asymmetricality of organisational relationships does not preclude mutuality. On the contrary such mutuality enables a sense of responsibility both for a particular role or function and for the whole organisational operation. The Mid Staffs case (Francis 2013) demonstrates how a narrow and unidirectional view of accountability led to the many different regulators and professionals losing any sense of responsibility for the whole healthcare project. Accountability involves plural identity.

The third mode focuses on shared responsibility for maintaining both the representation of core values and purpose, and the engagement of different actors to embody these values. This involves the exercise of the moral imagination (Lederach 2005; Werhane 1999; Nussbaum 1990; Bauman 1989); deliberation focused in the creation of possibilities. This creative response is as much about relationships as values or ideas.

The practice of developing narrative is critical to the development of identity, and thus integrity, at individual and organisational level: involving taking responsibility for authorship. In narrative identity, the person is not merely the one who tells the story, or merely the one about whom the story is told, but she/he 'appears both as a reader and the writer of its own life' (Riceour 2000, 246). This is close both to the idea of meta-cognition, the ability to reflect on how we think, and mindfulness, awareness of oneself in relation to others. van der Ven (1998; see also Freeman 2015) suggests that narrative enables 'distanciation', and thus perspective, from which to see the self in relationship, in effect to perceive the self as other (Riceour 2000).

Key to the second mode of responsibility is the practice of dialogue. Critical dialogue (Bakhtin 1984; Sidorkin 1999) enables an appreciation of difference and also challenge about core purpose and practice. As Bakhtin (1984) notes such dialogue differs from dialectic because it involves ontology; communicating something about the person as well as any discussion of propositions or practices. Dialogue also enables negotiation about shared responsibility and the development of the moral imagination (Lederach 2005).

Hence, the re-presentation of the self or organisation involves taking responsibility for developing identity over time and in relationship. This requires taking responsibility for meaning value and purpose, for giving an account of that, and working through shared responsibility in the light of that.

It is important to reinforce the point that this applies both to individuals and to organisations. First, personal identity is plural (Burkitt 2008; Covaleskie 2011; Raggatt 2012; Schlegel et al. 2009), informed by professional, organisational and wider community narratives as much as by family and friends. Hence, the personal, professional and political connect. Second, the organisation, institution or corporation may itself be said to be plural. Good examples of this are professional institutions. These engage the different narratives, of clients, members, corporations or other organisations which members work in, other professions who may share a wider purpose, future generations (through the different creations, from bridges to healthcare facilities). It also relates to wider society both through the pre-moral or moral goods, which form their key purpose and thus identity (Airaksinen 1994), such as health and well-being for the medical profession or justice for the legal professions. The identity of the profession is thus a function both of moral underpinning and of ongoing dialogue in the different relationships (Fawkes 2014).

Brown (2005; cf. Paine 1994) develops this theme for corporations, noting five dimensions of corporate integrity – cultural, interpersonal, organisational, social and natural. The first focuses on difference and disagreement in meaning, the second integration and wholeness, the third core purpose, the fourth on civic cooperation, and the final on the environment. Integrity in this light demands both commitment to core relationships but also awareness and appreciation of the plurality of relationships that form the social and physical environment. Organisational integrity in the light of this once more requires both attention to internal dialogue but also attention to shared narrative such as justice, or about the nature or purpose of the organisation (Nohria and Khurana 2008). Dialogue in this becomes key to an understanding of and taking responsibility for values and purpose in the organisation, and evidence suggests that it is infrequently practised in corporate of public governance (Macnamara 2015). A good example is remuneration. Corporate governance practises have focused on the narrow remuneration of leaders without any attention to an account of justice, involving the criteria of distribution and underlying compensation philosophy (Kolb 2006; Harris 2006). Such an account would require dialogue enabling all members of the organisation to understand and support (identify with) processes, and thus enable procedural integrity. Corporate governance remuneration sub-committees have precisely offered procedures without any substantive connection to values, worth or purpose.

This positive responsibility contrasts sharply with negative responsibility which is focused in denial of responsibility (Ricoeur 2000), defensive attitudes and cultures of fear. This leads to polarizing thinking, focused on defending narrow or exclusive narratives and associated views of integrity (Haidt 2013) which Polowczyk (2017) refers to as counterfeit integrity. In turn this leads to the dangers of: teleopathy (Goodpaster 2007); blindness to core purpose and consequences (Heffernan 2012); devaluing other narratives; dehumanizing other narrators in response to perceived threats; and precipitate action based in a convinced sense of rightness (Entine 2002; Pattison and Edgar 2011). Such blindness involves, in Jungian terms (cf. Fawkes 2014; Cottingham 2010), the shadow side. This is not a 'dark' or 'evil' side but rather the part of behaviour or thinking that has not been examined. Effective dialogue enables a continual testing of the 'shadow' side of the self or organisation and further presentation and development of the self/organisation identity.

Finally, such a view of integrity demands more than simply the development of systems of internal and external regulation to guard against corrupt practices. The danger of such regulation is that it focuses on avoiding corruption rather than practising integrity and associated virtues, in effect, as Moore (2012) suggests, 'crowding out' the virtues, intellectual, psychological and moral; 'dreaming of systems so perfect that no one will need to be good' Eliot (1934, 29).

I will now begin to explore how this view of integrity might apply to the university through a number of examples.

The University

A key aspect of integrity and the university is the first mode of responsibility and reflection on purpose, worth, values and social and economic context, and this immediately establishes the university as a complex institution. Dearing (1997) attempted to sum up the underlying very different senses of worth in terms of four purposes:

To inspire and enable individuals to develop their capabilities to the highest potential levels throughout life, so that they grow intellectually, are well equipped for work, can contribute effectively to society and achieve personal fulfilment.

To increase knowledge and understanding for their own sake and to foster their application to the benefit of the economy and society'.

To serve the needs of an adaptable, sustainable, knowledge-based economy at local, regional and national levels.

To play a major role in shaping a democratic, civilised, inclusive society.

This is brings together purposes which are: instrumental, such as contributing to the economy not least through developing students who are employable; of intrinsic worth, e.g. the focus on developing knowledge and understanding for its own sake; focus about contribution to wider significant meaning in society which is moral or pre-moral. Three questions are demanded of this list of purposes. First, do they reflect genuine worth and can we justify that judgement of worth (cf. Boltanksi and Thévenot 2006)? Second, if they are of worth (and I will assume they are), what connects them? Third, what do these purposes tell us about the identity of the university and how the university relates to the different narratives involved in Higher Education.

One of the most coherent answers to the second question come from Barnett's idea of higher learning (1994). This is based in the view that critical reflection is central, though not exclusive, to personal growth. Barnett (1994) argues that Higher Education is in essence emancipatory and holistic. In effect, it liberates the student from the narrow focus of the disciplines, enabling reflective thinking which can critique the assumptions of the discipline and look beyond to relations with other areas. Products of this process are 'self understanding and self empowerment', enabling students to 'come into themselves' (ibid.). This process of emancipation is something that is implicit in the idea of autonomous thinking, enabling the student to develop analytical and critical skills, and the capacity to think holistically and synoptically, i.e. across disciplines. This is higher order thinking, involving the development of 'analysis, evaluation, criticism and even imagination' (ibid. 85). This level of thinking transcends any narrow view of work centred skills, developing an awareness of the wider context and the capacity to learn about learning (cf. Rowan Williams 2005).

This holistic view of the worth provides a keystone to a critical understanding of the purpose of Higher Education. This is a pre-moral good as powerful as those of the health or legal professions; developing critical thinking which enables genuine autonomy. Of course, the idea is tested by attempts to polarise different elements, not least the view that the academic world is essentially abstract and thus distinct from practice. This, however, is to ignore the fact that academic engagement is in itself a practice and profession, founded itself in the first mode of responsibility. Other polarisations attempt to distinguish research and teaching. However, whilst there may different applications of these practices, they are essentially the same, part of the critical learning process (Ford 2004).

The first mode of responsibility demands then that some such idea of worth and purpose is critically established and that this is connected to the values of the organisation and to the practices of the organisation, involving internal and external relations. This includes showing how academic (intellectual), moral (including social responsibility) and organisational values relate to the core purpose. The obvious place to establish this meaning is in the organisations statement of Mission, Vision and Values. The danger at this point is to mimic corporate statements. These broadly try to capture meaning in terms of outcomes or product. Hence, some universities focus on narrow professional or business utility, with success perceived as the university's contribution to enterprise and the economy. Such success is often tied to the idea of the organisation becoming, over time, the leading institution of its kind.

Values then can easily become general without an anchor in pre-moral goods or plural purpose. One of the problems with this, like most corporate statements (King III 2009) is that 'values' are viewed as essentially moral values, and there is thus little attempt to articulate and connect intellectual, moral, socio-political, or psychological values. Hence, the holistic dimension of Barnett's higher learning is lost. Not surprisingly then, the logic of how this might connect to enterprise, or inform and strengthen professional practice (including skills), or relate to social as well as economic culture is also lost.

Of course, mission statements are not meant to be detailed and it could be argued that we should go elsewhere, for instance, to ethical codes or frameworks, to find the details and connections. There are two problems with this argument. First, setting out the core worth and purpose of the university is not a matter of length but of precision and the governing body is responsible for ensuring a statement which is both succinct and clear. Second, if there is not clarity about purpose and worth in the initial statement there is the danger that more detailed work will also lose focus. In ethical codes or value frameworks, for instance, there is the danger simply of listing values and assuming that the meaning is clear. Favourites amongst these are trust, empowerment, engagement, innovation, ambition, and learning and scholarship. These are without doubt important psychological and intellectual values but how do they connect to the worth of the institution and to moral values? Perhaps more importantly what do they actually mean? These are not abstract but practical questions; what do these values actually look like and how are they are practised? How often do staff and students reflect on them and how often are they developed, and in what way? Take the value of trust. Why is it important? How does it connect to the core mission and values and what does it mean? As O'Neill (2002) reminds us trust is focused less in transparency and more in getting relationships right, demanding open dialogue. Trust itself is based in other values. So how do all these values connect? The research of Gregory and Willis (2013) with corporate boards suggests that it is not an easy task to connect them in practice. Most board members could say what the values of the organisation were but could not identify how these were embodied in deliberation or procedures.

Another favourite values list is the Nolan principles of public life: Selflessness, Integrity, Objectivity, Accountability, Openness, Honesty and Leadership. However, important as these principles are it is not easy to understand them without a route map which shows how they are instantiated in individual and institutional practice. What is selflessness like in Higher Education? Is it the same as disinterestedness or altruism and how does it connect to the practice of teaching or research? Trust (O'Neill 2000) and integrity (Robinson 2016) are both contested concepts.

In fact, key principles can be seen to emerge directly from the purpose and practice of higher education. If the core purpose is developing higher learning then freedom, defined as critical autonomy, becomes a key principle. Alongside freedom comes equality, of respect and treatment. Partial treatment does not enable learning for all (Tawney 1930). This principle relates directly to the value of inclusivity. Closely related to that is the principle of justice. Justice can be defined both as fairness (Rawls 1972) and more broadly as equal distribution. Even these principles need to be bolstered by others, not least the principle of collegiality. Collegiality expresses the principles of care and community, i.e. providing an experience which supports students and staff to develop confidence in the practice of higher learning, including research. Learning involves risk associated with giving an account of one's thoughts and being prepared to see challenges not as personal threats. Connected to these principles is the principle of disinterestedness enabling a shared commitment to the focus of learning and research. All of these values inform academic freedom, but also a sense mindfulness, openness to the social and physical environment, to the creative possibilities of engaging with these, and thus for a continued search for truth in all aspects. Such principles can even begin to form the basis of understanding employability, bringing together critical thinking, relational consciousness and commitment, and creativity (Robinson 2005). With this higher learning is seen as informing all the Dearing purposes.

Of course, any connections are tested, along with the second mode of responsibility, accountability, once a major challenge occurs. This in turn questions the different narratives inside and outside the university: disciplinary, professional, social and political. Each of these brings different perspectives to purpose and value, not least their own view of pre-moral goods (such as health and justice). Such professions will in turn have different narratives. Medicine, for example, has narratives of specialisation such as research into cancer, essentially a scientific narrative, to wider narratives about public health and narratives about the medical profession and its leadership role in society (Lancet 2009). Other professions have a direct application to governance, not least accountancy (cf. ICAEW 2009). Such professions have developed a clear account of the meaning of integrity in practice, and thus have a direct contribution to any reflection on HE governance.

Another series of narratives comes from the student body. At one level this involves a narrative of consumerism, focused in contract. However, the student narrative includes a concern to develop higher learning, including complex social responsibility skills. This is a direct contribution to the dialogue on purpose and worth of the university and sets out students as partners, not consumers.

All of these different groups have a contribution to make to the identity of the university and their own identity within the university. All of them contribute to the connecting core value, worth and practice, informing debates, for instance, on the relation of values to practice and the connection of employability to wider issues of responsibility (Robinson 2005). All contribute to their own and the university's identity; in different ways enabling the connections between the Dearing purposes. The different perspectives they offer test and challenge the identity of other groups within the university. This demands effective dialogue developing a sense of mutual accountability to the different groups and mutual responsibility for the wider sense of purpose and identity of the university.

A good example of the absence of such dialogue is the well-known case of Nottingham Business School accepting substantial funding from British American Tobacco (BAT) for its Centre for CSR. What emerged in this case was little coherent practice of responsibility, or accountability. In the place of reflection on the identity of the university the VC Colin Campbell (2001) offered two sets of arguments to defend the controversial decision. First, procedures were followed and key stakeholders consulted. Second, the funding of university projects is always complex. In the first of these some contact was made with, for instance, Cancer Research UK and the medical faculty, and there was discussion in the University Senate which did not reveal major objections. The University then made use of a national protocol devised to ensure that monies from or resources funded by the tobacco industry should not be used by cancer researchers. Funding in a different faculty or school would not be covered by it (Campbell 2001). Hence, the university carefully focused the agreement in the Business School. However, there was little genuine dialogue with the wider groups in the university and even the 'consultation' with Cancer Research UK was not recognised by that body, who withdrew funding. There was also little effective dialogue with the medical faculty (from which 15 academics resigned) or with the Student Union. The use of the protocol in fact served to fragment any sense of shared responsibility around core purpose or any sense of mutual accountability between the Business School, the Medical School and the university. The accountability of the Business School to the University, to other professions, to the students or the Student's Union (which banned smoking), other disciplines or wider stakeholders was not explored.

The closest to a dialogue was the debate developed in the British Medical Journal between the editor (Richard Smith, a lecturer from Nottingham, 2001) and Campbell (2001). Smith raised the issue of BAT using the University for its own ends, and argued that accepting the funds would affect the reputation of the university. However, what that reputation involved was not actually addressed by either man precisely because there was no reflection on the values, purpose, identity and responsibility of the University, what its core purpose and beliefs were and how and to whom it was accountable. The dominant narrative became one of organisational sustainability. Campbell argued that the business environment within which universities operate, and to which they have to relate to survive, was irreducibly ambiguous, and the tobacco industry was simply a part of that. No business in Nottingham was free from the connection to tobacco.

Arguments were also presented to address some points about values. The Business School and BAT shared a concern for corporate social responsibility, and academic disinterestedness. The company had legal status and contributed (through taxes and gift) to social services. However, just how the Business School could remain disinterested (in other words how the value could be embodied in practice) was not explored. The wider issues of the nature of CSR (corporate social responsibility) and how it relates to human rights, and how business schools relate to industry or the effect this might have on academic as well as moral values (see Ghoshal 2005), were not critically examined. Perhaps not surprisingly, the contemporary investigation from the Department of Trade and Industry for allegations that BAT exploited smuggling around the world or the questions about the tobacco industry exploiting developing countries were not addressed.

The case then illustrates a lack of engagement of core purpose and worth, mutual accountability, or shared positive responsibility, with little clarity about identity or evidence of shared narrative or dialogue. The case also illustrates how a narrow view of accountability can lead to the uncritical acceptance of a dominant narrative; organisational sustainability. This is often characterised as 'managerialism' (De Vita and Case 2016). and is characterised by a philosophy of contract, involving targets and measurement of success. It also is also associated with an absence of dialogue. Macnamara's research (2015) in corporate leadership and communication suggests that whilst most leaders believe they practise dialogic leadership in fact the vast majority of communication is transmitted one way. It is perhaps not surprising that many issues in Higher Education reveal an absence of dialogue. The arrangement of space, for instance, often does not engage the core values. How, for instance, can the organisation of space in a university express core values such as collegiality, or enable sustained dialogue in teaching and learning (Robinson 2011)?

The philosophy of contract is also applied to relationships within the university and beyond. The university's relationship with external organisations is often viewed in terms of contract and product. Perhaps most striking is the relationship of the student to the university, as one of consumer and provider. Peter Mandelson argued for this essentially contract relationship as the proper focus for accountability. However, this is to assume that contract is the prime focus for accountability. But accountability does not have be a function of the consumer model primarily. It is already there in the academic community in the idea of thinking together, something that requires mutual accountability. Ramsden (2009) amongst others suggests that focusing on consumerism, often articulated as 'student-centred', runs the danger of developing a culture that is quite the opposite of collegiality, stressing satisfaction of individual rights rather than shared learning. It is focused on passive receipt of goods and is strongly affective, compared to a critical community that requires active engagement focused in purpose and shared responsibility. This demands greater focus on dialogue, and less on surveys to measure satisfaction, or encouraging organisational isomorphism (Thompson and Bevan 2013). The value of collegiality, focused in commitment and shared responsibility, has an element of the covenant (May 1987) which radically changes the nature of contract.

The Architecture of Dialogue

How realistic then is it to develop an architecture of dialogue which embodies integrity? Macnamara (2015, 19) argues that it begins with exploring the nature of listening, involving: 'recognition of others' rights and views; acknowledgement; paying attention; interpreting what is said to gain understanding of others' views; giving consideration to what is said; and an appropriate response'. In effect, the dynamics involves the practice of responsibility, ensuring that the voice of different actors is developed and heard, and that in turn this tests and supports the account of organisational identity.

Developing an architecture of dialogue then demands: a culture of dialogue; policies for listening; addressing the politics of dialogue; structures and processes, technologies, resources for dialogue; skills for listening; and articulation of dialogue to decision and policy making. Such an architecture enables all narrators in the organisation to be involved in governance, and therefore to take responsibility for the core purposes and sustainability of the institution. In more recent work in corporate and public governance, such as King III (2009) and IV (2017) Reports, it is explicitly argued that a great part of governance regulation should take place through stakeholder dialogue, avoiding over-reliance on external regulation. Once more this is focused in mutual accountability in which internal and external stake-holders are drawn into the dialogue.

A few examples must suffice. First, it is ironical that the UK government since the 1980s has favoured the old the corporate model, with governing boards are as small as possible. Small boards have the effect of diluting dialogue, focusing rather on swift decision making. Such boards can become distant from the community of practice, losing genuine accountability. Just as important as any sense of representation is the practice of dialogue which is founded in difference. Hence, the board has to demonstrate the quality of such dialogue (Robinson 2016). This places a lot of pressure on the chair of the board, to enable what MacIntyre (1990) calls the, 'institutionalisation of constrained conflict' fundamental to the nature of the university. It also places responsibility on board members to question the vice chancellor and the registrar's office. In corporate boards the logic of the non-executive director was to provide an external perspective that can ask critical questions that those paid by the institution might be afraid to ask.

There are, of course, different ways to develop this dialogue, from Councils and Senates to the suggestion of three courts that represent staff, students and external members (cf. Newman 2010). The argument against developing such governance frameworks is that it would set up different levels of accountability ad infinitum; the point being that the buck has to stop somewhere. This, however, misses the point. The integrity of the university demands leadership which enables responsibility to be shared in all its modes and across the university. Open dialogue in and beyond the board is as important as representation, subjecting narrative to open testing. Beyond board architecture there could be imaginative ways of opening the board members to unrehearsed critical dialogue; as distinct from the rehearsed practice of annual meetings. Some universities have developed annual gatherings of two or more days. These have included training and development events, open dialogue with stakeholders and board members (who are severally responsible for the direction of the university); developing open accountability and the narrative of the university. Allied to such dialogic architecture could be a regular review of mission and values. At the heart of this review would be an open process of critical conversation that might involve external figures, and engage all parts of the university, focusing on the responsibility of the university. This is one way of institutionalising the community of practice which Moore (2006) calls 'thinking with each other', something that goes right back to *universitas magistrorum et scholarium*, masters and scholars working side by side. At the heart of this is the everyday practice of the virtues (Moore 2012); intellectual, psychological, social and moral, which the articulation of ethical frameworks (such as CIHE 2005) can enable.

This suggests that a second architectural focus might be integrated thinking and reporting. The different regulatory agencies, including the Quality Assurance Agency, the Higher Education Funding Council for England and the Office of the Independent Adjudicator, to say nothing of sustainability agencies, tend to fragment reporting, and, with that, fragment the university narrative and sense of shared responsibility and mutual accountability. The framework for this involves the so called six capitals: financial, manufacturing (product/project); social and relational; intellectual and natural, which provides the environment within which the capitals (in effect values) sit (IIRC 2013). This is brings together different narratives and frames them in the university story. It is the logical outcome of the CIHE (2005) framework and helps the different stakeholders inside and outside the university to make sense of the purpose, values and project. Edinburgh University provide an excellent example of this approach, and such thinking is being developed by the Leadership Foundation in a universities project (https://www.lfhe.ac.uk/en/news/index.cfm/ITandRUnisconfirmed).

A third focus might be on everyday processes which enable critical dialogue. In the area of research ethics, for instance there have been great developments over the last 20 years, partly motivated by the funding councils. Research ethics protocols include guidance and codes and are increasingly focused in online applications. The best of these examples tie the practice to dialogue with research ethics coordinators in disciplines and sub disciplines who can work through any issues rapidly and also enable the development of a critical culture of research.

A final, connected, focus, is the integration of core purpose into the curriculum. One of the great dangers of the age of student massification is learning focused in the transmission of knowledge, the commodification of content rather than the practice of the core virtues of learning. Without dialogue the virtues are crowded out, and students practice only a limited sense of responsibility. The skills to do with this are what we are about not simply as members of a community or workforce but as human beings. As Oakshott (1962) suggests they are learned in a community of critical conversation, one that enables the student to hear the many voices, appreciate their difference and engage. This unrehearsed but disciplined conversation is key the practice of the three modes of responsibility and to the development of meta-cognition and mindfulness. This connects ideas to people and to the wider environment, engaging diverse narratives holistically; in cognitive, affective, and somatic terms (Oakshott 1962). This enerates the practice of a range of connected virtues: intellectual (wisdom); moral (courage, temperance, justice etc.), psychological (empathy, listening skills, negotiation skills), social (teamwork, communication skills). All focus on worth, ideas, values and practice. The development of this responsibility through critical and creative dialogue then can reflect the core purposes of the university and the core practices of governance.

The integrity of the university then demands that the modes of responsibility be at the centre both of governance and teaching. The challenge of providing an architecture for such dialogue, relationally and with the aid of technology, then becomes central to the purpose of the university, enabling mutual accountability that is both vertical and horizontal, individual and organisational. The responsibility for this project is then shared by all members, calling all members, but especially those with experience and authority, to push back against practice which fragments responsibility.

Conclusion

I have tried to show that integrity is focused in responsibility, and that this offers a vision of the university which is primarily about the quality of thinking and the quality of relationships inside and outside the university.

Graham (2002) argues that the university is primarily an intellectual beacon not a moral one, the betterment of society may come from the central value of critical discourse, but not necessarily. However, the danger in a primary focus on intellectual freedom is to settle for a passive tolerance of all values. The analysis of responsibility suggests that intellectual, psychological, social and moral are interconnected. Hence, as Jenkins (1988) suggests, the university should try to hold together many different purposes and their underlying values. It should be both an 'essentially critical place', and a place of betterment. This enables the university to subject its own and all the other purposes and values to critical scrutiny, amplifying Barnett's higher learning in the context of shared creative responsibility, individual, corporate and social; contributing to the moral imagination of the wider community (cf. Hardy 1992).

MacIntyre (1990) argues that universities are places where 'conceptions of and standards of rational justification are elaborated, put to working detail practices of enquiry, and themselves rationally evaluated, so that only from the university can wider society learn how to conduct its own debates, practical or theoretical, in a rationally defensible way'. I would add only two things to MacIntyre. First, the debates, as noted above, have moral content and implication. Second, the claim that the university is the only place where society can learn this practice is problematic. As I have suggested above other institutions, from schools to professions and various public and private corporations are based in the practice of responsibility; part of which may be to remind the university of it's responsibility.

References

Airaksinen, T. (1994). Service and science in professional life. In R. Chadwick (Ed.), *Ethics and the professions* (pp. 1–13). Aldershot: Ashgate.

Bakhtin, M. (1984). *The dialogic imagination: Four essays*. Austin: University of Texas.

Barnett, R. (1994). *The limits of competence, knowledge, higher education and society*. Berkshire: Oprn University Press.

Bauman, Z. (1989). *Modernity and the holocaust*. London: Polity.

Beebe, J., & Rosen, D. (2005). *Integrity in depth*. Austin: Texas A&M University Press.

Boltanksi, L., & Thévenot, L. (2006). *On justification: Economies of worth*. Princeton: Princeton University Press.

Brown, M. (2005). *Corporate integrity*. Cambridge: Cambridge University Press.

Burkitt, I. (2008). *Social selves: Theories of self and society*. London: Sage.

Calhoun, C. (1995, May). Standing for something. *Journal of Philosophy, XCII*(5), 235–260.

Callender, J. (2010). *Free will and responsibility*. Oxford: Oxford University Press.

Campbell, C. (2001, May). For and against: Should Nottingham University give back its tobacco money? For against. *British Medical Journal, 322*, 1118–1119.

CIHE. (2005). *Ethics matters in higher education*. London: Council for Industry and Higher Education.

Cooper-White, P. (2007). *Many voices*. Minneapolis: Fortress.

Cottingham, J. (2010). Integrity and fragmentation. *Journal of Applied Philosophy, 27*(1), 2–14.

Covaleskie, J. (2011). Integrity and identity: Judgment and the moral self. *Philosophy of Education Yearbook*, 308–315.

Curzer, H. (2014). *Aristotle and the virtues*. Oxford: Oxford University Press.

De Vita, G., & Case, P. (2016). 'The smell of the place': Managerialist culture in contemporary UK business schools. *Culture and Organisation, 2*(4), 348–364.

Dearing, R. (1997). *Higher education in the learning society*. London: HMSO.

Eliot, T. S. (1934). *The rock*. London: Faber and Faber.

Entine, J. (2002). Shell, Greenpeace and Brent Spar; the politics of dialogue. In C. Megone & S. Robinson (Eds.), *Case histories in business ethics*. London: Routledge.

Fawkes, J. (2014). *Public relations ethics and professionalism: The shadow of excellence*. London: Routledge.

Ford, D. (2004). Responsibilities of universities. *Studies in Christian Ethics, 17*(1), 22–37.

Francis, R. (2013). *The Mid Staffordshire Foundation Trust public enquiry*. www.modstaffspublicinquiry.com

Frankfurt, H. (1971). Freedom of the will and the concept of a person. *Journal of Philosophy, 68*, 5–20.

Freeman, M. (2015). *Rewriting the self*. London: Routledge.

Ghoshal, S. (2005). Bad management theories and destroying good management practices. *Academy of Management Learning and Education, 4*(1), 75–91.

Goodpaster, K. (2007). *Conscience and the corporate culture*. Oxford: Blackwell.

Graham, G. (2002). *Universities: The recovery of an idea*. Thorverton: Imprint Academic.

Greenblatt, S. (2012). *Renaissance self-fashioning: From more to Shakespeare*. Chicago: Chicago University Press.

Gregory, A., & Willis, P. (2013). *Strategic public relations*. London: Routledge.

Haidt, J. (2013). *The righteous mind: Why good people are divided by politics and religion*. London: Penguin.

Halfon, M. (1989). *Integrity: A philosophical inquiry*. Philadelphia: Temple University Press.

Hardy, D. (1992, September 9). *Theology in the public domain*. Unpublished paper given in the H. E. Chaplains' Conference, Hoddesden.

Harris, J. (2006). How much is too much? A theoretical analysis of executive compensation from the standpoint of distributive justice. In R. Kolb (Ed.), *The ethics of executive compensation* (pp. 67–87). Oxford: Blackwell.

Haste, H., & Abrahams, S. (2008). Morality, culture and the dialogic self: Taking cultural pluralism seriously. *Journal of Moral Education, 37*(3), 377–394.

Heffernan, M. (2012). *Wilful blindness*. New York: Simon and Schuster.

ICAEW. (2009). *Reporting with integrity*. London: ICAEW.

IIRC. (2013). *International Integrated Reporting Council capitals background paper*. http://integratedreporting.org/wp-content/uploads/2013/03/IR-Background-Paper-Capitals.pdf

Jenkins, D. (1988). What is the purpose of a university, and what light does Christian faith shed on this question? *Studies in Higher Education, 13*(3), 34–48.

King III. (2009). *Report on Corporate Governance*. Johannes burg: Institute of Directors in South Africa.

King IV. (2017). *Report on corporate governance*. Johannesburg: Institute of Directors in Southern Africa.

Lederach, J. P. (2005). *The moral imagination*. Oxford: Oxford University Press.

MacIntyre, A. (1990). *Three rival forms of enquiry*. London: Duckworth.

Macnamara, J. (2015). *Creating an architecture of listening in organisations*. https://gcs.civilservice.gov.uk/wp-content/uploads/2016/04/Organisational-Listening-Research-Report-16-1.pdf

Mason, M. (2001). The ethics of integrity: Educational values beyond postmodern ethics. *Journal of Philosophy of Education, 35*(1), 47–69.

May, W. (1987). Code and covenant or philanthropy. In S. Lammmers & A. Verhey (Eds.), *On moral medicine*. Grand Rapids: Eerdmans.

Moore, G. (2006). Managing ethics in higher education: Implementing a code or embedding virtue? *Business Ethics: A European Review, 15*(4), 407–418.

Moore, G. (2012). The virtue of governance and the governance of virtue. *Business Ethics Quarterly, 2*(22), 293–318.

Newman, M. (2010, February 8). Two-tier system should replace 'ramshackle' university governance. *Times Higher.* http://www.timeshighereducation.co.uk/story.asp?sectioncode=26&storycode=410296

Noelliste, M. (2003). Integrity: An intrapersonal perspective. *Human Resource Development Review, 12*(4), 474–499.

Nohria, N., & Khurana, R. (2008). It's time to make management a true profession. *Harvard Business Review, 86*(10), 70–77.

Nussbaum, M. (1990). *Love's knowledge: Essays on philosophy and literature*. New York: Oxford University Press.

Oakshott, M. (1962). *Rationalism in politics and other essays*. London: Methuen.

Paine, L. (1994, March–April). Managing organisational integrity. *Harvard Business Review*, 106–117.

Palanski, M., & Yammarino, F. (2007). Integrity and leadership: Clearing the conceptual confusion. *European Management Journal, 25*, 171–184.

Pattison, S., & Edgar, A. (2011). The problem with integrity. *Nursing Philosophy, 12*, 81–82.

Pianalto, M. (2012). Integrity and struggle. *Philosophia, 40*, 319–336.

Polowczyk, P. (2017). Organisational ethical integrity: Good and bad illusions. *Palgrave Communications, 3*, 46.

Raggatt, P. T. F. (2012). Positioning in the dialogical self: Recent advances in theory construction. In H. Hermans & T. Geiser (Eds.), *Handbook of dialogical self theory*. Cambridge: Cambridge University Press.

Ramsden, P. (2009, November 20). *A better student experience*. HEA.

Rawls, J. (1972). *A theory of justice*. Oxford: Clarendon Press.

Ricoeur, P. (2000). *The concept of responsibility: An essay in semantic analysis in the just* (D. Pellauer, Trans.). Chicago: The University of Chicago Press.

Robinson, S. (2005). *Ethics and employability*. York: HEA.

Robinson, S. (2009). The nature of responsibility in a professional setting. *Journal of Business Ethics, 88*, 11–19.

Robinson, S. (2011). *Leadership responsibility*. Oxford: Peter Lang.

Robinson, D. (2013a). Corrupting research integrity: Corporate funding and academic integrity. In *Global corruption report: Education* (pp. 202–210). London: Transparency International.

Robinson, S. (2013b). Hearing voices: Wisdom responsibility and leadership. In M. Thompson & D. Bevan (Eds.), *Wise management in organisational complexity*. London: Palgrave.

Scherkoske, G. (2013). *Integrity and the virtues of reason: Leading a convincing life*. Cambridge: Cambridge University Press.

Schlegel, R. J., Hicks, J. A., Arndt, J., & King, L. A. (2009). Thine own self: True self concept accessibility and meaning in life. *Journal of Personality and Social Psychology, 96*(2), 473–490.

Schweiker, W. (2010). *Responsibility and Christian ethics*. Cambridge: Cambridge University Press.

Sidorkin, A. (1999). *Beyond discourse: Education, the self and dialogue*. Albany: State University of New York Press.

Smith, R. (2001, May). For and against: Should Nottingham University give back its tobacco money? For against. *British Medical Journal, 322*, 1120–1121.

Solomon, R. (1992). *Ethics and excellence*. Oxford: Oxford University Press.

Solomon, R. (2007). *True to our feelings*. Oxford: Oxford University Press.

Tawney, R. H. (1930). *Equality*. London: Allen and Unwin.

Taylor, C. (1989). *Sources of the self*. Cambridge: Cambridge University Press.

The Lancet. (2009, May 16). Editorial, p. 1659.

Thompson, M., & Bevan, D. (2013). *Wise management in organisational complexity*. London: Palgrave.

van der Ven, J. (1998). *Formation of the moral self*. Grand Rapids: Eerdmans.

Werhane, P. (1999). *Moral imagination and management decision making*. Oxford: Oxford University Press.

Williams, B. (1973). Integrity. In J. J. C. Smart & B. Williams (Eds.), *Utilitarianism: For and against* (pp. 108–117). New York: Cambridge University Press.

Williams, R. (2005). Faith in the university. In S. Robinson & C. Katulushi (Eds.), *Values and higher education* (pp. 24–35). Leeds: Leeds University Press.

Wolf, S. (2009). Moral psychology and the unity of the virtues. *Ratio, XX*(2), 145–167.

Chapter 9
Universities and Unpaid Work: Louis Althusser Re-visited

Sabina Siebert

Abstract This chapter examines the practice of student work experience as a route into employment through the theoretical lens of Louis Althusser's ideological state apparatuses. In particular, I focus on unpaid work experience which is compulsory or highly recommended, but not formally facilitated by the university. Work experience such as this raises a concern about the exploitative nature of unpaid work. I investigate to what extent such consideration is evident in the universities' discourse of employability. Drawing on Althusser's notion of ideological state apparatuses I pose the question whether the universities' approach to employability, based on the values of individualism, can be held responsible for legitimising unpaid labour as a method of gaining access to paid employment.

Keywords Louis Althusser · Unpaid work · Employability · Work experiences · Neo-liberal

Introduction

This chapter focuses on unpaid work experience advocated by the university sector as a route into future employment. Despite recent media debates on the unfairness of unpaid placements and internships in the UK, the issue of why many young people consider it legitimate to work for free has not been widely discussed. In our earlier study on unpaid work experience (Siebert and Wilson 2013) I came across an apparently inconsistent finding. Evaluating unpaid work placement as many as 57% of students and recent graduates who participated in unpaid work placements considered these placements to be meaningful learning experiences, and 71% said they would be happy to recommend their placements to other students. Respondents saw gaining work experience as a necessity, as something that will put them 'ahead of

S. Siebert (✉)
University of Glasgow, Glasgow, UK
e-mail: Sabina.Siebert@glasgow.ac.uk

© Springer Nature Switzerland AG 2019

P. Gibbs et al. (eds.), *Values of the University in a Time of Uncertainty*,
https://doi.org/10.1007/978-3-030-15970-2_9

the rest', and 'the more work experience, the better'. At the same time 59% of these respondents felt that such unpaid work was 'exploitative'. Thus a question arises why so many respondents appeared to accept the practice of unpaid work and evaluated it positively while simultaneously a high proportion of them perceived it as exploitative.

In my attempt to explain these inconsistencies I argue that the University through its advocacy of employability plays a role in legitimising the practice of unpaid work. In our explanation I re-visit past scholarship and draw on theory that is rarely evoked in contemporary social science literature – Louis Althusser's (1971) ideological state apparatuses. Although Althusser wrote at a different historical moment and in a very different political context, his analysis of ideology is still relevant and illuminates some of the contemporary debates on employability.

Louis Althusser's Ideological State Apparatuses

Louis Althusser's most influential contribution to cultural studies has been his writing on ideology (Althusser 1971). Ideology for him was a set of discourses, images and ideas through which we live our relationship with historical reality (Feretter 2006). It was not something which existed in people's minds as an intellectual construct but in the real world as a practice through which people live their lives (Ritzer 2005). Althusser claimed that an ideology always exists as the product or practice of an ideology-producing system or apparatus, so that ideology for him had a material existence, i.e. it was present in practices that preceded and governed systems of ideas.

Althusser's (1971) significant development of Marxist theory of ideology was to draw attention to a body of institutions that function to reproduce dominant ideology. Thus he made a distinction between two overlapping but distinct sets of institutions – repressive state apparatuses, which were the focus of Marx's analysis, and ideological state apparatuses (ISAs). The repressive state apparatuses such as the army, the police, the prisons or the courts functioned primarily by violence, while ideological state apparatuses, which also reproduced power and power relations functioned primarily by ideology. ISAs could be religious, educational, legal, political or cultural, and include institutions such as the church, the family, the trade union, the arts, literature or sports. Both sorts of state apparatus ensure the cohesion and reproduction of certain practices (Feretter 2006) but in the case of the ISAs it is particularly clear that the practices of the institutions' members play a key role in sustaining the institutions, hence there are mutually constitutive relationships in play.

As a Marxist Althusser was primarily concerned to understand the paradox of the continued survival of capitalism with the apparent consent of those disadvantaged by it. How is it, he asked, that the exploited allow themselves to be exploited (Althusser 1971)? His answer to this question was in terms of the effective transmission of the dominant capitalist ideology by the ISAs. These institutions were in his view essential to reproducing capitalist relations of production by securing sufficient commitment to the system on the part of those who operated it, whether as workers, or as managers or as politicians. As a thinker deeply impressed by Lacanian psychology, Althusser was particularly ready to ascribe importance to those institutions that made their indelible impression on the younger members of society. This is because in their most formative years spent in the educational institutions children and young people are most vulnerable and susceptible to ideology – caught between the Family State Apparatus and the Educational State Apparatus (Feretter 2006).

Althusser's analysis of the reproduction of capitalist society is closely related to the place and time in which he was writing. Yet I will argue that the University remains a neat example of an ideological state apparatus promoting a collusive relationship between students and the corporate world which it is fair to describe as self-exploitation.

Employability

The notion of employability is a subject which invites critical evaluations from all ends of the political spectrum (Garsten and Jacobsson 2004; Moreau and Leathwood 2006; Cremin 2010; Clarke and Patrickson 2008; Bloom 2013; Beaumont and Gedye 2016; Qureshi et al. 2016; Pinto and Ramalheira 2017; Chen et al. 2018). As an educational aim, it is hard to argue against the notion of producing employable graduates, but even self-certifying educational aims do not guarantee results, and it is not clear how far employability is achieved in practice (Auburn 2007). The rhetoric of 'labour market preparedness' (Larner and Le Henron 2005: 854) is, however, widely current in universities and evident in the aspiration to produce 'work-ready' graduates equipped in the relevant knowledge and skills to secure and sustain employment. In an attempt to render graduates more employable, universities which are themselves 'increasingly corporately managed' (Prichard and Wilmott 1997: 287) help students identify and compete for work experience by compiling and distributing industry contacts; they also offer advice, and direct students to employers. They can then reasonably represent themselves as responding to pressures from both students and employers (Prichard 2012). It is unsurprising to note that this market-oriented discourse of employability can map smoothly onto a Marxist conception of capitalist ideology (Boltanski and Chiapello 2007), and can figure as a description of the desperate attempts of the alienated subject trying to come to terms with the uninterpretable Lacanian Other; 'never employable enough', 'functionally alienated from the capitalist modes of production' (Cremin 2010: 146), the subject flails about trying to conform to increasingly fluffy and non-operational specifications of 'graduateness'.

The Universities' employability agenda affects the structure of the labour market (Fejes 2010; Chertkovskaya et al. 2013), but it also affects the universities themselves. The need to achieve legitimacy through seeking to create employable individuals has been held to lead to 'academic self-hatred' (Taylor 2013: 852). And the new source of legitimacy may not even be coherent: employability is 'a condition that can never be fulfilled' (Cremin 2010: 139) and individuals through constantly enhancing their employability appear to maximisetheir self-alienation. Bloom (2013: 795) argued that 'the fantasy of employability directs desires for overcoming subjective alienation into an 'empowering' identity which paradoxically further conforms to the managerial desires'.

Work experience is an important aspect of the employability agenda in higher education. Work experience is often unpaid and as such it is often linked with the notion of work-for-labour, which Standing (2011: 120) defines as 'work that does not have exchange value but which is necessary and advisable' for those looking for jobs. In recent years work experience placements and internships have given rise to concerns about exploitation of young people, and about the ethics and legality of unpaid labour. After all, unpaid work even by an apprentice or learner creates value. Trade unions, pressure groups, news reports (e.g. Guardian 2012; BBC 2012) and campaigners, including web-based groups such as Cash for Interns, Rights for Interns, Interns Anonymous, Internocracy, or Intern Aware, have brought the controversies about internships to the fore of political and social debates. Numerous research reports and guidelines have raised awareness of the issue of fairness of unpaid work, and to a greater or lesser degree offered 'solutions' to the unpaid labour issue (Chartered Institute of Personnel and Development 2010; Institute of Public Policy Research/Lawton and Potter 2010).

So why is it that students appear to accept the practice of unpaid work and evaluate it positively while at the same time a high proportion of them perceived it as exploitative? I put forward the proposition that the university plays a role in shaping students' evaluations of unpaid work both by uncritical acceptance of the discourse of employability and by inadequate consideration of the issues that are associated with it.

The Study

With this proposition in mind I conducted a small-scale empirical study in which I examined the perspectives on unpaid work experience of two groups of stakeholders – students who took part in unpaid work experience and university staff from the programmes which had incorporated work experience in the curriculum. The primary data cited in this chapter were collected from undergraduate students on degree programmes related to the creative and cultural contexts, and university staff in two universities in the UK. Work experience was either compulsory or highly recommended, but not formally facilitated by the university on any of the programmes that I investigated.

The data was collected in the UK, and all participants were either students or staff working in the area of the creative and cultural industries (journalism, media studies, theatre studies, music, acting, events management). The study was carried out in two stages. In the first stage of the project I conducted a survey of students aspiring to secure a career in the creative and cultural industries and who have undertaken unpaid work experience in the relevant sector. A post-experience questionnaire was designed drawing on the research and policy literature on work experience. The questionnaire included questions in relation to the benefits that work experience brings to the participants and the employer, the ways placements were sourced, the accuracy of the placement description, whether the placement was seen as a valuable learning experience, and finally whether participants perceived their placements as exploitative. Fifty-six questionnaires were returned. Stage two of the project comprised eight semi-structured interviews with university staff who had a role in facilitating work experience. These included four university tutors, two career advisors, a placement officer, and one work placement manager. The interview data were analysed with a view to identifying themes and patterns emerging from the responses.

The message which appeared to dominate in the discourse of both universities was that in the aftermath of the global financial crisis graduate jobs are increasingly difficult to find, mainly due to an over-supply of candidates for jobs. Lecturers and career advisers warned their students that academic qualifications were no longer sufficient for securing employment; work experience was vital, and a candidate with relevant job experience was more attractive to employers than a graduate without any work experience. The benefits of work experience claimed by universities included: giving students a competitive advantage, allowing them to develop industry relevant skills, offering insights into the industry, and allowing the students to build networks.

The university staff emphasised to the students the importance of work experience, and enforced the requirement, but stressed that the university was not able to guarantee access to work opportunities. The most common method of student sourcing of work experience was reliance on students' own contacts, and University staff did not interfere in the process. Given a deficit of paid work experience opportunities, many students resorted to unpaid work in order to meet the University requirement and in order to improve their employability potential.

When asked about their experiences, the students rated the benefits as follows: they valued the insights into the way the industry worked, they got practical experience, they developed transferable skills, and they appreciated the opportunity to consider career options. The best placements made students feel that they were part of the team, that they took part in decision-making, that they were given responsibility for complex tasks, and that their efforts were recognised. Students appreciated it when they enjoyed an open and frank relationship with workplace staff and when they felt they were trusted to do a good job. Respondents also found it helpful to be assigned a variety of roles, effective training and constructive feedback on performance from management.

However, there is evidence that work experience did not always deliver the benefits anticipated, and our respondents raised concerns about the quality and value of work experience undertaken. The students reported dissatisfaction at the repetitive, low-skilled character of the work they were asked to undertake and being 'the runaround'. Some of them complained about 'having not enough to do', 'being left standing about', or being given 'tasks that paid employees did not want to do'. Others on the other hand were concerned about working very long hours without a break for lunch and having too much to do without support from paid staff. Placement descriptions were in many cases inaccurate and overemphasised the level of responsibility placed on participants (e.g. 'events management opportunities' turned out to be 'menial jobs') and underemphasised the amount of 'tedious repetitive work' that was expected. Lack of communication with staff, inadequate training and lack of supervision were also listed as concerns. A few participants explicitly commented on exploitation of their ideas, being 'taken advantage of' and feeling that 'you are there to reduce staff costs'. Some perks of the placement included 'after-show drinks', an 'opportunity to see the bands', free advance screenings of films, 'goody' bags, t-shirts and free dinners but over half of my respondents did not receive reimbursement of their expenses or any benefits-in-kind. Surprisingly, few students saw work placements as an effective way to link university study with the world of work.

When asked to comment on the feedback they received from students on their work experience, some staff admitted that 'issues occasionally arise', and that on the basis of bad experiences of students, the university had discontinued some arrangements with employers. One lecturer said that 'bad' work experience is also necessary from the point of view of learning about the negative aspects of the world of work, as it allows people to make more informed career choices. With regards to the duration of unpaid placements most staff acknowledged that long-term unpaid work is sometimes demoralising, and that the financial aspect of unpaid work experience also has detrimental effects on young people, who 'juggle paid and unpaid work', and consequently underperform in their studies.

There is also some evidence of university staff being aware of the potential risk of exploitation:

> They're asked to come in again for another two months and, to be honest, from my point of view it doesn't happen so often with our students and our courses but I am aware that you hear stories and people are occasionally are invited to work for free and we always advise people not to do that after a certain time period.

Another lecturer commented:

> We have students on our undergraduate degree – students very often go into work experience in public relations firms and it's quite common for them to be invited in to do a couple of weeks or one or two days a week for a number of weeks through a term. How we advise them is 'that's fine, but know your limits and after a certain amount, agree how long this is going to go on for. If at the end of that time if they say, 'can you keep coming in?', difficult though it may be, you need to raise with them the question of on what basis are you wanting me to come back in and if you have any concerns, they should ask us and we will advise them.

Career advisers and lecturers noted that in times of economic downturn there appears to be an increase in the numbers of employers seeking volunteers in the universities. Two university lecturers commented on the volume of 'requests for students' made by local organisations: in 'peak times' as many as two or three a day.

Despite the concerns voiced about work experience quality and the possibilities of exploitation, most of our interviewees believed that 'this is how things are' and appeared implicitly to accept the thesis of employability which pushes them to do unpaid work. Two questions arise from these findings – firstly, why do students engage in a practice which they evaluate negatively, and regard as exploitative? Secondly, why do university staff promote the practice of unpaid work even though they appear to be aware of ethical concerns?

Discussion

The idea that students might engage in their own exploitation and consent to it resonates with Louis Althusser's thesis – they are the targets of a great deal of ideological practice of a neoliberal individualistic flavour, channelled by the University and many other institutions. It would be unsurprising were they not to accept up to a point that 'this is how things are' and to live with the paradox of the 'benefits of exploitative work'. Not only would some such colouring by neoliberal ideology be inherently likely, it would also be favoured by the dominant position of the discourse of employability in the labour market. Thus Haasler (2013: 241) has argued that although both the labour market and employers promote employability, the individual remains the key actor in 'making employability work'. The measure of people's employability is judged on an individual basis (Chertkovskaya et al. 2013), and this emphasis on individualism recurs in universities' approach to work experience. The various ways in which the university supports students as they search for work experience opportunities are informed by individualistic values. A sense of individualistic values informs the guidance students receive about what to expect and how to behave on work experience, and how to judge workplace situations and actions, including their own. I move to the territory of rational choice theory here (Homans 1961; Coleman 1973; Becker 1981) informed by a version of methodological individualism which holds that 'the elementary unit of social life is the individual human action' (Scott 2000: 127). Developed by Homans (1961) and further expanded by Coleman (1973) and Becker (1981) rational choice theory holds that all human action is fundamentally rational in character, and that self-interested individuals calculate the likely cost and benefit of any action. In other words, in light of rational choice theory, social institutions, such as cultural trends, economic patterns or social divisions, are a consequence of people's behaviour, and behaviour is the product of the independent decision making of free individuals. This methodological individualism (Scott 2000: 127) means that students are faced with certain hard choices and they are inclined to follow the path which appears to lead most efficiently to their chosen ends.

From the point of view of the university, however, taking refuge in rational choice explanations and promoting these values of individualism, i.e. assuming that this is what the students want, has an element of bad faith. The paradox of embedded agency (DiMaggio and Powell 1991; Friedland and Alford 1991) with its ori gins in Giddens' (1976) structuration theory, reminds us that actors are embedded in institutions and this embeddedness conditions their behaviours. This is particularly true of educational institutions in which individuals are most susceptible to indoctrination (Althusser 1971). It is incumbent on such institutions to consider the role they play in shaping students' subjectivities, while remaining open to the role of other larger social institutions, including those 'supply-side' institutions which collude with the desires of individuals to shape the discourse of employability itself: cf. Cremin's summation (2010: 146): 'Alienation is realised as an exchangeable value'.

In the Neo-liberal university model higher education assigns markets central social value and supports corporate competitiveness. It would be hard for the universities on this basis to deny the right of corporate employers to specify those qualities which they require in the graduates they will employ, at least in so far as these requirements make sense: and however contested the discourse of 'teamwork', 'enthusiasm', 'presentation' may seem, there is almost certainly a real demand in the corporate world for people who can be 'proactive when faced with ill-defined circumstances' (Sennett 2006: 51; quoted in Cremin 2010: 133). If the employer wants work experienced graduates, but the graduates want work experience even more, then the likelihood is that the market rate paid to graduate trainees will be very low. The universities' advocacy of student work experience provides an implied justification of the right of employers to demand that prospective graduate employees have relevant work experience, which in many cases is unpaid.

What Can Universities Do?

The question what to do with unpaid work experience as part of the university study is linked to the broader debate about the role of the universities (Kavanagh 2009), and academic capitalism (Slaughter and Leslie 2001). Whose interests do the universities serve, and whose language do they speak? The 'distinctive neoliberal interpretation of fairness' (Lynch 2006: 3) dominating our universities is based on the supremacy of the market and is evident in the universities' approach to work experience. The supremacy of the market, in this case the supremacy of the labour market, stands in stark contrast to traditionally espoused theories of the fairness and equality of opportunity.

The voices against unpaid work experience as an entry into employment have to be counterbalanced by a duty of care for people at the start of their careers. Removing the work experience element completely from the curriculum might be seen as pulling a rug from under people's feet and making it even more difficult for them to gain employment. Also, a debate about the perils of unpaid work experience should not cast doubt over the laudability of gift-giving such as volunteering for a good cause. Should this work be given as a free gift and should universities be the agent complicit in providing it? The concerns about student and graduate unpaid work are unlikely to disappear, and universities may come under increasing pressure to regulate work experience and acknowledge the financial implications that such work places on students. Arguably the introduction of pay for compulsory work experience would come some way to addressing the contested issues – more young people would probably be able to afford to take up relevant work opportunities and both the employers and those who engage in work would have some rights and some responsibilities. However this remains the prerogative of governments through appropriate legislation, not universities, and legislation regarding unpaid work varies from country to country. In some countries such as the US, unpaid labour of young people appears to be a commonly accepted practice, while in other countries, mainly in Western Europe, more is done to regulate it.

There is a moral issue for universities to consider in their approach to employability. Kavanagh (2009: 587) has plausibly argued that the university is expected to provide 'a normative narrative and a critical interpretation of the world', and through its material processes it is expected to provide the semiotic nexus to interpret what is worthy and valuable. However, such a special status is always precarious and in our times the university is increasingly colonised by corporate practices which may be more effective in subordinating the life of the mind than many dominant institutions in the past. To take an example pertinent to my context, media reports portray universities as employers offering unpaid on-campus placements to students and graduates, and thus legitimising the practice (Murray 2011). The universities rarely acknowledge that students not only work for free, but they sometimes pay for the benefit of working by covering their own expenses, accommodation and sometimes, as some newspapers report, by paying for the privilege of work (The Student 2011).

So what can be done? Althusser's analysis of ideology may at least suggest an answer. Althusser argued that the ideological state apparatuses are not only the fundamental means of transmitting the dominant ideology – they are also a site in which oppositional ideology can be articulated: 'The resistance of the exploited classes is able to find means and occasion to express itself there, either by the utilisation of their contradictions, or by conquering combat positions in them in the struggle' (Althusser 1971: 140). There is some plausibility in this: after all, these are ideological apparatuses, they are not just repressive machines; ideas have to be voiced there, and in principle it is also possible to controvert and question them. By simply discussing the issues, by raising awareness about the dark side of the practice of unpaid work, the universities may expose to critical interpretation the employers' motives and bring students to an awareness and an enlightened concern for their citizen rights and responsibilities. Currently the discussion about the ethical and legal concerns behind the practice of unpaid work experience is conspicuously absent from the higher education discourse, and by not discussing these issues the university gives unpaid work a 'seal of approval'. Echoing Lynch's (2006) call, I argue that universities should challenge the prevailing orthodoxy of employability on employer terms, and offer an alternative narrative of employability – starting, but not finishing, with a collective understanding that working for no reward is a mark of exploitation – not just in the technical language of Marxian economics.

References

Althusser, L. (1971). Ideology and ideological state apparatuses. In *Lenin and philosophy, and other essays* (B. Brewster, Trans.). London: New Left Books.

Auburn, T. (2007). Identity and placement learning: Student accounts of the transition back to university following a placement year. *Studies in Higher Education, 32*(1), 117–133.

BBC. (2012). *HMRC minister David Gauke defends unpaid internship.* 20th March http://www.bbc.co.uk/news/uk-politics-17443200

Beaumont, E., & Gedye, S. (2016). 'Am I employable?' Understanding students' employability confidence and their perceived barriers to gaining employment. *Journal of Hospitality, Leisure, Sport & Tourism Education, 19*, 1–9.

Becker, G. (1981). *A treatise on the family.* Cambridge, MA: Harvard University Press.

Bloom, P. (2013). Fight for alienation: The fantasy of employability and the ironic struggle for self-exploitation. *Ephemera, 13*(4), 785–807.

Boltanski, L., & Chiapello, E. (2007). *The new spirit of capitalism.* London: Verso.

Chartered Institute of Personnel and Development. (2010). *Internships that work: A guide for employers.* London: CIPD.

Chen, T., Shen, C., & Gosling, M. (2018). Does employability increase with internship satisfaction? Enhanced employability and internship satisfaction in a hospitality program. *Journal of Hospitality, Leisure, Sport & Tourism Education, 22*, 88–99.

Chertkovskaya, E., Watt, P., Tramer, S., & Spoelstra, S. (2013). Giving notice to employability. *Ephemera, 13*(4), 701–716.

Clarke, M., & Patrickson, M. (2008). The new covenant of employability. *Employee Relations, 30*(2), 121–141.

Coleman, J. [1973] (2007). *Mathematics of collective action.* New Jersey: Transaction Publishing.

Cremin, C. (2010). Never employable enough: The (im)possibility of satisfying the boss's desire. *The Organ, 17*(2), 131–149.

DiMaggio, P. J., & Powell, W. W. (1991). Introduction. In W. W. Powell & P. J. DiMaggio (Eds.), *The new institutionalism in organisational analysis* (pp. 1–38). Chicago: University of Chicago Press.

Fejes, A. (2010). Discourses on employability: Constituting responsible citizen. *Studies in Continuing Education, 32*(2), 89–1-2.

Feretter, L. (2006). *Louis Althusser.* London: Routledge.

Friedland, R., & Alford, R. R. (1991). Bringing society back in: Symbols, practices, and institutional contradictions. In W. W. Powell & P. J. DiMaggio (Eds.), *The new institutionalism in organisational analysis* (pp. 2320–2363). Chicago: University of Chicago Press.

Garsten, C., & Jacobsson, K. (2004). Learning to be employable: An introduction. In C. Garsten & K. Jacobsson (Eds.), *Learning to be employable: New agendas on work, employability and learning in a globalizing world.* Basingstoke: Palgrave Macmillan.

Giddens, A. (1976). *New rules of sociological method.* London: Hutchinson.

Guardian. (2012). *Employment campaigners win pay settlements for interns.* Saturday October 20th.

Haasler, S. R. (2013). Employability skills and the notion of the 'self'. *International Journal of Training and Development, 17*(3), 233–243.

Homans, G. (1961). *Social behaviour: Its elementary forms.* Oxford: Harcourt, Brace.

Kavanagh, D. (2009). Institutional heterogeneity and change: The University as a fool. *The Organ, 16*(4), 575–595.

Larner, W., & Le Heron, R. (2005). Neo-liberalizing spaces and subjectivities: Reinventing New Zealand universities. *The Organ, 12*(6), 843–862.

Lawton, K., & Potter, D. (2010). *Why interns need a fair wage?* Institute for Public Policy Research http://www.ippr.org/publicationsandreports/publication.asp?id=765. Accessed 11 Apr 2012.

Lynch, K. (2006). Neo-liberalism and marketisation: The implications for higher education. *European Educational Journal, 5*(1), 1–17.

Moreau, M. P., & Leathwood, C. (2006). Graduates' employment and the discourse of employability: A critical analysis. *Journal of Education and Work, 19*(4), 305–324.

Murray, J. (2011). The 1994 group of universities advertises for graduate volunteers. *The Guardian.* September 21.

Pinto, L. H., & Ramalheira, D. C. (2017). Perceived employability of business graduates: The effect of academic performance and extracurricular activities. *Journal of Vocational Behavior, 99*, 165–178.

Prichard, C. (2012). Introduction: What are we to do with higher education? *The Organ, 19*(6), 879–880.

Prichard, C., & Wilmott, H. (1997). Just how managed is the McUniversity? *Organisation Studies, 18*, 287–316.

Qureshi, A., Wall, H., Humphries, J., & Bahrami, A. B. (2016). Can personality traits modulate student engagement with learning and their attitude to employability? *Learning and Individual Differences, 51*, 349–358.

Ritzer, G. (2005). *Encyclopedia of social theory.* London: Sage.

Scott, J. (2000). Rational choice theory. In G. Browning, A. Halcli, & F. Webster (Eds.), *Understanding contemporary society: Theories of the present.* London: SAGE.

Sennett, R. (2006). *The culture of the new capitalism.* New Haven: Yale UP.

Siebert, S., & Wilson, F. (2013). All work and no pay, consequences of unpaid work experience in the creative industries. *Work, Employment and Society, 27*(4), 711–721.

Slaughter, S., & Leslie, L. L. (2001). Expanding and elaborating the concept of academic capitalism. *The Organ, 8*(2), 154–161.

Standing, G. (2011). *The precariat: The new dangerous class.* London: Bloomsbury Academic.

Taylor, P. (2013). Putting theory to work – a.k.a. 'if you don't like academia, why don't you leave? *Ephemera, 13*(4), 851–860.

The Student. (2011). *University cashes in on internships.* 15 May, http://www.studentnewspaper.org/news/654-university-cashes-in-on-internships. Accessed 11 Apr 2012

Chapter 10
Values and the International Collaborative Research in Higher Education: Negotiating Epistemic Power Between the Global South and the Global North

Carolina Guzmán-Valenzuela

Abstract In this chapter, collaboration in the construction of knowledge in higher education between academics located in the North and in the South as part of internationalisation processes in universities is critically examined. By analysing patterns of publication of papers in journals in higher education in Latin America, attention is paid to the geopolitics of the production of knowledge. This chapter is focused especially on problematizing and deconstructing international collaboration. It also explores the weight of different cultural contexts, language issues, power relationships and values in shaping such collaboration. The chapter suggests that international academic collaboration and the construction of knowledge in the social sciences require spaces to think critically. The chapter ends by offering some ideas to promote new ways to re-shape international collaboration in the academia.

> Today, one does not have to be a postmodernist, relativist, or deconstructionist (key words in the culture wars of the Western academic world) to admit that political subjects are not mechanical products of their objective circumstances, that the link between events significantly separated in space and proximate in time is often hard to explain, that the kinds of comparison of social units that relied on their empirical separability cannot be secure, and that the more marginal regions of the world are not simply producers of data for the theory mills of the North. (Appadurai 2000: 4)

C. Guzmán-Valenzuela (✉)
Institute of Education and Centre for Advanced Research in Education, University of Chile, Santiago, Chile
e-mail: carolina.guzman@ciae.uchile.cl

© Springer Nature Switzerland AG 2019

P. Gibbs et al. (eds.), *Values of the University in a Time of Uncertainty*,
https://doi.org/10.1007/978-3-030-15970-2_10

Introduction

The terms 'collaboration' and 'partnership' usually have a positive connotation and are valued in educational settings and beyond (for example, within enterprises, diplomatic relationships, social programmes and so on). Through a collaborative and joint effort, individuals, groups, organisations and countries work together to pursue a shared goal.

However, in practice, social interactions involve uneasy relationships of power. This is particularly evident in academic research collaboration in a context of competition for financial resources and prestige where asymmetrical relationships come into play. Such asymmetry in research collaboration becomes even more critical when academics and universities from both industrialised and non-industrialised countries participate and share resources (of all kind) and aims.

This chapter tackles the pressures under which universities and their academics operate in relation to academic productivity, internationalisation and prestige so as to emulate the so called 'world-class universities'. A world class university is a university recognised on the basis of international reputation (Salmi 2009) and which works under standards of excellence especially in research terms (Altbach 2004). Specifically, the chapter critically examines one of the dimensions used to measure international reputation, that of research collaboration. In particular, it focuses on research partnerships in higher education established between academics from countries with well-advanced economies and academics from Latin America.

Firstly, the very concept of academic collaboration as a value in higher education is placed under examination. Secondly, the chapter revolves around the policies and institutional mechanisms that universities put into practice to promote processes of internationalisation so as to secure a position in international rankings. Thirdly, an examination of academic research collaboration is offered, deploying a geopolitical perspective. Fourthly, and to assist this analysis, the patterns in collaboration through publication in journals between academics located in the Latin American region and in countries in Europe and USA (mainly) are identified and examined. The chapter ends by offering insights and critical reflections about how to build new conceptualisations about research collaboration between the Global North and the Global South.

What Is Academic Collaboration and Partnership?

According to the Cambridge English Dictionary, collaboration involves a situation in which two or more people work together 'to create or achieve the same thing' (Cambridge Dictionary). Similarly, the concept of 'partnership' is defined as a 'relationship in which two or more people, organisations or countries work together as partners' (Collins Dictionary). 'The term "partnership" contains strong personal connotations and implies a form of social interaction that is supposed to entail a considerable degree of equality, mutual trust, shared vision, and mutual benefit among the different entities involved' (Obamba and Mwema 2009: 355).

In academia – as in other professional settings – processes of collaboration and partnership are valued since they make it possible to create new ideas, approaches and strategies in teaching, research and service that would not be possible to achieve individually. Through collaboration, academics pursue disciplinary and interdisciplinarity interests, combine efforts and engage in joint activities and discussions to reach their common goals. Departments and units in tertiary education usually promote collaboration and partnerships among colleagues within their own institutions, with external tertiary education institutions (locally, nationally and internationally) and beyond. Forming and extending partnerships, therefore, is not only an intrinsic value within an institution but also it has become a value promoted extrinsically. In the case of research collaboration, the formation of research networks plays an important role in pursuing the internationalisation of universities.

Particularly, through research, academic partnerships allow the creation of new knowledges and strategies to generate those knowledges.[1] This is what Knorr Cetina (2009: 1) called 'epistemic cultures', through which scientists with a common interest in a given field develop what is known and how it is known. In epistemic cultures, the formation of partnerships and collaboration has 'become ubiquitous, embedded in organisational cultures… Research partnerships can promote knowledge production and sharing; stimulate the pooling of financial and high level human resources across boundaries; and create synergies and complementarities among the diverse participants for mutual benefit' (Obamba and Mwema 2009: 349). Research collaboration also offers economic value that can be measured by indicators such as the Business Expenditure on Research and Development (BERD) proposed by the OECD. Research collaboration, therefore, is an activity highly valued by governments and universities since it allows the production of epistemic, social and economic goods, among others.

However, research collaboration in academia is far from being unproblematic. It involves asymmetrical relationships based on power of certain individuals, groups, institutions or countries over others. An imbalance of power in a relationship means that one of the parts of the collaboration enterprise dominates the interaction so as to obtain benefit to the detriment of the other part. This is particularly evident when collaboration involves countries and institutions from both industrialised and non-industrialised countries in terms of shared goals, financing and roles.

Internationalisation, Rankings and Global Cooperation: A Sword of Damocles?

The legend says that with great fortune and power comes also great danger. Collaboration and the formation of international partnerships in academia can be seen as positive actions that help to enhance creativity and promote new alliances in

---

[1] 'Knowledges' is used here following the concept of 'ecology of knowledges' (Santos 2014) in which each knowledge operates in specific contexts and is embedded in local practices.

the creation of knowledge. However, an examination of the drivers promoting international collaboration among academics and their institutions – such as international rankings, internationalisation and global policies of cooperation – is needed.

In an era when public funding of universities is scarce, the role of the state consists of regulating an educational market and where both competition for resources and prestige have become pivotal, the aspiration to become present in university league tables promoted by international rankings has gained traction (Hazelkorn 2017; Pusser and Marginson 2013). Prestige and reputation are valued assets and become a source of power and influence, which attract income in a global market (Marginson and Ordorika 2011; de Witt 2011). Well-known international rankings have become powerful tools to measure the extent to which universities are international institutions. 'Rankings have positioned themselves as a new form of gatekeeper for higher education, determining whom and what are valued, and to what degree' (Ordorika and Lloyd 2015: 4).

In order to respond to the demand imposed by international rankings, higher education systems across the globe have been developing policies and strategies to pursue internationalisation (Barnett 2016; Blessinger and Anchan 2015). According to Barnett 'each university (across the world) is now obliged to consider to what extent and in which ways it might became international' (2016: 51). Universities around the world – especially the most prestigious one – have been implementing a series of trans-national, national and institutional strategies to demonstrate how international they are, and, at the same time, to gain prestige and income. These strategies include the creation of international campuses; the promotion of on-line programmes that attract students from all around the world – and who can afford them; preferential access for, and enrolment of, wealthy international students – who usually pay double or treble the costs of local students; faculty mobility programmes (Qiang 2003); the recruitment of outstanding academics from around the world (Bennion and Locke 2010); and the promotion of international research networks (for example, within Europe or among regions) and research collaboration, among others.

In particular, international rankings give special weight to indicators such as academic productivity and research income. The latter has had a decisive impact on universities and academics who have organised their tasks and functions around these two indicators. As a result, the task of teaching has, to some extent, been relegated and labelled as a second-class activity while the research task is over-valued (Barnett 2005). In this context, obtaining competitive international research grants and publishing in well-regarded journals are paramount in addressing the demand in becoming international institutions.

In Chile, the National Funding Body (CONICYT) has implemented a series of strategies to promote and fund international research collaboration in academia with the expectation that such collaboration will improve research outcomes through the publication of papers in indexed journals. For CONICYT, collaboration is a matter of being strategic to produce more impact. CONICYT explicitly encourages and places a high value on the collaboration of Chilean scholars with partners in prestigious universities around the world (CONICYT 2015), and specifically CONICYT looks towards collaboration with countries such as the USA, Australia, Spain, Germany, France and the UK. This Chilean policy has borne fruit, with Chile occupying third place among OECD countries in terms of number of publications produced in collaboration with colleagues at an international institution (CONICYT 2015). Chile is not an isolated case. Universities and their academics around the world are under continuous pressure to obtain research income and gain international visibility through publication as a way to position themselves in an international conversation (Marginson 2016).

Additionally, global agencies such as the OECD and the World Bank have been orchestrating a series of initiatives to promote cooperation between industrialised and non-industrialised countries (OECD 2014; World Bank 2013). These initiatives have been shaping the type of research collaboration among universities across different regions of the world that differ in their economic development. In this context:

> partnership is increasingly an unavoidable conditionality for northern researchers or development practitioners wanting to conduct research or provide development assistance within the borders of developing countries. A large and growing number of northern governments and other bilateral donor agencies that provide funding for international development assistance and scientific research have made it a standard requirement for northern researchers to look for "partners" in the … South. (Obamba and Mwema 2009: 358)

The establishment of unequal partnerships between wealthy countries and poor countries have been established where both parties experience financial pressures (King 2008). As a result, relationships of mutual need and dependency have been promoted. This type of research collaboration necessarily involves 'varying configurations of power and resource flow asymmetries and geopolitics by promoting benevolent ventures designed to assist weak southern researchers' (Obamba and Mwema 2009: 349–366).

In this context, the very nature of collaboration among scholars and institutions belonging to regions with different degrees of industrialisation, the type of knowledge produced in the light of schemes of collaboration and the value attached to that knowledge deserve more attention and critical examination.

Research Collaboration and the Role of Universities from a Geopolitical Perspective

The geopolitical distinction between the Global North and the Global South refers to a differentiation of regions and countries in geographical and historical terms (Connell 2007) as well as in financial, educational, political and social terms. Countries in the Global North – such as the USA, Canada, Europe, Australia and New Zealand or what used to be called 'the first world' - usually disproportionately control global resources. In contrast, the Global South includes emerging-economy countries in Africa, Asia and Latin America which used to be called 'third world' and which are home to the majority of natural resources and population (Boggs 2016). Well-developed countries enjoy political and economic stability while countries with emerging economies are characterised for having fragile economies, political instability and a high proportion of their peoples in poverty. Historically, culturally and politically, most countries in the Global South were colonised by countries in Europe for centuries which meant the imposition of political, religious, language and cultural visions from countries in the Global North over countries in the Global South.[2]

The Global North/South distinction can also be explored in epistemic terms. Knowledge produced in the Global North tends to have primacy over knowledge produced in the Global South (Santos 2014, 2010; Connell 2007). Such a relationship is not only hierarchical but also interdependent. Santos coined the concept of 'abyssal thinking' which 'consists of a system of visible and invisible distinctions, the invisible ones being the foundation of the visible ones' (Santos 2014: 118). As a result of abyssal thinking, value is given to certain knowledge – that produced in the Global North – while knowledge produced in the Global South lacks value.

Similarly, in her book 'Southern theories', Connell analyses the ways in which countries in the North – what she called the 'metropole' – colonised the countries in the South – called 'peripheral countries'. The imposition of ways of thinking about the world and producing knowledge has been a result of the colonisation. In so doing, the North has used the South as a source to conduct experiments, and collect data and produce knowledge that is useful for its purposes (Connell 2007), so transforming the countries of the South into producers of data 'for the theory mills of the North' (Appadurai 2000: 4). Later on, the knowledge produced in the North is transferred to countries in the South to address local problems. However, according to Connell, the transference of knowledge from the North to the South fails to acknowledge the cultural and ethnic specificities of the southern countries.

The Global North/South distinction and the role of universities in epistemic, social and cultural terms and in the construction of knowledge are also relevant here. The very idea of the western university was born in Europe to respond to certain demands and challenges in the medieval period. The creation of the western university – with variants in England, Germany and France – has been shaping ideas about what a university is and how it should interact with the society over the years (Barnett 1994). The western university has also been systematically thought of as the predominant place where scientific knowledge is created (especially since the Enlightenment) although, currently, this idea may be in dispute and some claim that the university is only one of the places where knowledge is produced.

---

[2] The cases of Australia and New Zealand are interesting. Geographically, both are situated in the south and experienced process of colonization and the imposition of political, cultural and social values by colonisers. As such, for some authors, Australia and New Zealand are countries of the south. In this chapter, though, these countries are considered as being part of the Global North in terms of their wealth and the positions their universities occupy in the international rankings.

The idea of the European western university was imported into the regions of Africa and Latin America during processes of colonisation over the years, and through this importation, industrialised countries have been maintaining their domination over non-industrialised countries. In this respect, Altbach and Kelly (1978) offer a range of types of colonialism affecting education in the colonies. They point out that, during colonialism and after securing the land in the new world in the Americas, educational institutions were created to support the power exercised by the colonisers rather than to respond to the needs of the local population which were considered to be second-class citizens.

Currently, neo-colonialism is a perpetuation of that past of colonisation. This is particularly evident in educational institutions such as the universities which has given way to what Raju (2011) 'academic imperialism', that is, a dominance of a western model of the university which is specially focused on prestige gained through research and competition. Neo-colonialism entitles an epistemic domination that has remained unproblematised. It is a colonialism that has outlived colonialism, exhibiting continuing inter-dependency relationships:

> Nations involved in neo-colonial relationships have formally become independent, but as they continue to depend strongly on the support of the industrialised nations, the notion of independence is an illusion… Educational institutions located in the developing countries… are strongly dependent on the institutions located in the well-known academic centers. The reason for the maintenance of this link is very much related to the technological development of the centers, their advanced techniques and higher education performance. (Canto and Hannah 2001: 29)

In this context, a need for international collaboration to obtain research income, produce research outcomes and gain prestige has also permeated the Global South. Universities in the Global South are, though, in a fragile position to take on this role. By attempting to adopt a model of the world-class university, universities in the Global South give up to their identities and continuously look toward the Global North while, at the same time, universities in the Global North perpetrate and reinforce their supremacy over the rest.

In exploring processes of research and epistemic dependency in academia, in a recent chapter (Guzmán-Valenzuela and Muñoz-García 2018), a colleague and myself analyzed the patterns of international research collaboration between academics in Chile and academics at universities in wealthy countries, and pointing out that research collaboration among advanced-economy countries might be different from those between advanced and emerging countries. In that chapter, we referred to hegemonic and asymmetrical relationships between developing and industrialised countries. We paid special attention to the ways in which research agencies in Chile follow patterns dictated by international agencies such as the World Bank and the OECD which have imposed ways of collaborating mainly with academics at universities in the Global North. We critically reflected on these issues and the ways in which models imported from the Global North restrain academic freedom. We invited 'a rethink about the relationships between knowledge, collaboration, power and geography' (Guzmán-Valenzuela and Muñoz-García 2018: 184) and this chapter follows that suggestion.

Paper Publications in Higher Education Studies in Latin America: Empirical Study

So far, in this chapter, issues of academic research collaboration, the drivers underpinning a call for international research collaboration and the geopolitics in international research partnerships have been addressed. In examining such processes, in this section, attention is given to the patterns of publication in journals in higher education studies involving international collaboration between scholars in the Global North and in Latin America. Previous and detailed analyses of patterns of publications in higher education studies in Latin America were published recently (Guzmán-Valenzuela and Gómez 2018; Guzmán-Valenzuela 2017a, b). However, in this chapter, international collaboration in publications in higher education studies receives a special examination.

Papers in higher education indexed in Web of Science (WoS), SCOPUS and the Scientific Electronic Library Online (SciELO) were identified. WoS is a well-recognised database that includes the references of the main scientific publications of any discipline of knowledge. It is composed of its prestigious 'core collection' journals in sciences, social sciences, art and humanities and other indexes such as the Emerging Source Citation Index. It is managed by Clarivate Analytics, an independent and commercial company with branches in different countries in the Global North. SCOPUS is also a well-known index of citations across publications on similar research topics as the WoS which are published in journals and conference proceedings. It is especially present in Europe, Asia and Africa although it is also present in the USA and Latin America (Aghaei et al. 2013). WoS and SCOPUS are considered to be the most prestigious journals indexes (Vessuri et al. 2014: 656). In turn, SciELO is a leading index for emerging economies such as Latin America and Africa, and was created in Brazil. In 2013, SciELO was included in the WoS database although it is not part of its 'core collection'. SciELO works under a non-commercial policy of open access (Fischman et al. 2010).

Several searches were conducted in the WoS index core collection, SCOPUS and SciELO using similar keywords and categories. All of them addressed issues of higher education and were written by at least one scholar affiliated to a Latin American university. A total of 130 papers in the WoS core collection, 844 papers in SCOPUS and 1240 papers in SciELO published between 2000 and 2015 were identified.

The main results regarding patterns of collaboration are the following:

(a) *Papers published in higher education studies in Latin America*

Figure 10.1 shows a steady increase in the number of published papers with a remarkable production in SCOPUS and SciELO.

The fact that most of the papers were published in SCOPUS and SCiELO may be explained by language issues. Spanish and Portuguese are the two main languages spoken in Latin America and most SciELO journals are published in both Portuguese and Spanish while there are a good number of SCOPUS journals in both Portuguese and Spanish. In turn, most journals in the WoS index are published in

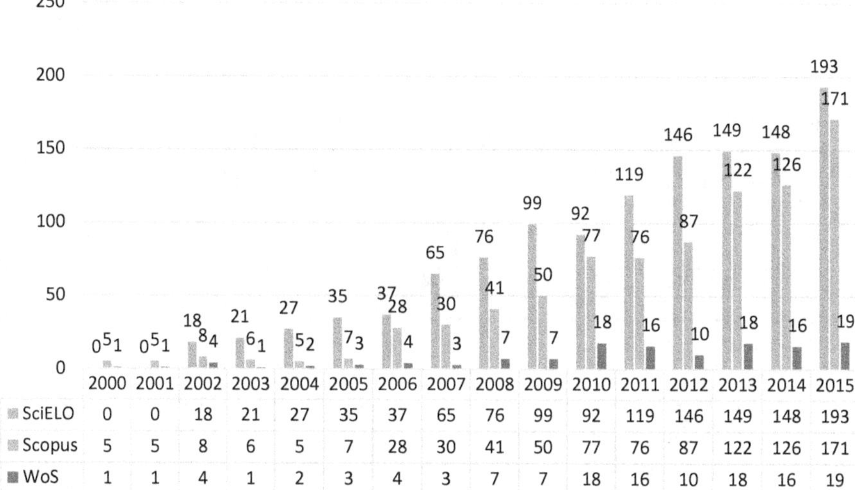

	2000	2001	2002	2003	2004	2005	2006	2007	2008	2009	2010	2011	2012	2013	2014	2015
SciELO	0	0	18	21	27	35	37	65	76	99	92	119	146	149	148	193
Scopus	5	5	8	6	5	7	28	30	41	50	77	76	87	122	126	171
WoS	1	1	4	1	2	3	4	3	7	7	18	16	10	18	16	19

Fig. 10.1 Number of papers in higher education studies in the WoS, SCOPUS and SciELO indexes

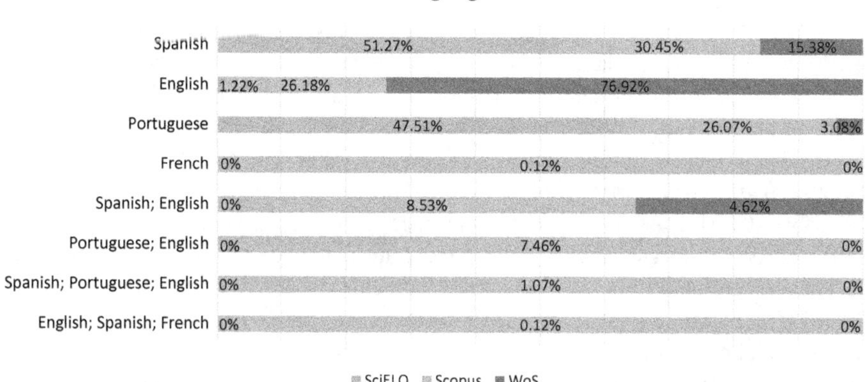

Fig. 10.2 Percentage of papers published in the WoS, SCOPUS and SciELO indexes according to languages

English and so researchers in Latin America tend to be at a disadvantage. Figure 10.2 supports this point and shows the percentages of papers published in each index according to languages.

In Fig. 10.2, it is observed that most of the publications in SciELO are in Spanish (51%) and Portuguese (47.5%) while in WoS most of publications are in English (76%). SCOPUS shows a more balanced production in terms of language (Spanish: 20.4; English and Portuguese: 26% each).

Table 10.1 Percentage and numbers of international paper collaboration in journals indexed in WoS core collection, SCOPUS, and SciELO between 2000 and 2015

	SciELO		Scopus		WoS	
	f	%	f	%	f	%
With international collaboration	85	6.94%	147	17.42%	50	38.46%
Without international collaboration	1140	93.06%	697	82.58%	80	61.54%
TOTAL PUBLICATIONS	1225		844		130	

Source: Author

A second possible and complementary explanation for this trend is the fact that publications in the social sciences and humanities – where higher education is anchored – typically use local languages to address local issues. The latter is different in hard sciences where the use of English is more common (Marginson 2016).

(b) *International collaboration in paper publications*

International collaboration is defined here as the extent to which Latin American scholars in higher education studies published with scholars from countries other than those in Latin America.

Table 10.1 shows the percentage of papers in higher education studies published by Latin American scholars with scholars outside their own countries. In this figure, it is observed that international collaboration is not high across all three indexes although it tends to be higher in WoS journals (38.4%, 50 papers).

In disaggregating international collaboration within and outside Latin America, another pattern can be observed (see Table 10.2).

Table 10.2 shows that a significant number (46 +1 paper with authors both within and outside Latin America) of WoS papers are produced by Latin American academics in collaboration with academics outside Latin America. In the case of SCOPUS, the number is higher (128 + 6). And, although – as seen above – international collaboration is rather low in SciELO papers, when it takes place, there is a marked tendency to collaborate with academics from outside Latin America (59+2) rather than within Latin America (24). Overall, Latin American academics tend not to publish with researchers within their own region. This phenomenon is noteworthy since, at least within SciELO papers, one might have expected more collaboration among academics within the Latin American region.

Having a further look to international collaboration across all three indexes with colleagues in countries outside Latin America, it is observed that:

– For WoS journals (see Table 10.3), most of the collaboration occurs with scholars in Europe (Spain and the UK) and the USA, followed by collaboration with academics in Portugal, Australia and Canada.

Table 10.2 International collaboration within and outside Latin America of papers indexed in WoS core collection, SCOPUS and SciELO (period 2000–2015)

	SciELO		Scopus		WoS	
	f	%	*f*	%	*f*	%
Collaboration breakdown	*f*	% (of total publications)	*f*	% (of total publications)	*f*	% (of total publications)
Outside LA	59	4.82%	128	15.17%	46	35.38%
Within LA	24	1.96%	13	1.54%	3	2.31%
Overlap *(both within and outside LA)*	2	0.16%	6	0.71%	1	0.77%

Source: Author

Table 10.3 Co-authorship of Latin American scholars in WoS papers jointly with colleagues from outside LA

WoS		%
Spain	16	30.8%
USA	16	30.8%
UK	7	13.5%
Portugal	4	7.7%
Australia	3	5.8%

– For SCOPUS journals (see Table 10.4), as in WoS journals, most of the collaboration takes place with colleagues in Spain, the US and the UK, followed by Canada, Portugal and Germany. Another pattern here, is that there is a wider range of countries with which Latin American scholars collaborate, including countries in Africa and Asia.

– For SciELO journals (see Table 10.5), Spain and Portugal lead international collaboration followed by the USA, the UK, France and Germany

These numbers and percentages across all three indexes are revealing since they show that Latin American scholars in higher education studies form publication partnerships with colleagues from countries in the Global North, and especially, Spain, the US and the UK.

Finally, when examining the leading authors of papers in which there was international collaboration, it is observed that out of 46+1 papers, most (26 papers) are led by authors from outside Latin America (see Fig. 10.3). Interestingly, most of these leading authors are from both the US (11 papers) and Spain (7 papers).

Table 10.4 Co-authorship of Latin American scholars in SCOPUS papers jointly with colleagues from outside LA

Scopus		%
Spain	55	34.0%
USA	29	17.9%
UK	21	13.0%
Canada	11	6.8%
Portugal	11	6.8%
Germany	5	3.1%

Table 10.5 Co-authorship of Latin American scholars in SciELO papers jointly with colleagues from outside LA

SciELO		%
Spain	27	43.5%
Portugal	16	25.8%
USA	9	14.5%
UK	2	3.2%
France	2	3.2%
Germany	2	3.2%

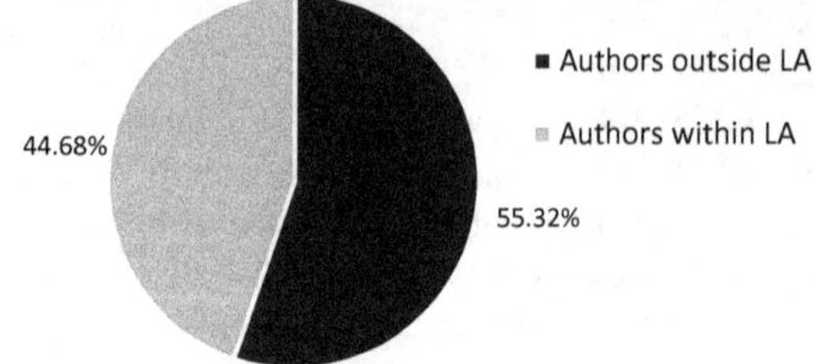

Fig. 10.3 Leading authors in WoS papers co-published by both Latin American authors and scholars from outside Latin America

To sum up:

(a) Papers in higher education studies in Latin America have been increasing in number. This is particularly evident in journals indexed in SCOPUS and SciELO although papers in WoS have also increased in numbers in recent years (Fig. 10.1).

(b) Most of the papers are published in both Spanish and Portuguese (Fig. 10.2). This is due to the fact that these two languages are vernacular languages in the region. SCOPUS and SciELO have a higher number of papers published in Spanish and Portugal unlike WoS journals which are mainly published in English.

(c) International collaboration in publications in higher education studies is rather low (Table 10.1).
(d) International collaboration with colleagues within and outside Latin America is rather low but tends to be higher for WoS papers.
(e) Although international publication is rather limited across all three indexes, when publishing in major journals – such as those in the WoS core collection – Latin American scholars prefer to co-publish with academics in the Global North (Tables 10.3, 10.4, and 10.5).
(f) In the case of WoS papers with collaboration outside Latin America, most of the leading authors are from the Global North (Fig. 10.3).

Hidden Patterns of Dominance in North-South Research Collaboration

Although international research collaboration and co-publication might be seen as an absolute value, this chapter offers an invitation to interrogate it. While objective indicators can be proposed so as to measure international research collaboration in terms of economic value or academic production, the very process of collaboration involves a clash of worlds with cultural visions, interests, values and knowledges in conflict. In the section above, through the examination of international publication patterns in higher education studies, we have seen that collaboration involves power relationships that put Latin American scholars and universities in a conflictual position which are not always explicit or evident. Indeed, in the academic world, the binomial relationship of dominant/dominated underpins international patterns of publication.

In the case of academic journals, that the most prestigious journals are managed by commercial and transnational companies located in the Global North and that most are published in English presents challenges to universities and academics not only in Latin America but also in non-English-speaking countries. In the experience of many Latin American colleagues, especially in the social sciences and in the humanities, it is not easy to express and write in a different language than their own. However, publications in English in well-regarded journals have become a strong desideratum for many of these academics not only because they need to maintain their university positions and demonstrate their productivity but also in order to be part of a 'single global conversation' in science (Marginson 2016: 19) that may bring them international recognition in their field.

In the process of joining this single conversation in English, many academics strategically use theories produced in the Global North to address problems that not always echo local needs in their countries but rather emulate research problems identified in the Global North to get their papers published (Guzmán-Valenzuela 2017a; Guzmán-Valenzuela and Gómez 2018). As a way of balancing the tension between publishing in English and addressing problems and publishing either in

Spanish or Portuguese to address local issues, some Latin American scholars have strategically opted for publishing in both local-southern journals and northern prestigious journals (Guzmán-Valenzuela and Gómez 2018). However, this tension is far from being resolved for many academics since a strategic pattern of publication requires academic capital acquired in the Global North and in English – for example, through obtaining a PhD degree in universities in countries in the Global North, or by initiating and keeping international networks with academics from those countries that facilitate joint research. Such academic capital, though, is within the reach of few universities and academics in Latin America. Even if such academic capital is within reach, academics might find themselves 'oscillating between strategy and identity, knowing that by position-taking on [the terms imposed by the global knowledge system] they are complicit in the very mechanisms that place them at a permanent disadvantage' (Marginson and Ordorika 2011: 94).

Another challenge in dealing with patterns of dominance in the world of publication in high-ranked journals faced by many in higher education in Latin America has to do with scholars' expectations of positioning local problems – which present in their own countries – in an international debate in such a way that might be useful for other countries or advance knowledge in the field. To do so, Latin American academics may try to position their analyses of local problems so as to understand global trends affecting other universities around the world. However, academic papers submitted by Latin American scholars may all too readily be rejected for being too parochial and for not tackling what some editors call 'international problems'. The use of quotation marks – 'international problems' – is deliberate here since it seems that international problems are just those affecting the countries in the Global North.

These are just a few examples to illustrate the hidden patterns of dominance of the Global North over the Global South and the tensions experienced by Latin American academics when publishing in well-regarded journals. Probably academic readers from Latin America and South Africa can find many more. What is more, researchers from southern countries in Europe (such as Spain, Portugal or Italy) might find similar challenges and tensions in their attempt to become visible and be valued in an international single conversation dominated by Anglo-Saxon countries or northern Europe.

Moving Beyond: Is There a Future for International Research Collaboration Between the Global North and the Global South?

There is present a global conflict in epistemic value, with different sets of epistemic value operation in the Global North (reputation, competition and 'world-classness') on the one hand, and the Global South (locality and societal contribution), on the other hand. As a result, there are many geopolitical barriers in research collaboration that are imposed upon academics in countries in the Global South, especially in the social sciences and humanities.

However, aside from interrogating and questioning the ways in which international research collaboration takes place in relation to academics and universities from the Global North and the Global South, it seems productive to envisage new and imaginative ways to put into practice a type of collaboration that takes into account the richness that can be provided from both zones.

Appadurai wonders about the possibility to democratize research in a context of globalisation in which 'certain dominant forms of critical knowledge… have come to be organised by the social sciences in the West' (Appadurai 2000: 4). Aligned with Appadurai's question and following Drake et al. (2000) and Obamba and Mwema (2009), it is proposed here that a first step in the democratisation of collaborative research and the construction of knowledge may consist of creating a common space of collaboration in which shared vocabularies, concepts and theories come together so as to value ways of thinking from different places and experiences. This provides spaces for both consensus and dissensus in academia that allows the interrogation of hegemonic knowledge (Guzmán-Valenzuela and Muñoz-García 2018) and promotes and values a multiplicity of knowledges. In this new space of democratised collaboration, values such as democracy, opening to dialogue, empathy tolerance and respect are pivotal.

A second step consists of giving weight to the need 'of building research capacity within collaborating institutions in the South' (Obamba and Mwema 2009: 366) so as to promote and consolidate them. This needs a political will within southern countries, the implementation of planned national research policies and joint transnational efforts among them. Also, policies promoting collaboration among research institutions within the Global South by global organisations such as the OECD, UNESCO and the World Bank are also key here. In building a research capacity within the Global South, the value of recognising local capacities and strengths in the construction of knowledge that is useful and meaningful for the Global South is enhanced.

These two steps will help and shape new ways of research collaboration between the Global North and the Global South so as to obtain mutual benefit. Nations, global organisations, higher education systems and academics from both parts of the world have a responsibility in promoting these new ways of valuing knowledge and putting into practice research collaboration.

References

Aghaei Chadegani, A., Salehi, H., Yunus, M., Farhadi, H., Fooladi, M., Farhadi, M., & Ale Ebrahim, N. (2013). A comparison between two main academic literature collections: Web of science and scopus databases. *Asian Social Science, 9*, 18–26.

Altbach, P. G. (2004). The costs and benefits of world-class universities. *Academe, 90*(1), 20.

Altbach, P. G., & Kelly, G. P. (1978). *Education and colonialism.* New York: Logman.

Appadurai, A. (2000). Grassroots globalisation and the research imagination. *Public Culture, 12*(1), 1–19.

Barnett, R. (1994). *The limits of competence: Knowledge, higher education and society.* Buckingham: Society for Research into Higher Education & Open University Press.

Barnett, R. (2005). *Reshaping the university: New relationships between research, scholarship and teaching*. Berkshire: McGraw-Hill Education.

Barnett, R. (2016). *Understanding the university. Institution, idea possibilities*. Abingdon/New York: Routledge.

Bennion, A., & Locke, W. (2010). The early career paths and employment conditions of the academic profession in seventeen countries (European review [Supplement on the Academic Profession]). *Journal of the Academia Europaea, 18*(1), S7–S33.

Blessinger, P., & Anchan, J. P. (Eds.). (2015). *Democratizing higher education: International comparative perspectives*. New York: Routledge.

Boggs, G. L. (2016). Economic impact of digital media: Growing nuance, critique, and direction for education research. In B. Guzzeti & L. Mellinee (Eds.), *Handbook of research on the societal impact of digital media* (pp. 178–207). Hershey: IGI Global.

Canto, I., & Hannah, J. (2001). A partnership of equals? Academic collaboration between the United Kingdom and Brazil. *Journal of Studies in International Education, 5*(1), 26–41.

Cetina, K. K. (2009). *Epistemic cultures: How the sciences make knowledge*. Cambridge, MA: Harvard University Press.

CONICYT. (2015). *Principales Indicadores Cienciométricos de la Actividad Científica Chilena*. Retrieved on 30 September, 2017, http://www.conicyt.cl/informacioncientifica/tag/indicadores-cienciometricos/ from Santiago-Madrid-Viña del Mar: [Main Science Indicators of the Chilean Research Activity].

Connell, R. (2007). *Southern theory: The global dynamics of knowledge in social science*. Cambridge: Polity Press.

de Witt, H. D. (2011). Internationalisation of higher education in Europe and its assessment: towards a European certificate. In H. d. Wit (Ed.), *Trends, issues and challenges in internationalisation of higher education* (pp. 39–44). Amsterdam: Hogeschool van Amsterdam.

Drake, P., Ludden, D., Nzongola-Ntalaja, G., Patel, S., & Shevtsova, L. (2000). '*International scholarly collaboration: Lessons from the past'*, *Inter-regional working group on international scholarly collaboration*. New York: The Social Science Research Council.

Fischman, G. E., Alperin, J. P., & Willinsky, J. (2010). Visibility and quality in Spanish-language Latin American scholarly publishing. *Information Technologies and International Development, 6*(4), 1.

Guzmán-Valenzuela, C. (2017a). The geopolitics of research in teaching and learning in the university in Latin America. *Scholarship of Teaching and Learning in the South, 1*(1): September 2017.

Guzmán-Valenzuela, C. (2017b). Internationalisation of higher education studies in Latin America. In P. Teixeira & J. Shin (Eds.), *Encyclopaedia of international higher education systems and institutions*. Dordrecht: Springer.

Guzmán-Valenzuela, C., & Gómez, C. (2018). Advancing a knowledge ecology: Changing patterns of higher education studies in Latin America. *Higher Education, 77*(1), 115–133.

Guzmán-Valenzuela, C., & Muñoz, A. L. (2018). (De) colonizing international collaborative work: Exploring new grammars for academic partnerships in Chile. In L. Gormall, L. Sweetman, & B. Thomas (Eds.), *Exploring consensual leadership in higher education: Co-operation, collaboration and partnership* (pp. 171–189). London: Bloomsbury.

Hazelkorn, E. (Ed.). (2017). *Global rankings and the geopolitics of higher education: Understanding the influence and impact of rankings on higher education, policy and society*. Abingdon: Routledge.

King, K. (2008). The promise and perils of partnership. *NORRAG News, 41*(December), 5–6.

Marginson, S. (2016). Global stratification in Higher Education. In S. Slaughter & B. J. Taylor (Eds.), *Higher education, stratification, and workforce development, higher education dynamics. Competitive advantage in Europe, the US, and Canada* (pp. 13–34). Dordrecht: Springer.

Marginson, S., & Ordorika, I. (2011). El Central volumen de la fuerza. Global hegemony in higher education and research. In D. Rhoten & C. Calhoun (Eds.), *Knowledge matters: The public mission of the research university* (pp. 67–129). New York: Columbia University Press.

Obamba, M. O., & Mwema, J. K. (2009). Symmetry and asymmetry: New contours, paradigms, and politics in African academic partnerships. *Higher Education Policy, 22*(3), 349–371.

OECD. (2014). *Recommendation of the OECD council concerning international co-operation on competition investigations and proceedings*. Avaialable at: http://www.oecd.org/daf/competition/2014-rec-internat-coop-competition.pdf

Ordorika, I., & Lloyd, M. (2015). International rankings and the contest for university hegemony. *Journal of Education Policy, 30*(3), 385–405.

Pusser, B., & Marginson, S. (2013). University rankings in critical perspective. *The Journal of Higher Education, 84*(4), 544–568.

Qiang, Z. (2003). Internationalisation of higher education: Towards a conceptual framework. *Policy Futures in Education, 1*(2), 248–270. https://doi.org/10.2304/pfie.2003.1.2.5.

Raju, C. K. (2011). *Ending academic imperialism: A beginning*. Penang: Multiversity and Citizens International.

Salmi, J. (2009). *The challenge of establishing world-class universities*. World Bank Publications.

Santos, B. (2010). *Refundación del Estado en América Latina: perspectivas desde una epistemología del Sur*. Lima: Plural Editores.

Santos, B. (2014). *Epistemologies of the South: Justice against epistemicide*. Santiago: LOM.

Vessuri, H., Guédon, J. C., & Cetto, A. M. (2014). Excellence or quality? Impact of the current competition regime on science and scientific publishing in Latin America and its implications for development. *Current Sociology, 62*(5), 647–665.

World Bank. (2013). *Financing for development post-2015*. Available at: https://openknowledge.worldbank.org/bitstream/handle/10986/16310/82800.pdf?sequence=

Part III
Caring for Others

Chapter 11
Love and Revolution in the Post-truth University

Victoria de Rijke

Abstract

The scholar and the world! The endless strife,
The discord in the harmonies of life!
The love of learning, the sequestered nooks,
And all the sweet serenity of books;
The market-place, the eager love of gain,
Whose aim is vanity, and whose end is pain!

Henry Longfellow's poem of 1825 may as well have been written for the class of 2025, given that in our market-driven higher education economy, love of learning now comes at a price. (£9000 this year, and if students love their universities enough, perhaps £12,000 in the next). If in 1968 the Brazilian educationalist Paolo Freire (1921–1997) famously accused education of 'banking sickness' (Freire P, Pedagogy of the oppressed. Bloomsbury, London, 2000), where knowledge was seen as a gift bestowed by those who consider themselves knowledgeable upon those whom they consider to know nothing), 50 years later, it is surely bank robbery. This chapter will explore the role of love in institutions of higher education – what Henry Giroux calls the 'military-industrial-academic complex' – where Friedrich Nietzsche noted 'they're so cold, those scholars'. It has been claimed that love creates ontological panic in educrats, yet surely 'Logos without Eros becomes sadistic' (Thomas Moore). From literature to research studies, and from classical to revolutionary models, an 'epistemology of love' will be presented as the true heart of higher education.

Introduction

Harry Lewis, the former Dean of Harvard College (one of two schools within Harvard University granting undergraduate degrees), lamented in his book, Excellence Without a Soul (2007) that our universities, for all their academic and

V. de Rijke (✉)
Middlesex University, London, UK
e-mail: V.deRijke@mdx.ac.uk

© Springer Nature Switzerland AG 2019
P. Gibbs et al. (eds.), *Values of the University in a Time of Uncertainty*,
https://doi.org/10.1007/978-3-030-15970-2_11

research brilliance, have lost sight of their core mission, which is to foster human beings in our full humanity. By this he means human beings with passion, compassion and a larger sense of purpose than career and success. A key reason for academic "blindness" to community and higher purpose, perhaps, is the deep cultural split between knowing and loving, yet:

> At bottom, knowing and loving significantly overlap each other: there are passions of the mind that are almost indistinguishable from passions of the heart in the energy they generate. That is why the eleventh-century theologian St. Simeon described the deepest form of human knowing as the result of thinking with 'the mind descended into the heart. (Palmer and Zajonc 2010, p. 29)

Peter Le Breton (2012) contends that unchecked rationality, the worshipping of a scientific (or scientistic) worldview that maintains the fiction of value-neutrality and objectivity is a root cause of higher education dilemmas, suggesting, as Thomas Moore put it: 'Logos without Eros becomes sadistic' (de Quincey 2005, p. 270). Evidently such a complex matter for any scholarly enquiry, it has been claimed that 'love creates ontological panic in educrats' (Gidley 2010, p. 353.). What follows nonetheless is an exploration of the role of love in higher education with special attention to metaphor- where the current danger is that post-truth universities have become part of what Henry Giroux (2007) calls the 'military-industrial-academic complex,' – about which Friedrich Nietzsche in an earlier era had noted: 'they are cold, these scholars' (Nietszsche 1888, p. 217) From literature to research, and from classical to revolutionary models, an epistemology of love will be presented as the true heart of higher education.

If 'Love and education, go together like a train and station' (with apologies to Frank Sinatra) and in the face of the train wreck that is current education legislation, this chapter is a discussion of love and education pictured running on interconnected tracks: (1) self-love and authenticity; (2) revolutionary love; (3) love and freedom, and (4) love and playful affiliation. But first, to tackle the terms 'love' and 'truth'.

What Is Love, Anyway?

What is love, anyway? (Howard Jones, Human's Lib album 1983)

Defining love in the educational context is no simple matter. One of the key problems is the polysemous nature of the word 'love' itself. Its meanings are legion.

Socrates' statement from the Symposium that 'love is the desire for the perpetual possession of the good' or a searching for beauty, reminds us that love does set up a belief that the beloved embodies the good. In Plato's view love is cerebral (hence the term Platonic love) and involves our best love organ: the brain. If classical theories gave us three types: 'Eros' (desire) 'Philia' (community) and 'Agape' (humanity), in late consumer capitalism, is nothing left but the first?

Alfred North Whitehead (1916) described the essence of education as religious in its deep connections to reverence, closely aligned to Rudolf Steiner's spiritual position. In 1909 Steiner named love and devotion – the two sides of reverence- as the 'best educators of the Soul', and the selfless educative forces capable of developing humanity's next stage of consciousness (Steiner cited in Gidley, 2010, p.352). In a later anthroposophical lecture 'Love and its meaning in the world' (Zürich 1912) Steiner separates the values of love, wisdom and strength, arguing that neither love nor wisdom are egoistic, comparing wisdom to the flowering of a plant in maturity, as 'an advanced stage of development', but seeing love as 'the creative force in the world' (Steiner's emphasis). Interestingly, Steiner also sees love as having no vested interest in the future but, in fact, pictured on an evolutionary timeline, 'as a payment of debts incurred in the past'. Acts of love can therefore pay off the debt for our existence. Teaching has a special relationship to both truth and love, as:

> To teach seriously is to lay hands on what is most vital in a human being. It is to seek access to the quick and the innermost of a child's or adult's integrity…Poor teaching, pedagogic routine, a style of instruction which is, consciously or not, cynical in its merely utilitarian aims are ruinous. They tear up hope by its roots. Bad teaching is, almost literally, murderous, and, metaphorically, a sin. (Steiner 2003, p. 18)

In 1988 psychologists Robert Sternberg and Michael Barnes created an anthology of then contemporary theories of love, each author presenting their own taxonomies, but Zick Rubin's preface and critique of the volume (1988), that no one taxonomy or definition was maintained by the collection of authors, and that 'love researchers might do well to move to a more common vocabulary' (p. ix) has ironically not been realised by the newer edition (Sternberg and Weis 2006). In a key socio-psychological study (Fehr and Russell 1991, cited in Sternberg and Weis 2006) college students were asked to list as many forms of love as came to mind. After collapsing syntactic variants, 216 separate types of love were named, (mother-love, friendship-love, animal-love, etc.) and of those, 93 were named by more than one person.

Avoiding the types or subheadings attached to love in preference for its qualities, physicist Arther Zajonc developed what he calls an 'epistemology of love' (2005), organised around principles such as sustained attention, openness to diverse and contradictory possibility, respect for the views of others and gentle yet rigorous enquiry. Somewhat similarly, psychologist Ellen Berscheid's (2006) taxonomy of love offers psychological, religious and philosophical frameworks with which to explore attachment and compassion, and she has more recently explored 'love in the fourth dimension' (2010) or temporal love; that which is sustained over time through the values of compassion and shared interest rather than personal benefit.

If these principles might be love, what might then be truth, particularly in relation to higher education? A vision in the service of truth might perhaps sound more suited to a faith university, but Thomas Aquinas' truth as 'adaequatio rei et intellectus,' (conformity of the intellect with the thing itself) presumably marks the foundation of all institutions of higher education. As outlined in the Dominican

University vision, commitment to truth is 'both a virtue and a passion' for Dominican scholars. Thomas Aquinas' scholastic practice of disputatio, a method that seeks to resolve difficult questions by finding the truth in each, was required of medieval masters and students, 'as it does today of teachers and learners, a rigorous exploration of multiple ways of resolving a question, ways leading to the one resolution that can be best supported by reason and evidence' (DU 2012, p. 5).

However, what becomes of truth in an era when reason and objective facts may be less influential in shaping public opinion than appeals to emotion and personal belief? In 1938, looking back on the misinformation around the Spanish civil war, George Orwell confessed that he felt frightened by the possibility that: 'The very concept of objective truth is fading out of the world… Lies will pass into history.' (Orwell 1968, p. 258). 'New truth regimes' do emerge, argued Michel Foucault, with each new corpus of knowledge, technology and scientific discourse, entangled with its own current 'multiple restraints' of power (Foucault in Lynch 2001, p. 317). Objective truth or facts are thus equally relative to any given paradigm. Is it possible that universities, with their post-Enlightenment conviction of unlearning truth in preference for Kant's 'dare to know', their post-modern hostility to grand narratives, their post-positivist outlook, have left themselves vulnerable to the idea of truth being open to endlessly relativist interpretation? Sydney University's recent research on the topic claims that

> in this context, it is possible to view post-truth discourse as the radicalisation of the Enlightenment. Specifically, in the realm of knowledge production, it is the democratisation of epistemology… [and that] post-truth finds intellectual legitimation in the necessary and critical approach to the construction of knowledge that is taken as a given in academia. (Wright 2017)

Joshua Forstenzer, Vice Chancellor's Fellow for the Public Benefit of Higher Education at the University of Sheffield declared in 2017 that he would never have 'believed that the very notions of "truth" and "expertise" would become objects of scorn and vilification in the media and the politics of advanced democracies'. He cites the Robbins Report of 1963, where universities were originally 'tasked with four functions: "instruction in skills" and "the promotion of the general powers of the mind so as to produce not mere specialists but rather cultivated men and women", as well as "the search for truth", and the transmission of a common culture and common standards of citizenship' (Forstenzer 2017, npn). If only!

However, the central 'post-truth paradox' is that, under these apparently privileged conditions, democracy in higher education seems to be regressing rather than progressing. In their urgent need to recruit, retain and be highly rated by fee-paying students, the sector is becoming increasingly corporatised and marketised (Neary and Winn 2009), with universities branding themselves with vision, mission and universal truth claims: 'putting students first', 'making the world better', and so on. With as yet little research on whether universities actually 'embody the values they espouse' (Elwick 2017) there is some evidence (Arcimaviciene 2015) that the metaphors used (in this case of a study of 20 European university mission statements): staff 'assets'; student 'intake'; 'producing' excellence, and so on, demonstrate that 'the modern narrative of higher education is based on consumerism and property ideology, and this manner of representation is expected to be audience appealing' (p. 11) in a climate of corporate exchange. In post-truth discourse, trust in account-able evidence-based research has eroded to the extent that identity and populism can outrank argument or expertise. Coupled with a populist revolt against elites or the idea of expertise, higher education is potentially in significant trouble. Frustrated by media misinformation and outright lies, academics such as technical scientists have been pushed to online gestures such as the 'pro-truth pledge' with its long list of commitments including the increasingly rare values of 'balance', 'clarity', 'com-passionate education' and 'honour' (ProTruthPledge 2017). But where, amongst all this, are love and authenticity?

Self-Love and Authenticity

> You gotta have the mindstate like: 'I'm so great,' and can't nobody do it like you do.
>   Miraculous, phenomenal and ain't nobody in here stopping you. (Conceited album, Remy Ma 2006)

Self-love, or regard for one's own well-being and happiness should not be despised as a moral flaw. Where Shakespeare makes the silly vain Malvolio 'sick of self-love', … 'and taste with a distempered appetite' (Twelfth Night ACT1, Sc1), Erich Fromm resists the immoralities of such self-indulgence and narcissism by viewing self-love simply as the act of taking care and responsibility for oneself, as others may for you. The polemic Teaching as a Subversive Activity (1969) recom-mended, along with

> 7. Prohibit teachers from asking questions they already know the answers to', …14. Require each teacher to provide some sort of evidence that he or she has had a loving relationship with at least one other human being. (Postman and Weingartner 1969, p. 136)

Accounts and research studies by early childhood educators are careful to acknowledge that love of teaching and love of the taught involves respecting the rights of others with a sense of fairness – which directly contributes to 'feelings of professional authenticity' (Goldstein 1997, p. 99). For me, professional authenticity has a relationship to self-love, in the sense that I cannot really imagine one able to exist without the other. Teaching requires a strong sense of self confidence and responsibility if one wants to encourage students to question and challenge the teacher's or the institutional position. Self-love seems central to why, for example, I have stayed in teaching for over three decades.

By self-love, I do not refer to self-branding or the "professionalising" of higher education academics for University marketing or social media, since that patently has a competitive – even divisive- commodifying effect (Duffy 2017). Elizabeth Barratt Browning's lines from Sonnet 43: 'How do I Love thee? Let me count the ways,' reminds us we cannot count if we 'love freely, as men strive for right' (Barret Browning 2009). Rudolf Steiner pointed out at the turn of the twentieth century that all forms of self-measurement or that of others (in our times, Ofsted, REF, TEF, student/staff surveys, league tables and so on) are nothing more than an illusion, as love cannot operate freely in the interest of self-perfecting. Simon Blackburn's study of self-love acknowledges its near-relationship to self-mastery, self-respect and self-esteem, plus of course 'arrogance, vanity, narcissism and others' (2014, p. 10). Philosopher and writer Iris Murdoch was savage in her criticism of such self-delusions, insisting that 'the love which brings the right answer is an exercise of justice and realism, and really looking' (Murdock in Rowe 2010 p. 114); aiming, as she did in her writing, for serious objective attention to things other than ourselves. Feminist thinker Carol Gilligan's theories of connectedness and 'the intelligence of the heart' (1993) has equally long resisted patriarchal, stereotyped perspectives for a wider, more interdisciplinary discourse. Her notion of Higher Education teaching and research 'starting from a place of genuine curiosity', 'making oneself vulnerable to discovery' and striving for 'authentic listening', challenges the idea of a purity or singularity of evidence-based single-discipline research or practice, as much as it reminds the academic of the need to open love up to the other 'who stands at the door of understanding' (McLaren 2000, p. 171.)

Part of Gilligan's research practice noting 'the structure of the narrative, the voices and points of view, the symbolism, patterns of repetition, omissions' (Gilligan 2009) led, in my case, to noting the role of metaphor, as an associative, relational device. Hence, remarks such as 'I love that book', 'I love her lectures', 'I love grammar' or 'I love my job' which may appear glib, light or passive, function actively, descriptively and associatively at the metaphoric level. The verb love stands for commitment or application to, engagement with, scholarly interest and deep satisfaction in – in this case- teaching and learning. Etymologically speaking, the word 'love' from the Middle English word 'luf' is akin to another Old English word, 'lēof' which means 'dear'. The Latin 'lubere', 'libere,' 'to please', associated with lībere, means 'freely' or 'boldly'. Therefore, we might equally say 'that book is dear to me', 'that lecture pleased me', 'grammar frees me', or 'I am bold in my job', all of which highlight the sense of love as offering a security of emotional attachment as the necessary precondition for freedom, risk and resilience. Current formal measures of student evaluation of teaching do not wholly reflect actual teaching effectiveness, as the study 'Love me, Love my lectures?' (Shevlin et al. 2000) found, and there is apparently also 'not much love for the TEF' (Teaching Excellence Framework) in its current manifestation (McCrae 2017), either for academics or heads of higher education departments.

Higher education could thus aspire to Martin Luther King's 'love that does justice' (Edwards 2005); a radical, equality-seeking force that sees self-love as the necessary step to self and other empowerment, allowing for relations based on truth and authenticity. Self-accepting love requires eradicating self-righteous superiority or false consciousness over others, so, as part of professional authenticity, I believe we should acknowledge the role of love towards freedom.

Love and Freedom

> All we have to do now
> Is take these lies and make them true somehow
> All we have to see
> Is that I don't belong to you
> And you don't belong to me
> Freedom. ['Freedom', George Michael, Listen Without Prejudice album, Vol.1. 1990]

Brazilian educationalist Paolo Freire argued that a genuine act of love always generates 'other acts of freedom; otherwise, it is not love. Because love is an act of courage, not of fear, love is a commitment to others. No matter where the oppressed are found, the act of love is commitment to their cause-the cause of liberation.' (Freire in McLaren 2000, p. 171) He does not see the educationalist as shaping student lives, but guiding them to becoming. In Pedagogy of the Oppressed (1968) he wrote:

> The teacher is of course an artist but being an artist does not mean that he or she can make the profile, can shape the students. What the educator does in teaching is to make it possible for the students to become themselves… Education is thus constantly remade in the praxis. In order to be it must become. Its "duration" (in the Bergsonian meaning of the word) is found in the interplay of opposites: permanence and change. (Freire 2014, p. 213)

The concept of 'duration' borrowed from philosopher Henri Bergson (1859–1941) suggests that love and becoming offer a special continuity over lived times of static and change.

For Charles Isaacs, in his study Praxis of Paulo Freire (1972), Freire's discussion casts the limit-situation in such an optimistic light that it seems in danger of losing its meaning. For him and other critics this is a weakness in the Freirian dialectic, as he appears to equivocate between idealism and materialism. Freire has been found inconsistent, even sexist, failing to define terms such as 'humanisation' more specifically in terms of men and women, black and white or other forms of socially defined identities… but perhaps for him, love was blind. Despite feminist criticisms of his male-centred world view, for Freire, the false generosity of paternalism is not healthy; neither is cruelty, such as the subjection of women, for love must be fair, and plural. Oppressive relationships are inherently unfair and thus lack love.

For me, Freire brings the dialectic relation between the sentimental and the intellectual universe of the human being into relief, reversing technocratic rationalism which shatters and degrades the presence of the student into simple sets of abilities and measurable skills. Freire describes the teacher, pedagogy and praxis: "I personally, just do not love the world, but also the process itself of getting to know the world" (Freire in Gadotti 1994, p. 153).

Following Freire, American cultural critic bell hooks, argues, 'Even when we cannot change ongoing domination and exploitation, love gives life meaning, purpose and direction' (2001), p. xxiv.). Hooks' borrowing of Freire's "education as the practice of freedom," refers to 'that quality of education that is enabling and empowering and that allows us to grow.' For Hooks, the heart of education as a practice of freedom is to promote mental, cultural and societal growth (Hooks 1994).

She cites German social psychologist Erich Fromm's (1956) four elements that for him make up love: 'care, responsibility, respect and knowledge', informing, for her, a career bemoaning the absence of love as the defining characteristic of contemporary academic life, especially the intimate connections between race, class, gender, teaching and love. While other educators seek cautiously neutral, non-romantic or non-sexualised definitions born broadly out of attachment theory, reluctant perhaps to recognisethat intimacy is part of pedagogic eros, hooks has no fear of it.

For Rudolf Steiner, in fact, 'transmuted anger is love in action… we can call it the teacher of love' (Steiner 1909) which Freire transforms as the freedom for political and personal self-determination:

> I have the right to be angry and to express that anger, to hold it as my motivation to fight; just as I have the right to love and to express my love for the world, to hold it as my motivation to fight, because while a historical being, I live history as time of possibility, not of predetermination. … My right, my justice is based on my disgust towards the denial of the right to "be more" which is etched in the nature of human beings. (Freire 2004, pp. 58–59)

Freire's vision of love as the embodiment of and solution to struggle continued to resonate into the twenty-first century. Michael Edwards' claim that 'a healthy civil society depends on the development of our collective capacities to talk, argue, innovate, learn and ultimately solve our problems together through a process of social reason', or a "politics of freedom", in which no one has a monopoly of truth and everyone shares an obligation to negotiate their interests with each other' (Edwards 2005, npn), reads as so ideal it might be revolutionary.

Love and Revolution

> It is time for a love revolution
> It is time for a new constitution
> You are a child of the most high
> There is nothing you can't do and that is no lie
> You were designed
> To use your mind
> 'Love Revolution' Lenny Kravtiz, It is Time for a Love Revolution album, 2008

In times of social strife and cultural turmoil, love resists despair and apathy. As argued above, active, politicised love carries a radical' significance, particularly in Freire's last works, where the notion of love is a continuous topic of reference. As Peter McLaren observes, 'love, for Freire, always stipulates a political project, since the love for humankind that remains disconnected from liberating politics does a profound disservice to its object' (McLaren 2000, p. 171). Moreover, Freire's concept of love is never standardised or static. On the contrary, he re-orientates the meaning of the notion, aligning it with a revolutionary essence, conceiving love as an act of freedom that becomes the pretext for other actions that lead to true emancipation, with passion and commitment.

For Freire, love transgresses unilateral psycho-sentimental interpretations. He re- defines love again as a combative 'for those that are sure of the right and duty to fight, to denounce and announce' (Freire 2009, p. 147). The ethics of love forms the active, spirited (but not aggressive) attitude of the radical teacher, encouraging radical students. The denunciation of the de-humanizing structure and the announcement of a humanised structure is a commitment to participate in the social and political transformation of real conditions (Freire 1985). This notion of love springs from Freire's deep faith in humanity and a world 'in which it will be easier to love' (Freire, in Mayo 2004, p. 4), by bringing together revolution and love, embracing the rationale of Che Guevara (Gadotti 1994). The genuine rebel is motivated by a strong emotion of love. In 1965, Che wrote: 'At the risk of seeming ridiculous, let me say that the true revolutionary is guided by a great feeling of love. It is impossible to think of a genuine revolutionary lacking this quality.' He went on to warn against 'dogmatic extremes, cold scholasticism, or an isolation from the masses', since it is the 'we' that will 'make the human being of the twenty-first century' (Che 2003, pp. 225–227).

Knowing and loving significantly overlap each other: there are passions of the mind that are almost indistinguishable from passions of the heart in the energy they generate. But we can be shallow. Che demanded, 'Everyday people straighten up the hair. Why not the heart?' (Deutschman 2003).

In pre-Castro Cuba, universities were the preserve of the privileged few, and autonomous from government. Following the 1959 revolution, the Association of Students of the Engineering Faculty at Havana university assumed control in 1960 and dismissed two professors, spurring the government into supportive action. Whilst much followed the Soviet model, this aspect was revolution as Hannah Arendt condones it, not out of pity or love for the poor, but the respect and solidarity that can follow the groundswell of groups claiming a place in political life (Arendt 2006).

Cuba's acknowledgment of the complexity of university higher education and its responsibilities for political change informs their teacher training at this level. It is common for the best graduates to be approached by their own university to consider tertiary level training as their career. These candidates embark first on a higher research degree, and after 3 years of laboratory and observational work, may reach Assistant Professor and teach small seminar groups for 5 years, moving to Associate Professor able to lecture for 2 more years, and finally full Professor: 10 years in total (MacDonald 1996). Cuba's universities now contribute significantly to global development in areas such as primary public health and agriculture, climate change and sustainable water management, with programmes that stand unique in variety of length, flexibility of access and governance. Despite the country's economic difficulties under the US trade embargo, plus small island vulnerability to natural disaster and climate change, education continues to be free at all levels, and Cuba's generosity in cases of disaster and medical assistance overseas is an example of what love and revolution can bring to education for the wider global good.

Love and Playful Affiliation

Teacher's pet (pa dum pa dum), I wanna be teacher's pet (pa dum pa dum)
I wanna take home a diploma and show Ma that ya love me, too
['Teacher's Pet' sung by Doris Day, composed Joe Lubin 1958]

To be fair, all that most students probably want is for their parents and teachers to love them and to graduate without completely crippling debt. Kings College QAA Report 'Student Expectations and Perceptions of Higher Education' (2013) concluded with many recommendations for better practice, including the need for universities to explain the relationship of fees to the quality and value of the degree, better responsivity and support for very different student needs, an acknowledgment of student preference for face-to-face interaction and a focus on process rather than product. As students are no doubt aware of the gap between graduate salaries and the debt they are incurring, something like Paul Frijters' 'economic theory of greed' emerges, where 'love-investment' (2013, p. 354) is far less likely in the pursuit of self-interest (for both students and teachers in a competitive market).

Psychologist David McClelland called love *affiliation* in his well-known model of need and motivation within organisations – mutual trust, value, care and warmth (McClelland 1984, p. 6). Like McClelland, Irving Singer sees love as bestowed value, as 'the beloved has become valuable for their own sake' where reciprocity allows for shared value; what Martin calls 'a 50-50 distribution to benefits and burdens' (Martin 1996, p. 105). Our higher education finance and human remains (resources) departments could learn much from this equation.

Martin identifies virtues of care, fairness, fidelity which enable love to 'combine aspirations with earthiness' (Martin 1996, p. 3)- as much for ourselves as others, guided by an attitude that we are worthy of such attention. With this self-affirmation is assurance about the potential of oneself and others, particularly in teaching, as one is passing on the idea of confidence and delight in existence. Daniel Cho (2005) argues that love can unite the teacher and student in the quest for knowledge, where love of learning can empower students to challenge knowledge, thereby pushing its limits (p. 79). Pedagogic passion for Cho is akin to an exuberant desire for knowledge, caring about relationships and connections. Loreman (2011) sets great store by kindness as the environment in which love as pedagogy can flourish, and, out of an assumption of affiliated kindness towards and between students and teachers, my own experience has been that of developing pedagogies of playfulness. This includes teasing as well as praising, deliberate silliness as well as earnestness, and shock as well as gentleness.

Acknowledging the active role of the learning subject (teacher and student) in the construction of knowledge and culture, we affirm processes of agency, difference, resistance and democracy. Given the most common resistances to schooling (non-performance, truancy, disruptive behaviour) generally result in academic failure, it follows that those students who reach higher education are likely to have been more conformist. This means that teachers in HE have a particular responsibility to resist the possibility for insidious and unconscious reproduction of passive conformity.

David Trend has argued that popular pedagogic programmes such as "learning how to learn' can be simply another method of regularising behaviour', rather than 'pressing students to move toward subjective autonomy' (Trend 1992, p. 151). Similarly, academics are under increasing pressure to demonstrate a kind of generic, corporatised excellence (measurable by student survey and the TEF). Obedience to institutionalised markers of 'quality', 'environment' or 'learning gain' may -in actuality- muffle any revolutionary sensibilities, in favour of taking shallow breaths in such a stifling culture of conformity. Palmer and Zajonc (2010) point to this hypocritical orthodoxy:

> Academic culture might celebrate "critical thinking," often elevating that capacity to its number-one goal for students. But academic culture is sometimes dominated by orthodoxy as profoundly as any church I know. If a mode of knowing, pedagogy, a life experience, or social perspective is not regarded as kosher in the academy, it too often does not get a fair hearing (p. 23).

In the interplay of opposites, of permanence and change, the armed loved - the fighting love of those convinced of the right and the duty to fight, to denounce and to announce, love of subject, love of study, playful affiliation, and above all things love of resistance and curiosity is the love that – in John Berger's felicitous phrase – 'holds everything dear' (2008). 'Dear' also means expensive, of course. Higher education is becoming dear.

Love and Revolution in the Post-truth University: A Hopeful Conclusion

Have we have lost sight of education as fostering complete human beings? Past expectations of a degree guaranteeing any prospects of employment no longer apply, as graduates find getting a job at McDonalds as hard as anyone else. Policy-makers and knee-jerk fluctuating university missions seem to be heading us for Freire's worst nightmare, that of anti-dialogue: a 'loveless, arrogant, hopeless, mistrustful and acritical' future (1973, p. 46).

Cynically, if higher education is largely for keeping young people off the streets and government unemployment figures for 3 years or so until it spits them out to financial debt and dependency on their parents or the state, how love features in this experience could at least make a difference to their mental health. I came into University teaching to freely educate future teachers to love the learning, the job and the learners. I stayed at it for 30 years. Now university education is a £9000 a year training to meet national standards struggling nationally to recruit, and, once trained, a majority of teachers stay in post less than 5 years after graduating (EPI 2018). I think we can now assume no-one is loving it.

Yet higher education is more important than ever in a post-truth world. To Forstenzer,

> universities exist, at least partially, to serve as a place where a society comes face-to-face with itself. Do they truly succeed in this? Rarely, if ever. But does that mean they should stop trying? I think not. Now, perhaps more than ever, we need universities to find ways to enrich our understandings of ourselves and others. That is why I hope that this commitment to serving the public will ultimately be reflected in the legal definition of the "university." (2017, npn)

We should not be complacent about the need for love and revolution, though examples such as 'The Centre for Contemplative Mind' in Massachusetts, with a programme dedicated to love and compassion in the academy, are rare. Even more unusually, Case Western University's Institute for the wonderfully titled 'Study of Unlimited Love' offers a liberal education for the twenty-first century based on service to humanity where 'students can put aside self-interest and dedicate their lives to helping others through benevolent love' (Mac Labhrainn 2016). I have yet to discover a university combining love with Freire's 'pedagogy of laughter', or a playful practice of freedom. To 'play for love' is to play for no stakes, after all, but the play alone.

'Here, at the intersection between love and reason, lies the future of the University, of that I am sure… [yet] where *stands* the University in this regard, and where stand *we*?' (Mac Labhrainn 2016). Edwards believes the one force that counterbalances the destructive interplay of reason and post-truth is love, love that is able to signify 'the deliberate cultivation of mutually reinforcing cycles of personal and systemic change'. He argues that it is the *combination* of the two seemingly opposing qualities – 'love, and forcefulness, rigour or reason – that defines the relationships central to the democratic resolution of social problems.' His vision is of a 'social science of love,' capable of transforming politics, economics. social and international relations. As Steiner also argued, teachers and learners are in debt to what is past: facts, thoughts, ideas, values; all the teaching and education that has gone before, and Edwards' vision carries deep resonances of past radical love revolutionaries Steiner, Freire, Che Guavara, Postman and hooks:

> This love is universal love, unconditional love, attached only to the equal and general welfare of the whole. This is love that contains a radical equality-consciousness, a force that breaks down all distance and hierarchy. This is a love that respects the necessary self-empowerment of others, eschewing paternalism and romanticism for relationships of truth and authenticity, even where they move through phases of conflict and disagreement, as all do. (Edwards 2005, npn)

Love of this magnitude is a tall order. In 1874, Longfellow was urged to write a poem for the 50th anniversary of the graduation of his college class to be held the next summer, and that long poem, reluctantly written, was titled "Morituri Salutamus" translated as 'those who are about to die salute you'- famously the last words of gladiators to the emperor before they fought to the death. The poem suggests that, whilst we cannot stop the march of time, if we have learnt something in life, we may become better as we age. Whilst many of the poet's images are cautionary rather than revolutionary: lasting education as 'not the blaze of noon' in youth but the 'living sparks' in embers; 'enough to warm but not enough to burn'; the poem also concludes hopefully, with 'nothing is too late' (Longfellow 1875).

Love and revolution have a strong association with our species' survival, as both set up challenges and risks that only our ingenuity can master. Over two centuries after Steiner's elemental metaphor 'Love is the moral sun of the world' (1912), I would call for more love in higher education and more revolution, lest we risk moral extinction.

References

Arcimaviciene, L. (2015). EU universities' Mission statements: What is popularised by metaphors. *SAGE Open, 5*(2), 1–12.

Arendt, H. (2006). *On revolution*. Harmondsworth: Penguin.

Barret-Browning, E. (2009). *Sonnet 43. Sonnets from the Portuguese*. The Floating Press.

Berger, J. (2008). *Hold everything dear: Dispatches on survival and resistance*. New York: Knopf Doubleday Publishing Group.

Berscheid, E. (2006). Searching for the meaning of "Love". In R. J. Sternberg & K. Weis (Eds.), *The new psychology of love* (pp. 171–183). New Haven: Yale University Press.

Cho, D. (2005). Lessons of love: Psychoanalysis and teacher-student love. *Educational Theory, 55*(1), 79–96.

de Quincey, C. (2005). *Radical knowing: Understanding consciousness through relationships*. Rochester: Simon & Schuster.

Deutschman, D. (2003). *Che Guevara reader: Writings on politics and revolution*. Melbourne: Ocean Press.

DU. (2012). *The Dominican Charism in higher education: A vision in service of truth*. River Forest: Dominican University, IL.

Duffy, B. E. (2017). *(Not) getting paid to do what you love: Gender, social media and aspirational work*. New Haven: Yale University Press.

Edwards, M. (2005). Love, reason and the future of civil society, *Open Democracy*. https://www.opendemocracy.net/globalisation-vision_reflections/love_3149.jsp. Accessed May 2018.

Elwick, A. (2017). *Do universities embody the values they espouse?* Research proposal srhe.ac.uk

EPI (Education Policy Institute). (2018). *Analysis: Teacher Labour Market Pressures*. https://epi.org.uk/publications-and-research/the-teacher-labour-market/. Accessed May 2018.

Forstenzer, J. (2017). We are losing sight of higher education's true purpose, *The Conversation*. https://theconversation.com/we-are-losing-sight-of-higher-educations-true-purpose-73637. Accessed May 2018.

Freire, P. (1985). *Pedagogy of the oppressed*. London: Bloomsbury.

Gadotti, M. (1994). *Reading Paolo Freire: His life and work*. Albany: Albany State University Press.

Gidley, J. (2010). Evolving higher education integreally: Delicate mandalic theorizing. In S. Esbjorn-Hargens, J. Reams, & O. Gunnlaugson (Eds.), *Integral education: New directions for higher learning* (pp. 345–361). Albany: SUNNY Press.

Gilligan, C. (1993). *In a different voice*. Cambridge, MA: Harvard University Press.

Gilligan, C. (2009). Making oneself vulnerable to discovery, Carol Gilligan in conversation with Mechthild Kiegelmann. *Forum: Qualitative Social Research, 10*(2), 1–19. http://www.qualitative-research.net/index.php/fqs/article/view/1178/2718. Accessed May 2018.

Giroux, H. (2007). *University in chains: Confronting the military-industrial-academic complex*. New York: Routledge.

Goldstein, L. (1997). *Teaching with love: A feminist upproach to early childhood education*. New York: Peter Lang Publications.

Hooks, B. (1994). *Teaching to transgress*. London: Routledge.

Isaacs, C. (1972). The praxis of Paolo Freire: A critical interpretation. *Critical Anthropology, 2*(2), 5–30.

Le Breton, P. (2012). Evoking love in higher education: Towards a sustainable future. *Journal of Conscious Evolution, 8.*

Longfellow, H. W. (1875). *Morituri Salutamus: Poem for the fiftieth anniversary of the class of 1825 in Bowdoin College.*

Loreman, T. (2011). *Love as pedagogy.* Springer.

Lynch, M. P. (2001). *The nature of truth: Classical and contemporary perspectives.* London: MIT Press.

Mac Donald, T. (1996). *Schooling the revolution: An analysis of developments in Cuban education since 1959.* London: Praxis Press.

Mac Labhrainn, I. (2016). *Higher education and civic engagement: International perspectives.* London: Routledge.

Martin, M. W. (1996). *Love's Virtues.* University Press of Kansas.

Mayo, P. (2004). *Liberating praxis: Paolo Friere's legacy for radical education and politics.* CA: Greenwood Publishing Group.

McClelland, D. C. (1984). *Motives, personality and society.* Praeger: University of Michigan.

McCrae, A. (2017). *[Ex-] head of department's blog, the TEF: Measuring excellence or adequacy?* https://headofdepartmentblog.wordpress.com/2015/08/03/the-tef-measuring-teaching-excellence-or-teaching-adequacy

McLaren, P. (2000). *Che Guevara, Paulo Freire, and the pedagogy of revolution.* Rowman & Littlefield.

Neary, M., & Winn, J. (2009). The student as producer: Reinventing the subject experience in higher education. In L. Bell, H. Stevenson, & M. Neary (Eds.), *The future of higher education: Policy, pedagogy and the student experience* (pp. 192–210). London: Continuum.

Nietzsche's Last Notebooks 1888, 20 (98) Daniel Fidel Ferrer.

Orwell, G. (1968). *The collected essays, journalism and letters of George Orwell: My country right or left, 1940–1943.* Harmondsworth: Secker and Warburg.

Palmer, P. J., & Zajonc, A. (2010). *The heart of higher education: A call to renewal.* San Francisco: Jossey-Bass.

Postman, N., & Weingartner, C. (1969). *Teaching as a subversive activity.* Harmondsworth: Penguin.

Pro Truth Pledge. (2017). https://www.protruthpledge.org/. Accessed May 2018.

Rowe, A. (2010). *Iris Murdock and morality.* Springer.

Shevlin, M., Banyard, P., Davies, M., & Griffiths, M. (2000). The validity of student evaluation of teaching in higher education: Love me, love my lectures? *Assessment & Evaluation in Higher Education, 25*(4), 397–405.

Sternberg, R. J., & Weis, K. (2006). *The new psychology of love.* London: Yale University Press.

Steiner, R. (1909). GA 58 – Metamorphoses of the soul paths of experience Vol. 1 – Lecture 2: The mission of anger – Munich, 5th Dec.

Steiner, R. (1912). Love and its meaning in the world lecture Zurich, 17th December, https://wn.rsarchive.org/Lectures/19121217p01.html. Accessed May 2018.

Steiner, G. (2003). *Lessons of the masters.* Cambridge, MA: Harvard University Press.

Trend, D. (1992). *Cultural pedagogy: Art/education/politics.* London: Bergin & Garvey.

Wright, C. (2017). *The conversation.* https://theconversation.com/uk/topics/post-truth-32226. Accessed May 2018.

Zajonc, A. (2005). Love and knowledge: Recovering the heart of learning through contemplation. Unpublished Mimeo, Amherst College: Physics Department.

Chapter 12
Kindness, Communication and Academic Responsibility in Higher Education

Martin G. Erikson

Abstract The purpose of this paper is to discuss functions of kindness in social practices guided by values in higher education. Definitions of kindness are briefly discussed and kindness is handled as a quality in social interactions between teacher and students, and between students. It is argued that kindness must be seen in a framework of values of higher education that are guiding the social interactions discussed – interactions that in turn are presumed to promote and communicate such values and facilitate an academic development in line with these values. Quality of communication is suggested as an overall value for this purpose, as it is argued that quality of communication in a broad sense is at the core in every academic endeavour, both in research and in higher education. Communication is further related to academic freedom and academic responsibility, seen as two sides of the same coin. The overall discussion focuses on how kindness can promote communication in higher education, and on how kindness as thus can be seen in terms of academic responsibility for both teachers and students. A caveat is that kindness is not about delimiting what can be said in an academic discourse, as this is guided by academic freedom, but of how it ought to be said to enable the best outcome in relation to academic values. It is also discussed how communication and academic freedom, in relation to kindness, are influenced by whether students are seen as customers, as victims, or as free adults being academic partners in the construction of knowledge.

Keywords Kindness · Communication · Proficiency · Academic value · Academic freedom

M. G. Erikson (✉)
University of Borås, Borås, Sweden
e-mail: martin_g.erikson@hb.se

P. Gibbs et al. (eds.), *Values of the University in a Time of Uncertainty*,
https://doi.org/10.1007/978-3-030-15970-2_12

Introduction

Social interaction of various kinds is at the core of higher education. Still, the literature on higher education tends to focus on particular kinds of interactions, and more general qualities of this interaction are given less attention. For example, there is a substantial literature on the functions of feedback in higher education, but the qualities of the social interaction where this feedback is given is seldom discussed (this is illustrated by, for example, Merry et al. 2013). One such quality, or set of qualities, concern what we might label kindness. Binfet (2015) reviewed a number of educational studies where kindness is discussed in relation to children's behaviour, but the concept has received less attention in higher education. Clegg and Rowland (2010) is a notable exception, and they saw kindness as a concept with subversive powers in higher education (se also Rowland 2009, as well as Cramp and Lamond 2016, who based their work on Clegg and Rowland). While there are challenges in adopting the notion of kindness as an academic concept that will be discussed below, I argue that the concept can help us understand and hopefully support interaction in higher education regardless of any ambitions of subversion. The purpose of this paper is to discuss how kindness can be understood as an aspect of social interaction in higher education and in what ways kindness can be beneficial for this interaction. I will start by suggesting a few demarcations that place the concept of kindness in an academic framework, and continue the discussion by looking at kindness from some different angles within this framework.

Defining Kindness as an 'Academic' Concept

Kindness is a concept that can be difficult to include in an academic discourse, for at least two reasons. The first reason is that kindness is something inherently positive. The second is that kindness is so embedded in our everyday discourse. To lay a foundation for a more profound discussion of kindness in higher education, the two problematic aspects and their consequences must therefore be handled.

Kindness as Inherently Positive

Kindness is something intrinsically good that should be promoted whereas unkind behaviour should be prevented. To use kindness as a general point of departure in a discussion of social interaction in higher education therefore places us at risk of using a concept that can be made to cover too much through its positive connotations, making it difficult to say something significant (perhaps except that we ought to be kind to each other). If we want our students to look at things from new perspectives, we might argue that it is important that they are pushed out of their comfort zones.

If we believe that students benefit from being pushed out of their comfort zones, it can be claimed that we are 'kind' to them by doing so. Similarly, if we believe – with good reasons – that it is impossible for students to learn and develop without sometimes failing, it can be claimed that we are 'kind' to our students by failing them. Hence, if we are not careful we can end up with a more or less implicit notion that cruelty is kindness. I suggest that this has two consequences. First, kindness will in this paper refer to the way we interact in higher education. We can fail our students kindly or unkindly, or we can push them outside their comfort zones kindly or unkindly. However, it can also be claimed that failing students, or pushing them outside their comfort zones, are unkind actions in themselves. Clegg and Rowland (2010) discussed this in terms of the kindness being erroneously interpreted to imply leniency or a 'therapeutic' approach to teaching. That brings us to the second consequence: I suggest that a discussion of kindness in higher education must be seen in a framework of values that we believe should guide higher education ventures; values that are at the core of the purposes of higher education. The kindness of specific acts can then be evaluated in relation to these values.

Kindness as an Everyday Concept

The second reason that kindness is problematic to include in an academic discourse is because it is an everyday concept, and so very rooted in our everyday discourse that it would be impossible to include it in a theoretical model independent of our understanding of everyday human interaction. As an everyday concept, kindness is usually understood as acting for the good of others, without expecting something in return – a definition that can be traced at least to Aristotle's *On Rhetoric* (1991, trans). Still, this can take many forms. The Oxford Dictionary has defined kindness as "The quality of being friendly, generous, and considerate", which includes a broad set of qualities or traits. On the other hand, academic psychology tends to avoid the concept of kindness. For example, Reber's (1985) comprehensive diction-ary of psychology does not include the concept. Further, Binfelt (2015) argued that the psychological literature on the prevention of unkind behaviour, such as bullying, greatly outnumbers the literature on the promotion of kind behaviour. Therefore, it might not be surprising that no common definition is found in the psychological literature, where the concept is used in different ways in different contexts, in the few studies where it is adopted. In these studies, the concept of kindness is defined in various ways, from denoting a motivation to be kind to denoting social norms and rules of expected social behaviour, in many cases vaguely defined (for brief reviews of the psychological literature on the concept of kindness, see Binfelt 2015, as well as Canter et al. 2017). In the study by Canter et al. (2017), empirical evidence sug-gested that 'benign tolerance' and 'empathetic responsivity' were important compo-nents of kindness, but that also a general 'core kindness' could be distinguished, more or less as a personality trait opposite to psychopathology. Such discussions are in line with the everyday use of the concepts, where there are also no clear boundaries for what to consider as kindness. Further, there are other examples of the ambiguous boundaries of kindness outside academic discourse: when St. Paul listed kindness as an attribute of those living in accordance with the Holy Spirit (Galatians 5: 22–23), it was together with other attributes such as patience and gentleness, which we – in particular if lacking theological subtlety – could find it difficult to separate from our everyday understanding of kindness. Here, we also see that even if we in everyday life can agree about what to regard as kindness, it is deeply connected to cultural norms, including religious teachings, with ensuing expectations in particular situations. A conclusion is that kindness therefore should be regarded as context dependent, which also is in line with the demarcations based on academic values adopted above. The potential multitude of definitions of kindness – more or less ad hoc – is in itself an argument against an attempt to make too technical a definition. In this paper, I will therefore use kindness in an everyday sense, and as a general term for a way of behaving, including, for example, patience, gentleness, empathy, generosity and tolerance, for the good of others, without expecting any personal gains in return. As Clegg and Rowland (2010) argued, we recognise kindness as present or absent in social settings regardless of formal definitions and it is a component in good teaching even if it is seldom discussed explicitly (see also Rowland 2009). Further, in this paper kindness is about intentional overt behaviour, and not about any feeling of kindness not expressed in behaviour. I will focus on kindness as a reflected and intellectual effort to reach out and make social interaction pleasant. Kindness, in the way discussed here, is closely related to respect, but I suggest that respect is a more elementary feature than kindness. In higher education, respect can be seen as a basic mark of professionalism. Kindness in the sense discussed here is taking this a step further.

Communication as an Academic Value

It was stated above that kindness in higher education should be seen in relation to a context of educational values. If so, we need to explicate these values, and their relation to purposes of higher education. For the sake of simplicity, it would be desirable to define such values on as general a level as possible, with the aim of making them acceptable over a wide spectrum of approaches and assumptions in higher education. For the present discussion it is also beneficial if we can se a connection between academic values and social interaction, thus leading us to situations where kindness can be a relevant factor. I suggest that such a general value is proficiency in communication of clear and coherent ideas. This proficiency in communication would concern both sender and receiver, and would include not only the ability but also the motivation to communicate.

In everything we do in academia, communication is at the core – as Polanyi (1947) argued, without communication there would not be any science. Findings not based on the communications of others (in terms of citations) are not regarded as scientific. Further, to be part of the scientific knowledge base, new findings must be communicated to the scientific community, and accepted by it, through complex patterns of communication (including peer-reviews and publications and citations). For example, Merton's (1973) norms, usually accepted as defining an ethos of science, can to a large extent be analysed in terms of how to communicate and how to assess communication. Higher education is equally dependent on proficiency in communication of clear and coherent ideas, for teachers as well as for students. Humboldt (1970) saw teaching and scientific publishing as two instantiations of the same activity – both are about communicating knowledge-claims to others for whom they are a novelty. Students must be able to expect such proficiency from teachers and ought to strive for it themselves, and it is also the teachers' responsibility to support students' development of such proficiency. Lectures, textbooks, seminars, and student essays are all about communication, and certainly not just between teacher and student. The seminar is as much about communication between students as about communication between students and teacher. A further example is assessment, dependent on students being able to communicate their competence after which their teachers, communicating back to them, give them feedback. Higher education not only depends on complex patterns of present day communication, but our students are also trained to communicate and to use communication according to certain standards (e.g. according to norms of academic writing). This, they are expected to continue to do in the future. Further, communication can clearly be seen as vital for the development and assessment of a central purpose of higher education: critical thinking. Unless critical thinking becomes an apparent element in students' academic output, it is hard to argue that there is any critical thinking going on at all. In the cases when critical thinking calls for a deeper understanding of a problem in order to take a stand, engaging in clear communication can also be a vital part of critical thinking (e.g., Andrews 2015; Barnett 2011, 2015; Ennis 2015). Taken together, proficiency in academic communication ought to be an uncontroversial basic value in higher education. It even ought to be acceptable across the various ideological assumptions inherent in conceptions of higher education purposes (see, e.g. Filippakou 2011; Friberg 2015). Of course this definition of a value is a very blunt instrument for many purposes. Still, I argue that it is useful as a point of departure for a discussion of kindness, because it gives a general framework for what kindness ought to promote, as well as a framework based on social interaction. A further advantage of a focus on communication, which will be explored below in relation to kindness, is the close connection between communication, academic freedom and free speech, as discussed by, for example, Searle (1971).

Kindness and Proficiency in Communication

Academic communication covers a lot of practices that include more or less direct social interaction. In these interactions, we criticise and dissent, and propose hypotheses and arguments and invite others to accept or refute. This involves complicated social processes where we are expected to be objective and neutral and impartially consider arguments alone, and the way we communicate is part of the process. In higher education in particular, a lot of this social interaction is either face-to-face or written communication in one-to-one social relationships, which in turn elicit further interaction face-to-face – situations of interpersonal communication where kindness can be an influential factor. Further, higher education is abundant with such forms of communication, where students have a junior position in relation to a teacher, and the latter also has the power to assess and examine. It can be suggested that kindness in higher education should be seen in terms of how it can support these kinds of communication.

It should be noted that academic communication involves an unavoidable rhetorical aspect – if we cannot convince others that we are correct, it does not matter what we have found in our studies (see for example Harris 1997, for a discussion of rhetoric in academic communication). When Aristotle discussed kindness, it was not primarily as a virtue but in the context of rhetoric, though not the least in relation to the possibilities of making an opponent seem unkind (see Aristotle 1991, trans. – while this is a completely different way of handling kindness compared to the approach in this paper, it is worth pointing out the possibilities of expanding a discussion of kindness as a rhetorical device beyond Aristotle's angle). However, while rhetorical elements are unavoidable, we should not let this overshadow the fact that kindness has broader functions in higher education. Here, I suggest a metaphor: that kindness can be seen as drops of oil that facilitate communication. There are two ways in which kindness can have this function. The first way is direct, by creating trust in personal relationships. The second way is indirect, by creating a good learning environment where students dare to try and are confident enough to learn from failure, if needed, in the process of learning.

Consequences of the Academic Delimitation of Kindness

When placing kindness in the context of academic communication, we must also avoid possible misunderstandings by a clear caveat: clear communication of ideas and arguments come first. Kindness, delimited by the boundaries of academic values, is not about protecting students from difficulties and demands. It is not about avoiding criticism and it is not about avoiding discussions that can be disturbing and hurt feelings.

Kindness and Criticism

As pointed out by Clegg and Rowland (2010), kindness is not to ask either students or senior academics to refrain from being critical. However, kindness is about the expectation that criticism should be presented in a way that enables communication. There is in particular an unavoidable responsibility to react to bad scholarship. In a discussion of academic freedom, Barrow (2010) explicitly includes the right of teachers to criticisethe work of students when not meeting the standards because "the university is concerned with standards of understanding; it is not a therapeutic or rehabilitation centre" (Barrow 2010, p. 186). Still, the right to be unkind does not follow from this. It is even possible to make a pragmatic argument for this: not only would kindness help create a relationship of trust and a good learning environment, but we can also assume that lack of kindness in criticism would in general not be beneficial for learning. Kindness is about how we express ourselves and how we handle others' reactions in order to facilitate trust and – through that – communication. The aim is not to protect students from failure or critique, but to make such experiences beneficial for the students' learning and self-confidence.

Kindness and Comfort Zones

To a certain degree, higher education includes creating uncertainty and perhaps even confusion for students. Already in Wilhelm von Humboldt's vision for the Berlin University, written in 1809 or 1810, the need for students to understand the uncertainty of knowledge was stressed (Humboldt 1970). As Barnett (2011, p. 124) wrote: "It is the university's direct responsibility to bring students to confront accounts of the world that are new to those students. It is the university's implicit responsibility, therefore, to disturb the students with strangeness." This position is also supported by cognitive learning studies, as shown by Clark and Bjork (2014), who used the term *desirable difficulties*. In other words, a goal of higher education is to push students out of their comfort zone. Barnett (2011) took the role of uncertainty further. It is not only the responsibility of the university to generate epistemological uncertainty for the students and foster a critical reasoning relating to this uncertainty. The student will also become uncertain about the self; about who she or he is, or is about to become, which Barnett described as an ontological uncertainty (see also Biesta 2005). In response to this, the students need support to handle this ontological uncertainty. For Biesta (2005), these educational goals meant that students have to be prepared to take risks, and Biesta saw learning as a reaction to disturbance, challenges or even irritation. This is not an easy process, and Biesta goes as far as describing it as a violent dimension to education. From this point of view, it is reasonable to argue that the more secure the students feel in their educational environment, the more willingly can they take the risks associated with confronting the uncertainties and the challenges. A central source of such security is the students' relationship with the teacher: "One way to express this, is to say that one of the constituents of the educational relationship and of education itself is trust (Biesta 2005, p. 61)." This is also a matter of supporting the student in taking responsibility for their knowledge, helping them to dare to try out arguments and accept being contested (see also Dewey 1910). As shown by Barnett (2007), a reluctance to meet the challenges can be a matter of shyness or cultural factors (see also Lun et al. 2010). It can also be a matter of an instrumental convenience, where the student tries to avoid challenging situations. Here, a well-functioning educational project will add a challenge for the student also on a meta-level – the challenge to confront the espoused approach to study, and the student's responsibility for his or her knowledge. Here, there are wide implications for kindness as an influence on how educational environments are constructed, and as Clegg and Rowland (2010) argued, kindness is about understanding the students' perspective. However, this can be taken further, as I will argue that kindness also should be about students trying to understand the teachers' perspective as part of student transformation.

Kindness in higher education is not about restricting what we can say or discuss, neither in terms of to-the-point academic criticism nor in terms of the selection of topics as 'acceptable' for an academic discourse. This freedom of expression includes both which ideas and aspects the teachers are allowed to communicate and what ideas and arguments the students are allowed to communicate to their peers and to their teachers. Kindness is about how these communications are carried out and the aim must always be communication, never silence. For example, if an institution of higher education gives in to students' demands for safe spaces or trigger warnings, or gives in to students' protests against lectures or guest speakers with subjects or perspectives seen as unacceptable by groups of students, this is not a matter of kindness as defined in this paper. Instead, it is a matter of giving up the academic value of communication and freedom of expression. For an institution to give in to students' demands for 'safe spaces' is to give up the responsibility to foster communication and it can be questioned to what extent such an institution meets the purposes of higher education and contributes to society. The notion of learning as an effect of epistemological and ontological uncertainty is a direct antithesis to the idea that learning should be without psychological struggle, which, for example, Vatz (2016) saw as the rationale behind trigger warnings (see also Morris 2015). Summing up so far, some pertinent points can be made. A university should provide safe spaces for the free communication of arguments and ideas, and they should be provided and protected always and for everyone. Everyone should be able to find something they regard as disturbing in a good education. An education without disagreement is an education without critical thinking. By combining this framework with mutual expectations of kindness, an educational environment can be supported where proficiency in communication can be developed.

Adding a Dimension: Academic Freedom

We have seen above that freedom of expression has an important role in the communicative practices of higher education; this can be discussed in terms of academic freedom. The notion of academic freedom is well rooted in academic discourse and was, in particular, established in the writings of Humboldt (1970, trans) but also, as shown by Åkerlind och Kayrooz (2009), the concept is used in different ways, covering different perspectives. Still, some common ideas are found in the writings of, for example, Polanyi (1947), and the relation between academic freedom and freedom of expression is discussed by, for example, Searle (1971). Academic freedom and academic communication are inseparable. Academic freedom is the freedom to communicate: As argued by Watson (2014), it is certainly not the freedom to be left alone or to be allowed to say whatever we want without being contradicted. Instead, it is the freedom to argue and to contradict – a freedom to communicate with peers and students out of scholarly expertise and the scientific findings of self and others.

If the communication of teachers and students is set within a framework of academic freedom, we can also see that academic responsibility is the other side of the coin: academic freedom and academic responsibility cannot be separated. This position is implicit but unavoidable in the writings of Humboldt and explicit in the works of his followers, such as Helmholtz (1877/1995) and Jaspers (1946/1959). In a more modern context, also related to higher education, this relation between academic freedom and responsibility is argued for by, for example, Kennedy (1997) and Swinnerton-Dyer (1995). Academic freedom is the freedom to communicate but we also have the academic responsibility to communicate in a way that promotes others' understanding of our points and that promotes our understanding of the points of others. It was stated above that kindness is not a matter of delimiting what can be said. This is a right defined by academic freedom. However, we can also conclude that this freedom at the same time gives us a matching responsibility to facilitate communication and promote proficiency in communication amongst the students, so that they will be able to take advantage of the same freedom. If kindness is a tool in this process (the drops of oil) it can be argued that we have an academic responsibility to use this tool when we support them in the development of their academic responsibility (including their responsibility for adopting kindness as a drop of oil). We can also distinguish different levels of academic responsibility. The first level is to give students a nuanced image of their subject, which is a basic responsibility of all academic teachers (e.g. Hunt 2010; Swinnerton-Dyer 1995). On the next level, we have the responsibility to support our students by creating an atmosphere that supports communication. As an example, Erikson et al. (2016) found that students expected their teachers to take an active role in securing a good atmosphere that would promote good and respectful communication. A way of doing that is to show our students that we believe in them and care for their wellbeing In other words: kindness as a drop of oil promoting a positive learning environment. It can be argued that this drop of oil has more influence in some areas than in others. The first such area would be teaching and learning activities concerning potentially controversial topics. A second area would be when dealing with students who do not believe in their abilities, which can be defined, for example, in terms of self-efficacy (see Bartimote-Aufflick et al. 2016, for a recent review). This issue can be expanded in various directions, and it opens up for empirical research: for example, would a lack of self efficacy in a higher education setting makes it more difficult to show kindness? That could be a potential problem for teachers as well as for students, as also the teachers' self-efficacy is a vital parameter in an educational environment. The third area where the drop of oil would be especially beneficial would be when promoting widening participation, with students from non-traditional backgrounds who are feeling uncertain about the benefits of higher education and/or the practices and expectations involved (see Wilkins and Burke 2015 for a recent review on widening participation). In this context we also have the issue of the teacher as a role model. For some students, higher education will offer their first encounter with successful and acknowledged international experts (and all students have the right to meet such teachers in higher education). The extent to which such a teacher shows kindness towards a student, uncertain of his or her place in academia or the world at large, can be life changing. As discussed by Erikson (2018), even expectations about such behaviours from teachers or peers in the future can influence a young person's decision to engage in higher education at all. Here, widening participation also gives a clear example of Barnett's (2011) notion of ontological uncertainty as discussed above, suggesting that the challenges of widening participation can in fact be beneficial for learning, but the directions in which it can lead the students and the teachers might offer surprises. Still, a bit of kindness can make that journey easier for all concerned.

Kindness, Communication and Conceptions of Students

It can be argued that communication can be used as an analytic framework for defining various features of higher education, in the sense that such features are reflected in patterns of communication, enabling or weakening the academic qualities of this communication (a further issue that calls for empirical research). It is of course possible to use other theoretical approaches to discuss these mechanisms, in particular various forms of discourse analysis. However, the more simplistic notion used in this paper will hopefully suffice to make the main points about the function of kindness.

In relation to kindness, the way we see our students and the way they see themselves can be an interesting example. Of all concepts in the higher education literature, 'student' is probably the concept most taken for granted. Let us therefore consider three conceptions of students, with ensuing differences in educational values, and their implications for kindness. In the first position, the student is as a customer or consumer, with the right to place demands on a seller – we might not take it as far as to claim that 'the customer is always right', but at least we state that we see knowledge as a commodity offered to a buyer – see, for example, Nixon et al. (2016), for a critical discussion of this perspective. This is the conception of student that has received most interest recently, also in relation student's self-concept as a customer from various perspectives (e.g. Bunce et al. 2017; Tomlinson 2017). In the second position, not necessarily completely separated from the first, the students are victims, struggling through the insensitive and elitist labyrinth of academia desperately fighting for their rights (see Friberg 2015, for a critical discussion of this perspective). In the third position, the student is regarded a responsible adult with a free will, a junior academic and thus a co-creator of knowledge (see, for example, Jaspers 1946/1959, and, for a discussion in a more modern higher education setting, Macfarlane 2017). If we see our students as customers, kindness to a certain extent becomes a matter of servility: the servants bowing to their masters. With the students as victims, kindness is at risk of becoming a matter of feeling pity towards the students. If students are seen as customers, kindness can be demeaning for the teacher and if students are seen as victims, kindness can be demeaning for the students. In neither of these situations does the teacher have a position where clear demands about communication can be placed on the students. Further, these positions also reduce the expectations of kindness that can be placed on the students. This not only undermines a fundamental principle of higher education but also weakens the social interaction and thus the role of kindness (the drops of oil). If we, on the other hand, see students as adults, voluntarily engaging in a joint project of higher education as novice academics, the relation between teacher and student is suddenly much more equal and focused on the common goal of knowledge acquisition (e.g. Jaspers 1946/1959; Macfarlane 2017). Here, a mutual expectation of kindness can be seen as a natural position in an interaction between adults.

Conclusions and Implications

The purpose of this paper was to discuss how kindness can be understood as an aspect of social interaction in higher education and in what ways kindness can be beneficial for this interaction. While the discussion above show that kindness concerns behaviour that can be of great importance to higher education, the conceptual problems of kindness might lead to the conclusion that kindness is not necessarily be the best label, and alternative concepts are worth considering. For example, we could call it benign interest instead, or perhaps benevolence. On the other hand, the use of an everyday concept might be an advantage if we want it to denote an everyday activity and a personal relation, rather than a strictly defined psychological concept or set of behaviours. Without having to treat kindness as an exact academic concept, we are free to see human interaction in higher interaction in a broader perspective – in the case of the present paper, discussed in terms of communication. The use of an everyday concept might also reduce the risk that some over-zealous policy-maker would start creating performance indications for kindness, which otherwise is a truly horrible vision.

An advantage of the explicit discussion of kindness is that it makes it possible to distinguish what kindness in higher education is not. This concerns at least two dimensions. The first is the risk of confusing kindness and academic leniency, illustrated by student demands for 'safe spaces', or a misguided striving to avoid criticizing bad scholarship or a reluctance to press students outside their comfort zones. The second dimension is the potential to use assumptions about kind behaviours as a foundation for reflections on practices of social interaction in the educational settings. When we have decided on what kindness is and is not, we can also identify the opposites of kindness to be avoided. Whereas aggression might come to mind as the opposite of kindness, indifference as well as attitudes of superiority or arrogance are probably far more common. It can also be assumed that they represent behaviours that are not the result of reflection, instead being a result of an institutional culture where social relations are not discussed or considered important (aggression would be more of an individual characteristic). This shows the importance of a reflexive component in the notion of kindness used in this paper. On the other hand, to see virtue as an element of action, reached through reflexivity, has been a central position in western philosophy at least since Aristotle (2009, trans.). In the educational context, the concept of kindness might offer a possible addition to Macfarlane's (2004) model of 'teaching virtues' – either as a conceptual tool to give more nuance to virtues such as Respectfulness and sensitivity, or as an added virtue.

The greater the distance there is between people, in worldviews, in conceptions of humanity and society, in theoretical and methodological approaches or in cultural assumptions, the more demanding is the communication we are striving for, and the more challenging is therefore the development of the proficiency we are striving for. The greater distance, the more important it is to reach out to make the other understand our position, and to understand their position. It is a matter of effort, a matter of respect and a matter of the open mind that is a fundamental part of the striving for communication. Kindness can be a vital tool in this process. Here, kindness is a manifestation of the tolerance that comes from having opted to learn and approach the perspectives of others with an open mind.

References

Åkerlind, G. S., & Kayrooz, C. (2009). Understanding academic freedom. In M. Tight, K. H. Mok, J. Huisman, & C. C. Morphew (Eds.), *The Routledge international handbook of higher education* (pp. 453–467). New York: Routledge.

Andrews, R. (2015). Critical thinking and/or argumentation in higher education. In M. Davies & R. Barnett (Eds.), *The Palgrave handbook of critical thinking in higher education* (pp. 49–62). New York: Palgrave Macmillan.

Aristotle. (1991). *On rhetoric* (G. A. Kennedy, Trans.). New York: Oxford University Press.

Aristotle. (2009). *Nicomachean ethics* (D. Ross, Trans.). Oxford: Oxford University Press.

Barnett, R. (2007). *A will to learn*. Maidenhead: McGraw-Hill.

Barnett, R. (2011). *Being a university*. Abingdon: Routledge.

Barnett, R. (2015). A curriculum for critical being. In M. Davies & R. Barnett (Eds.), *The Palgrave handbook of critical thinking in higher education* (pp. 63–76). New York: Palgrave Macmillan.

Barrow, R. (2010). Academic freedom: Its nature, extent and value. *British Journal of Educational Studies, 57*, 178–190. https://doi.org/10.1111/j.1467-8527.2009.00433.x.

Bartimote-Aufflick, K., Bridgeman, A., Walker, R., Sharma, M., & Smith, L. (2016). The study, evaluation, and improvement of university student self-efficacy. *Studies in Higher Education, 41*, 1918–1942. https://doi.org/10.1080/03075079.2014.999319.

Biesta, G. (2005). Against learning. *Nordisk Pedagogik, 25*, 54–66.

Binfet, J.-T. (2015). Not-so random acts of kindness: A guide to international kindness in the classroom. *The International Journal of Emotional Education, 7*(2), 49–62.

Bunce, L., Baird, A., & Jones, S. E. (2017). The student-as-consumer approach in higher education and its effects on academic performance. *Studies in Higher Education, 42*, 1958–1978.

Canter, D., Youngs, D., & Yaneva, M. (2017). Torwards a measure of kindness: An exploration of a neglected interpersonal trait. *Personality and Individual Differences, 106*, 15–20. https://doi.org/10.1016/j.paid.2016.10.019.

Champ, A., & Lamond, C. (2016). Engagement and kindness in digitally mediated learning with teachers. *Teaching in Higher Education, 21*(1), 1–12.

Clark, C. M., & Bjork, R. A. (2014). When and why introducing difficulties and errors can enhance instruction. In V. A. Benassi, C. E. Overson, & C. M. Hakala (Eds.), *Applying the science of learning in education: Infusing psychological science into the curriculum* (pp. 20–30). Washington, DC: Society for the Teaching of Psychology.

Clegg, S., & Rowland, S. (2010). Kindness in pedagogical practice and academic life. *British Journal of Sociology of Education, 31*(6), 719–735. https://doi.org/10.1080/01425692.2010.515102.

Dewey, J. (1910). *How we think.* Boston: D. C. Heath & Co.

Ennis, R. H. (2015). Critical thinking: A streamlined conception. In M. Davies & R. Barnett (Eds.), *The Palgrave handbook of critical thinking in higher education* (pp. 49–62). New York: Palgrave Macmillan.

Erikson, M. G. (2018). Potentials and challenges when using possible selves in studies of student motivation. In H. Henderson, J. Stevenson, & A.-M. Bathmaker (Eds.), *Possible selves and higher education: New interdisciplinary insights* (pp. 13–26). London: Routledge.

Erikson, M., Erikson, M. G., & Punzi, E. (2016). Student responses to a reflexive course evaluation. *Reflective Practice, 17*, 663–675. https://doi.org/10.1080/14623943.2016.1206877.

Filippakou, O. (2011). The idea of quality in higher education: A conceptual approach. *Discourse: Studies in the Cultural Politics of Education, 32*, 15–28. https://doi.org/10.1080/01596306.2011.537068.

Friberg, T. (2015). A holistic, self-reflective perspective on victimization within higher education in Sweden. *Critical Studies in Education, 56*, 384–394. https://doi.org/10.1080/17508487.2014.969287.

Harris, R. A. (Ed.). (1997). *Landmark essays on rhetoric of science: Case studies.* Mahwah: Hermagoras Press.

Hunt, E. (2010). The rights and responsibilities implied by academic freedom. *Personality and Individual Differences, 49*, 264–271.

Jaspers, K. (1959). *The idea of the university* (H. A. T. Reiche & H. F. Vanderschmidt, Trans.). Boston: Beacon Press. (Original work published 1946).

Kennedy, D. (1997). *Academic duty.* Cambridge, MA: Harvard University Press.

Lun, V. M.-C., Fischer, R., & Ward, C. (2010). Exploring cultural differences in critical thinking: Is it about my thinking style or the language I speek? *Learning and Individual Differences, 20*, 604–616.

Macfarlane, B. (2004). *Teaching with integrity: The ethics of higher education practice.* London: Routledge.

Macfarlane, B. (2017). *Freedom to learn – The threat to student academic freedom and why it needs to be reclaimed.* London: Routledge.

Merry, S., Price, M., Carless, C., & Taras, M. (Eds.). (2013). *Reconceptualising feedback in higher education.* Abingdon: Routledge.

Merton, R. K. (1973). The normative structure of science. In R. K. Merton (Ed.), *The sociology of science: Theoretical and empirical investigations* (pp. 267–278). Chicago: University of Chicago Press. (Original work published in 1942).

Morris, L. V. (2015). Trigger warnings. *Innovative Higher Education, 40*, 373–374.

Nixon, E., Scullion, R., & Hearn, R. (2016). Her majesty the student: Marketised higher education and the narcissistic (dis)satisfactions of the student-consumer. *Studies in Higher Education.* Advance on-line publication. https://doi.org/10.1080/03075079.2016.1196353.

Polanyi, M. (1947). The foundations of academic freedom. *The Lancet, 249*(6453), 583–586. https://doi.org/10.1016/S0140-6736(47)91856-4.

Reber, A. S. (1985). *Dictionary of psychology*. London: Penguin.

Rowland, S. (2009). Kindness. *London Review of Education, 7*(3), 207–210.

Searle, J. R. (1971). *The campus war*. New York: World Publishing Company.

Swinnerton-Dyer, P. (1995). The importance of academic freedom. *Nature, 373*, 186–188.

Tomlinson, S. (2017). Student perceptions of themselves as 'consumers' of higher education. *British Journal of Sociology of Education, 38*(4), 450–467.

Vatz, R. E. (2016). The academically destructive nature of trigger warnings. *First Amendment Studies, 50*(2), 51–58.

von Helmholtz, H. (1995). On academic freedom in German universities. In D. Cahan (Ed.), *Science and culture* (pp. 328–341). Chicago: The University of Chicago Press. (Originally published 1877).

von Humboldt, W. (1970). On the spirit and the organisational framework of intellectual institutions in Berlin (E. Shils, Trans.). *Minerva, 8*, 242–250. (Originally published 1903).

Watson, D. (2014). *The question of conscience*. London: Institute of Education Press.

Wilkins, A., & Burke, P. J. (2015). Widening participation in higher education: The role of professional and social class identities and commitments. *British Journal of Sociology of Education, 36*, 434–452. https://doi.org/10.1080/01425692.2013.829742.

Chapter 13
Taking Responsibility: Truth, Trust, and Justice

Jon Nixon

Abstract In this chapter I refer to ideal collegial relationships as relationships of virtue and draw on the Aristotelian notion of virtuous friendship to clarify and ground the argument. I also presuppose a heterogeneous category of what I term 'educational professionals' that comprises a wide range of occupational groupings. We live in a society that is not only increasingly professionalised, but increasingly pedagogicised: a society, that is, in which professionals in different walks of life and different institutional settings define their professionalism, and mediate their professional practice, in increasingly pedagogical terms. Professionals are now expected to explain, persuade, mediate, consult, negotiate, and learn from, and with, their clients. That is all for the good, but it suggests new forms of collegiality across professional boundaries and new forms of public-professional engagement. It also suggests a renewed sense of intellectual solidarity: the 'we' and the 'us' that Said (Humanism and democratic criticism. Columbia University Press, New York, 2004) had in mind when he refers to 'scholar-teachers', carrying forward what he saw as a radical tradition of 'critical humanism', or the notion of 'we scholars' that Damrosch (We scholars: changing the culture of the university. Harvard University Press, Cambridge, MA, 1995) evoked in his brave attempt to envisage 'the next intellectuals'.

Keywords Responsibility · Truth · Trust · Justice · Virtuous friendship

> Education is the point at which we decide whether we love the world enough to assume responsibility for it and by the same token save it from the ruin which, except for renewal, except for the coming of the new and young, would be inevitable. (Arendt [1961] 1977, 196)

J. Nixon (✉)
The Education University of Hong Kong, Tai Po, Hong Kong

Middlesex University, London, UK

© Springer Nature Switzerland AG 2019

P. Gibbs et al. (eds.), *Values of the University in a Time of Uncertainty*,
https://doi.org/10.1007/978-3-030-15970-2_13

Introduction

Aristotle maintained in Book VIII of The Politics that '[i]n matters that belong to the public, training for them must be the public's concern'. He was thinking here not just of military training, which was supremely important for the survival of the city state, but also of those qualities and dispositions that promote the form of political life that the citizenry will collectively lead. Thus, he continues, 'it is not right either that any of the citizens should think that he belongs just to himself; … for each is part of the state; and the responsibility for each part naturally has regard to the responsibility for the whole' (Aristotle 1992, 452). Education, in other words, permeates every aspect of civil society; a society for which the citizenry bears collective responsibility.

We have lost that sense of education as a collective endeavour that reaches across civil society, informing the culture and ethos of our public institutions and affecting the quality of our civic and professional relationships. This chapter is premised on the assumption that an effective education system requires not only organisational systems and institutional structures (important though these are), but also inter-personal and inter-professional relationships based on the recognition of both individual difference and equal worth: education conceived as a continuum of learning stretching across, and deeply grounded in, social and cultural relations.

I ground my argument in an initial discussion of what constitutes a good institution. To imagine such an institution, I argue, requires hope in our capacity to develop and sustain relationships based on mutuality and trust. Drawing on the Aristotelian notion of 'virtuous friendship', I refer to such relationships as 'relationships of virtue': relationships in which each cares for the material and moral wellbeing of the other. Without such care, I argue, justice becomes an empty shell. Indeed, justice may well under such circumstances incline towards injustice. A just and caring society is one in which we learn to reason together and acknowledge the vital link between being true to one another and trusting one another.

In addressing the question of what constitute the values of the university, we must grapple with the post-truth realities of untruth, mistrust, and injustice; and, crucially, find ways through to a very different social order based on truth, trust and justice, and a very different political order based on a recognition of the tensions and contradictions that are historically layered into that social order. The prime task of the university is, I argue, the renewal of society through a steady insistence on the fact that truth matters; that trust is impossible without a commitment to truthfulness; and that justice relies – always precariously – on the possibility of trust and truth. The responsibility of the university is to make justice matter not only in its mission statements, but in the institutional practices that inform its ethos.

Good Institutions

John Hall was right to assert that 'civil society is fragile, and it needs to be extended' (Hall 1995, 27). Over a quarter of a century later, however, the need to deepen, as well as extend, civil society seems equally urgent. Engagement, membership and participation comprise the depth dimension of civil society. Good institutions are – from a neo-Aristotelian perspective – constructed around good relationships that in turn are based upon the mutual recognition of equal worth and the reciprocity of trust that such recognition generates. Moreover, good institutions become better institutions through the growth of mutuality and reciprocity at the level of the inter-personal. The quality of civil association in any institution is a significant indicator of the wellbeing of the institution as a whole.

This is not an assumption that carries much weight among those responsible for the management of corporate institutions. In what the late Zygmunt Bauman char-acterised as these 'times of disengagement', one counter assumption at least carries a much heavier punch: namely, that 'power consists in decision-making and resides with those who make the decisions' (Bauman 2001, 39–49). Power, in other words, belongs to those who make the decisions rather than those who implement them. It is the former who determine the organisational structures, which in turn frame the systems of institutional communication and deliberation, which then seek to cir-cumscribe the culture or ethos of the institution. In resisting such circumscriptions 'persons in relation', to draw on the moral philosopher John MacMurray's terminol-ogy, find for themselves and one another spaces in between the institutional systems and organisational structures (MacMurray 1961).

These spaces-in-between can be imagined only through recourse to a way of talking about academic practice that not only avoids but deliberately resists the lan-guage of market-management – a language that dominates the education sector as a whole but has a particularly tight hold on higher education. 'We are', as the historian Ross McKibbin put it in his powerful rejoinder to what he saw as the destruction of the public sphere, 'familiar with the way this language has carried all before it':

> We must sit on the cusp, hope to be in the centre of excellence, dislike producer-dominated industries, wish for a multiplicity of providers, grovel to our line managers, even more to the senior management team, deliver outcomes downstream, provide choice. (McKibbin 2006, 6)

In the 10 years or so since McKibbin wrote these words, the language of mana-gerialism has pervaded every nook and cranny of the higher education sector: indeed, education conceived as a public good is imperilled at every level by both government policy (austerity, centralisation, privatisation …) and institutional man-agement (target-driven, competitive, top-down …).

Human beings are by definition subject to unpredictable changes of fortune and circumstance. We are vulnerable creatures. A managerial perspective that seeks, by implication, to redefine humanity in terms of some notion of perfectibility is doomed to failure. It renders our institutions inhuman and in so doing puts at risk the civil society of which those institutions are an essential component. The 'fragility of goodness', to evoke Nussbaum's (2001) telling phrase, is a defining feature not only of what it means to be human, but what it means to build and sustain institutions within which human beings can flourish.

The Necessity of Hope

Being good is difficult. The difficulty lies not only in the occasional lassitude of will towards goodness, but in contingent factors: the conditions underlying the wellbeing of the self, of the institutions of which we are members, and of wider society. The moral project is not one which we can undertake alone or in isolation. Because of the nature of goodness – its dependence upon dispositions that are acquired in and through practice – we can only grow into goodness through our relationships with others. (Even when thinking alone – or talking to oneself – we are engaging in what Hannah Arendt called the 'two-in-one' of thinking) (Arendt 1978, I, 179–193). Coping with not being perfect is part and parcel of whatever becoming better might mean.

That is why we require something like hope. 'Hope alone', as Jürgen Moltmann in the first volume of his great theological trilogy put it, 'is to be called "realistic", because it alone takes seriously the possibilities with which reality is fraught. It does not take things as they happen to stand or lie, but as progressing, moving things with possibilities of change'. It is precisely because our experience of the world continually brings home to us the sheer contingency and unpredictability of human affairs that hope is essential: 'Only as long as the world and the people in it are in a fragmented and experimental state which is not yet resolved, is there any sense in earthly hopes' (Moltmann 1967, 25).

There is, as MacMurray pointed out, a complex and crucial relation between our capacity to act in the world and our incapacity to fully comprehend that world. Our agency can only be exercised in a world that is ultimately unknowable and unpredictable in its outcomes:

> In action we presuppose that we determine the world by our actions. The correlative of this freedom is that the world which we determine in action must be indeterminate, capable of being given a structure that it does not already possess. We can only know a determinate world; we can only act in an indeterminate world. (MacMurray 1957, 55)

He clinches his argument in the following terms: 'Therefore, if we really do act, if our freedom of will is not an illusion, the world in which we act must be unknowable' (MacMurray 1957, 55). Agency is enacted in an indeterminate and, in that sense, an unknowable world.

In elaborating this seeming paradox, MacMurray implied that agency, the capacity to act in an indeterminate and therefore unknowable world, is always reliant upon some human capacity that is not dissimilar to what Moltmann (1967) understands by hope. Action, involving as it always does an element of incalculable risk, is an expression of our hope that the risk factors are not entirely insurmountable – or, if insurmountable in the short term, may, in some unforeseeable and wholly unpredictable long-term, work in the interests of the common good.

History is not some inescapable fate. It can, sometimes at great cost, be remade, reworked, reconceptualised. 'Meaning and value', as the literary theorist and historian Tzvetan Todorov put it, 'only come from human subjects questioning and judging the past …Sanctifying the past robs it of all effectiveness in the present' (Todorov 2003, 176). It is in the remaking of the past within the present that we begin to imagine possible futures.

The social content of hope focuses on both relationship and justice: relationships of virtue are inconceivable without a notion of justice; but, conversely, a just society is unthinkable without a social practice inclusive of virtuous relationships.

Virtuous Relationships

In Books VIII and IX of the Nicomachean Ethics Aristotle was clear that the highest form of friendship – variously translated as virtuous friendship, perfect friendship, and character friendship – is founded on the mutual recognition of equal worth and of the desire to enhance the worth and wellbeing of the other:

> Only the friendship of those who are good, and similar in their goodness, is perfect. For these people each alike wish good for the other … And it is those who desire the good of their friends for the friends' sake that are most truly friends, because each loves the other for what he is. (Aristotle 1976, 263)

He also acknowledged, however, that friendships differ in kind and quality. The political historian Horst Hutter (1978, 115) has suggested that 'what Aristotle seems to be saying is that if we understand the psychodynamics of friendship in the narrow sense, we thereby also understand the nature of other human associations. All human associations are forms of friendship, even if only imperfectly'.

Friendship may, for example, be tactical and therefore provisional and conditional: a kind of strategic alliance based upon the mutuality of either self-interest or pleasure. Friendship, in either of these two senses, is a matter of being part of the club, part of the enclave – a category which excludes those who are not part of the club, not part of the enclave. Pahl (2000, 21), in his sociologically oriented study of friendship, neatly summarises this set of distinctions in terms of 'friends of utility, friends of pleasure and friends of virtue'.

Much hinges on these distinctions, not least the notion of equality. 'Friends of utility' and 'friends of pleasure' are likely to be useful and pleasurable to one another precisely because of their economic and social commonalty: who has access to which influential networks; who can afford to dine out at which fashionable restaurants. But 'friends of virtue', who may be diversely positioned in terms of their economic and social conditions, may still be useful and pleasurable to one another since the virtuous friendship to which they aspire morally re-orientates 'the useful' and 'the pleasurable' towards 'the good': friendship 'which has virtue as its base and aim is also pleasant and useful. It combines all three aims, since the good in character, when friends, also find each other's company pleasant and useful' (Hutter 1978, 108).

Such relationships, argued Randall Curren in his study of Aristotle's notion of public education, constitute 'a partnership in pursuit of the best life … this third and rarest, but also most unifying, category of civic friendship' (Curren 2000, 132–133). Simone Weil, in one of the now classic statements on friendship, emphasises this idea of an equal partnership between autonomous, non-dependent individuals and based on mutual respect: 'all friendship is impure if even a trace of the wish to please or the contrary desire to dominate is found in it'. She continues: 'In a perfect friendship these two desires are completely absent. The two friends have fully consented to be two and not one, they respect the distance which the fact of being two distinct creatures places between them.' Although it is a bond between two people, she maintains that 'it is in a sense impersonal. It leaves impartiality intact' (Weil 2005, 287).

The kind of virtuous friendship to which Weil directs our attention is almost always an aspiration and very rarely an achieved state. As a concept, it is what Hutter called 'a theoretical searchlight' or 'a guiding norm' by which actual relationships can be evaluated (Hutter 1978, 104–105). It is a teleological concept which enables us to grasp, ontologically, the underlying purposefulness of the kind of relationship which Anthony Giddens characterised as 'pure' in its adherence to 'the imperative of free and open communication' (Giddens 1993, 194).

Such relationships exist between those who consider each other to be of equal worth. Mutuality of recognition, of respect, is central. Such relationships are neither provisional nor instrumental, but unconditional in terms of what is good for oneself and the other: they are both inward-looking and outward-reaching. They are premised on the assumption that we become better people through the reciprocity afforded by our shared aspiration to help one another become so. That is why, as Pahl put it, 'friends of virtue' are also 'friends of hope' and 'ultimately friends of communication': 'our friends who stimulate hope and invite change are concerned with deep understanding and knowing' (Pahl 2000, 79). Relationships of virtue are, by this reckoning, learning relationships; they are, from first to last, pedagogically inspired and pedagogically purposeful.

The notion of virtuous friendship, as referring to a kind of relationship that privileges the recognition of equal worth, is central to our understanding of the conditions of learning. Such relationships are a precondition not only of the deliberative process whereby we ascertain what constitutes right action for ourselves and others; they are also the means by which such processes endure and enjoy some albeit fragile security. They inform our agency, while at the same time providing us with relational structures within which to recognise the agency of others.

What Aristotle understood by virtuous friendship becomes, then, a means of rethinking what we aspire to in terms of self-recognition and the recognition of the other through mutuality and reciprocity. It becomes a means of reconfiguring, not only our notion of the just society as hypothetical space, but the practice of justice as meeting place: the life-world of associative, civil, and institutional reality. As such it is crucial to our understanding of what it means to be an educator and – crucially – what the university should aspire to in support of those who practice within it.

Justice *and* Care

The link between relationship and justice is contentious. Paul Ricoeur claimed that friendship, as conceived by Aristotle, is akin to justice, but not in itself a form of justice: 'Aristotle's analysis of friendship in his Nichomachean Ethics has to do with the conditions most propitious for mutual recognition, that form of recognition which brings friendship close to justice. Without being a type of justice, Aristotle says, friendship is akin to it. This is a crucial distinction which requires some elaboration. The suggestion is that justice and relationships of virtue are mutually dependent while at the same time distinct. Why is that? In what sense are they different? In what sense are they, as Ricoeur put it, 'akin' but not the same 'type' of thing? (Ricoeur 2005, 221).

Nel Noddings, in her philosophical work on the nature of care and justice, was concerned with these kinds of questions and seriously raised the stakes by arguing that not only are justice and relationships of virtue distinct, but that they are also potentially at odds with each other. 'Debate on care and justice', she argued, 'has often taken the form of strong opposition, care versus justice. It has also often concentrated on an alleged gender difference – women favouring care and men favouring justice' (Noddings 1999, 7). Thus, 'the need to move beyond frameworks of justice', while acknowledging 'that the emphasis on justice and rights has made an enormous contribution to human welfare' (p. 8). Even notions of distributive justice – justice as fairness – only take us so far: 'the justice orientation often prescribes formulaic remedies and then pronounces the problem theoretically solved … Care hesitates to make decrees; it would prefer cooperative decisions, a variety of desirable outcomes, and multiple options to achieve them' (p. 12).

Care picks up where justice leaves off (i.e. when a judicial decision has been reached). Writing from what she terms a 'care perspective', Noddings argued:

> We do not suppose that ethical responsibility is finished when a just decision has been reached. Indeed, it is especially at this point that we must ask: What happens now to relationships? What happens to communities? What happens to the quality of experience for those who will undergo the consequences of our decision?' (Noddings 1999, 12) (See also Noddings 1984)

The political and moral philosopher Onora O'Neill defines the problem with reference to what she sees as the monopoly that abstract and totalising theories of justice seek to impose. In her study of justice and virtue she posed the rhetorical question: 'Might justice be enough?' Acknowledging that 'this is the view of many contemporary writers on justice', she argued that the 'contemporary friends of the virtues find the view unconvincing and repugnant. They aim to make a complete break with "abstract" theories of justice and with inclusive principles of all sorts.' If, she argued, 'virtue need no more be unprincipled than justice need be implacably uniform, a choice between them may be neither necessary nor plausible' (O'Neill 1996, 184).

From this perspective caring for one another – respecting one another at the inter-personal level as being different but of equal worth – is not something we do in addition to justice. Rather, it is the means whereby we work towards a fair and just society. It provides the anti-structure, the counterbalance, to codes of justice that would otherwise, as the philosopher Charles Taylor put it, run the risk of rigidity and atrophy: 'all codes need to be countervailed, sometimes even swamped in their negation, on pain of rigidity, enervation, the atrophy of social cohesion, blindness, perhaps ultimately self-destruction' (Taylor 2007, 50). The codes of justice are not in themselves enough; just societies – and the institutions that shape and sustain them – require also the practice of care, the recognition of equal worth, and space for reciprocity and mutual respect.

Reasoning *Together*

In addressing these kinds of concerns Martha C. Nussbaum has introduced and developed a significant body of literature on functional capabilities. Among these capabilities, which she sees as essential to human wellbeing, Nussbaum privileges practical reasoning and affiliation. These two capabilities, she has argued, are fundamental to our functioning as human beings: 'To plan in one's own life without being able to do so in complex forms of discourse, concerns, and reciprocity with other human beings is … to behave in an incompletely human way' (Nussbaum 2000, 82). In elaborating this argument with reference to work and employment, she insists that, to be a truly human mode of functioning, work

> must involve the availability of both practical reason and affiliation. It must involve being able to behave as a thinking being, not just a cog in a machine; and it must be capable of being done with and toward others in a way that involves mutual recognition of humanity. (Nussbaum 2000, 82)

To make of work something other than alienated labour requires the capabilities of both practical reasoning and affiliation.

Nussbaum defines practical reasoning as 'being able to form a conception of the good and to engage in critical reflection about the planning of one's own life' (Nussbaum 2000, 79). Work requires of the worker both a conception of the good and the capacity to apply that conception, through practical reasoning, to particular ends and purposes. So, for example, if I am a medical practitioner, I seek through practical reasoning to align my practice to the ends and purposes of healing; if I am a lawyer, I seek to align it to those of justice; if I am a teacher, to those of learning. Professional practice, insists Nussbaum, requires a sense of moral purposefulness on behalf of the practitioner. Through practical reasoning the practitioner meets this moral requirement; the moral requirement, that is, for practice to become morally purposeful and for purposes to be imbued with practical import.

To reason together requires wisdom, circumspection, and evaluation in respect of one's own and others' best interests. It involves prudence, discernment and deliberation. 'Practical wisdom', as Ricoeur put it, 'is this discernment, this quick glance, in a situation of incertitude, in the direction of the suitable action. This is inseparable from an agent of action who we can say is prudent' (Ricoeur 2005, 88). This orientation towards practical reasoning or practical wisdom is, of course, directly related to the Aristotelian notion of phronesis and of the person who is committed to acquiring that disposition: the wise one, the phronimos. Practical wisdom, so conceived, cannot be reduced to a set of skills or techniques. 'There is', as the philosopher Alasdair MacIntyre argued, 'no set of rules to invoke, nothing therefore that corresponds to Kantian maxims or to the rules of the rule-utilitarian'. So, 'the phronimos has in the act of practical judgement no external criterion to guide her or him. Indeed, practical knowledge of what criteria are relevant in this particular situation itself requires phronesis' (MacIntyre 2006, 28, 4).

Nor, according to MacIntyre, does practical reasoning necessarily involve any application of theoretical knowledge or even any sustained reflection upon the ultimate ends and purposes of human existence:

> A phronimos who happens never to reflect on the ultimate end of human beings is not a contradiction in terms. And, for many of us at least, our own experience of the best human beings that we have known attests that human goodness and inarticulateness about, indeed lack of interest in reflection upon ultimate ends can indeed be found together. (MacIntyre 2006, 25)

Practical reasoning is acquired, then, not through abstract theory or even philosophical reflection, but through habitual practice. It depends, the philosopher Jeffrey Barash suggested, 'upon an ethos, upon a whole series of dispositions, as a basis of prudent choice' (Barash 1999, 35). A major constitutive element of that ethos – that whole series of dispositions – is what Nussbaum calls affiliation. Our habitual practice is shaped to a large extent by the nature and quality of our affiliations – the company we keep, the relationships we form, the associations we develop.

In defining affiliation Nussbaum draws a distinction between, on the one hand, being 'able to imagine the situation of another and to have compassion for that situation; to have the capability for justice and friendship', and, on the other hand, of 'being able to be treated as a dignified being whose worth is equal to that of others; … being able to work as a human being, exercising practical reason and entering into meaningful relationships of mutual recognition with other workers' (Nussbaum 2000, 79–80). What emerges from this distinction is the importance of reciprocity: the way in which 'the capability for justice and friendship' is crucially dependent upon 'being able to be treated as a dignified human being whose worth is equal to that of others'. My capability for justice and friendship towards others is, in other words, dependent upon the capability of others for justice and friendship towards me. The capability of affiliation, like that of practical reasoning, is fundamental because without it there is no way of ensuring that our other capabilities can become functional. To reason is to reason together – in affiliation and association with others.

Truth Matters

If practical reasoning and affiliation are mutually dependent capabilities, each is also dependent upon what the philosopher Bernard Williams called 'the virtues of truth'; 'qualities of people that are displayed in wanting to know the truth, in finding it out, and in telling it to other people' (Williams 2002, 7). A person who has no desire whatsoever to know the truth, to find it out, or to tell the truth to others would be incapable of what Nussbaum understands by affiliation or what, following Aristotle, she and MacIntyre understand by practical reasoning. He or she would lack the qualities necessary for the formation of mutually respectful forms of affiliation and deliberative modes of reasoning together.

But what is truth? Here I draw on a distinction that Arendt made in her essay on 'Truth and Politics' – the distinction, that is, between 'rational truth' and 'factual truth'. 'Facts and events', she argues, 'are infinitely more fragile things than axioms, discoveries, theories – even the most wildly speculative ones – produced by the human mind'. Moreover, once a factual truth is lost, no rational effort will ever bring it back:

> Perhaps the chances that Euclidian mathematics or Einstein's theory of relativity – let alone Plato's philosophy – would have been reproduced in time if their authors had been prevented from handing them down to posterity are not very good either, yet they are infinitely better than the chances that a fact of importance, forgotten or, more likely, lied away, will one day be rediscovered. (Arendt 1977, 231–232)

Politicians and pundits are well aware of the fragility of 'factual truth', which is why the more unscrupulous among them routinely dismiss it as 'fake news' and seek to replace it with 'alternative facts'. Lies have now become an unavoidable feature of the political landscape, as populist and authoritarian leaders seek to blur the distinction between truth and untruth.

The philosopher Richard J. Bernstein, in commenting upon the continuing relevance of Arendt, warns of the risk that this routine recourse to untruth has on democratic politics:

> What happened so blatantly in totalitarian societies is being practiced today by leading politicians. In short, there is the constant danger that powerful persuasive techniques are being used to deny factual truth, to transform fact into just another opinion, and to create a world of 'alternative facts.' (Bernstein 2018, 74)

Democracy, within such a context, becomes – as the political thinker Sheldon S. Wolin puts it – 'managed', 'incorporated', 'fugitive'. Ultimately, it runs the risk of becoming a form of what he termed 'inverted totalitarianism': populism coupled with authoritarianism operating as a totalising ideology (Wolin 2010, 2016).

The prime responsibility of the university, and all those who work within the higher education sector, is to insist, through both their espoused values and their pedagogical practice, that truth matters – and to challenge any attempt, covert or otherwise, to blur the distinction between truth and untruth. This involves, to return to Williams's philosophical inquiry into truth and truthfulness, 'the virtue of Accuracy': 'the virtue that encourages people to spend more effort than they might have done in trying to find the truth, and not just to accept any belief-shaped thing that comes into their head' (Williams 2002, 87–88). This virtue, Williams goes on to argue, is closely related to another of 'the virtues of truth'; namely, 'the virtue of Sincerity'. For, as he puts it, '[i]f we are to rely on what others tell us, they had better be not just sincere but correct; moreover (in the other direction so to speak) if we take care to be right, we need to be honest with ourselves' (Williams 2002, 94).

Truth – and specifically 'the virtues of truth' as exemplified by 'the virtue of Accuracy' and 'the virtue of Sincerity' – is, then, connected with trust. The word 'truth' – as, again, Williams remarks – originally meant fidelity, loyalty, or reliability, with the transition to the modern sense probably having occurred by the fourteenth century. (The archaic phrase 'plighting one's troth' harks back to the earlier sense)

(Williams 2002, 93–94). To trust someone is to be assured that what they say or write is not only sincere in the sense of being an honest expression of their beliefs, but that those beliefs are correct in the sense of being an accurate reflection of the way things are. Insofar as higher education is concerned with 'encourag[ing] people to spend more effort than they might have done in trying to find the truth', it is therefore necessarily concerned with establishing the conditions necessary for mutual trust.

The crucial point here is the symbiotic relation between truth and trust. We do not establish the truth and then gain the trust of one another. Nor do we gain that trust and then establish the truth. The two, as it were, go hand in hand, with mutual trust achieved through the process of 'spending more time than [we] might have done in trying to find the truth' – or, to turn that point on its head, with a greater sense of truthfulness achieved through the creation of a discursive environment in which each can rely on what the other says.

This point is, I believe, highly relevant in any attempt to understand the nature of teaching and learning, since it provides an educational justification for placing human relationships at the heart of the pedagogic process. It thereby avoids the unhelpful distinction (or, to my mind, the false dichotomy) between 'the pastoral' and 'the academic', with the former being so often pushed to the periphery of what is seen as the 'core business' of the university. To follow the logic of Williams's argument is to acknowledge that our regard for the truth and our regard for one another are inextricably linked.

In acknowledging that link we are in effect acknowledging that education is necessarily an ethical endeavour. By that I do not mean that it may have some ethical outcomes – or beneficial side effects – that are somehow independent of the processes and practices of teaching and learning; but, rather, that those processes and practices involve the acquisition of certain dispositions that enable us to flourish as interdependent and mutually respectful human beings. In short, they contribute to the building and sustainability of a just society, in which justice is informed and shaped not by regulatory codes but by mutual care and the recognition of equal worth.

Conclusion

What we value – and how we value it – matter enormously. A just society requires its citizens to take responsibility for the world through their capacity to reason together regarding right action and the common good. Such citizens establish and maintain the conditions necessary for mutual trust and recognition through their insistence on truthfulness and their rejection of untruth. They maintain, in other words, our albeit fragile polity. Those responsible for the education of others – in whatever professional capacity – have a duty of hope that such a society is possible and attainable. They require what the other Williams – the cultural and literary critic Raymond Williams – called 'the resources of hope' (Williams 1989).

To be accounted good, the institutions and organisational frameworks within which educational professionals work should be judged not against some bureaucratically imposed target of 'excellence', but with reference to their determination to create the conditions necessary for truth, trust and justice. That requires universities to measure up to a very different notion of the good institution than the various versions peddled in a time of post-truth. Hannah Arendt, in the words quoted at the head of this chapter, points a way forward:

> Education is the point at which we decide whether we love the world enough to assume responsibility for it and by the same token save it from the ruin which, except for renewal, except for the coming of the new and young, would be inevitable. (Arendt [1961] 1977, 196)

The world is constantly made and remade though our own pursuit of truth, trust and justice. These are, I would suggest, the foundational building blocks of a democratic system of education and of the institutions that sustain it. The future of the university – as a cornerstone of liberal democracy – depends upon its commitment to build upon those foundations.

References

Arendt, H. (1961/1977). *Between past and future: Eight exercises in political thought*. New York: Penguin Books. (First published by Faber & Faber, 1961, and with additional material by Viking Press, 1968).

Arendt, H. (1978). *The life of the mind*. San Diego/New York/London: The University of Chicago Press.

Aristotle. (1976). *The ethics of Aristotle: The Nicomachean ethics* (J. A. K. Thompson, Trans., & Revised by H. Tredennick). London: Penguin Books. (First published by Allen and Unwin, 1953).

Aristotle. (1992). *The politics* (T. A. Sinclair, Trans., & Revised and re-presented by T. J. Saunders). London: Penguin Books.

Barash, J. (1999). The politics of memory: Reflections on practical wisdom and political identity. In R. Kearney & M. Dooley (Eds.), *Questioning ethics: Contemporary debates in philosophy*. London/New York: Routledge.

Bauman, Z. (2001). *Community: Seeking safety in an insecure world*. Cambridge, MA: Polity Press.

Bernstein, R. J. (2018). *Why read Hannah Arendt now*. Cambridge, MA/Medford: Polity Press.

Curren, R. R. (2000). *Aristotle on the necessity of public education*. Lanham/Boulder/New York/Oxford: Rowman and Littlefield.

Damrosch, D. (1995). *We Scholars: Changing the Culture of the University*. Cambridge MA: Harvard University Press.

Giddens, A. (1993). *The transformation of intimacy: Sexuality, love and eroticism in modern societies*. Cambridge, MA: Polity Press.

Hall, J. A. (1995). In search of civil society. In J. A. Hall (Ed.), *Civil society: Theory, history, comparison* (pp. 1–31). Cambridge, MA: Polity Press.

Hutter, H. (1978). *Politics as friendship: The origins of classical notions of politics in the theory and practice of friendship*. Waterloo: Wilfred Laurier University Press.

MacIntyre, A. (2006). *Ethics and politics: Selected essays* (Vol. 2). Cambridge: Cambridge University Press.

MacMurray, J. (1957). *The self as agent* (1st volume of the Gifford Lectures delivered in the University of Glasgow, 1953–54). London: Faber and Faber Ltd.

MacMurray, J. (1961). *Persons in relation* (2nd volume of the Gifford Lectures delivered in the University of Glasgow, 1953–54). London: Faber and Faber Ltd.

McKibbin, R. (2006). The destruction of the public sphere. *London review of books, 28*(1), 3–6.

Moltmann, J. (1967). *Theology of hope: On the ground and the implications of Christian eschatology* (J. W. Leitch, Trans.). London: SCM Press Ltd.

Noddings, N. (1984). *Caring: A feminine approach to ethics and moral education*. Berkeley: University of California Press.

Noddings, N. (1999). Care, justice, and equity. In M. S. Katz, N. Noddings, & K. A. Strike (Eds.), *Justice and caring: The search for common ground in education* (pp. 7–20). New York/London: Teachers College Press, Columbia University.

Nussbaum, M. C. (2000). *Women and human development: The capabilities approach*. Cambridge: Cambridge University Press.

Nussbaum, M. C. (2001). *The fragility of goodness: Luck and ethics in Greek tragedy and philosophy* (Revised ed.). Cambridge: Cambridge University Press.

O'Neill, O. (1996). *Towards justice and virtue: A constructive account of practical reasoning*. Cambridge: Cambridge University Press.

Pahl, R. (2000). *On friendship*. Cambridge, MA: Polity Press.

Ricoeur, P. (2005). *The course of recognition* (D. Pellauer, Trans.). Cambridge, MA/London: Harvard University Press.

Said, E. W. (2004). *Humanism and Democratic Criticism*. New York: Columbia University Press.

Taylor, C. (2007). *A secular age*. Cambridge, MA/London: The Belknap Press of Harvard University Press.

Todorov, T. (2003). *Hope and memory: Lessons from the twentieth century* (D. Bellos, Trans.) London: Atlantic Books.

Weil, S. (2005). *An anthology*. London: Penguin Books.

Williams, R. (1989). In R. Gable (Ed.), *Resources of hope: Culture, democracy, socialism*. London/New York: Verso.

Williams, B. (2002). *Truth and truthfulness: An essay in genealogy*. Princeton/Oxford: Princeton University Press.

Wolin, S. S. (2010). *Democracy incorporated: Managed democracy and the specter of inverted totalitarianism*. Princeton/Oxford: Princeton University Press.

Wolin, S. S. (2016). *Fugitive democracy and other essays* (N. Xenos, Ed.). Princeton/Oxford: Princeton University Press.

Chapter 14
Islamic and Western Liberal Secular Values of Higher Education: *Convergence or Divergence?*

Abdullah Sahin

Abstract This chapter aims to discuss critically the changing values in higher education within the context of culturally, ethnically and religiously plural modern European societies with a special focus on the case of emerging European Islamic higher education institutions. The inquiry argues for the need to rethink the core values in Islamic and western liberal, secular higher education in order to facilitate a new creative engagement between these two distinctive perspectives on higher education that share an intertwined intellectual legacy. The focus of the study is framed by the following questions: Do central educational values of Islam and western secular higher education remain in conflict? To what extent can a critical dialogue of convergence be facilitated between the educational/pedagogic cultures of Islamic and western higher education? Why should such a critical engagement be based on a shared relational ethics of respecting the dignity of difference and recognition of mutual interdependence? The study adopts a phenomenology-infomed critical, comparative analysis method while exploring the topic within its historical and contempoaray dimensiosns. The original contribution of the inquiry lies in its reflective engagement with the Islamic and western values of higher education and developing a distinctive conceptual framework to facilitate a new pedagogic dialogue among the communities of learners and teachers coming from these educational cultures who increasingly share the same social space. After presenting the aims and context of the inquiry, a brief historical account of Islamic and western values of higher education will be provided. This will be followed by discussing the arguments supporting the incompatibility of Islamic and western values of education. The incompatibility thesis will be deconstructed by critically examining its logic of binary literalism. By drawing on the evidence suggesting presence of a shared reflective, critical educational heritage between Islam and the West, the chapter argues for the need to revive these forgotten traditions of pedagogic curiosity and critical openness to inspire a new cross-pollinating dialogue capable of acknowledging the dignity of being different and recognizing the reality of sharing an interdependent world.

A. Sahin (✉)
Centre for Education Studies, University of Warwick, Coventry, UK
e-mail: A.Sahin@warwick.ac.uk

199

P. Gibbs et al. (eds.), *Values of the University in a Time of Uncertainty*,
https://doi.org/10.1007/978-3-030-15970-2_14

Keywords Islam · Liberal Education · Comperative Education · Islamic Higher Education · Pedagogic curiosity · Islamic Critical Pedagogy

Introduction: Aims, Methodology and Context of the Study

This chapter critically considers the changing values in higher education within the context of culturally, ethnically and religiously diverse modern European societies with a special focus on the case of the European Muslim communities. This politically contentious, but sociologically undeniable, Islamic presence poses a dual challenge: European Muslims struggle to reconcile their faith with the values of secular liberal democracy which in turn finds it difficult to extend its principles and values of inclusivity to accommodate faith-based demands of European Muslims. There are complex dynamics informing this contentious relationship. The current wave of nationalist, authoritarian populist politics, threating the hard-earned liberal values of an open society in the West, gravely undermines the possibility of a constructive dialogue and mutual trust to emerge. Within the context of higher education, which is the focus of current study, persistence of structural inequalities stemming from the intersection of class, gender and economic income, for example, can cause access issues that potentially hindering eh social mobility among the most disadvantaged communities in the society. These barriers can be more intensely experienced by the members of minority ethic and faith communities who are overwhelmingly underrepresented in the faculties of academia. The increasing negative public perception of Islam and Muslims that has direct negative impact on Muslim students' campus experience illustrates the latter concern (National Union of Students, 2018).

An inclusive model of higher education embracing cultural plurality of contemporary European societies can play a significant role in facilitating a critical engagement and dialogue between the educational heritage of Islam and the West. This, however, requires rethinking both Islamic and western core values of higher education within the cultural diversity of the modern world. This inquiry aims to engage critically with this urgent task of rethinking by posing the following questions: Do central educational values of Islam and western secular higher education remain in conflict? To what extent can a critical dialogue of convergence be facilitated between the educational/pedagogic cultures of Islamic higher education and the contemporary western liberal secular university? Why should such an educational dialogue and engagement between modern Islam and the West be facilitated through observing a relational ethics of respecting the dignity of difference and recognition of mutual interdependence?

In terms of methodology, this conceptual inquiry adopts a critical/comparative thematic analysis in engaging with the pedagogic ideas, values and practices in Islamic and western higher education. The study will be guided by a broad phenomenological approach originally suggested within the latter work of E. Husserl (1970). Husserlian phenomenology offers a rigorous method by which to understand how meaning(s) are generated in human experience which also form the intersubjective fabric of individual and collective 'life-worlds'. The study argues for a reciprocal dialogue in which cultural and religious difference which defines diverse 'life-worlds' is dignified and not simply tolerated but, most significantly, the reality of a wider context of inter-dependency and inter-relationality is firmly recognised. Every genuine encounter is also an opportunity of being moved and redefined by one another. Islamic and western liberal education, often perceived within a distorted essentialist binary, have distinctive differences but also commonalities that challenge such a stereotyping. The pedagogic values of 'critical openness and critical faithfulness' are shared by both educational traditions. Such values, if nurtured within higher education, can enable diverse communities of learners to show competence for critical self-reflexivity, an important feature of contextual self-understanding(s) needed to achieve better social cohesion, harmony and justice in plural societies.

Islamic and western educational cultures now inform the wider educational experience of millennial European Muslims. A reflective conversation between the traditions of higher education in Islam and the contemporary West can lead to the emergence of a more inclusive, just and meaningful modern higher education system within which the civic values of trust and the common good as well as a vision of a caring global learning and citizenship can be fostered. The gradually emerging European Islamic higher education institutions, established as a result of the communities' post-Second World War migration history, can no longer narrowly focus on reproducing certain identity narratives privileged by the transnational religious movements. Instead of trying to forge young peoples' identities, it would be much more meaningful for these institutions to offer a broad and balanced education capable of enabling young people to develop contextual understanding of their faith heritage, its diversity and encourage them to form a reflective religious agency capable of articulating Islam within the everyday reality of their life-worlds. In this regard, collaboration between mainstream and faith-heritage universities is crucial. Such a collaboration should not be based on a pragmatic motive of simple degree- validation/income-generation but in order to place Islamic higher education in the mainstream. This can be achieved through facilitating exchange and dialogue leading to the formation of a genuine reflective pedagogic culture, *a modern critical/ reflective Muslim paideia*, rooted in the transformative/holistic conception of education in Islam, namely *tarbiyah* (Sahin 2014, 2017, 2018). With such an integrative educational ethos, these intuitions would be in a better position to facilitate a contextual Islamic faith leadership education in the modem world and more effectively respond to the educational needs of students under their care.

Values in Islamic and Western Higher Education: An Intertiwined Legacy in Transition

Before rethinking the ethos and values of higher education within the cultural plurality of modern world, it is important to briefly reflect on the concept of education and highlight how it is an integral feature of human existence. Inspired by the Husserl's phenomenology, Maurice Merleau-Ponty (2013) stressed the embodied nature of human experience and its embeddedness in a concrete physical evivorment, bodily presence and an in an inseparable cultural context. Values are culturally-embedded enduring beliefs and attitudes that shape sense of purpose, meaning, trust, truth and worth in people's lives. Education, a defining feature of human experience, is a fundamental organising principle of human existence that articulates diverse 'life-worlds', value systems, crystallised in specific historical, cultural settings, and forms different interpretations of being human. Crucially, educational activity in its formal and informal embodiments both reflects as well as promotes a given society's ideal values. However, the perception of education in contemporary universities appears to be more vocational, designed to respond to the needs of the labour market. Hence, it overwhelmingly reflects a narrow competence-based epistemological function. The focus on imparting certain bodies of knowledge and skills comes at the expense of ignoring the deeper ontological power of educational practice in facilitating human flourishing. Critical educational theorists (Giroux 2011; Nemiroff 1992) argue that the capitalist market priorities dominating western societies have shaped the educational culture and values of higher education too. The role of universities in preparing young people for employment, economic prosperity and independence are crucial (Gibbs 1998: 14); however, questions whether one can trust in such a competence-focused, industrialist university model where 'moral trust is replaced with the unsupported notion of competence of trust, which ultimately dilutes the moral dimension of higher education'. Furthermore, rapid demographic changes, increasing cultural diversity, mass migration coupled with the growing socio-economic inequalities and environmental concerns challenge universities to rethink their educational mission in a fast-changing world.

Naturally, Education Studies within academia is expected to be more directly involved with this rethinking process. Education Studies is a relatively recent field, rather than a discipline, where interdisciplinary research designs are utilised to understand the complexity informing different levels and forms of educational process including further and higher education (Bartlett and Burton 2016; McCulloch 2002). However, the distinction between a field and discipline does not seem to be always clear-cut. Phenomenologically considered, the possibility of a distinctive educational way of looking at life, an ability to think educationally, does enable 'Educational Studies' to be considered a discipline making claims to a special branch of knowledge, methods of inquiry and analysis. In western academia, international/comparative education studies are popular, often advancing the international development agendas of western countries in the so-called underdeveloped world. However, as Levine and White (2017) note, the study of diverse educational cultures and their philosophies and values of human development have not yet been given due space and recognition in western academia.

The Latin word 'Universitas' refers to a guild or corporation of students and masters. (Coincidentally, the word 'corporation' also derives from the Latin and refers to a 'body of people'.) According to some historians (Makdisi 1981, 1990; Goodman 2003), the early Islamic higher learning institution, the *Madrassah* and its religiously- sanctioned voluntary funding framework, *waqf*, might have had some influence on the formation of universities in western Europe such as Bologna (1088), Oxford (1096) and Paris (1160–1170). The values informing the tradition of collegiality and commensality – that is, the manner in which college educational life forms the relationships of its members, tutors and students, associated with Oxford and Cambridge (Tapper and Palfreyman (2010) – is very similar to the organisation of the traditional Islamic college system. *Madrassah*, literally 'place of study', originally emerged as a private affair formed around inspiring religious teachers, small study circles (*halaqa*) taking place in special meeting places (*majlis*) where the values of intellectual engagement, friendship and sense of a 'learning community' were nurtured. Learning was not confined to knowledge retention but, as in its original Arabic, knowledge, *'ilm*, meant to be a sign pointing towards sensing a deeper reality. Like its equivalent in the Hebrew Bible, *yada* (Snaith 2009), *'ilm* meant developing inner engagement, inspired intimacy, attachment and embodied awareness among the learners. Higher education remained private and, thus, scholars kept their independence until the emergence of proper 'scholar-bureaucrats', mainly during the Ottoman Empire (Atçıl 2017), who were openly aligned to the ruling classes and incorporated into the Muslim imperial order. *Madrassahs* were often attached to a mosque where worship, learning and study were integrated. The word for such a large mosque compound is *al-Jaami* which is related to the modern Arabic word for university, *al-Jamiaa*. The modern University of Al-Qaraouiyine, founded in Morocco by Fatima al-Fihri in 859 AD, is considered by some to be the oldest degree-granting university in the world.

The *Madrassah*, particularly in its most creative period (eighth to thirteenth centuries) integrated the transmitted religious sciences (*naqliyaat*), via a strong provision for auxiliary sciences (*aliyyat*) such as the study of language and logic, with the philosophical and natural sciences (*aqliyaat*). This attracted European students who were prevented by the medieval Church to engage in free and critical inquiry. In today's popular Muslim discourse the latter point often gets exaggerated and idealised. However, western students, encouraged by the open educational culture of the Muslim learning institutions, were re-connected with the ancient Greek philosophical and scientific heritage that in turn had stimulated the emergence of Renaissance humanism. The latter stimulated medieval Europe to reform itself around a new reason/science-based secular Enlightenment narrative and to create institutions of higher learning that eventually eclipsed the no longer dynamic Muslim *Madrassah*. Makdisi (1981) attempts to confine classical *Madrassah* to the transmitted religious sciences (naqliayat) and sees it as not more than a specialist guild of higher legal training (*Sharia*). However, he nevertheless appears impressed with the elaborate and innovate pedagogic practices such as reflective debate (munazara/jadal) and licencing/authorising (*ijaza*) students who mastered certain sciences that formed the basis of modern degree confirmation and certification. He seems, however, to neglect the fact that *Madrasah*, inspired by core educational values of Islam, included theological focus as well as specialisms in natural sciences, including medicine and astronomy, where foundational religious and spritual sciences were also taught.

The curriculum of medieval education in the West consisted of a seven-subject syllabus, based around particular books, and composed of the preparatory trivium (grammar, logic and rhetoric) and the quadrivium (geometry, arithmetic, astronomy, and music), known as the seven liberal arts at the heart of the idea of a liberal education. The early modern period did see humanism taking root in the western universities, challenging medieval 'scholasticism' with its emphasis on free will, ethical values and individualism. However, philosophy and the values of 'scholasticism' dominated the Medieval university which held biblical truth as pre-eminent in what was essentially a defence of Christian dogma: the pursuit of divine truth and learning. The humanists' goal for liberal education was the well-rounded development of the student. Education become human-centred, defining a key aspect of western secular modernity facilitating its new scientific spirit that nurtured the values of free inquiry, question and curiosity. In the nineteenth century, Cardinal Henry Newman (1996) stressed that university is only for intellectual pursuits, an end in itself. However, it was the context of the industrial revolution whereby a heavy instrumentalist and utilitarian perception of science gave rise to a technology and skills-focused university model. It was the University of Berlin in 1810, which became known as the first of the 'Humboldtian' universities, whose philosophy and structure have shaped contemporary universities (Scott 1993).

B. Clark, in his seminal work (1983) analysing the nature of modern higher education in a cross-national perspective, suggested four basic values – namely 'social justice, competence, liberty, and loyalty' – as required to shape the future of higher education policy. The emphasis on loyalty was interpreted as referring to the values fostering the greater 'national integration and identity'. It appears that, within such a liberal analysis, the conserving function of education, central to the formation and survival of the nation states, was predominant. The diversity of cultures in western societies largely facilitated by the need to draw on global human resources had not yet been properly recognised. However, with the increasing marketisation of higher education, loyalty and fidelity have been gradually replaced by the values of 'accountability, efficiency and excellence' all of which came to define a regime of outcome and measurement-based 'quality control' dominating modern higher education.

As a consequence, the performative, procedurial set of skills and values, rather than personal transformation or human happiness and fulfilment, appear to have been prioritised. In reaction to this, at the beginning the early twentieth century, a person-centred humanist educational movement briefly re-emerged to emphasise the liberating, empowering character of the educational process that was an integral part of wider family and community life. Consequently, a progressive agenda, couched not in terms of bureaucratic efficiency but rather in terms of transformative pedagogic values (Dewy 2011) promoting 'personal development, fulfilment, happiness' as wellas nurturing civic social values necessary to maintain a democratic way of life, gained priority.

Critical pedagogy is a radical approach combining education and Critical Theory and represented by the work of philosophers like Habermas (1973). Habermas, unlike other influential twentieth century liberal political theorists such as Rawls

(2005), advocated a notion of public reason and ethics in secular western societies that is inclusive of their growing cultural and religious plurality and mindful of the inequalities caused by their capitalist economic system. Critical pedagogy stresses the significance of integrating 'reflection' with 'criticality' so that the former does not turn into a self-serving introspection. It operates from an understanding that the basis of education is 'political' hence it emphasises critical reflexivity to prevent misuse of power producing inequalities. P. Freire's concept of 'conscientisation', or critical consciousness is a good illustration of this perspective and refers to 'learning to perceive social, political and economic contradictions, and to take action against the conditions forming oppression in human individual and social life' (Freire 2000; Giroux 2011; Goodson and Scherto 2014).

The study by Allen and Bull (2018:23) shows how even the values informing research and policy in UK universities, due to financial pressure, become vulnerable to the ideological influences exhorted by big corporations and increasingly international organisations with neoconservative and evangelical religious ideology. They discuss the US-based John Templeton Foundation's recent large investment in shaping research and policy development in character education in the UK which, they argue, aims 'to promote values of free market, individualist and socially conservative worldview'. Incidentally, to promote its anti-secular and religion compatible view of science, the same organisation has recently funded several projects aiming to overcome what it percives to be a concerning 'science-religion conflict' in Muslim societies simply assuming that such a conflict exists in all cultures (Templeton Grant Date Base 2016, 2017). Generously funded by the Templeton, these projects suggest improving the educational standards in current traditional Muslim theological seminaries through introducing 'a religious friendly science literacy' to facilitate a pedagogic reform in these institutions (Religion News Service 2018). These projects strangely seem to be uninterested in critical, reflective historical thinking skills of social sciences and humanities, for example, to be integrated into traditional seminary education. It this the latter social scientific competence that these traditional seminaries desperately need inorder to be able to facilitate contextual learning and teaching of Islam and its diverse historical expressions.

Clark et al. (2018) offered a critique of neoliberal educational discourse which often uses positive-sounding values such as 'entrepreneurship', 'widening access to higher education' and 'serving students as clients'. Their analysis suggests how these values – 'at face value reflecting the principles of democratic access, inclusion, social justice and benefiting from economic opportunities' – actually hide the reality of growing inequality in global economic systems. Furthermore, as Smith (2018) points out, while access to universities is widening, inequalities in higher education participation persist. What is more concerning is that the value of higher education itself has been increasingly put into question as there is less evidence linking having a 'university degree' with the desired outcome of positive social mobility.

With the reality of globalisation, there is also a growing presence of international students in western universities who are mostly seen as an easy revenue source. However, the responsibility for higher education institutions to provide learning opportunities that are transcultural in terms of ethos, values, place/environment of study, content and pedagogic experience has also become apparent (Matus and Talburt 2015; Gu et al. 2010). Higher education is increasingly associated with the values of 'global learning', a term which originated with the founding of the Global Learning Division of the United Nations University (UNU) in 1982. The aim was to develop educational practices that would enable people of different cultures to understand and respond to transnational challenges such as poverty, conflict, environment and ethical dilemmas that face global human society. Furthermore, it suggests a strong sense of learning to think globally: that is, recognizing the interconnected nature of the modern world (Soedjatmoko and Newland 1987). This has paved the way for the idea of modern 'global citizenship' (Hovland 2006) and the recognition of serving the 'global public good' (Kehm 2014) signifying the need to have a sense of shared interdependent futures.

The market-driven performance- and measurement-centred values defining most higher education systems have been widely criticised (Goodson and Gill 2014; McLaren 2009; Tight 2009). In their vision and mission statements, most universities do emphasise certain aspirational values such as fostering 'values of learning, inquiry, enterprise and contributing to social cohesion, well-being of the society, responding to the needs of global citizenship' (Scott 2005). However, the everyday reality of universities increasingly resembles a corporate life where students are seen as units of income and spending. Alternative models and philosophies of higher education have been put forward: university as a house of wisdom (Maxwell 1984), as civic spaces (Nixon 2018), a 'thinking and thoughtful' university where involvement, care and societal engagement complements the openness of thought itself (Bengtsen and Barnett (2018) and an ecological university where education is embedded in the physical environment, social relations and human subjectivity (Barnett 2017). The debate on the changing values in higher education urgently needs to take seriously the diversity of educational and pedagogic cultures increasingly sharing the same social space within contemporary societies. Universities, as places of global learning, can serve a culturally and religiously diverse student community and operate within an interconnected world.

The increasing Islamophobia and the negative impact of the official Prevent policy in the UK that now adds universities to its web of surveillance, makes constructive conversation on such sensitive issues very difficult. Although there are an estimated 300,000 Muslim students in the UK in further and higher education, there is very little empirical research exploring the campus experiences of Muslim students. The existing small-scale research, however, suggests alarming findings. A recent survey by the National Union of Students (2018), based on a sample of 578 participants, found that one third of respondents reported being negatively affected by the Prevent strategy, and 43% of them felt uncomfortable in expressing their views and engaging with debates on the campus due to the fear of being reported. One in three of the participants reported to have experienced some type of abuse and female students were mostly worried about their presence due to having visible Islamic dress such as a headscarf. Similarly, an official government report (Social Mobility 2016) suggests that there is a relatively high level of Muslim participation in higher education. The findings, however, also indicate that Muslim students are more likely to find themselves on unsatisfying study programmes, to experience higher dropout rates and, most likely, (particularly females) not be able to gain access, to post-university job markets.

Towards an Educational Dialogue of Convergence Facilitating a Shared Sense of Human Dignity and Common Good

A binary view of Islam and secular West held by some Muslim and non-Muslim educators such as Bilgrami and Ashraf (1985), Tan (2014) and Al-Attas (1980) often stresses the presence of an unbridgeable gap in the perception of education between Islam and the secular liberal West. Such a dichotomy has largely emerged as a reaction to the trauma of colonial experience whereby western secular education was enforced, in an authoritarian style, on the majority of Muslim nations. Therefore, one can appreciate to some extent such a strong negative reaction within the context of the colonial/postcolonial Muslim world. However, it is very concerning that such a binary mind set, transplanted from the grievance-ridden narrative of the post-colonial Muslim world, persists within the European Muslim diaspora. This has direct implications for the self-understanding of European Muslim youth and the way I which they relate to the cultural plurality in their lives.

The table offers a summary of an often-perceived incompatibility between Islamic and western secular values of education (Table 14.1).

However, this binary view reflects an ahistorical, literalist and reified perception of both Islam and the West. Although some of the observations may well be based on contemporary Muslim educational practices or Muslim impressions of western

Table 14.1 A binary view of Islamic and western educational values

	Western Liberal Secular Education	Islamic Education
Educational Pedagogic Values Vision & Perception	Human-centred	God-centred
	Learner-led	Teacher/text-led
	Freedom, autonomy	Obedience, reverence
	Scepticism, rationality, criticality	Certainty, trust, piety, fidelity
	Individualistic, personal fulfilment	Collectivist/ religious fellowship (*ummah*)&discipleship
	Free inquiry-based knowledge	Revelation, tradition-based knowledge,
	Materialistic, market driven, dualistsecularism	Spiritual, moral, holistic
	Discovery, questioning	Instruction, memorisation, transmission, indoctrination
	Progressive/linear time perception	Cylical, apocalyptic time perception
	Literate, organised, intellectual, scientific	Oral/aural, story-shaped nurture, unscientific
	Democratic, open	Authoritarian, inward-looking.
	Measured, assessed, outcomes based	Informal, repetitive, unmeasurable
	Civic, inclusive	Intolerant to religious, gender, cultural difference
	Interpretative plurality	Essentialist conformity, no role for personal interpretation
	....	....

education, the categorical difference is largely formed out of a mutual prejudice and stereotyping of both educational cultures. It certainly disregards the educational self-understanding of Islam and the historical experience between the educational cultures and thoughts of early Islam and the West. Crucially, it ignores the open educational attitude of the Qur'an and prophetic tradition that had motived first Muslims to adopt an educational curiosity about the diverse cultures with which they came into contact. The reminder of this this chapter offers a brief deconstruction of this binary literalism by drawing on the relevant historical evidence and discussing the nature of educational values in diverse traditions of Islamic higher education.

Seeing the world from a relational, holistic educational vision enshrined in the Qur'an stimulated early Muslims to engage with the indigenous thought and wisdom of the traditions of Persia, India and ancient Greece that in turn have contributed to the emergence of Islamic civilization (Sahin 2014). A key literary, educational and moral concept that shaped Muslim higher education – particularly its humanities curriculum, the *Adab,* which meant refinement of character, manners and aesthetic, literary taste – was developed out of interaction with the Indio-Persian heritage that Muslims inherited (Metcalf 1984). Ibn al-Muqaffa (d.670), a convert from Persia is usually credited with the development of the literary- and moral education-focused *adab* genre. It is significant that, when first Muslims reached Southeast Asia, largely through trade, instead of dismissing the deeply-rooted values of Hinduism and Buddhism of the region, they simply integrated and creatively expressed Islam within this rich civilisational tapestry. The morally and spiritually redefined Islamic *Adab* become easily adopted by people who mostly voluntarily converted to Islam. The *Adab* complemented and was richly reinterpreted within the indigenous educational cultures. For example, it was infused into the sense of being an 'educated person' as depicted in the *Darangen*, the pre-Islamic oral epic poem of the Maranao people of Southern Philippine (Milligan 2005). It is not surprising to note that so many contemporary Muslim thinkers in the Southeast Asia, like Al-Attas (1980) in Malaysia, have preferred the concept of Adab to be at the centre of their understanding of education in Islam.

Perhaps the largest outside influence contributing to the early flourishing of Muslim civilisation came from the encounter with ancient Greek thought, mainly Aristotelianism and Neoplatonism, that had already shaped Christianity and to some extent Judaism. Muslims preserved, studied and expanded ancient Greek philosophy and science (Gutas 1998; Walbridge 2001) without much serious hindrance from their faith. Most of early Muslim moral and educational thought was actually modelled on ancient Greek works. Even Muslim theologians, the *mutakallimun*, could not resist adopting the systematic thinking habits of the ancient Greeks. It was mostly the educated Christian Arabs who possessed the required linguistic competence and were encouraged by the Caliphs to translate Greek philosophical and scientific works into Arabic (Ephat 2000). Muslim philosophers like Al-Farabi (d.951), in his well-known book on 'attaining happiness', not only commented but developed these original works to the point of attempting to reconcile the philosophies of Plato and Aristo. Ibn Sina (Avicenna) (d.1037) even began to subdue Islam within the thinking habits of ancient Greek philosophy which he took to be superior to the religious language of Islam that he merited only as a good source of general public moral education. Muslim theologians like Al-Ghazali (d.1111) and Ibn Taymiyah (d.1328), who had mastered Greek philosophy and classical Islamic sciences, eventually offered a much more nuanced and critical reading of the ancient Greek legacy. The former exposed the incoherence in the philosophical discourse of Muslim philosophers like Ibn Sina and the latter written influential works on refutation the Aristotelian logic (Hallaq 1997). However, even the pioneers of early indigenous Islamic rationality, Mutazilah, could not resist using the categories of philosophical thinking which had led to the emergence of Islamic philosophical theology. The Andalusian philosopher Ibn Rushd (Averroes) (d.1198), working in the early Muslim western context of Spain, persuasively argued for the strong compatibility between Islam (Sharia) and Greek philosophy. As S. Gunter's short comparative study (2015) demonstrates, as a result of being nourished by ancient Greek ideas, both the Muslim Averroes and the Christian Thomas Aquinas's philosophies of education exhibit stark similarities. Such a dialectical engagement enriched classical Muslim thought as it enabled a synthetic and integrated Muslim educational self-understanding to flourish. It cannot be stressed highly enough that contemporary Muslims need to have confidence in their tradition and revive this early Muslim spirit of learning and critical education in order to creatively engage with the challenges facing them.

Most of classical Islamic ethical thought and moral education, with few exceptions, have parallels with, if not modelled on, early Greek thinking. This was not a simple borrowing but a creative appropriation and integration into the core revelation-based Islamic values. For example, the books written within the genre of Adab were mostly entitled as 'refinement of character' (*Tahdhib al-Akhlaq*) and modelled on the original Greek inspired work by the Christian Ibn 'Adi (d.974). Naturally, Ibn 'Adi's book (Al Takriti, 1978) has no reference to the Qur'an but the equivalent works by Muslim scholars – such as al-Raghab al-Isfahani (d.1109) and even philosopher Ibn Miskawayh (d.1030) who penned a work with the same title – integrated the core Greek ethics with insights gleaned from the Qur'an and prophetic traditions. It appears that the philosophical and educational ethics in Islam were deeply shaped by ancient Greek concepts (Bucar 2018) such as *phronesis*, referring to the kind of practical wisdom and virtues, in Muslim tradition *hikma*, needed for developing a good sense, judgment and following the best course of action in one's life. The epistles of *Ikhwan al-Safa*, the brethren of purity, in eighth/tenth century, is another integrated model of an early comprehensive work on Islamic public education (Sahin 2012). Muslims adopted an educational learning attitude towards their own faith but, most crucially, towards the wisdom embedded in humanity's collective memory. As the 20-volume work, Book of Songs, by Abu al-Faraj al-Isfahani (d.967) illustrates, even the pre-Islamic Arab oral traditions of singing, poetry, humour, and story-telling were diligently studied and used as educational resources.

The above dichotomic perception does not square with the nature and character of educational self-understanding in Muslim core sources and the diverse traditions relating to its higher education institutions. There is no space to explore the dynamic educational theology and hermeneutics that shaped Muslim intellectual heritage:

suffice it to say that while Muslim higher education was open to the values developed within diverse pedagogic and ethical models outside the Muslim world, it managed to interpret them within a higher Islamic educational value system. For example, as mentioned above, the classical Greek ethical idea of *sophrosyne* ('excellence of character, perfect harmony') that also refers to the 'power of self-control, training and controlling passion with reason' influenced Muslim educational ethics and its perception of the perfect human being. However, the Qur'an and the prophetic traditions put forward a much more holistic perception of human nature and its perfection into a balanced maturity that integrates bodily, rational, moral and spiritual elements. The idea of human excellence, harmony and just balance is expressed not with the brute power of control or possession of abstract knowledge but with the concept of ihsaan: that is, perfecting one's conduct in life and showing values of kindness, compassion, generosity, hospitality and openness. The inner control is tied with increasing self-awareness and being God-consciousness (*taqwa*). Furthermore, a rigorous application of educational hermeneutics on the Qur'an reveals that that the value of gratitude (*shukr*) defines the nature of Islamic faithfulness and brings about a grateful humanity iat the heart of its critical and reflective pedagogy (Sahin 2017).

Finally, the values of educational ethics in Islamic and western civilisation in its secular and religious foundations rests on the notion of human dignity. For example, within the Judeo-Christian tradition there is a clear emphasis on the idea that humanity is created in the image of God (Gen 1:26–28) and, therefore, the dignity and sanctity of all humanity, regardless of colour and creed, needs to be respected. Moreover, within prophetic monotheism there is a clear demand that practising justice and addressing inequality should be part of faithfulness. In the Muslim tradition, contributing to the 'common good' (maslaha) and ensuring the dignity (karamah), well-being and security of all, regardless of communities' ethnicity and religious affiliation, are fundamental educational and ethical values. Read within such a contextual hermeneutics, theology (that is, the virtual dimension of faith, or God-centredness) becomes an anthropology (that is, collapses into a human-focused horizontal dimension articulated as an ethical demand to facilitate human well-being, justice, happiness and fulfilment). As such, faith becomes a liberating educational force facilitating human formation and flourishing (*tarbiyah*), nurturing values of gratitude (*shukr*), respect for human dignity (*karamah*) and emphasising the need to remain open to difference (*taaruf*). For a detailed analysis of these critical educational concepts in Islam, see Sahin (2014).

Islamic Higher Education in Secular Context: Forming an Islamic Critical Pedagogy of Reconciliation

As mentioned at the start of the chapter, there is a complex set of challenges that arise from the presence of diverse Muslim communities in Europe today. Challenges are often perceived, interpreted and responded to differently by the minority Muslim communities in Europe and the wider secular European states and societies. Instead of a dialogical convergence, there seems to be a politics of divergence at work when framing this sensitive issue. The widespread policies of surveillance and feeling of being under suspicion severely undermine Muslim civic rights, recognition and participation within the democratic polity that professes to be open and inclusive of cultural and religious plurality. There is a growing number of promising Muslim individual and group initiatives that aims to create a positive change within the British Muslim communities (Lewis and Hamid 2018). However, it is regrettable that during the last two decades Muslim communities, by and large, have been very reluctant to acknowledge the rise of religious extremism in their midst while policy-makers have simply assumed that a security-focused approach will solve the problem of radicalisation and violent extremism. Within such a polarised context, it is difficult to discern constructive ways with which to address the challenges that are strongly felt and voiced by both Muslim communities and wider society.

In such a volatile socio-political context, it is important find out how Islamic higher education institutions respond to the educational challenges facing the community. In the UK alone, there are more than 25 traditional Muslim higher education institutions (the theological seminaries known as *dar-al-uluum/hawza*) none of which are recognised by the mainstream UK education system. There is a handful of independent hybrid Muslim higher education institutions which offer externally validated degrees. Most of these institutions have been set up by contemporary transnational Islamic movements, networks belonging to majority Sunni and minority Shia Islam. Most of these movements have come out of the trauma of the postcolonial Muslim world and largely shape the religiosity of Muslims in the UK and wider Europe. Mainly due to access issues, there has not been any serious study of these institutions exploring the student-intake, duration, curriculum, and the expected religious- and employment-related outcomes of such a long educational process that includes a parallel offered study provision for completing GCSE and A levels. The existing few ethnographic studies on Muslim seminaries are too anecdotal to be taken seriously. The educational culture in these institutions and the impact of the teaching/learning experiences on the formation of students' identity and values are among the areas needing to be urgently researched.

Often set up by charismatic personalities, these institutions show more interest in reproducing the existing power structures, expanding their influence among the young by perpetuating certain interpretations of Islam. It appears there is less interest in building an open reflective Muslim educational culture that adopts a professional attitude to education and that puts student needs at the heart of its pedagogic mission. For over a decade, I have been exploring the formation of religiosities among Muslim youth, faith leaders and graduates of traditional Islamic seminaries in Britain (Sahin 2014). The data was gathered through a 'Semi-Structured Muslim Subjectivity Interview Schedule' (MSIS) which includes an 'attitude towards Islam scale, a self-characterisation sketch' and several theological/ socio-political themes that the participants are invited to discuss. The interviews were analysed by applying a set of assessment criteria constructed to discern psycho-social processes of 'commitment and exploration' as articulated within the religious life of the participants.

This longitudinal study has revealed four types of 'religiosities' amongst the students and the graduates of Muslim higher education institutions in the UK. The first is an 'exploratory' religious identity, mostly observed among female and younger age groups, who wanted the relevance of Islam to be demonstrated rather than merely asserted; the second is a 'diffused identity' where Islam only functions as a cultural sentiment; the third is a 'foreclosed' religiosity, potentially rendering individuals vulnerable to radical voices, the third being the dominant of the three. These two latter religiosities – coupled with increasing Islamophobia, socioeconomic inequalities, the reality of inter-generational change and what is perceived to be unjust and unethical Western foreign policy towards the Muslim world – have created a fertile ground for religious extremism to emerge. The fourth, 'achieved mode' of religiosity signifying an exploratory and confident sense of religious agency showing willingness to accept diverse interpretations of Islam and engage with the cultural plurality has not been observed among the study participants. Two recent empirical studies (Khan 2015; Zaheer 2018) using Sahin's MSIS show that the educational and pedagogic culture which is overwhelmingly 'text-teacher-centred/transmission-oriented', observed in current traditional Muslim theological seminaries, and the hybrid Muslim higher education institutions appear to be largely reproducing the dominant 'foreclosed type' of religiosities and hence perpetuating the leadership crises affecting Muslim communities.

Research in the traditional Muslim seminaries in the UK is scarce. As such, what is even less known is the female students' experience of studying in these institutions and whether they are able to effectively prepare the formation of Muslim female education and faith leadership in the UK. A recent qualitative case study (Sahin 2019), consisting of 25 in-depth interviews conducted among the female graduates of traditional seminaries in the UK, indicates the presence of concerning pedagogic, educational and student-welfare related issues. Students mostly attend seminaries out of strong family encouragement and fear of secular university that is perceived to be alienating young people from their faith and culture. Participants appreciated the opportunity of studying their faith but felt uncomfortable with the discontinuity in their educational experience gained in mainstream schooling and the dar al-uluum. The latter, they opined, was a much more controlling educational culture, centred around the authority of the teacher(s) and contributing less to formation of their personal agency. It is not surprising that the participants noted that many of their friends after a year or two would simply leave, pointing to the reality of high drop-out rates in these institutions.

The educational culture at the universities in Muslim majority societies faces similar challenges that need be taken up by a separate study. There are (a) few encouraging attempts, particularly in Indonesia, to develop an integrated model of Islamic higher education (Woodward 2015). It appears that an indigenous sense of 'Islamic civic, democratic educational vision' is starting to shape Indonesian Islamic universities. Such an inclusive educational philosophy grounded in Islamic educational values needs to be followed by the rest of the Muslim world. However, suffice it to say that the Islam/West binary (explored above) continues to frame higher education in most of the so-called hinterland of the Muslim world. As several Arab Human Development Reports (2016) have shown, there is little evidence suggesting that higher education is actually contributing to positive social change, even in oil-rich Arab Gulf states. The increasing colonisation of higher education space by the western universities, mainly motivated by business interests, appear to be making little positive impact. In fact, it only reinforces the dichotomy between western liberal arts/science education and traditional perceptions and values of education in these societies (Guessoum 2018).

Mainly due to its popularity, many non-specialist academics in Social Sciences feel the urge to produce books on Education, Islam and Islamic Education. (For a recent comprehensive critical review of this literature see Sahin 2018). With very few exceptions, most of the literature on contemporary Islamic Education and more specifically Muslim higher education adopt a narrow historical or socio-political focus while neglecting engagement with educational and pedagogic culture within these institutions. A meaningful integration of Islamic higher education within the mainstream university system in the West requires collaborative partnerships. Above all else, it requires the presence of a professional approach to Islamic Education as well as a critical/reflective holistic Muslim education philosophy that is not hindered by the simplistic dismissal of western liberal secular education. Similarly, western liberal educators need to be part of this critical dialogue showing curiosity about the educational thought of Islam rather than simply dismissing Islamic education as mere religious indoctrination.

Most hybrid Islamic Higher Education institutions are based on highly pragmatic collaborative partnerships with mainstream universities validating their academic degrees. Such a collaborative provision, which in principle is a positive development that needs to encouraged, increases the legitimacy and academic reputation of the former institutions. However, despite such partnerships having existed for almost two decades now, there is hardly a single convincing case where it has led to a formation of a reflective educational academic exchange and dialogue between Islamic institutions and their validating university partners. The educational/ pedagogic culture and the wider academic environment within these institutions almost always remain the same: a variation of a teacher-text centred provision that hardly encourages students to develop reflective critical learning skills and facilitate an open engagement with the curriculum. Therefore, such partnerships often do not go beyond an initially set short period and have not facilitated enough academic capacity-building that could enable these institutions to offer their own degrees and become the first models of trusted and inclusive Islamic higher education institutions in Western Europe.

Young European Muslim leadership needs to be resourced with a reflective *Muslim paideia* – the interpretive and imaginative pedagogic skills – that facilitate indigenous Islamic expressions of being European, and European articulations of Islam. Islamic higher education appears very distant from bringing about such an urgently needed education model in both majority and minority Muslim societies. In continental Europe, due to the pressure to mitigate against perceived Islamist extremism, there is now state-sponsored academic provision for Islamic theology and teacher training which, due to space limitation, has not been evaluated here. In the UK, the first Islamic Education access course that is focused on bridging the pedagogic gap between the educational culture of the traditional Islamic higher education institutions and mainstream university is offered at the University of Warwick where Islamic Education Studies is a recognised interdisciplinary field of research, scholarly study and professional development (For further details see: https://warwick.ac.uk/newsandevents/pressreleases/uks_first_access/).

Conclusion

Contemporary societies are increasingly defined by cultural and religious plurality. Making sense of such hyper-cultural diversity, enabling it to become a positive resource for enriching humanity and inspiring peaceful and just coexistence, is among the central challenges facing the twenty-first century world. The irrational fear of the 'other' and cultural plurality have begun to put humanity into a regressive mode of desiring to return to an 'imagined' past seeking solace in an idealised 'pure identity narrative'. This threatens the inclusive nature of democratic societies and deepens the structural inequalities in these societies. This chapter has discussed the importance of creating a reflective dialogue among contemporary diverse cultures, tradtions and values of higher education in order to facilitate mutual understanding and a desire to better relate to one another, leading to a community of global learners and just and peaceful coexistence. Young generations need to be given the opportunity for developing intercultural competence and educational values inspiring them to learn and remain critically open to one another. The chapter has deconstructed the perceived binary incompatibility thesis between Islamic and western higher educational values. In its place, it has offered evidence for the presence of a shared reflective and critical educational heritage between Islam and the West and argued for the need to revive this forgotten tradition of pedagogic curiosity to inspire a new cross-pollinating dialogue capable of acknowledging the dignity of being different and recognizing the reality of sharing an interdependent world. The gradually emerging Muslim higher education institutions and wider mainstream universities need to embed the educational values of critical openness and dialogue so that they can better respond to the changing needs of students under their care.

References

Al Takriti, N. (Ed.). (1978). *Yahya Ibn 'Adi: A critical edition and study of his Tahdhib al-Akhlaq*. Beirut/Paris: Editions Oueida.

Al-Attas, S. M. N. (1980). *The concept of education in Islam: A framework for an Islamic philosophy of education*. Kuala Lumpur: IITC.

Allen, K., & Bull, A. (2018). Following policy: A network ethnography of the UK character education policy commu-nity. *Sociological Research Online, 23*(2), 438–458.

Atçıl, A. (2017). *Scholars and sultans in the early modern ottoman empire*. Cambridge: Cambridge University Press.

Bartlett, S., & Burton, D. (2016). *Introduction to education studies*. London: Sage.

Barnett, R. (2017). *The ecological university; a feasible utopia.* London: Routledge.

Bengtsen, S. S. E., & Barnett, R. (Eds.). (2018). *The thinking university a philosophical examination of thought and higher education.* London: Springer.

Bilgrami, H. H., & Ashraf, S. A. (1985). *The concept of Islamic University.* London: Arnold Overseas.

Bucar, E. M. (2018). Islamic virtue ethics. In N. E. Snow (Ed.), *The Oxford handbook of virtues.* Oxford: Oxford University Press.

Clark, J., et al. (2018). Ideology in neoliberal higher education: The case of the entrepreneur. *Journal for Critical Education Policy Studies, 16,* 238–260.

Dewy, J. (2011). *My pedagogic creed.* Boston: Applewood Books.

Ephat, D. (2000). *A learned society in a period of transition.* Albany: State University of New York.

Freire, P. (2000). *Pedagogy of the oppressed.* London: Penguin.

Gibbs, P. (1998). Competence or trust: The academic offering. *Quality in Higher Education, 4*(1), 7–15.

Giroux, H. A. (2011). *On critical pedagogy.* London: Bloomsbury Publishing USA.

Goodman, L. E. (2003). *Islamic humanism.* Oxford: Oxford University Press.

Goodson, I., & Gill, S. (2014). *Critical narrative as pedagogy.* London: Bloomsbury Academic.

Goodson, I., & Scherto, G. (2014). *Critical narrative as pedagogy.* London: Bloomsbury Academic.

Gu, Q., et al. (2010). Learning and growing in a 'foreign' context: Intercultural experiences of international students. *Compare: A Journal of Comparative and International Education, 40*(1), 7–23.

Guessoum, N. (2018). Is liberal arts education a good model for Arab Universities? In E. Baydoun & J. R. Hillman (Eds.), *Universities in Arab countries: An urgent need for change* (pp. 175–187). Cham: Springer.

Gunter, S. (2015). Averroes and Thomas Aquinas on education. In M. Pom-erantz & A. Shahin (Eds.), *The heritage of Arabo-Islamic learning* (pp. 250–283). Leiden: Brill.

Gutas, D. (1998). *Greek thought, Arabic culture: The Graeco-Arabic translation movement in Baghdad and early 'Abbasaid society (2nd-4th/5th–10th c.).* London: Routledge.

Habermas, J. (1973). *Theory and practice* (J. Viertel, Trans.). Boston: Beacon.

Hallaq, W. (1997). *Ibn Taymiyya against the Greek logicians.* Oxford: Oxford University Press.

Hovland, K. (2006). *Shared futures: Global learning and Liberal education.* Washington, DC: Association of American Colleges and Universities.

Husserl, E. (1970). *The crisis of European sciences and transcendental phenomenology, an introduction to phenomenological philosophy* (D. Carr, Trans.). Evanston: Northwestern University Press.

Kehm, B. M. (2014). Beyond neo-liberalism: Higher education in Europe and the global public good. In P. Gibbs & R. Barnett (Eds.), *Thinking about higher education.* Heidelberg: Springer.

Khan, I. (2015). *The development of leadership through Islamic education: An empirical inquiry into 'religiosity' and the styles of 'educational leadership' experienced by contemporary graduates of Muslim Institutes of Higher Education in the UK.* Unpublished PhD thesis, University of Gloucestershire.

Levine, R. A., & White, M. I. (2017). *Human conditions: The cultural basis of educational developments.* London: Routledge.

Lewis, P., & Hamid, S. (2018). *British Muslims new directions in Islamic thought, creativity and activism.* Edinburgh: Edinburgh University Press.

Makdisi, G. (1981). *The rise of colleges: Institutions of learning in Islam and the West.* Edinburgh: Edinburgh University Press.

Makdisi, G. (1990). *The rise of humanism in classical Islam and the Christian West: With special reference to scholasticism.* Edinburgh: Edinburgh University Press.

Matus, C., & Talburt, S. (2015). Producing global citizens for the future: Space, discourse and curricular reform. *Compare: A Journal of Comparative and International Education., 45,* 226–247.

Maxwell, N. (1984). *From knowledge to wisdom.* Oxford: Blackwell.

McCulloch, G. (2002). Disciplines contributing to education? Educational studies and the disciplines. *Educational Studies, 50*(1), 100–119.

McLaren, P. (2009). Critical pedagogy: A look at the major concepts. In A. Darder et al. (Eds.), *The critical pedagogy reader* (pp. 61–84). London: Routledge.

Merleau-Ponty, M. (2013). *Phenomenology of perception*. London: Routledge.

Metcalf, B. (Ed.). (1984). *Moral conduct and authority: The place of Adab in South Asian Islam*. Berkeley: University of California Press.

Milligan, J. A. (2005). *Islamic identity, postcoloniality, and educational policy*. New York: Palgrave Macmillan.

National Union of Students. (2018). *The experience of Muslim students*.

Nemiroff, G. (1992). *Reconstructing education: Toward a pedagogy of critical humanism*. New York: Bergin & Garvey.

Newman, J. H. C. (1996). *The idea of a university*. New York: Yale University Press.

Nixon, J. (2018). Universities as civic spaces: In the footsteps of Arendt and Jaspers. In R. Barnett & M. A. Peters (Eds.), *The idea of the university: Contemporary perspectives v.2* (pp. 447–461). New York: Peter Lang.

Rawls, J. (2005). *A theory of justice*. London: Harvard University Press.

Religion News Service. (2018). *Madrasa discourses equip tomorrow's Islamic scholars with scientific literacy*. https://religionnews.com/2018/12/03/madrasa-discourses-equip-tomorrows-islamic-scholars-with-scientific-literacy/. Accessed 20 Dec 2018.

Sahin, A. (2012). The role of educational theology in reconciling faith and reason in Islam: Reflections on the case of Ikhwan al-Safa. *The Muslim World Book Review, 32*(4), 6–17.

Sahin, A. (2014). *New direction in Islamic education: Pedagogy and identity formation* (Rev ed.). Leicestershire: Kube Academic.

Sahin, A. (2017). Education as compassionate transformation: The ethical heart of Islamic pedagogy. In P. Gibbs (Ed.), *The pedagogy of compassion at the heart of higher education* (pp. 125–137). Heidelberg: Springer.

Sahin, A. (2018). Critical issues in Islamic education studies: Rethinking Islamic and Western liberal secular values of education. *Religion, 9*(11), 335.

Sahin, A. (2019). Challenges of female faith leadership formation in British Muslim diaspora: Exploring female students' educational experience in Muslim seminaries (dar al-auluums). In A. Sahin (Ed.), *Islamic education in contemporary world: Traditions, rearticulations & transformation, special issues of religions*. Basel: MDPI. (Forthcoming).

Scott, P. (1993). The idea of the university in the 21st century: A British perspective. *British Journal of Educational Studies, 41*, 4–25.

Scott, P. (2005). The university and civic values. In S. Robinson & C. Katulushi (Eds.), *Values in higher education*. London: Aureus Publishing.

Smith, E. (2018). *Key issues in education and social justice*. London: Routledge.

Snaith, N. H. (2009). *Distinctive ideas of the old testament*. New York: Wipf & Stock Pub.

Soedjatmoko, & Newland, K. (1987). The United Nations University: A new kind of university. *The Washington Quarterly, 10*, 215–224.

Tan, C. (2014). *Islamic education and indoctrination*. London: Routledge.

Tapper, T., & Palfreyman, D. (2010). *The collegial tradition in the age of mass higher education*. London: Springer.

Templeton Foundation. (2016). *Grant data base*. Available at: https://www.templeton.org/grants/grant-database

The Social Mobility Challenges Faced by Young Muslims. (2017). The Social Mobility Commission.

Tight, M. (2009). *Higher education in the United Kingdom since 1945*. Buckingham: Open University Press.

Woodward, K. E. (2015). Indonesian schools: Shaping the future of Islam and democracy in a democratic Muslim country. *Journal of International Education and Leadership, 5*(1), 10–25.

Zaheer, M. (2018). *Modes of religiosity and attitude towards community cohesion and social integration among British Sunni Muslims: an empirical case study*. Unpublished PhD thesis, University of Gloucestershire.

Chapter 15
The Values of Liberté, Égalité, Fraternité 50 Years on: Why the 'Free Speech' Debate Makes It Even Less Likely That Mai '68 Could Happen in Britain Now Than It Was Then

Alison Scott-Baumann

Abstract In May 1968 there was a strong sense of left-wing camaraderie that drew many French university students into collaboration with the workers' unions to rise up against de Gaulle's government. It is highly unlikely that British campuses could be gripped by these values of solidarity and shared agency in a common cause: what can that tell us about Britain? In Britain there are assumptions on the part of many young adults that we are free, equal and fraternal. The parallel digital world that they inhabit so comfortably appears to encourage and facilitate consumer behaviour and freedom of expression: it seems possible to buy and write online almost exactly what you like without consequences. Yet against a backdrop of crass populist discourse there are urgent issues regarding ethical behaviour: online and offline use of language is sharply racialised and gendered. People of colour and women of all ages are frequently attacked. Hate speech is poorly controlled and legal restraints are lagging behind the global digital empires. In addition, on campus the British government is intervening much more than ever before, which makes some students less free, less equal and less fraternal than others. Free speech is being constrained. Populism is on the rise, framed by political alienation. Finally, precarity affects the young in their responses to university: is it worth incurring the debt of high fees? The philosophy of Ricoeur and Lorey show how to interrogate dominant discourses and attempt a better world.

Keywords Prevent · Free speech · Populist discourse · Solidarity · Hate speech

A. Scott-Baumann (✉)
School of Oriental and African Studies, University of London, London, UK
e-mail: as150@soas.ac.uk

© Springer Nature Switzerland AG 2019
P. Gibbs et al. (eds.), *Values of the University in a Time of Uncertainty*,
https://doi.org/10.1007/978-3-030-15970-2_15

Introduction

In twentieth century France the ideas of Karl Marx took many forms and provided students with various models for challenging the state and showing solidarity with workers. Not only is Marxism largely lacking in Britain, but also political activities of all types are being actively discouraged on campus. There are two ways in which government achieves this. Firstly, the 2015 Counter Terror and Security Act has spawned a set of guidelines (the Prevent Duty Guidance) that advises reducing discussion of Islam and the Muslim world, in case students are radicalised into committing acts of terror. There is no evidence that this has ever happened on campus but it is taken seriously nevertheless. This approach affects three important aspects of university campus life: student society activities, visiting speaker invitations and the curriculum. Secondly, the student unions have recently been constrained by the Charity Commission to behave like charities and become apolitical. This discourages student society activities about anything that does not directly concern the local welfare of students on that campus. My research shows that these two regulatory mechanisms are having a chilling effect on freedom of expression and that the instruction from the Charity Commission to avoid discussing, for example, environmental issues, whale hunting, Prevent, Israel/Palestine and the state of political prisoners abroad is having an oppressive influence upon students. There are complex reasons for this that require analysis, at a time 50 years on from May 1968 when urban French campuses are again in turmoil from militant student action and British campuses are, again, not rising up. In the context of this chapter these issues of Prevent and the Charity Commission can only be summarised. More detailed analyses are provided by Heath-Kelly (2017), Scott-Baumann (2017a, b, 2018a, b), and Scott-Baumann and Perfect (2019) (in preparation).

Free, Equal and Fraternal in 1960s Europe

In May 1968 I was an English teenager, I wore my skirts and my hair long, and I read Mao's little red book and Baudelaire's poetry. All that summer I sat on the floor with my penfriend in Strasbourg and we spoke very seriously about freedom and identity, read *Les Fleurs du Mal* to each other and opined on the rebellious, cool dudes manning the barricades in Paris. Perhaps we were quite relieved that they were a long way away. Later I wondered if much at all had happened and, when I went to university in England, I was not in the least interested in, or cognisant of, political activism among the student body. That level of inactivity was then, and still is, characteristic of students in well-established democracies – except for the French and possibly the Germans, who coined their own terms: the *soixante-huitardes* and the *Achtundsechziger* respectively.

However, Vinen's suggestion that there was a lack of sincerity during the 'long '68' seems unjust and inaccurate (Vinen 2018). Believing in ideals, even when some behaviour was frankly ridiculous, gives us values to honour. The image of young adults walking 20 abreast down a boulevard in Paris, Lille or Lyon, arms linked, heads held high, proselytising zeal flashing in their eyes about something or nothing in particular, is an 'iconic' one that we can conjure up easily because we have seen it often in black and white photographs from the late 1960s and early 1970s. British students don't have the same reputation. Indeed both then and now, levels of political literacy on campus appear to be low: French students are revolting again in 2018 but British students don't seem to have noticed the chilling effect orchestrated by the Prevent Duty Guidance agenda and by the Charity Commission. In fact this chilling effect intensified soon after 9/11 and was present even before that with regard to certain topics that had already been discouraged for some time, most notable of which is Israel/Palestine.

So What Happened in May 1968 in France: Sex and Drugs and Rock 'N' Roll

This was photogenic stuff: we witnessed fighting on the streets, burning cars and Gauloises-smoke-filled rooms heady with Marxist debate. In fact France was moved: President de Gaulle fled the country briefly, the government of France nearly fell and when it was all over the French workers had secured considerable improvements in their working conditions (*salles de réunions, panneaux syndicales*; staff rooms and union noticeboards) and salaries. Students had won the right to sit on management committees (*cogestion* co-management) although that turned out to be somewhat illusory. These changes came as a result of this socialist type of left wing populism and France felt chastened and relieved. At that time in Britain, the Labour working class was strongly united in values based on equality but, after that, the 1970s miners' strikes led to the destruction of Labour's main base, the workers (Ali 2018:6). Thus in 1968 there was a great deal of counterculture but the middle classes did not unite with the workers. It was not politics at the barricades, it was cultural politics: rebellious music, theatre, clothes and sex. The sex was very present on French university campuses too; while French students' support for workers' strikes had led to improved pay and working conditions, students were also keen on liberating each other.

For Paul Ricoeur, French philosopher and witness to these events, it seemed that one could actually attribute the events of May 1968 partly to a sexual revolution (Ricoeur 1974). Ricoeur attributed the unrest also to the mixing of socio-economic groups (middle-class and working class, broadly speaking). Surely we must also see the febrile world context. Many French students knew about and regretted their country's and others' colonial actions and made attempts to retrieve some good from them: they recalled 1954 Dien Bien Phu, 1955 Bandung, 1959 Cuba, 1960 African colonial independence, they despised the French government's dealings with Algeria ('freed' in 1962), they noted the 1966 tricontinental conference and there was always Vietnam. British students tended to use music lyrics, fashion statements and art to express their understanding while French students rioted.

In France, Ricoeur found the Sorbonne system oppressive, inefficient and impersonal. He had great hopes for the new campus at Nanterre, mud pits in the suburbs that he hoped would create a blueprint for a new university system. The social revolution that ensued, starting at Nanterre with features of a political revolt, was in fact a great disappointment to him. His work on the violence of language and the necessity for balance in dialectical provisionality and debate would have benefited the students greatly if they had been in a state of mind to listen. We can still learn from Ricoeur's sophisticated versions of thought from that turbulent time, trying to lessen the impact of Hegel in order to admire and critique Freud. Meanwhile the British university system, although still elitist and sexist, already represented the practical approaches for which Ricoeur longed; tutorial systems, smaller lecture halls than France and academic staff on site available for discussion.

The Situation in Twenty-First Century Britain

There are economic and ideologically driven values at stake on the British campus. In economic terms neoliberal marketisation has made the student-as-customer and debtor into the single unit that defines the modern university and colleagues on mainland Europe commiserate on our loss of the independent British university system that Ricoeur admired so much 40 years ago (Collini 2018: 39). This is in stark contrast to the nineteenth century sense that knowledge will empower the individual to enrich society culturally, economically and even morally. These older values can still be seen occasionally on campus, particularly because of the unusual nature of the university community, a vibrant place where young people of different backgrounds, cultures and socio-economic means can meet who would otherwise never do so. Yet there are ideological values embedded in the surveillance policy structures I've mentioned that militate against frank discussion of controversial matters, let alone revolt.

In 2017 the Higher Education Policy Institute (HEPI) published their analysis of free speech on campus (*Keeping Schtumm*); they found that students are ambivalent about free speech, which is perhaps no surprise, as it is a complex issue. In March 2016 HEPI had conducted a student survey about free speech on campus. HEPI found that over 50% of the student sample they worked with believed that it is reasonable for universities to work closely with the police and security services to identify students at risk. They also supported the training of staff to recognise people who might support terrorism. One in five of the sample of students indicated they do not know what their personal opinion is. When asked about the NUS's non-platforming policy, 76% agreed wholly or partly with it and 48% support a safe space policy. It is difficult to know from these findings whether students were considering the issues around self-censorship and whether it is commonly perceived to be necessary to ensure that a segment of the population do not express their thoughts.

This may be thought of by many as a necessary evil: ring-fencing the possible danger from one small group can be accepted grudgingly as a utilitarian necessity when seeking to preserve the wellbeing of the majority. What is not clear is whether these students were aware that some students might feel freer to speak openly than others. This possibility was clearly understood from empirical data collected during the 2016–2017 academic year for the 3 year AHRC project based at SOAS, 'Re/presenting Islam on campus'. From a sample of nearly 300 staff and students at six university campuses, over 80 expressed concern about Prevent and its effects:

> And, as I say, I don't think terrorism is something that is … I mean, it's ludicrous to me to suggest that terrorism would be a concern with my students. But, at the same time, you know, I can imagine that they might feel intimidated by this sort of a climate of policing of their thought, and their ability to express ideas. (Academic staff member, AHRC research project)

How can we understand students now: are they transformers of a nation's cultural imagination or are they 'snowflakes' that melt at the slightest whiff of controversy? Our evidence suggests that they feel constrained by the surveillance atmosphere and may become unwilling transmitters of a restrictive cultural imagination. In 1968 in Paris it was different: they daubed obscene or political slogans on lecture hall walls and used quotes from classical philosophy to show their erudition – sometimes misspelt! This was 'move fast and break things' but not as we see it now multiplied by the internet (Taplin 2017). Taplin analyses how, over the last few decades, this mantra has inspired and shaped much about Silicon Valley. Contrasted with what happens in digital media now, the 1968 revolts seemed positively wholesome, because they were visible to all and physically enacted in public spaces by humans, not controlled by algorithms, disseminated by memes or secreted in supposedly private hate-filled chatrooms that periodically are 'outed' by a shocked chatroom member, as we shall see through discussion of events at Exeter and Warwick in spring 2018.

What we now have in 2018, in politicised spaces such as digital chatrooms and the right wing press, is a different and worrying tendency to use language to make non-dialogical and extreme assertions that are offensive, unproven and unprovable. These assertions make conversation impossible. In 1967, when the French student activism and desire to improve the French university system was beginning to build up, Ricoeur wrote an essay entitled Violence and Language, in which he demonstrates the dangers of these incompatible impulses becoming conjoined. Violence is quintessentially an imbalance of power, and this is currently manifested in language through non-dialogic utterances that discount the possibility of an interlocutor. These linguistic features have become characteristic of the amorphous yet dangerous political impulse called populism, often seen as a 'thin ideology' that cannot stand alone and that is parasitic upon another ideology from which it feels alienated, usually liberal democracy.

Populism is thus often based upon perceived alienation from political agency, a dichotomy between a pure people and a corrupt elite, as well as a demand to retain popular sovereignty (Mudde and Kaltwasser 2017). Unlike communism or fascism that are recognisably themselves, populism is a chameleon and can be left wing or right wing or both. What characterises populism currently across Europe and N. America is its dependence upon the use of extreme language as just described. This is so extreme and aggressive, often racist and hate filled, that students seek to avoid open contact with such utterances, perhaps believing that they cannot counter them. Students who engage in racist and sexist abuse online do not usually do so publicly and therefore cannot be challenged. This often creates a vacuum that populist assertions can fill, becoming strong without being challenged. Therefore I take populism as a challenge to us: a challenge to the language we have become accustomed to, online as well as off, a challenge to our memories of May 1968 and a challenge to our future agency after May 2018.

Public and Private Spaces

If May 1968 represented an attempt by students and workers to create a populist movement, shouting about everything they wanted and attempting to create liberté, égalité and fraternité, then populism presents a very different challenge for students in 2018. Outspoken talk has gone underground, i.e. online and has taken a very unpleasant turn: there is a specific example of this that shows how vulnerable students may have become to the illusion that the digital world is simultaneously liberating, egalitarian and fraternal. In spring 2018 it became public knowledge that two separate groups of students, one at Warwick University and one at Exeter, had been posting apparently racist and sexist messages to each other on what they believed to be private groups on Facebook and WhatsApp. Presumably a member of their group took a dislike to their posts and reported them. For some of these students this reportedly led to them losing their work placement at a law firm and being expelled from their university, for others it led to suspension. Lawyers became involved and there was much public discussion and newspaper coverage about these two episodes. I believe it would be inappropriate to comment upon the punishments meted out by the two universities, because I do not know the exact details of each event. Nevertheless it seems likely that university managements in general find themselves perplexed as to how to respond, because of the potential reputational damage to the institution and the possibility that any punishment could be unfair, given the likelihood that there is a great deal of such online behaviour that remains undetected/ unreported.

Public and Private Behaviour

The values ostensibly at stake in monitoring online behaviour are those enshrined in the Human Rights Act, Article 9 (freedom of thought, belief and religion) article 10; (freedom of expression), and article 11 (freedom of assembly and association). In addition these are protected by article 14; (protection from discrimination in respect of these rights and freedoms). Recently I was briefly interviewed on the Today programme on radio 4 about the Exeter and Warwick cases – and I had time to make two points: first, nothing online is ever private. Secondly, the illegal/borderline illegal nature of the hate speech that was used make it the responsibility of universities to warn students of the dangers of using such language and to put in place censuring and even punishment procedures. Certainly SOAS has a section in its code of conduct about such behaviour, on and offline. All students sign up to that upon arrival and the possibility of sanctions, including suspension and expulsion, are clear.

It is, however, possible that universities need to be more proactive in guiding students about online etiquette. I say this not least because of the tenor of the conversation threads that follow the newspaper articles that reported these events and the tone of my interlocutors in my radio interview. In both contexts there was a strong view that the young do make mistakes, they should be allowed to say unacceptable stuff and anyway they were writing privately. This is all true to a degree, but the debate indicates that there is therefore a general failure to acknowledge what Plato worked out a long time before the internet, namely that once you write something down, you cannot be responsible for it anymore. Nothing is private on the internet. There is also a possible failure of empathy: the perpetrators were young white men, writing obscene and racist posts about women and people of colour. Empathy can be considered to be a value that is highly prized in modern society. As the ability to understand another person's point of view, empathy can also be used ruthlessly in business, for example. However, it can be argued that a core principle of equality is the requirement that we should follow a broadly Kantian model, in treating others as we would wish them to treat us. Normally this means treating others with respect. Thus, while the parallel digital world appears to encourage and facilitate freedom, there are major issues regarding ethical behaviour. Mostly the digital world is remarkably, even shockingly, little regulated. In addition, the philosophical traditions and legal limits of free speech are poorly adhered to Lee and Scott-Baumann (2019).

One of the great triumphs of populism is that it creates the impression that the privileged majority are in fact suffering at the hands of others (such as immigrants) as if they were a beleaguered minority: we see this on a small scale with these micro-aggressions that relatively privileged students feel entitled to write down online.

Intrusion onto Campus Activities: The Charity Commission and Prevent

In contrast with the unregulated digital world, central government is intervening much more than ever before in student activities on campus, which I will show makes students less free, less equal and less fraternal. We are told by the media and by government that there is a moral crisis on campus: free speech is being hampered by students using no-platforming and safe spaces, such that they render themselves incapable of dealing with difficult concepts and ideas. Beloff asserts that he was no-platformed, perhaps almost as a badge of honour (Beloff 2018: 13). We are told how Germaine Greer and Peter Tatchell were no-platformed. From this debate we have the idea of the snowflake generation (Wonkhe 2017).

In fact the situation in this 'moral crisis' is rather different to the one being discussed so much: universities are unusual settings, where young people have to mix and socialise and learn together who otherwise might well avoid each other. In our daily lives after formal education we choose who we spend time with but at university we are thrown together. Over two million students study each year, and although they are a privileged minority, they also represent many different and potentially incompatible viewpoints, religious approaches and cultural backgrounds. Yet, despite this rich heterogeneity, on each university campus thousands of public events take place every year, and most of them pass without incident. Germaine Greer and Peter Tatchell were not no-platformed after all, they were able to speak, although costly security was probably necessary, because of the adverse publicity generated beforehand.

Yet it seems that there is some chilling of speech happening on campus. Not only are we receiving malinformation, but also there is undoubtedly some censorship, as it is harder than it used to be to discuss certain topics: Student Union (SU) officers report that they have to fill in a lot of paperwork for outside speakers and that they are more careful about what they discuss with students than they used to be (Scott-Baumann and Perfect in preparation 2019). This comes from the recent re-categorising of the SUs as full, no longer exempt, charities. By coming directly under the regulation of the Charity Commission, SUs have to accept CC regulations: SU behaviour must conform by being apolitical and by avoiding not only illegality but also controversy. Being controversial seems to be measurable on a Google test: if a prospective speaker is vilified online, they may be considered too controversial to invite. This is having a chilling effect on those campuses where there are Muslims. Moreover, it accords a great deal of power to the media to create controversy that becomes damaging even if unfounded.

This creates ethical dilemmas for student unions. As the Joint Committee on Human Rights pointed out in the final report about its investigation of free speech on campus:

> the generic guidance on protecting a charity's reputation does not place due weight on the fact that inhibiting lawful free speech can do as much damage to a student union's reputation as hosting a controversial speaker. (pp 36–7 JCHR final report)

Legal experts warn of the dangers of this and when Helen Mountfield QC gave evidence to the same JCHR investigation of free speech on campus she expressed her concern:

> The Charity Commission's view is that that expression of opinion goes beyond the student union's charitable objects and I think that rather depends on the way in which the opinion is presented. I think it goes too far and may suppress speech that is actually lawful and within the student union's charitable objects. (p 34 JCHR final report)

Precarity Conditions Students' Responses to University

Students are now encouraged to see themselves as customers, consumers of the education that they require in order to secure good jobs with their university degree. The idea of knowledge as intrinsically valuable, a good in itself seems to have fallen by the wayside. Annually over two million students are attending UK universities. Debt and difficulties in securing jobs are major factors in many of these young people's lives and yet the state we inhabit is still relatively stable: as integral components of the necessary balances in a mature democracy, the judiciary is still relatively independent of government and although education may no longer be, it is at least aware to some extent of its dependency (Collini 2018). Lorey demonstrates how the neoliberal approach functions within this stable state to create the impression of instability which makes us easier to govern. This is achieved partly by increasing fears about security, manifested in the perceived need for enhanced police and military support, surveillance regimes, and discourse about freedom and insecurity, not about freedom and security (Lorey 2012:64). Because it is becoming difficult for students to be confident about job prospects, economic instability is, relatively speaking, a major concern that may not be demonstrably improved by attending university. The shrunken state apparatus increasingly functions to construct this impression of social insecurity, which makes the precariousness of living well into a reality. The Brexit discourse is perfectly attuned to amplifying this pervasive sense of insecurity whereby 'insecurity becomes a normalised mode of government' (Lorey 2012: 65). It seems unlikely that students in Britain would rebel when they find themselves increasingly embedded in insecurity, although of course Britain is still a safe and stable country. In challenging and addressing these phenomena, the young have a unique role to play. A university education allows for higher-level formation of abstract and practical ideas, which should encourage a critical approach to extremisms, as well as higher chain production where developed western economies can compete on a global scale – led by university education, innovation and research.

Populism is creating societal tensions and we ask why it is that the young seem unable to see the dangerous possibilities of populism in its current forms. We know that youth activism erupts at times when established political structures and players prove unable or unwilling to tackle a problem: racism in Birmingham Alabama 1963, capitalism in Paris 1968, Russian control in the Prague spring 1968, oppression in Soweto 1976, desire for democracy in the Arab spring 2011, gun control protests in USA 2018, and there are many more. Students protest against injustice, they protest for specific change, and they are capable of achieving a mood swing in a population that can put inescapable pressure upon the political classes. Of course we know that young people are less likely to vote and are often infantilised by their elders (who mock the young as 'snowflakes'), cannot withdraw their labour because they are students, and thus often have less of a say in the issues that finally cause them to erupt in protest. Young people also interact in many different ways with political ideologies: they voted for Margaret Thatcher in 1979 and 1983 and many voted for Trump in 2017. Yet the young are also known to be good diffusers of innovations (Rogers 2003).

This possibility of successful diffusion of knowledge can only be achieved when there is legal protection of free expression, as emphasised by the JCHR final report on free speech on campus:

> This right to free speech is a foundation for democracy. It is important in all settings, but especially in universities, where education and learning are advanced through dialogue and debate. It underpins academic freedom. Universities are places where ideas are developed, a diverse range of interesting–and sometimes controversial–topics should be debated. Students are among those particularly affected. (JCHR final report 2018:3)

Conclusions and Recommendations

When young people group together to act, their activism can be said to be a necessary (although not a sufficient) trigger for progressive change. However, currently they are apparently not ready, willing or able to take on populism. Current outbreaks of populism in Europe and elsewhere are providing a platform for hate speech, racial discrimination, and social division, online and offline. Liberty, freedom and fraternity are under pressure. In Italy the young "hipster fascists" who support a return to fascism believe this is the only way. We may find that these populist movements are indeed based on reasonable questions about corrupt elites and the voice of the people being ignored, but they can lead to the wrong answers, such as giving the people a referendum vote on a subject they do not understand (Mudde and Kaltwasser 2017).

A remarkable feature of the current British and European situation is that young people do not seem to be asking for explanations or for justice and many seem to accept the drift to extreme politics, while often despising it. Of course there are counter examples, such as the use of digital media by groups within the Labour Party such as Momentum, which galvanised thousands of young Britons in the run up to the most recent British election (Ali 2018: 8–9). Students on campus are the most potentially powerful group to act upon the negative use of digital platforms, yet they are not reacting, except perhaps to avoid these issues or select a different path, such as leaving their country to find work, as young Italians are doing. One correlational, possibly even causal factor in this mix is the use of populism on campus which has the effect of chilling free speech. The counter terror agenda serves the government as a populist ploy playing into fears of terrorism. The Charity Commission is endorsing such an ideology by having a chilling effect on 'controversial' topics.

A potentially important reason to focus on students is because they can have a valuable role as innovators and leaders in developing innovative ways of thinking about society's ills and then diffusing these innovations into society. There are precedents for these ideas about the characteristics of innovators in society. Rogers's (2003) seminal work on the diffusion of innovation, which has been used in numerous programme designs and empirical studies, proposes a model whereby innovation diffuses through a population as a normal distribution. He believed that innovators and opinion leaders, making up about 2.5% of the population, develop or take on new ideas first and then assist in the diffusion of these to other parts of society. According to Rogers' model, these innovators tend to be younger in age than the general population and higher in social class. They often have greater financial resources, have large social networks including other innovators, and have access to scientific sources. In short, university students share many important characteristics with innovators, facilitating the diffusion of innovation to the remainder of society. Students can be more flexible when it comes to activity changes. After establishing a family, people need more stability and have different responsibilities from those of students.

Lorey shows how being deprived of economic freedom creates a less equal society, but one that should make use of ideals of liberty, equality and fraternity in order to resist governmental pressures and inspire a better world. It should be possible to support students in becoming innovators in society and this would involve them becoming more critical of the digital world to which they are addicted. Research funding could be used to develop novel digital tools and activities which would support interventions to understand and respond critically to identified populism challenges. Relevant challenges may be directly on campus in terms of sensitizing students or research personnel to populism. It would be feasible to propose and develop mitigating strategies through the development of digital tools, such as online platforms, chatbots and apps. Such approaches could facilitate students' ability to debunk misinformation, and to recognise and understand populism. It is also possible to imagine meetings that bring together students on campus with researchers and members of the public, in order to plan to raise awareness of populism. Tools could be developed to support interventions in the curriculum or make additions to course structures. Additionally there could be on-campus campaigns or initiatives to consider how digital media can be used to address populism challenges and to establish arenas for debate and activism: the most potent value of all is exercising the right to (controlled) free speech for the good of society. We are a long way from that at present.

Acknowledgements NOTE: This chapter draws some of its material from a keynote I delivered on 3 May 2018 at King's College London for a conference on Mai 1968, convened by Prof Ziad Elmarsafy for KCL and Paris Diderot.

The author disclosed receipt of the following financial support for the research, authorship, and/or publication of this article: This research is supported by the AHRC: 'Re/presenting Islam on campus: gender, radicalisation and interreligious understanding in British higher education' (2015–2018), [AH/M00841X/1] for which Scott-Baumann is PI, with Cheruvallil-Contractor, Guest, Naguib and Phoenix.

References

Ali, T. (2018). That was the year that was *London Review of Books*, pp. 3–10.

BBC. (2018a). Exeter university students suspended over racism and rape claims. *BBC News*. Retrieved from https://www.bbc.co.uk/news/uk-england-devon-43473517.

BBC. (2018b). University of Warwick suspends 11 students over hate posts. *BBC News*. Retrieved from https://www.bbc.co.uk/news/uk-england-coventry-warwickshire-44052070.

Beloff, M. (2018, June 15). Learning for earning's sake. *Times Literary Supplement*. pp. 12–13.

Collini, S. (2018, May 10). *Diary London Review of Books*, pp. 38–39

Higher Education Policy Institute Keeping Schtum. (2016). http://www.hepi.ac.uk/wp-content/uploads/2016/05/Hepi_Keeping-Schtum-Report-85-Web.pdf.

Heath-Kelly, C. (2017). The geography of pre-criminal space: Epidemiological imaginations of radicalisation risk in the UK prevent strategy, 2007-2017. *Critical Studies on Terrorism, 10*, 297–310.

JCHR. (2018). *Freedom of speech in universities* (Fourth Report of Session 2017–19 HC 589/HL Paper 111). London: UK Parliament. House of Commons and House of Lords.

Lee, Y., & Scott-Baumann, A. (2019). Digital ecology of free speech: Authenticity, identity, and self-censorship. In S. Yates & R. E. Rice (Eds.), *The Oxford handbook of digital technology and society*. Oxford: Oxford University Press.

Lorey, I. (2012). *State of insecurity*. London: Verso Books.

Mudde, C., & Kaltwasser, C. R. (2017). *Populism: A very short introduction*. Oxford: Oxford University Press.

Ricoeur, P. (1974). In D. Stewart & J. Bien (Eds.), *Violence and language in political and social essays*. Athens: Ohio State University Press.

Rogers, E. M. (2003). Elements of diffusion. *Diffusion of Innovations, 5*(1.38).

Scott-Baumann, A. (2017a). Ideology, utopia and Islam on campus: How to free speech a little from its own terrors. *Education, Citizenship and Social Justice: Special Issue on Prevent*. https://doi.org/10.1177/1746197917694183.

Scott-Baumann, A. (2017b, October). No platform and safe spaces aren't the real dangers to freedom of speech. *Guardian* HE online. https://www.theguardian.com/higher-education-network/2017/oct/25/no-platform-and-safe-spaces-arent-the-real-dangers-to-freedom-of-speech.

Scott-Baumann, A. (2018a). Trust within reason: How to trump the hermeneutics of suspicion on campus. In A. Yaqin, P. Morey, & A. Soliman (Eds.), *Muslims, multiculturalism and trust*. New York: New Directions Palgrave.

Scott-Baumann, A. (2018b). 'Dual Use Research of Concern' and 'Select Agents': How researchers can use free speech to avoid 'Weaponising' academia'. In *Special issue on exploring radicalisation and securitisation from Islamic studies and religious studies perspectives. Journal of Muslims in Europe (Brill), 7*(2).

Scott-Baumann, A., & Perfect, S. (2019). *Freedom of speech on British university campuses: Islam, charities and counter-terrorism*. London: Routledge In preparation.

Taplin, G. (2017). *Move fast and break things*. New York: Little, Brown and Company.

Vinen, R. (2018). *The long '68*. London: Allen Lane.

Part IV
Making a Difference

Chapter 16
Quality Improvement with Compassion: Developing Healthcare Improvement Science in the European Health Professions' Education

Manuel Lillo-Crespo and M. Cristina Sierras-Davó

Abstract Patient-centred care should be the golden thread that runs through all healthcare education and continuing professional development nowadays. However, the values and attitudes supposed to be part of healthcare professions, such as compassion, address an important gap in training today. As compassion is a complex, culturally-based value, the challenge for healthcare educators consists in providing and evaluating compassionate care practice in a global society within contexts with different social and cultural value systems.

Developing an educational culture specific for European health professions that promotes improvement as a core value within the health education programmes and connecting compassion as the baseline was the purpose of the ISTEW Project (Improvement Science Training for European Healthcare Professionals) funded by the European Commission. Its main contributions were a consensus definition of Healthcare Improvement Science (HIS), four accredited HIS educational modules and a HIS Evaluation Framework. Since July 2016 an annual international summer programme named as "Immersion to Healthcare Improvement Science" takes place in the Faculty of Health Sciences at University of Alicante (Spain). This summer course has the potential to introduce students as future professionals in healthcare into improvement science and critical thinking with the scope of compassionate care by using the ISTEW outcomes. All this body of work and knowledge generated aims to improve patient outcomes, health system performance and population health.

Keywords Compassion · Health care · Patient-centred care · Training programme · Spain

M. Lillo Crespo (✉) · M. C. Sierras-Davó
Faculty of Health Sciences, University of Alicante, Alicante, Spain

Patient-centred care should be the golden thread that runs through all healthcare education and continuing professional development nowadays, what requires a constant commitment to quality, with a willingness to engage with and helps extend the evidence base for practice, and to develop reflective practice and critical judgement. However, the values and attitudes supposed to be part of healthcare professions, such as compassion, address an important gap in training today all over the world. We expect compassion from frontline staff though they are not always well served by compassionate leadership and not even trained for (McMahon and White 2017). Therefore, it is necessary to highlight the essential features of healthcare education and the types of support for newly registered professionals to create and maintain multidisciplinary teams of competent, compassionate workforce to deliver current and future health and social care services with the highest quality. Consequently, our education systems must produce healthcare professionals who have both intellect and compassion, not one or the other.

Concretely, European healthcare systems face daunting challenges in the years ahead. Increasing costs, patients' and professionals' mobility within the European Union, differences in access to care, and variability in the quality of care delivered threaten their long-term viability. Many factors contribute to the financial pressures plaguing the European healthcare systems, including an aging population, a fragmented healthcare organisational system, defensive medicine, advances in technology, and discordant incentives between the people who deliver and utilisehealthcare services. However, a primary driver of dysfunction in healthcare across Europe is a lack of emphasis on person-centred values which should start in the first steps of healthcare training in higher education institutions (HEIs). Although some authors have pointed out that value in healthcare can be defined similarly as in any industry by a ratio of the benefits accrued and the budget spent to achieve those benefits (Porter 2010), outcomes and benefits in healthcare include both the quality and patient experience associated with the provision of healthcare services (Bozic 2013). Currently, our healthcare systems are value-agnostic and this fact has been indirectly assumed by generations of future professionals who later have repeated the same when they are in practice. In many placements providers are incentivised based on the volume and intensity of healthcare services they provide to their patients, with little emphasis on or motivation to maximise populations' health outcomes and their lived experiences regarding the perceived values within the health systems. Patients who utilise healthcare services have little or no skin in the game, with very little direct responsibility for the cost of the care they consume, no voice and almost no information available to them regarding the cost or quality of care delivery by the providers from whom they seek care. Improvements are interpreted as a measurement instead of a patient-centred value; while compassion does not even appear as part of the healthcare scenarios and is unfortunately far from becoming an evaluable indicator or at least a sign of improvement.

The creation of a positive organisational culture that promotes innovation and quality has to have compassion as a central value and belief if we are to consider populations' voice. People feel safest when they are surrounded by understanding and compassion which determines the quality improvement. Leaders who model compassion, inclusion and dedication to improvement in all their interactions are the key to creating cultures of continuous improvement in health and care. Compassionate and inclusive leadership creates an environment where there is no bullying, and where learning and quality improvement become the norm. At this point, healthcare educators, professionals and managers should wonder the number of hours they have spent on this and the time they are dedicating to train and educate the future workforce on improvement and compassion and how both terms are related. The research evidence shows that compassion in healthcare practice is understood as an improvement, also creating psychological safety, such that staff feel more confident in speaking out about errors, problems and uncertainties. They feel more empowered and supported to develop and implement ideas for new and improved ways of delivering services. And they are likely to work more cooperatively and collaboratively in compassionate cultures, in climates characterised by cohesion, optimism and efficacy (West 2017a).

As compassion is a complex culturally-based value, the challenge for healthcare educators consists on providing and evaluating compassionate care practice in a global society within contexts with different social and cultural value systems. Moreover, health service leaders are under pressure to meet targets amid financial constraints, but a culture of cooperation and support is crucial for better care. In the absence of compassion, however, the quality of care falls and terrible situations are experienced by patients determined by a lack of compassionate care. In line with this, West (2017b) stated that over 50% of all NHS staff in the UK were not able to successfully attend their work demands. A high percentage (40%) suffer from stress as a result of all these constraints. Additionally, around half of all the staff reported a lack of energy leading to different medical errors with all their consequences. Concentrating on compassion, it is not something new, or even a new trend. This concept appeared recurrently associated as a religious and secular value and virtue, as an emotion, a psychological process, a political phenomenon, a core value in health professional practice and as a topic of empirical research for some time. However, the concept is still developing and is often presented in an idealistic form – as something that simply and automatically takes place in the provision of healthcare rather than a concept that could potentially change or improve how healthcare services can be delivered and experienced (Sinclair et al. 2018). The complexity of developing improvement with compassion in healthcare education and practice is directly linked with the scarce level of development and understanding of both terms in healthcare scenarios.

Currently, across Europe, an estimated 8–12% of patients hospitalised suffer adverse events and medical errors whilst receiving healthcare attention, as the World Health Organisation (2018) states, infections associated with health care affect an estimated 1 in 20 hospital patients on average every year. There is a real concern amongst policy makers about negligible patient care and the lack of compassion related with the preparation that clinicians and future professionals received for the demanding context in which they practice (Sinclair et al. 2016). Therefore, the contribution of improvement methods, compassionate care and the science of implementing effective change in clinical practice to improve patient safety, outcomes and satisfaction is increasingly recognised as being an essential component of the healthcare worker's role though there is not one unique framework based on consensus and useful for academics and clinicians to support this.

Since the Bologna Reform in the European Higher Education System, there is a growing interest in evaluating attitudes and values specifically within Health Professions' Training and Education. In the last years, some reports around UK and Ireland have made it clear that there is a lack of compassion in the clinical context and the standards of nursing care are not good enough, highlighting the need to develop appropriate "compassion" into the nursing core codes and day to day work (White et al. 2014). There is no other report or evidence about this across other European countries. Specifically, in Southern European countries such as Spain, the term is assumed as part of the communication relation between patient and professional and considered a synonym of "human sensitivity" with little interest from the academic perspective. As Paul Gibbs stated in 2001, HEIs in their curricula are not providing students with sufficient tools to confront their expectations and values versus the real contexts in a safe environment. However, universities, as the highest education institutions, should help to develop these values, competences and awareness to improve the future professionals' outcomes in a way that the economic market or politics are not able to do (Gibbs 2001). In the case of health professions, the interventions oriented to promote a value-centred education in both scenarios, the academic context and the real practice, may become more challenging and complex due to the fact that students co-live during their training within both environments which are different and where values are understood, interpreted and practiced differently.

Even though the Bologna Reform (1999–2010) in the European Union remarked from the beginning the importance of a value-centred education across Europe, in health studies and concretely in the case of the Faculty of Health Sciences at the University of Alicante (Spain) efforts have focused since then on identifying, describing and evaluating professional competencies and skills indirectly including values that professionals should learn at HEIs and apply in real contexts. Compassion is one of those values that population relates with the fact of being a physician and a nurse. From an academic point of view, health professions' competencies are evaluated in Spain from three different scopes according to the Spanish National Agency of Higher Education Quality (ANECA): theoretical competencies (those taught at the academic contexts), practical skills (putting in practice the previous ones in labs or simulation contexts and later within real placements) and attitudes (regarding those values and behaviors that professionals should experience and develop in the previous types of competencies). There is not any explicit reference to professional values in the competencies' description not even in the academic contents. If we have a look at the documents about health professions' competencies, we realisethere is much stress on the communication skills within the group of attitudes and therefore we could assume that values such as compassion would be included underneath communication. An explanation for this could be that the term compassion in the Spanish language has a religious connotation and has not been openly linked with academic aspects, though it is indirectly expressed in terms of human sensitivity. In fact, compassion is not a concept that can be easily seen in documents and publications related to Spanish healthcare professions, far from the Academic and research fields. However, it is something culturally taken for granted and understood as part of being human and concretely as part of health professions' practice. Moreover, those documents referring to attitudes do remark the importance of values from a generic scope though there is not any in-depth description about what types of values should be practiced and not even any sort of intervention to promote those values and evaluation to measure or describe the impacts.

With the aim of filling this gap, the Faculty of Health Sciences at the University of Alicante has organised since July 2016 an annual international summer programme named as "Immersion to Healthcare Improvement Science" with the participation of students from Health Studies arriving from different countries who are invited to reflect upon and discuss how a value-centred healthcare education should be by analysing the differences and similarities amongst cultures, health systems' organisations and professional competencies to later propose initiatives of improvement for real contexts. This summer programme appeared as the need of continuing working on a European Commission funded project called ISTEW (Improvement Science Training for European Healthcare Workers) after its end in September 2015. Developing an educational culture specific for European health professions that promotes improvement as a core value within the health education programmes and connecting compassion as the baseline was the purpose of the ISTEW Project (Improvement Science Training for European Healthcare Professionals) that began in 2013. Seven European countries' partners (Scotland, Spain, Italy, Slovenia, England, Poland and England) participated with a variety of research and evidence-gathering activities that focused on person-centered care, evaluating and measuring values and improvement in European healthcare systems and its educational programmes (Macrae et al. 2016; Erasmus+ 2016). This project's main contribution was a consensus definition of Healthcare Improvement Science, named as the "Bled" definition as the generation of knowledge to cultivate change and deliver person-centred care that is safe, effective, efficient, equitable and timely. It improves patient outcomes, health system performance and population health by putting the person in the first line. Healthcare Improvement Science states that educators are increasingly required to evaluate the impact of the education they teach their students and the difference this makes in practice focusing mainly on patient-centred values such as compassion by building a bridge between theory and practice for the future healthcare professional workforce.

Focusing on the literature search conducted about Healthcare Improvement Science during the ISTEW Project's ongoing; some important key findings were revealed on which it is worth emphasizing. The lack of a standard definition for HIS in their literature was revealed. Issues vary according to the country's healthcare context and therefore work needs to be done to help translate proven 'bench' theory into 'bedside' practice, but there is no standard and agreed model for how this should be done (Lillo-Crespo et al. 2017). Additionally, partner narratives revealed a wide range of settings in which HIS tools and techniques were being practised, but as with the definition, in the main, these did not link back to a common definition or agreed way of working. Given that there has been worldwide concern regarding quality, compassionate care and patient safety, as well as international and national initiatives on improvement, the lack of agreement, and lack of robust evidence obtained might indicate that there are distinct challenges, some unspoken, in the definition and implementation of Healthcare Improvement Science. Furthermore, a key theme in relation to articles describing the education of healthcare professionals was the paucity of literature directly concerned with this topic. Themes highlighted by the various countries included empowerment; the need to follow through on the interest of healthcare professionals through formal and on-the-job training; and the need for further research in this area to demonstrate the link between effective training and improved healthcare outcomes. Healthcare Improvement Science as a recognised inter-disciplinary subject was still in its beginning and it was therefore difficult to describe the impact it is having on the healthcare system as a whole. Overall, the limited amount of literature revealed through the systematic search could be argued to underscore the huge need for a continuing project which could develop standard principles, and deeper understanding of healthcare. Underscored was the need for further research in this area to demonstrate the link between effective training and improved healthcare outcomes (Lillo-Crespo et al. 2017).

These findings demonstrate there is not enough empirical awareness of compassion in healthcare and education, pointing up the lack of patient, family and professional voices in compassion research. A broader understanding of the core behaviors and attitudes that lead to improved patient-reported outcomes through compassionate care is necessary (Sinclair et al. 2016). This is a complex task as there are specific difficulties in defining, developing, documenting and reproducing educational interventions in which many influencing factors meet particularly in healthcare education in which students move constantly from academic contexts to real practice. However, despite those complexities practitioners as service users at the front line of healthcare delivery are very well positioned to identify improvements that can be made to curricula and would impact in healthcare contexts.

University education in Europe for multidisciplinary healthcare professionals covers a wide spectrum from diploma to PhD and includes both online and face-to-face taught programmes. As Skela-Savic et al. (2017) stated, Healthcare Improvement Science (HIS) and its education has not been equally developed in all European countries. About compassion, there is a gap in relation with how it works, how it can be included in healthcare staff skills and how it can be measured or sustained. So, as a consequence, there is a need for developing interprofessional study programmes and other materials addressing this gap in the European curricula, ensuring that compassion in association with improvement science becomes a core competency for all healthcare graduates (Skela-Savic et al. 2017).

As part of the ISTEW Project results, four accredited HIS educational modules that can be delivered by Higher Education Institutions (HEIs) across Europe were developed (Macrae et al. 2016). The four modules were Systems Thinking, Models for Improvement, Measurement for Improvement and Managing Change and Communication in Healthcare (UWS 2014). Those modules compiled the ideas of improvement and compassion as core values of healthcare professions education and training. As we mentioned before, nowadays the ISTEW Modules are being piloted in the annual summer programme developed by the Faculty of Health Sciences of the University of Alicante in Spain and named as Immersion in Healthcare Improvement Science. The summer course has the potential to introduce students as future professionals in healthcare into improvement science and critical thinking with the scope of compassionate care. Instead of considering what the university needs from the process or the system to create the modules, some reflection should be done on what the student/future professional needs, expects, sees, hears, and feels as they're going through that process or system (Howard 2018).

Furthermore, an evaluation framework was designed during the ISTEW Project to be used by the educational institutions to capture the impact of HIS into the educational modules through an evaluation tool. This Evaluation Framework is being piloted in the annual summer programme with compassion as an added value integrated into its content's evaluation. The framework created has the potential to effectively identify strengths, weaknesses, and gaps in HIS education across Europe, as well as a way to test if there is a relationship between quality and compassion in health care or not. During the construction of the HIS Evaluation Framework, the Kirkpatrick's Model was used as the theoretical framework although some changes were introduced. The Evaluation Framework is divided into five levels that represent the different learning stages. The first level ("Reaction") is about students' initial response to the educational proposal, second level ("Learning") evaluates the knowledge gained and how students interpreted the learning process, third level ("Behaviour") is related to the training transfer from theory to practice, and finally fourth level ("Results") is for measuring how the change in behaviour affects the organisations. Additionally, ISTEW partners added a fifth level (named as "Return on Investment") which is a long-term analysis about the results scaled up. The framework was developed considering the different samples involved in the learning process, including students, professional staff and mentors, managers and academics (Lillo-Crespo et al. 2017) and the tool designed for the evaluation is able to collect data from the different samples through questionnaires consisting of open-ended questions and closed ones easily answered through likert scales. Values, improvement and compassion are transversally evaluated in the different levels and with the different samples and have also been explored in the different European contexts in which the evaluation framework has been piloted and validated.

Summarizing, Healthcare Improvement Science (HIS), is an emerging science, particularly in Europe, where it is less well developed than it is in the United States of America, where it has been gaining momentum since the 1980's though focusing in other values mainly concentrated on management. Healthcare Improvement Science (HIS) in Europe frames, studies and improves the quality of health and social care interventions. It is thus an umbrella term for all actions (practice, education, science and policy), which can lead to better health treatment outcomes (health), better system performance (care) and better professional development (learning) and also healthier communities. HIS encompasses anything that helps fulfil the U.S. Institute of Medicine attributes of quality healthcare: safe, effective, efficient, equitable, timely and person-centred care (IHI 2018). Healthcare

Improvement Science incorporates patient safety and quality improvement into the daily work of health and social care professionals. As such it involves the structure, practices and contexts of healthcare. HIS is thus holistic, covering all aspects of health and social care, and is thus a multifactorial concept, involving the use of a wide variety of tools, to deliver comprehensive, multi-dimensional understandings of health and social care.

In line with these both areas of work, improvement and compassion, it is imperative that everyone in decision-making healthcare teams is included, and central to this are patients, as well as professionals and students. Both demand open-mindedness in all of those involved. From this we can all understand ourselves as co-learners in a learning system, with everyone working together and learning together. Although challenging to achieve, shared understandings are essential. Compassion in care as a core value within Healthcare Improvement Science education is critically important in responding to the demands of twenty-first Century healthcare and must bridge multiple professions, and also develop shared understandings between research and practice.

Both interventions, as well as the examples of improvement educational initiatives described before, are understood as key points for developing Healthcare Improvement Science in European health professions' education. Initiatives such as the HIS annual summer programme in the University of Alicante helps in engaging students as future professionals with Improvement Science, also as a tool to evaluate the Framework for assuring HIS education quality in educational contexts. Moreover, the ISTEW Alicante Team, composed of academics and researchers in healthcare, have included HIS-related items in subjects such as: Healthcare Management and Administration; Quality Management in Health Services; and Qualitative Research at different educational levels (undergraduate, postgraduate, master degree and PhD) with a multidisciplinary scope mainly represented by future nurses and nutritionists though also with professionals from other health studies. This initiative is also being evaluated nowadays with the HIS Evaluation Framework and recently new initiatives are being implemented also in Latin America, concretely in Mexico with the aim of spreading the HIS knowledge and ISTEW outcomes in Spanish-speaking countries as well as to continue piloting the HIS Evaluation Framework in new contexts.

Investing in a better-educated professional staff regarding the scope of HIS and compassionate care could improve the quality of patient care, contributing to the development of an improvement culture in healthcare contexts. One of the difficulties in the implementation of improvement and compassion within the health professions' educational contexts could be that both are culturally-centred and based on experiential learning, with scarce scientific evidence published to support their existence. On the contrary, health professions' education has been traditionally focused on the positivist paradigm, far from qualitative aspects of health.

In conclusion, healthcare systems worldwide are in the midst of transformational change and higher education institutions play a core part in this transition by training future healthcare providers in those values we are missing nowadays. If we aim to stablish compassion in practice, a self-evaluation of all healthcare and educational roles should be promoted to make them aware of their own responsibility, showing empathy and creating the best conditions possible to make compassion to flourish. As McMahon and White stated in 2017, "There is no simple solution, no quick fix."

As providers of valuable, quality-of-life enhancing services, healthcare professionals are well-positioned to play pivotal roles in the conversion of our healthcare systems from ones focused on the volume and intensity of services provided to ones that incentivisehigh value, patient-centered care, improvement and compassion. Long-term success is predicated on the creation of patient-centric value creation in line with a Healthcare Improvement Science culture which is compassionate. Achieving success in value-based contexts requires an organisational culture that emphasises and facilitates high-quality, safe, patient-centered, cost-effective care. It also requires strong professional leadership and a willingness to change often long-standing practice patterns and systems of care.

References

Bozic, K. J. (2013). Improving value in healthcare. *Clinical Orthopaedics and Related Research, 471*(2), 368–370.

Erasmus+. (2016). *Creating opportunities for the UK across Europe. Higher education projects.* Avalaible at: https://www.erasmusplus.org.uk/higher-education-projects. Accessed 2 May 2018.

Gibbs, P. (2001). Higher education as a market: A problem or solution? *Studies in Higher Education, 26*(1), 85–94.

Howard, P. (2018). *How to overcome "Improvement Resistant" Challenges* [online website]. The Institute for Healthcare Improvement. Science of Improvement About Us. Available at: http://www.ihi.org/communities/blogs/how-to-overcome-improvement-resistant-challenges?utm_campaign=tw&utm_source=hs_email&utm_medium=email&utm_content=62411239&_hsenc=p2ANqtz%2D%2DdwnNQyGFiZQZGIzItSNAUuLcBFtERXVhylTF76cMbXQ2v0zf1iRRyG73mSf8r_9zyqkWoPsmZPxUnMQZL8U5C6t4__NxQJtOXyB4_3_GO8m6pxic&_hsmi=62411239. Accessed 2 May 2018.

Lillo-Crespo, M., Sierras-Davó, M. C., MacRae, R., & Rooney, K. (2017). Developing a framework for evaluating the impact of healthcare improvement science education across Europe: A qualitative study. *Journal of Educational Evaluation for Health Professions, 14*, 28.

MacRae, R., Rooney, K. D., Taylor, A., Ritters, K., Sansoni, J., Crespo, M. L., & O'Donnell, B. (2016). Making it easy to do the right thing in healthcare: Advancing improvement science education through accredited pan European higher education modules. *Nurse Education Today, 42*, 41–46.

McMahon, A., & White, M. (2017). Compassion in practice: Connected, contested, conflicted, conflated and complex. *Journal of Research in Nursing, 22*, 3–6.

Porter, M. E. (2010). What is value in health care? *New England Journal of Medicine, 363*(26), 2477–2481.

Sinclair, S., Norris, J. M., McConnell, S. J., Chochinov, H. M., Hack, T. F., Hagen, N. A., et al. (2016). Compassion: A scoping review of the healthcare literature. *BMC Palliative Care, 15*(1), 6.

Sinclair, S., Hack, T. F., Raffin-Bouchal, S., McClement, S., Stajduhar, K., Singh, P., et al. (2018). What are healthcare providers' understandings and experiences of compassion? The healthcare compassion model: A grounded theory study of healthcare providers in Canada. *BMJ Open, 8*(3), e019701.

Skela-Savič, B., Macrae, R., Lillo-Crespo, M., & Rooney, K. D. (2017). The development of a consensus definition for healthcare improvement science (HIS) in seven European countries: A consensus methods approach. *Slovenian Journal of Public Health, 56*(2), 82–90.

The Institute for Healthcare Improvement. (2018). *Science of improvement* [online website]. About us. Available at: http://www.ihi.org/about/Pages/ScienceofImprovement.aspx. Accessed 2 May 2018.

University of the West of Scotland. (2014). *ISTEW project*. Retrieved from: http://www.uws.ac.uk/improvementscience/

West, M. (2017a). *Compassion and innovation in the NHS*. Organisational Culture. Retrieved from https://www.kingsfund.org.uk/blog/2017/09/compassion-and-innovation-nhs

West, M. (2017b). *Michael West: Collaborative and compassionate leadership*. Organisational Culture. Retrieved from https://www.kingsfund.org.uk/audio-video/michael-west-collaborative-compassionate-leadership

White, M., Wells, J. S., & Butterworth, T. (2014). The productive ward: Releasing time to care™ – what we can learn from the literature for implementation. *Journal of Nursing Management, 22*(7), 914–923.

World Health Organization. Regional Office for Europe. (2018). *Data and statistics* [online website]. Patient Safety. Available at: http://www.euro.who.int/en/health-topics/Health-systems/patient-safety/data-and-statistics. Accessed 2 May 2018.

Chapter 17
Understanding and Creating Compassionate Institutional Cultures and Practices

Kathryn Waddington

Keywords Compassion · Institutional cultures · Practices · Psychodynamic psychology · Academic engagement

Introduction

This chapter identifies and explores the values and assumptions underpinning compassionate institutional cultures and practices. It presents, and further develops, a conceptual framework for creating conditions for compassion outlined in Waddington (2017). Theoretically, the chapter is informed by insights and evidence from psychodynamic psychology, work and organizational psychology. It also draws lightly upon empirical material and findings from a small-scale mixed methods study exploring Human Resource Management (HRM) strategies and academic engagement in six universities in the UK (reported in Lister and Waddington 2014; Waddington and Lister 2010, 2013; Waddington 2012). A key finding from this study was that HRM strategies and practices were often viewed in a negative light, described in language that implied a sense of conflict:

> A HoD [Head of Department] referred to perceptions of HR in the following terms: '*HR is essentially used to implement unpleasantness*'. They went on to talk about senior management '*taking HR out of the drawer*' when there was something unpleasant to implement, then putting it away afterwards. This reflected an underlying perception and sense of HR as a '*tool in the management armoury*'. (Waddington and Lister 2013: 20)

An armoury is a place where weapons are kept, implying battles, conflict, casualties and trauma. Conflict is therefore used as an organizing metaphor in the chapter, to illustrate the tensions and potential for suffering in a higher education landscape dominated by neoliberal ideology and values (e.g. Berg and Seeber 2016; Calvard and Sang 2017; Smyth 2017). Culture is an organisational concept that exemplifies how work gets done, how individuals are rewarded, developed, managed and led.

K. Waddington (✉)
University of Westminster, London, UK
e-mail: K.Waddington@westminster.ac.uk

© Springer Nature Switzerland AG 2019

P. Gibbs et al. (eds.), *Values of the University in a Time of Uncertainty*,
https://doi.org/10.1007/978-3-030-15970-2_17

Culture includes an organisation's values, its power dynamics, decision-making processes, allocation of resources, behavioural expectations and the level of risk it accepts and encourages (Hogan and Coote 2014; Schein 2017). A key assumption underpinning this chapter is that compassion is a core component of healthy and humane workplace cultures.

Universities have a duty of care – a moral and a legal obligation to ensure that everyone associated with the organisation, whether employee, student or the general public, is fully protected from any personal physical and/or emotional harm. Care and compassion are not separate from being professional; rather, they represent fundamentals of humanity in the workplace. Being human 'implies a particular moral status: having moral value, agency, and responsibility' (Bastian et al. 2011: 469). Being human refers to essential characteristics such as openness, emotionality, vitality, and warmth. Barnard and Curry (2011) assert that humanity is fostered through self-compassion, which entails: (i) being kind and understanding toward oneself in times of pain or failure; (ii) acknowledging one's own suffering as part of a larger human experience; and (iii) holding painful feelings and thoughts in mindful awareness. Universities should care about compassion and it is vitally important that their institutional cultures reflect these central aspects of humanity.

The chapter includes activities that encourage readers to question and critically reflect on the organisational dynamics, issues and challenges they have experienced and/or are facing in their work, signposted as ***Slowdown and Think***. This term is deliberately chosen in order to disrupt the relentless pressures and demands of university life, in support of the concept of 'slow science'. Slow science is based on a feminist ethics of care that challenges such working conditions, arguing instead for strategies that 'foreground collaborative, collective, communal ways forward' (Mountz et al. 2015: 1237). ***Slowdown and Think*** activities are also included in response to Berg and Seeber's (2016, xiii) call for us all 'to think harder about what is really valuable in teaching, scholarship and collegiality'.

Slowdown and Think #1
- What inspired you to buy/read this book? What are you hoping to achieve after reading this chapter?

The chapter begins with an elaboration of a conceptual framework for creating the conditions for compassion and consideration of the need for compassionate values and practices in the academy. Schein's (2017) definition and model of organisational culture provides a core theoretical lens. The chapter concludes outlining a new paradigm for creating and sustaining compassionate cultures, which includes critical reflection, action learning and coaching.

Creating Conditions for Compassion

In Waddington (2017) a framework for creating compassionate institutional cultures and practices was presented, as summarized in Box 17.1.

> **Box 17.1: Conditions for Compassion**
> 1. Being open-minded and self aware
> 2. Having an understanding of the science of mindful compassion
> 3. Exposing and illuminating the dark side of university life
> 4. Applying theoretical insights, ideas, concepts and frameworks from psychodynamic psychology
> 5. A commitment to working together to shift cultural patterns and behaviours at individual, group and organisational levels
>
> Source: Waddington (2017: 67).

The approach outlined in Box 17.1 acknowledges the relevance of mindfulness and mindful compassion at the individual and neuroscience levels of analysis, but *extends* this to embrace a whole systems approach to achieving cultural change. It draws on insights and concepts from psychodynamic psychology, such as unconscious processes that can thwart the most well-intentioned organisational cultural change initiatives and interventions. From a psychodynamic standpoint, systems theory is based on the open systems approach and perspectives developed by family therapists (see Huffington et al. 2004; Waddington 2017). Systemic ideas and thinking locate the institution in context, enabling a greater understanding of the interplay between the parts that constitute the whole, and also between the institution and the external environment (Zagier Roberts 1994). Systems theory also relates to teamwork, and the way that teams work in both coordinated and co-operative ways, and/or in dysfunctional and fragmented ways (Ballatt and Campling 2011).

A whole systems approach is necessary for effective organisational change (Holman et al. 2007). However according to Bushe (2017), it has been estimated that an overwhelming 75% of organisational development (OD) interventions – including culture change programmes and initiatives – fail. Based on this uninspiring failure rate, Bushe proposes three criteria that can be used as a checklist to interrogate OD and cultural change interventions in order to foster more collaborative work systems:

Criterion 1: The more developed a system, the more aware it is of itself; it can talk to itself about itself. This criterion draws upon the psychoanalytic method that promoted self-analysis as a path to health and growth. Highly developed organisations all include the capacity for authentic communication, transparency and employee voice, based on the principle that people in the organisation/team are able to talk to each other honestly and courageously about what they really think, feel and want. This requires skillful, appreciative discourse, which values diversity and difference as a source of learning and innovation.

Criterion 2: The more developed a system, the less it is driven by reactive, unconscious emotions, motivations and cognitive frameworks and the more decisions and actions are based on reason, rationality and cognitive complexity. Again, this criterion draws upon Freudian thinking, and the idea that powerful motivations lie outside of conscious awareness. Awareness of our own emotions and defences, for example denial that change is necessary, leads to levels of emotional development where people are ever more aware of their feelings and motivations. The emphasis here is increasing capacity to think about thinking and feeling. In a developed group/team, people are not afraid to have courageous conversations if these discussions are fundamental for attaining the organisation's purpose.

Criterion 3: The more developed the system; the more it is able to actualize its potential. While the notion of actualisation is most frequently associated with Maslow (1954), it is latent in psychoanalytic thinking with regard to the realisation of an individual's self though integration of opposites, for example Jung's (1933) notion of the 'shadow self'. A developed organisational system embodies awareness of capabilities at individual and team levels that create previously unknown synergies that lead to organisational development, creativity and innovation. This is about growing and nurturing capacities, competencies, core strengths and values.

Bushe's criteria have clear links to the conditions for compassion outlined above in Box 17.1 with regard to: (i) being open-minded and self aware; (ii) understanding that individuals and institutions have a 'dark side'; (iii) application of insights from psychodynamic theory; and (iv) a commitment to challenging cultural patterns and behaviours.

Slowdown and Think #2
- How comfortable do you feel about having courageous conversations that challenge the status quo and the values that stifle compassion?

Organisational Culture

There is much ambiguity and variation with regard to the nature and definition of organisational culture, and the term is more frequently used as an umbrella concept and way of thinking about cultural and symbolic phenomena in organisations (Alvesson 2013). Schein (2017: 6) offers a dynamic definition of culture as:

> The accumulated shared learning of [a] group as it solves its problems of external *adaptation* and internal integration; which has worked well enough to be considered valid and, therefore, to be taught to new members as the correct way to perceive, think, feel, and behave in relation to those problems. [It] is deliberately focused on the general process of how *any culture is learned and will evolve* (emphasis added).

This definition does not specify the size or location of the group or social unit to which it can be reasonably applied. There are *macro* cultures, which may be national, ethnic, disciplinary, or organisational, reflecting diverse, and potentially conflicting, values (see Fig. 17.1).

Fig. 17.1 Levels of culture – artwork by Hannah Waddington

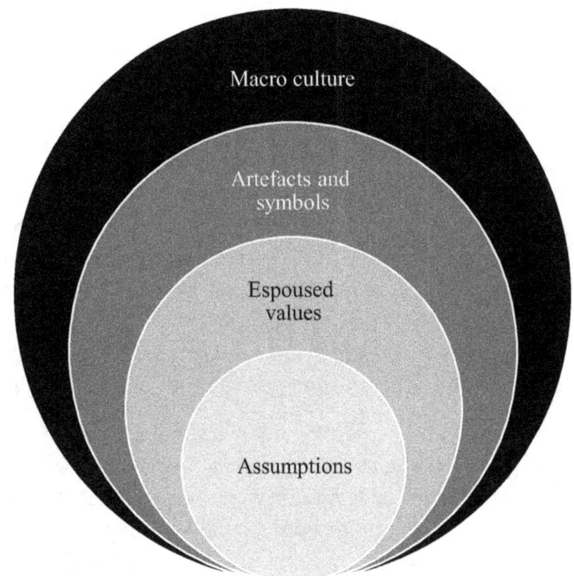

Schein's work is widely used in the organisational culture literature (e.g. Ganon et al. 2017; Hogan and Coote 2014; Longman et al. 2018) and his three level model of organisational culture provides an overarching theoretical lens for this chapter. The three levels are: (i) artefacts and symbols; (ii) espoused values and beliefs; and (iii) underlying assumptions, as illustrated in Fig. 17.1.

Manifestations of organisational culture **'as the organisation says it is'** are artefacts and symbols which are visible both internally and externally and which in some respects are, quite literally, 'superficial'. These are the evident in things like architecture, websites, content on visual display screens, logos, patterns of behaviour in meetings and so forth. Artefacts and symbols are things that can be seen and heard, but they do not necessarily tell you *why* you are seeing and hearing them. Manifestations of organisational culture **'as it really is and experienced'**, take the form of espoused values and beliefs, and deeper underlying assumptions. Espoused values are formal, 'official' statements, presentations and documents that communicate the strategies, principles, ethics, values and vision of the organisation. Arguably all universities' values and strategies say essentially the same thing, albeit in different ways, as a Human Resources (HR) Director commented when interviewed about the relationship between their HR strategy and their university strategy:

> We started with the university strategic plan and looked at what that says the organisation is here to achieve but as I'm sure you know most university strategic plans, if you boil them down all say the same thing – we will be brilliant at teaching and brilliant at research and brilliant at contributing to the community. (Waddington and Lister 2010: 6)

Some authors argue that organisational culture and strategy are synonymous (Weick 2008), and that organisational culture should be an integral factor when considering strategic human resource management (Harrison and Bazzy 2017).

> **Box 17.2: Culture Eats Strategy for Breakfast**
> The University of Arbitrary County (a pseudonym – obviously) provides a short case example of disengagement, disconnected and dissonant communication processes:
>
> *The VC* [Vice Chancellor] *announced a new strategy, which they had discussed with the senior management team* [SMT] *that was brilliantly espoused in a series of presentations. And in my time in the sector we have never been able to focus upon one thing that is so conceptual and so easily graspable. Yet the staff survey showed a lack of engagement with staff and almost an impermeable membrane. There was a feeling* [in the SMT] *that the message was not getting down.* (HR Director)
>
> Compare the above with a comment from an academic who described the poor communication practices of management: *'The cries going up and down the corridors'*. The underlying meaning was that the cries went unheard, yet the SMT also recognised that: *'Sometimes the ideas that are coming up from the shop floor are brilliant and we need to absorb them'*.
> Source: Waddington (2012: 92).

However Peter Drucker's often quoted phrase: *culture eats strategy for breakfast* still rings true. As reported in Waddington (2012), there is frequently disengagement, disconnection, and dissonance between formally communicated documentation of organisational strategies and values, and day-to-day experience of organisational culture, as illustrated in Box 17.2.

The **'essence of organisational culture'** therefore is found in the underlying tacit assumptions, the taken for granted and jointly learned values and beliefs. These are sometimes described as the things that you stop noticing after working 6 months in a new organisation. As such, this notion as culture as a set of taken-for-granted assumptions and values can lead to blind spots: 'a fixed world within which people adjust, unable to critically explore and transcend existing social constructions' (Alvesson 2013: 17). The core underpinnings of organisational culture can be revealed through use of metaphor, and recognition of the role of language as a core element of organisational culture (Hogan and Coote 2014). Adopting this approach enables us to see culture as always emergent and enacted, rather than static and stable. When we do this, it brings organisational culture and change *theory* closer to organisational culture and change *practice*.

Slowdown and Think #3
• Ask yourself: If my organisation were something else what would it be? Think further and critically, why this particular metaphor? What does it reveal about tacit assumptions and values?

Use of metaphor is a powerful method for exposing and understanding deeper assumptions and values, and the extent to which they are reflected – or not – in the visible artefacts, symbols, and experience of students and staff. I have used metaphor when teaching students about organisational culture. Metaphors generated by students can provide subtle insights that may not necessarily be picked up by 'sledgehammer' metrics. The critical thinking process of working with metaphor is illustrated in the following anonymized (and lightly altered to preserve confidentiality without significantly altering meaning) dialogue:

Kathryn: *If* the university were something else what would it be?
Students: A mobile phone
Kathryn: *Why* a mobile phone?
Students: Because there are some parts of the university where there is a really good signal; in other parts you can't get a signal at all!
Kathryn: *What* kind of a phone would it be? – E.g. a state of the art latest version iPhone contract phone?
Students: Oh no, just a pay-as-you go basic phone!
Kathryn: *Why* pay-as-you-go?
Students: Because you pay every time you come in – with your emotions!

Metaphors and associated imagery may be interrogated and questioned further to uncover deeper layers of assumptions and values. Pay-as-you go is more commonly used to describe a system of payment in which bills are paid when they are due or goods and services are paid for when they are bought (Merriam-Webster Dictionary, accessed 6th August 2018 – https://www.merriam-webster.com/dictionary/pay-as-you-go). It reflects a slightly 'old fashioned' approach, and I have also had students use metaphors such as the university is 'like a classic car' – nice to look at but it can be difficult to get replacement parts. More broadly, a lily pond has been advanced a metaphor for levels of culture, with the visible leaves and blossoms seen as a result of the quality and amount of water in the pond, root systems and nutrients. In other words, as a result of the invisible 'DNA' of the pond (Schein 2017: 27). If you want different colour lilies, painting them a different colour will not work. Leaders intending to change culture must locate the cultural DNA and change some of that.

The Evolution of Compassionate Organisational Cultures

Schein's (2017) definition of organisational culture, outlined above, is deliberately dynamic, in order to highlight the evolutionary nature of culture in terms of what a group learns in its quest for survival and growth. This chimes with contemporary perspectives on Charles Darwin's theory that evolution is about adaptation and collaboration (Gardner 2017). Crucially, 'scientists have shown that the notion of *"survival of the kindest"* explains more evolutionary success than the "survival of the fittest"' (Kukk 2017: 13, emphasis added). Indeed it is a myth that Darwin coined the phrase 'survival of the fittest'; this has been attributed to Herbert Spencer. In contrast, Darwin in *On the Origin of the Species* argued that communities that included the greatest number of the most sympathetic members would flourish best (Browne 2002). Kukk (2017: 11, citing Paul Ekman) argues that what Darwin called sympathy 'today would be termed empathy, altruism or compassion'. It is important to note however that compassion is not necessarily the *same* as empathy, altruism, pity or sympathy. Gibbs (2017a: 3) offers an 'opaque' view of compassion, arguing that only '*attentiveness to, and an agency or willingness to alleviate the suffering of others in order to increase their chosen contentment can be considered compassion*' (emphasis in original).

Similarly, Worline and Dutton (2017) define compassion in terms of a four-part process: (i) noticing that suffering is present in an organisation; (ii) making meaning of suffering in a way that contributes to a desire to alleviate it; (iii) feeling empathic concern; and (iv) taking action. Compassion therefore involves both feelings *and* a response; inclusion of responding differentiates it from related concepts like empathy. Compassion can also be understood as an individual response *and* organisational process involving emotions and action (Waddington 2016). Atkins and Parker (2012) note that in order to enhance compassion in organisations the processes through which compassion can be enhanced in individuals needs to be better understood. They go on to advance the notion of 'psychological flexibility', defined as 'mindfulness combined with *values-directed action* [which] motivate effort to engage in compassionate action' (524, emphasis added). However, the notion of psychological flexibility is potentially problematic if individual values of compassion do not align with organisational values, culture and climate. For example, in the HRM strategies and academic engagement study an academic focus group respondent commented:

> *I have heard people say that academic staff are an endangered species here, they are seen as a problem... there is a view that academics have become some kind of beast that has to be controlled.* (Waddington and Lister 2013: 17)

Compassion (with associated aspects of kindness and empathy) and control (with associated aspects of power and regulation) do not sit well together. The resulting tension can lead to suffering and harm, and is manifest in higher education cultures.

Higher Education Cultures

Suffering is happening in universities for staff and students. Almost a decade ago, Watson's (2009) exploration of morale in UK universities found that while 'at their best they can achieve remarkable things; *at their worst they can be petty, corrosive, even dangerous* (141, emphasis added). Things have not improved. The Institute for Public Policy Research (IPPR) reports increasing numbers of students suffering with mental health problems (Thorley 2017). The Universities UK (2017) *Step Change Framework* aims to encourage university leaders to adopt a strategic, whole organisation, whole population approach to staff and student mental health by providing a:

- Case for a strategic approach
- Vision
- Whole-institution approach
- Eight-step framework for achieving the vision.

Smyth's (2017) sociological critique of contemporary higher education cultures and practices challenges the neoliberal ideology that has resulted in academics' sense of loss, damage and despair Compassion is stifled in environments where instrumental relations and values have dominance, 'where people are used as a means to an end, as commodities rather than respected citizens' (Ballatt and Campling 2011: 139). In higher education, such instrumental attitudes combined with relentless managerialism, marketisation and metrics create toxic environments, and persecutory and overwhelming cultures that can fatally undermine staff morale. Neoliberal ideology and higher education policy models that emphasize the value of free market competition are seemingly at odds with the values of compassion. This has been captured well by Hansen and Trank (2016: 352, emphasis added) who argue:

> Our increasingly managerialist perspective seems to go hand in hand with a dispassionate approach to scholarship and a focus on narrowly defined metrics of effectiveness and efficiency. As our scholarship has pursued these narrow economic objectives over the public good and society, we have become a less happy and healthy profession ... It appears *we could not care less* about making a contribution to society and exist to publish for the sake of having been published.

Furthermore, Bergquist and Pawlack (cited in Longman et al. 2018: 4, emphasis added) describe dominant higher education cultures, as 'a *world of the blade*, with a strong emphasis on often subtle but nevertheless quite powerful competition and striving for prestige and dominance'.

The organisational cultures, structures and processes that operate in universities and the relentless political drive on standards, results and student satisfaction, while laudable in principle, can also erode morale. Ineffective management systems were identified by Watson (2009: 139) as one of the 'pathologies' that also undermine positive morale, and which are a source of 'institutional crisis'. Similarly, Hawkins and Shohet (2012: 229) identified patterns of 'dysfunctional organisational cultural dynamics', which are manifest in the following ways:

- Driven by crisis – where there is little time for reflection, thinking and the development of sustainable relationships between different parts of the organisation
- An over-vigilant and bureaucratic culture – which is high on task orientation but low on personal relatedness, and driven by fear of complaints.

Nevertheless, despite this 'dark side' of university life, there is also a brighter side emerging in the evidence-base for compassion.

The Evidence-Base for Compassion

Increasingly, university leaders, scholars and researchers are coming to recognize the importance of compassion in the academy (e.g. Gibbs 2017b; Kanov et al. 2017). In order to nurture cultures of compassion, organisations require their leaders – as the carriers of culture – to embody compassion in their leadership (West et al. 2017). There is now a growing body of evidence to support the argument that compassion in the work environment improves staff well-being and positively impacts the bottom line (see Kukk 2017; Poorkavoos 2016, 2017; Worline and Dutton 2017). Box 17.3 summarizes the evidence-base for compassion.

Universities as care-giving organisations need to nurture organisational cultures that ensure the delivery of high-quality research and compassionate pedagogy (Gibbs 2017b; Kahn 2005). According to Schneider et al. (cited in West et al. 2017: 4), organisational cultures evolve a result of three influences:

Box 17.3: The Evidence-Base for Compassion

- Those who experience compassionate leadership at work are more likely to report an emotional commitment to their organisation and to talk about it in positive terms
- Compassion breeds compassion – those who experience compassion are then more likely to demonstrate it towards others
- Managers who perceive that their organisation values their well-being are more likely to show supportive behaviour towards the people they manage
- There are mutual benefits: (i) for people receiving compassion; (ii) the person demonstrating compassion; and (iii) also colleagues who witness compassionate acts
- Experiencing compassion at work: (i) reduces employee turnover and increases organisational citizenship; and (ii) connects co-workers psychologically and results in a stronger bond between them
- Relationships based upon compassion are stronger, more positive and collaborative
- People working in compassionate care-giving organisations (which includes universities) are less likely to experience stress and burnout
- Compassion also can help with growing trust between individuals and creates psychological safety
- This can create a willingness to discuss and learn from errors and failures, talking about them more easily and learning from those mistakes
- Compassionate cultures can result in improved innovation and creativity

Created from: Poorkavoos (2016, 2017), West et al. (2017), and Worline and Dutton (2017).

1. The founding values of the organisation
2. The early experiences acquired values, norms and behaviours of those joining the organisation, via formal and informal induction and organisational socialisation processes
3. The behaviour of its leaders.

While founding values are important, they should not tether institutions to 'old-fashioned' ways of working, as illustrated in the metaphors of classic cars and pay-as-you-go phones discussed earlier in the chapter. If the **'essence of organisational culture'** lies in underlying tacit assumptions, values and beliefs – the things that you stop noticing – then observations and feedback from newcomers is important. With regard to the behaviour of leaders, West et al. (2017) set out four components of compassionate leadership: attending; understanding; empathizing; and helping. Importantly, a *collective approach to leadership* is necessary. Borrowing from Alexandre Dumas's 'all for one and one for all' approach this means everyone taking responsibility to support each other, and embodying the collective organisational values of compassion. There is shared, rather than dominant, team leadership and a commitment to team development, characterized by openness, curiosity, kindness, authenticity, appreciation and above all compassion. Conversely then, hierarchical and top-down approaches to leadership are ineffective ways of creating compassionate cultures. In summary, a compassionate organisation is one:

> where people trust each other and feel it is acceptable to talk about their problems and to seek help and support. In such an organisation people know that if they talk about their problems, other colleagues will not judge them and will listen and try to help. (Poorkavoos 2017: 5)

However, notions of help seeking and support are in conflict with dominant higher education cultures and there are still barriers to compassion that need to be overcome.

Overcoming Barriers to Compassion in Universities

Worline and Dutton (2017: 207) comment: 'Just as the possibility of human responsiveness to pain is inherent in every system, so too is the possibility that we will turn away from suffering'. They argue that 'hearts turn to stone' when interpersonal relationships are characterized by disrespect, incivility and/or a sense of injustice. In organisational cultures of self-interest and a punitive blame approach, it is far less likely that people will view the well-being of others as part of their work. Furthermore when systems offer little room for creative job crafting – the ways in which employees use opportunities to customize their jobs by actively changing their tasks and interactions with others – people are less likely to build compassion into their work practices. Workplaces characterized by overload lead to 'empathy fatigue', a form of emotional exhaustion which makes it less likely that people will notice other people's suffering and limits feelings of concern.

Poorkavoos's (2016, 2017) mixed methods research across a range of industries (public sector, private sector, manufacturing, and not for profit) found that barriers to compassion reported by participants fell into one of three categories:

1. *Organisational culture related barriers*: These related to cultural norms of what is perceived as acceptable/inacceptable in the work place and performance pressure from senior management. Additionally some managers did not feel empowered to make decisions themselves that would enable them to act in a compassionate manner.
2. *Individual circumstances related barriers*: These related to time pressures, and being too busy to stop and show care, and being fearful of crossing unseen boundaries. Low emotional intelligence and an instrumental focus on getting the job done whatever the cost were also cited as barriers.
3. *Policy and procedural related barriers*: These related to a perception that HR policies were too restrictive and rigidly followed, which did not allow for adaptation to individual circumstances.

Slowdown and Think #4

- Step back and think about time when you may have missed an opportunity to give or receive compassion because of the above organisational culture, individual circumstances, or policy/procedural barriers?

Missed opportunities for compassion can be re-framed as 'critical moments', which:

> Occur wherever people make *meaning and coordinate actions with each other.* [They] occur everywhere: at dinner tables, in conference halls and boardroom … when responding to emergencies, in classrooms and consultations, during political campaigns and public hearings. (Pearce 2007: 11–12, emphasis added)

Critical moments occur when we experience dissonance, for example a conflict of values. Compassion grows when we enhance our ability to discern those critical moments, and then act wisely into them. For example, in Waddington (2016) I reflected upon critical moments, which were formed of multiple fragments from conversations with colleagues, observations made during meetings and emails. Words like *'terminated'*, *'excluded'*, *'viability'* and *'obsolete'* when used to describe students, courses and modules reflect an undercurrent of indifference. Importantly, as Koutselini (2017: 204) notes, there must be 'a reflective and responding character in compassion'. Universities are sites of learning and education; storied worlds where narratives of care and compassion can be surfaced through reflecting and responding, in order to:

- Challenge the 'objectification and measurement' of students and staff, which reduces people to faceless resources to be manipulated and managed.
- Be more attentive to the language and representations of compassion in everyday experience.

Reflection upon critical moments, combined with individual and organisational development methods, for example action learning and coaching, creates a powerful new paradigm for creating and sustaining compassionate cultures and practices.

A New Paradigm for Universities?

Returning to Bushe's (2017) criteria introduced earlier in the chapter, successful organisational and cultural change rests upon the following paradigmatic assumptions:

- The more developed a system, the more aware it is of itself; it can talk to itself about itself
- The more developed a system, the less it is driven by reactive, unconscious emotions, motivations and cognitive frameworks and the more decisions and actions are based on reason, rationality and cognitive complexity
- The more developed the system; the more it is able to actualize its potential.

The question mark over this part in the chapter is because arguably the paradigm, which draws upon psychodynamic systems thinking and humanistic psychology, is simply 'old wine in new bottles'? However, I contend that when combined with: (i) critical reflection; (ii) coaching with compassion; and (iii) action learning, it offers a strong steer for individual, team and organisational development and culture change in our universities. Pässilä and Vince (2016) identify four characteristics of critical reflection that differentiate it from other approaches to reflection. Firstly, the reflective task is to identify and question taken-for-granted beliefs and values. Secondly, particular attention is paid to the analysis of power relations and the relationship between power and knowledge. Thirdly, critical reflection implies a shift in focus away from an individual perspective towards a collective, situated process. Finally, reflection on socially constructed, collective experience highlights political, emotional and ethical dimensions and dynamics.

Turning now to coaching with compassion, Boyatzis et al. (2012: 156) propose that this enhances the adaptability of organisations through creating norms and relationships of caring and development. Its aims are to:

> Further the coachee's development by focusing on their Ideal Self and on their strengths more than their weaknesses. Instrumental coaching and coaching toward the Ought Self can be called *coaching for compliance*, defined as coaching another to comply with an authority's or an organisation's view of how they should act, often inducing a defensiveness or sense of guilt. We argue that coaching with compassion leads to more positive outcomes than coaching for compliance and deficit-based coaching. (emphasis in original)

Importantly, Boyatzis et al. offer an expanded view of compassion, challenging the assumption that compassion must *always and only* be a response to distress, pain, or suffering. Under this expanded view they argue that a manager can also demonstrate compassion by noticing an employee is excited and optimistic about, for example, moving to a new role in the organisation. Coaching with compassion in this instance would involve helping them understand what they need to do to effectively prepare themselves for transition and change. This also re-frames coaching in a positive light, away from deficit-focused instrumental coaching, promoting greater acceptance of a coaching culture.

Harding (n.d.) and Kapoutzis (n.d.) describe the stages and processes involved in creating and developing coaching cultures in two UK universities. These include senior team engagement, developing a strong business case, and building the external and internal coaching capacity. All of this takes time, and requires some fundamental shifts as Kapoutzis (p. 4) notes:

> For us to achieve what felt at the beginning to be a very nebulous and highly utopian coaching culture, fundamental rules and habits of interacting, managing and engaging with each other had to shift.

Action learning is a method of supporting people through organisational cultural change (e.g. see Waddington and Hardy 2014). It involves a continuous process of learning and reflection that occurs with the support of a group or 'set' of colleagues working collaboratively. Working with action learning presumes core values, assumptions and ideas (McGill and Brockbank 2004), which include:

- Membership of a set is voluntary
- Confidentiality and trust
- Commitment to the process
- Learning as a social and collaborative process
- Support and challenge
- Quality of attention
- Empathy

Action learning is therefore a powerful vehicle for developing compassionate cultures and practices (Waddington forthcoming/2019). By way of a brief example from my recent experience of participating in action learning, a small but significant action was to pay more attention to, and *notice,* the tone and content of email and other forms of communication. This was coupled with the notion of being an 'active bystander' and calling attention to positive examples of compassionate practices. However it is naïve to assume that action learning can only be, and always is, 'a good thing'. It is important to have an understanding of how emotions, power and politics influence the processes of action learning in volatile, uncertain, chaotic and ambiguous (VUCA) environments. Critical action learning, which incorporates critical, collective reflection as outlined above, is an appropriate approach, which ensures:

> Individuals' questioning insight is undertaken in the context of collective emotional dynamics, linked to unconscious processes and complex inter-personal relations, as well as the everyday politics that surround them. (Vince 2012: 213)

VUCA is a U.S. military term for an unpredictable, turbulent and rapidly changing organisational context, characterized as:

- **V**olatile: Change happens rapidly and on a large scale

- Uncertain: The future cannot be predicted with any precision
- Complex: Challenges are complicated by many factors and there are few single causes or solutions
- Ambiguous: There is little clarity on what events mean and what effect they may have before becoming disastrous.

Stewart et al. (2016: 241), writing in a higher education context, note:

> VUCA forces will present businesses with the need to move from linear modes of thought to problem solving with synthetic and simultaneous thinking. They cannot be ignored as hidden in the challenges are the essential opportunities that are necessary for survival and sustainability.

Schein (2017) argues that as the world becomes more turbulent, a greater degree of flexibility is required because, paradoxically, the process of creating organisational culture is potentially dysfunctional because it stabilizes things. Therefore we need to ask: What would a culture look like that favored perpetual learning and flexibility?'

Bringing It All Together

In conclusion, and to answer the question 'what might a compassionate learning culture look like?' I return, for the final time, to Schein's (2017) *Organisational Culture and Leadership*. Schein identifies ten components of a learning culture, all of which can be infused with compassion, summarized here as: 'noticing another's need, empathizing, and acting to enhance their well-being' (Boyatzis et al. 2012: 153). Schein's components/approaches to creating and leading a learning culture are:

1. *Proactivity:* this approach rejects fatalistic assumptions of passive acceptance of change, advocating instead confident, proactive problem solving and learning. However it is more important to be *committed to the learning process,* than to identifying any particular solution to a problem.
2. *Commitment to 'learning to learn':* a learning culture needs in its DNA a 'learning gene' – the shared assumption that learning to learn is a skill which requires investment (of time and resources), reflection, experimentation and action. It also includes willingness to ask for – and accept – help, and also accept errors and failure as learning opportunities.
3. *Positive assumptions about human nature:* learning leaders need to have faith in people, and a belief that ultimately human nature is essentially good, and in any case, malleable. Assumptions that people are lazy and self-seeking create cynical attitudes and self-fulfilling prophecies.
4. *A belief that the environment can be managed:* this relates to the shared assumption that the environment is to some extent manageable and is reflected in the concept of 'lead and disrupt'. Organisations that survive and thrive retain their

core values and simultaneously build new and adaptive cultures and ways of working.

5. *Commitment to 'truth' through inquiry and dialogue:* this is the shared assumption that solutions to problems and learning are derived from a deep commitment to inquiry and a pragmatic search for 'truth'. Learning is a shared endeavor, and requires leaders at all levels to build personal, open and trusting relationships with colleagues at all levels.

6. *Positive orientation towards the future:* this involves thinking far enough ahead to judge the consequences – intended and unintended – of actions, and simultaneously thinking in terms of the near future to judge whether or not actions are working.

7. *Commitment to full and open task-relevant communication:* a learning culture is built on the assumption that communication and information are central to individual and institutional well-being. Full task-relevant information is built upon trust and truth telling.

8. *Commitment to cultural diversity:* the more turbulent the environment, the more likely it is that organisations with culturally diverse resources are better able to cope with and adapt to unpredicted events.

9. *Commitment to systemic thinking:* in an increasing complex and interdependent world it is necessary to abandon simplistic linear thinking in favour of more complex mental models.

10. *Belief in the value of internal cultural analysis:* this involves collective reflection and analysis in order to reveal and better understand the organisation's values, power dynamics, decision-making processes and expectations.

In summary, a compassionate leader, as well as being a compassionate person, encourages compassion and caring in the wider organisation. A compassionate leader encourages employees to talk about their difficulties *and* opportunities for growth and development (Boyatzis et al. 2012; Poorkavoos 2016; West et al. 2017). Compassionate leadership is about trying to create a culture whereby seeking or providing help is not just acceptable but is seen as the norm.

Slowdown and Think # 5

- Which of the ten components of a compassionate learning culture can you apply to your own role and practice in order to promote and provoke change in your workplace?

The idea for *Slowdown and Think* activities came to me at a structured writing retreat when working on an early draft of this chapter. To recap, the term was chosen in order to disrupt the relentless pressures and demands of contemporary university life. The pressure to publish is universal, and research is a priority in every university strategy. However, as Murray and Newton (2009: 551) note, 'the writing element of research is not universally experienced as a mainstream activity'. We need 'pauses' in our work in order to be kind to ourselves, and others, and also to protect and enhance the quality of our work (Berg and Seeber 2016). I would argue that this also enables a return to the core values of the university – intellectual curiosity, thoughtful dialogue and courage to challenge existing paradigms and ideologies.

I will end with a final note of caution: *The commodification of compassion must be avoided at all costs.* In the current climate, I fear it may be all too easy for compassion to become the panacea for papering over the cracks in dysfunctional institutional systems and cultures. There is a danger of compassion becoming just another 'flavour of the month' buzzword, and a consequent risk that it could lose its power and potential to influence change in organisational values and cultures. As Davis's (2008: 67) critique of 'intersectionality as a buzzword' argues, it is crucial to maintain a critical perspective. As discussed earlier, a critical perspective is one that acknowledges the influence of power and power dynamics and relations in organisations. There is a further risk that individualistic, reductionist psychological perspectives, which emphasize personal responsibility for well-being, happiness and resilience, fail to take into account wider organisational, social and contextual realities. Academic leaders, managers and human resources organisational development practitioners must resist the commodification of compassion, and look beyond individualistic approaches in order to create conditions for compassionate university cultures to flourish.

References

Alvesson, M. (2013). Organisational culture: Meaning, discourse and identity. In N. M. Ashkanasy, C. P. M. Wilderom, & M. P. Peterson (Eds.), *The handbook of organisational culture and climate* (2nd ed., pp. 11–28). Thousand Oaks: Sage.

Atkins, P., & Parker, S. (2012). Understanding individual compassion in organisations: The role of appraisals and psychological flexibility. *Academy of Management Review, 37*(4), 524–546.

Ballatt, J., & Campling, P. (2011). *Intelligent kindness: Reforming the culture of healthcare.* London: RCPsych Publications.

Barnard, L. K., & Curry, J. F. (2011). Self-compassion: Conceptualisations, correlates, & interventions. *Review of General Psychology, 15*(4), 289–303.

Bastian, B., Laham, S. M., Wilson, S., Haslam, N., & Koval, P. (2011). Blaming, praising, and protecting our humanity: The implications of everyday dehumanisation for judgments of moral status. *British Journal of Social Psychology, 50*(3), 469–483.

Berg, M., & Seeber, B. K. (2016). *The slow professor.* Toronto: University of Toronto Press.

Boyatzis, R. E., Smith, M. L., & Beveridge, A. J. (2012). Coaching with compassion: Inspiring health, well-being, and development in organisations. *The Journal of Applied Behavioral Science, 49*(21), 153–178.

Browne, J. (2002). *Charles Darwin: The power of place.* London: Jonathan Cape.

Bushe, G. R. (2017). *Where organisational development thrives.* Horsham: Roffey Park.

Calvard, T. S., & Sang, K. J. C. (2017). Complementing psychological approaches to employee well-being with a socio-structural perspective on violence in the workplace: An alternative research agenda. *International Journal of Human Resource Management, 28*(16), 2256–2274.

Davis, K. (2008). Intersectionality as buzzword: A sociology of science perspective on what makes a feminist theory successful. *Feminist Theory, 9*(1), 67–85.

Ganon, M. W., Donegan, J. & Rotondo, G. (2017). Embedding values in corporate culture: Applying Schein's organizational theory to Lehman brothers. *International Journal of Business and Applied Sciences, 6*(1), 20–33.

Gardner, A. (2017). The purpose of adaptation. *Interface Focus, 7*, 20170005. https://www.ncbi. nlm.nih.gov/pmc/articles/PMC5566815/. Accessed 10 Aug 2018.

Gibbs, P. (2017a). Higher education: A compassion business or edifying experience? In P. Gibbs (Ed.), *The pedagogy of compassion at the heart of higher education* (pp. 1–16). Cham: Springer.

Gibbs, P. (Ed.). (2017b). *The pedagogy of compassion at the heart of higher education*. Cham: Springer.

Hansen, H., & Trank, C. Q. (2016). This is going to hurt: Compassionate research methods. *Organisational Research Methods, 19*(3), 352–375.

Harding, C. (n.d.). *Bournemouth University: Creating a coaching culture*. London: Leadership Foundation for Higher Education.

Harrison, T., & Bazzy, J. D. (2017). Aligning organisational culture and strategic human resource management. *Journal of Management Development, 36*(10), 1260–1269.

Hawkins, P., & Shohet, R. (2012). *Supervision in the helping professions* (4th ed.). Maidenhead: Open University Press.

Holman, P., Devane, T. & Cady, S. H. (Eds.) (2007). *The change handbook: The definitive resource in today's best methods for engaging whole systems*. San Francisco, CA: Berrett-Koehler.

Hogan, S. J., & Coote, L. V. (2014). Organisational culture, innovation, and performance: A test of Schein's model. *Journal of Business Research, 67*(8), 1609–1621.

Huffington, C., Halton, W., Armstrong, D., & Pooley, J. (2004). *Working below the surface: The emotional life of contemporary organisations*. London: Karnac Books.

Jung, K. G. (1933). *Modern man in search of a soul*. New York: Harcourt.

Kahn, W. A. (2005). *Holding fast: The struggle to create resilient caregiving organisations*. Hove: Brunner-Routledge.

Kanov, J., Powley, E. H., & Walshe, N. D. (2017). Is it ok to care? How compassion falters and is courageously accomplished in the midst of uncertainty. *Human Relations, 70*(6), 751–777.

Kapoutzis, N. (n.d.). *University of Westminster: Developing a coaching culture*. London: Leadership Foundation for Higher Education.

Koutselini, M. (2017). The reflective paradigm in higher education and research: Compassion in communities of learning. In P. Gibbs (Ed.), *The pedagogy of compassion at the heart of higher education* (pp. 203–212). Cham: Springer.

Kukk, C. L. (2017). *The compassionate achiever: How helping others fuels success*. New York: Harper Collins.

Lister, J., & Waddington, K. (2014). *Academic-practitioner knowledge sharing inside Higher Education Institutions*. London: Leadership Foundation for Higher Education.

Longman, K., Daniels, J., Bray, D. L., & Liddell, W. (2018). How organisational culture shapes women's leadership experiences. *Administrative Sciences, 8*(8), 1–16.

Maslow, A. H. (1954). *Motivation and personality*. New York: Harper and Row.

McGill, I., & Brockbank, A. (2004). *The action learning handbook*. London: RoutledgeFalmer.

Mountz, A., et al. (2015). For slow scholarship: A feminist politics of resistance through collective action in the neoliberal university. *ACME: An International E-Journal for Critical Geographies, 14*(4), 1235–1259. https://www.acme-journal.org/index.php/acme/article/view/1058. Accessed 10 Aug 2018.

Murray, R., & Newton, M. (2009). Writing retreat as structured intervention: Margin or mainstream? *Higher Education Research & Development, 28*(5), 541–553.

Pässilä, A., & Vince, R. (2016). Critical reflection in management and organisation studies. In J. Fook, V. Collington, F. Ross, G. Ruch, & L. West (Eds.), *Researching critical refection: Multidisciplinary perspectives* (pp. 48–62). Abingdon: Routledge.

Pearce, W. (2007). *Making social worlds: A communication perspective*. Malden: Blackwell.

Poorkavoos, M. (2016). *Compassionate leadership: What is it and why do organisations need more of it?* Horsham: Roffey Park.

Poorkavoos, M. (2017). *Towards more compassionate workplaces*. Horsham: Roffey Park.

Schein, E. H. (2017). *Organisational culture and leadership* (5th ed.). Hoboken: Wiley.

Smyth, J. (2017). *The toxic university: Zombie leadership, academic rock stars, and neoliberal ideology*. London: Macmillan Publishers Ltd..

Stewart, B., Khare, A., & Schatz, R. (2016). Volatility, uncertainty, complexity and ambiguity in higher education. In O. Mack, A. Khare, A. Krämer, & T. Burgartz (Eds.), *Managing in a VUCA world* (pp. 241–250). Cham: Springer.

Thorley, C. (2017). *Not by degrees: Improving student mental health in the UK's universities*. London: IPPR.

UUK. (2017). *The universities UK framework*. London: UUK.

Vince, R. (2012). The contradictions of impact: Action learning and power in organisations. *Action Learning: Research and Practice, 9*(3), 209–218.

Waddington, K. (2012). *Gossip and organisations*. New York: Routledge.

Waddington, K. (2016). The compassion gap in UK universities. *International Practice Development Journal, 6*(1), 1–9. https://www.fons.org/library/journal/volume6-issue1. Accessed 10 Aug 2018.

Waddington, K. (2017). Creating the conditions for compassion. In P. Gibbs (Ed.), *The pedagogy of compassion at the heart of higher education* (pp. 49–70). Cham: Springer.

Waddington, K.. (forthcoming/2019). *Towards the compassionate university: From golden thread to global impact*. London: University of Westminster Press.

Waddington, K., & Hardy, S. (2014). Comrades in adversity: Weathering the storm of NHS reform through action learning. In S. Hardy (Ed.), *Towards creative action: Transformations and collaborations in practice* (pp. 23–30). Manchester: Manchester Metropolitan University.

Waddington, K., & Lister, J. (2010). *HRM strategies and academic engagement*. London: Leadership Foundation for Higher Education.

Waddington, K., & Lister, J. (2013). Human Resource Management (HRM) strategies and academic engagement in UK universities: Reflections on an academic-practitioner study. *European Work and Organisational Psychology in Practice, 5*, 12–25.

Watson, D. (2009). *The question of morale: Managing happiness and unhappiness in university life*. Maidenhead: Open University Press.

Weick, K. E. (2008). Strategy is culture is strategy. In H. Mintzberg, J. Lampel, & B. Ahlstrand (Eds.), *Strategy bites back* (pp. 201–204). Harlow: Pearson.

West, M., Eckert, R., Collins, B., & Chowla, R. (2017). *How compassionate leadership can stimulate innovation in health care*. London: The King's Fund.

Worline, M. C., & Dutton, J. E. (2017). *Awakening compassion at work: The quiet power that elevates people and organisations*. Oakland: Berrett-Koehler.

Zagier Roberts, V. Z. (1994). The organisation of work: Contributions from open systems theory. In A. Obholzer & V. Z. Roberts (Eds.), *The unconscious at work* (pp. 28–38). London: Routledge.

Chapter 18
Improving Well-Being in Higher Education: Adopting a Compassionate Approach

Frances A. Maratos, Paul Gilbert, and Theo Gilbert

Abstract This chapter directs attention to calls to integrate compassion training in curricula throughout the education system. Following a review of current Higher Education (HE) aims and objectives, and the potential psychological impacts that these can have on staff and students, we outline a case for compassion based initiatives in education. We discuss the nature and functions of compassion, as well as how compassion can heighten prosocial competencies. We then consider how compassion based approaches can be - and have been - implemented in education settings, including HE, to promote the health and well-being of staff and students, as well as academic performance. We argue that elements of compassion should underpin the training of lecturers (and teachers), as well as students, if UK institutes of learning truly embrace the various core values they advertise.

Keywords Well-being · Compassion-based motives · Higher education · Resilience · Competences

Overview

This chapter directs attention to increasing calls to integrate compassion training in curricula throughout the education system. Compassion-based initiatives are now beginning to be utilised within a wide range of organisational, health and educational settings. One reason is that a large body of evidence is now well established – and growing rapidly – that demonstrates focusing on the cultivation of compassion-based motives and affiliative emotions has important effects on mental states and well-being. Indeed, compassion training is now known to have a range of physiological effects and improve both moral and prosocial behaviour and to

F. A. Maratos (✉) · P. Gilbert
University of Derby, Derby, UK
e-mail: F.Maratos@derby.ac.uk

T. Gilbert
University of Hertfordshire, Hatfield, UK

© Springer Nature Switzerland AG 2019

P. Gibbs et al. (eds.), *Values of the University in a Time of Uncertainty*,
https://doi.org/10.1007/978-3-030-15970-2_18

enhance connections between people that are rescuing, sustaining and rational. In universities and schools, the call for compassion training is set against a growing concern with the consequences of the increasingly self-focused competitive nature of education.

While some degrees of competitiveness can be useful, individuals who are overdriven in competitiveness can become narcissistic and callous, while those who feel they are failing can become stressed, self-critical, anxious, depressed and generally mentally unwell (Gilbert 2009, 2017a). In Higher Education (HE) it is growing harder and harder to mediate such cultures when neither staff nor students have experience, in their teacher training, nor school backgrounds, of even a basic education in the psychobiological nature of compassion. Key players in government too appear to misunderstand or overlook how such a grounding plays a vital role in combining socio-emotional and subject education. Compassion builds mental and emotional resilience.

In this chapter we review current HE aims and objectives, and the potential psychological impacts that a metric-based educational system can have on both staff and students, including the values it creates. We also outline the importance of having a clear understanding of the nature of compassion as a form of courage and focus, and explore the processes and evidence for a particular form of compassion training – 'compassionate mind training' or 'CMT' – on wellbeing, including in terms of social relating. In addition, we discuss how to implement compassion-based practices in HE, enabling universities to embrace the core values they often advertise, e.g. statements suggesting they champion the health and well-being of their communities, as well as academic performance. In sum, we argue that elements of compassion should underpin the training of lecturers (and teachers), as well as students (and pupils), if UK institutes of learning are to truly embrace the core values they advertise and promote the health and well-being of their staff and student body.

Higher Education and the Concept of Compassion

The landscape of higher education is changing. The shift to funding through student tuition fees combined with the lifting of student quota controls has led to a competitive market, where universities increasingly allocate much larger monetary amounts to capital investment (i.e. marketing and advertising, as well as redesigning buildings/infrastructure etc.) and senior management pay (UCU 2018). Concurrent with this is the metricisation of higher education, with UK universities competing for top-ranking research status (as measured via the Research Excellence Framework 2018), top-ranking teaching status (as measured via the Teaching Excellence Framework 2018), and most recently their ability to demonstrate transfer of knowledge out of academia (in accordance with the yet to be finalised 'Knowledge Exchange Framework' 2018). According to Universities UK (2018), a key idea of this metricisation is to enable a *consistent* approach to research, teaching and knowledge exchange in higher education across the UK – yet to what detriment?

Potentially, a system of metricisation comes with the de-professionalisation of teaching and research, where innovative pedagogical practices are feared by academics (given the potential for poor student ratings, despite greater learning); and research is increasingly guided by the strategic aims of the specific university and/or academic department rather than the domain of the academic. Bizarrely, however, for staff, this is at odds with a number of UK university aims and objectives (as of June 29th, 2018), which state they are a place of providing *'innovation'* for their students (e.g. University of Huddersfield, Imperial College London, University of Birmingham, University of Bristol, Durham University, etc.) or *'personalised students' learning experiences'* (e.g. University of Nottingham, University of Oxford).

For the student, a system of metricisation, potentially leads to the narrow focus of higher education becoming the pursuit of qualifications that leads to graduate employment, as measured by a further metric the 'Destination of Leavers from Higher Education' (2018). Here, transformational values, such as becoming an inspired learner who actively seeks out broadening knowledge, as well as engages in prosocial behaviour for genuine reasons, is often side-lined in order to prioritise 'assessment-focus' and an encompassing CV. This prioritising of private enterprise is very much echoed in a number of UK University mission and/or value statements e.g., as of June 29th, 2018, *'to produce graduates distinguished by their intellectual capabilities'* (University of Manchester), *'educating our students to become future leaders'* (University of Bath), *'to be the best in all we do'* (University of Southampton) and the value of *'ambition and drive'* (University of Warwick).

Given these conflicting aims and objectives of UK universities for academic staff, and the highly competitive nature of HE to students and staff alike, it is unsurprising that the well-being of University staff and students is a current focus of attention. This includes the formation of the 'Education Support Partnership' in 2015, which claims to be *'the only charity dedicated to improving the health and wellbeing of the entire education workforce'* and Universities UK (2016), introducing a new programme to address mental health and wellbeing in universities, with major aims including: to: (i) *'Set out the case for institutions to see **mental health** as a strategic priority and to develop a whole-institution framework in support'* and (ii) *'Establish baseline data on the **mental health** of our populations and the effectiveness of interventions in place'*. (Embolded text, authors own).

Importantly, one potential type of mental-health initiative/intervention that is not only demonstrating a range of beneficial effects, including the promotion of prosocial behaviour (e.g. Kirby and Gilbert 2017; Ricard 2015; Singer and Bolz 2012), is that based on the ethos of compassion, and in particular compassion-focused therapy (CFT) and compassionate mind training (CMT). CMT is demonstrating increased utility in applied settings including education. For example, based on both CFT and CMT, a pragmatic understanding of the micro skills of compassion – a compassion-focused pedagogy (CfP) – has been developed for HE group and team work. Using extensive ethnographic studies of HE classroom behaviours in various disciplines, these evidence-based micro skills have been studied for their effects on student social and learning experience in group work with comparisons made between intervention and control groups (Gilbert 2016; Doolan et al. submitted). Based on results so far, this kind of CfP is being used and explored further in some universities as a practical approach to students' management of their group work.[1] However, to understand why CFT and CMT initiatives are gaining favour (as well as results) in applied settings, it is necessary to first briefly outline what compassion is, its premises as an intervention and its growing evidence base.

Understanding the Nature and Functions of Compassion

The evolution of compassion owes its origins to the evolution of caring behaviour between infant and parent (Mayseless 2016). This major shift in reproductive strategies was to have a profound effect on the subsequent evolution of mammalian species, partly because of the social challenges and opportunities that interpersonal closeness created (Gilbert 1989/2016; Mikulincer and Shaver 2007). Evolution created physiological systems that enabled parents to be sensitive and responsive to the needs and distress of their infants and for infants to be physiologically organised around inputs from the parent. Over the subsequent 100 million years evolution adapted these physiological mechanisms significantly, such that distress responsiveness and preparedness to help, even by putting oneself at risk, now operates in a range of relationships. For example, all medical and rescue services depend on this fundamental motive. Similarly, while some individuals may go into teaching as a 'job' others choose it as a vocation because they have a genuine interest in helping support the learning of the next generations. Many studies have revealed that the desire to be helpful to others is one of humans' most meaningful goals (Gilbert 2009, 2017b; Ricard 2015).

It is now well recognised that caring behaviour in contrast to competitive behaviour organises a range of physiological systems in very different ways and supports moral behaviour and well-being in a way that self-focused competitiveness may not (e.g. Weng et al. 2013, 2018). In addition, being a recipient of caring behaviour has major physiological effects which are quite different from experiencing oneself as a competitor with potentially indifferent or even critical and hostile others (Gilbert 2017a, b, 2018a, b). It is additionally now known that early life experiences associated with caring behaviour have a range of impacts including gene expression, immune system functioning, cardiovascular functioning, and maturation of the autonomic nervous system/frontal cortex to name just a few (Cowan et al. 2016). Importantly too, children who grow up in a secure, caring environment in contrast to a neglectful or hostile one, demonstrate quicker learning, and are more flexible, creative and demonstrate greater explorative play (Mikulincer and Shaver 2016).

---

[1] https://www.youtube.com/watch?v=3jFVTCuSCOg

Compassion Heightens Pro-social Cognitive Competencies

Compassion is more than caring though, and utilises specific human cognitive competencies. To expand, about 2 million years ago our human ancestors began to evolve very rapidly new types of brain that enabled new types of cognition. This involved self-awareness, abilities to reason and think systematically, abilities to use symbols and language and, critically, the ability to develop knowing intentionality. When these new cognitive competencies are used in the service of caring they are called compassion (Gilbert 2017b). So compassion can be defined as a motivation that is focused on the sensitivity to suffering in self and others, with a commitment to try to alleviate and prevent it (Gilbert and Choden 2013; Gilbert 2009). With respect to this there are two elements; these are stimulus detection and response proficiency. First is stimulus sensitivity whereby different stimuli activate and orientate attention which, for compassion, is some kind of need or distress. Second is response proficiency. This is the capacity for empathically understanding what would be helpful in that specific context. This definition clearly highlights that compassion is more than just intentionality. To illustrate, seeing somebody fall into a river and, consequently, jumping in to save them may be a compassionate intention but it will be ineffective, and potentially even problematic, if one cannot swim. In this case, one lacks the wisdom of knowing how to behave or act appropriately. This is where compassion training underpins effective and helpful behaviours, as well as social relating, by enabling individuals the skills to develop compassion for themselves, as well as compassion for others, and being open to compassion from others.

Compassion training focuses on how to orientate to need and/or distress in both the self and others, and how to work out appropriate empathic responses. Individualistically competitive environments, however, tend to do the opposite and close down interest in the needs and distress of others in favour of self-focused achievement and concern with self-presentation and positive social comparison. For example, Crocker and Canevello (2008, 2012) asked University students to rate the degree programme they were taking, in terms of "compassionate" goals such as wanting to be helpful to people and being sensitive to their needs in contrast to "self-image" motives and goals, such as wanting others to see that you are right and avoid showing mistakes. Results revealed that these two motivations were related to quite different potentials for social and mental health outcomes. Compassionate goals were linked to feeling connected, to lower levels of conflict, and better mental health. Conversely, self-image goals were negatively related to these outcomes. Indeed, the more self-focused, competitive and shame-focused individuals are, the more prone to depression they may be (Crocker et al. 2010).

There are a number of slightly different approaches to compassion training all of which have some evidence to support them (Kirby 2017; Kirby and Gilbert 2017; Seppälä et al. 2017). One is called compassionate mind training (CMT), which forms part of compassion focused therapy (CFT) developed for individuals who have high levels of self-criticism and shame and/or are vulnerable to depression and anxiety (Gilbert 2009, 2010). However, whereas CFT involves developing a therapeutic relationship and detailed formulation of a particular problem, then tailoring interventions for the specific individual, CMT is a set of practices and psychoeducation that are designed to cultivate both physiological and psychological processes that are conducive to well-being, creativity, moral and prosocial behaviour.

These practices and processes can be utilised outside of a therapeutic setting, as well as in larger group settings, including in schools, colleges and universities, and for staff as well as students (Gilbert 2009, 2016; Maratos et al. submitted).

CMT is an integrative and multidimensional approach to compassionate mind training that includes: emotion and body awareness, breathing and voice tone practices to stimulate affiliative physiology (Arch et al. 2014; Chang et al. 2013; Maratos and Sheffield in preparation), a range of attentional, imagery and behavioural practices to promote compassion (Duarte et al. 2015; Rockliff et al. 2008) as well as education as to the nature of 'being human' drawn from research science (e.g. neuroscience, evolutionary psychology, social psychology, developmental psychology etc., see Gilbert 2014; Richardson et al. 2016).

Additionally, and also of key importance, CMT focuses on three orientations of compassion. Firstly, there is the compassion we can feel for others and how we seek to reach out to others; and there is now increasing evidence that practising being helpful to others has major impacts on our physiological systems that are conducive to well-being and brain changes (Weng et al. 2018). Second is being open and receptive to compassion from others including experiencing joyful (not obligatory) gratitude (Wood et al. 2010). Here again this is linked to a large literature on the value of feeling supported and cared for in one's personal environment (Wang et al. 2014). Third is our ability to be self-compassionate rather than harshly self-critical. It is known, for example, that it is not so much the content of criticism but the emotional tone of criticism that is harmful (Gilbert 2010). Adding to this, it is when criticism becomes hostile or contemptuous that depression is more likely. Hence compassionate mind training teaches individuals to be sensitive to the emotional tone of their own thinking and try to generate a friendly rather than hostile tone (ibid).

There is now evidence that even a very short-term (2 week) intervention based on this style of training has a range of beneficial effects including decreased reports of stress, increased reports of compassion (to the self and others) and improved heart rate variability; the latter being an indicator of increased physiological well-being (Matos et al. 2017, 2018; see also Kirby et al. 2017). If the aim of education is to create a secure, safe and encouraging base for learning that promotes not only critical thinking, but also moral and ethical awareness, then addressing the dynamics of how to create a conducive environment for this is key. This is especially important given the changing nature of educational environments, particularly the move towards an overly self-focused competitive and threat-based educational system in the UK over recent decades that was noted above. Indeed, many of the increases in poor mental health and suicide in student populations appear to be linked to fears of failing in this intense competitive environment (see, for example, Hjeltnes et al. 2015).

We consider the adverse effects of these educational environments in a little more detail in the following section. Then we detail how CMT has recently been shown to be effective in school settings and how compassion-focused pedagogy (CfP) is being created in the modern context of Higher education.[2]

The Need for Compassion Based Initiatives in Educational Settings

In the context of HE, the Times Higher Education (July, 2018) reports Professor Gail Kinman's recent finding that over half of a sample of 6539 university teaching staff had experienced levels of mental health-damaging stress. (Only staff in the prison sector, she points out, experience more). Untenable workloads, including being required to mark 418 scripts in 20 days for example – pushed a UK university's father of three, Dr. Malcolm Anderson, to commit suicide in February (Grove 2018). Only months later, in June, the UK's Universities Minister delivered a speech to the country's Higher Education Policy Institute on the need for some HEI's to work harder on "Delivering Value for Money" – with none of the above reality factored in (Gyimah 2018). Schools, colleges and universities are championed as learning environments that facilitate creating a safe and secure base for teaching and learning, cultivate critical reasoning, and promote prosocial behaviour/moral awareness as part of the educational experience. But this is too often not the case for either staff or students.

Indeed, the individualistically competitive nature of the working and learning environment, and its impact on student, as well as staff, mental health is increasingly evident in universities. Levels of clinical anxiety and depression amongst students globally continue to rise (Hamilton and Schweitzer 2000; Mitsui et al. 2013). The HE sector in England and Wales is no exception, and increasing numbers of student suicides are reported by the Office of National Statistics (2017). In the 1st months of 2018, for example, the UK media's coverage of seven student suicides in a single UK university in just 18 months galvanised public protest at the neoliberal model of a marketised, business-minded, profit-focussed HE sector, when HE's original fundamental purpose is to serve the public good. The Vice-Chancellor of the above university has pointed out quite rightly, that these human disasters are a feature of the HE sector as a whole. There are around 130 universities in the UK. It is argued, mostly by a currently right-wing government, that a business model for HE is

---

[2] In this paper the taught and assessed use of the micro skills of compassion for use in group work, are only one example of a burgeoning development of empirically driven, CMT-based, compassion-focused pedagogy that is being developed in some universities.

perfectly acceptable. This is irrational. Governments in most countries would be constrained by law to close down any business whose *service* product was so frequently associated with customer deaths.

Mirroring HE, there is also growing evidence that primary and secondary schools are becoming increasingly stressful environments for both teachers and pupils. In primary education (7–11 years), rates of anxiety and panic attacks are on the rise, with an increase of 78% over the past 2 years (The Key 2017). Adolescent mental health issues, including teenage suicide, are also on the rise. Here, Rodway et al. (2016) indicate antecedents include exam pressures in 27%, and bullying in 22%, of cases. More general reports reveal an increase in fear of academic failure (76%) and depression (55%), among these young populations (Mental Health Foundation 2016), as well as a significant impact on pupils' capacity for learning.

In respect to teacher health, a recent UK government report states that 30% of teachers left the profession within the first 5 years for reasons of excessive workload and bureaucracy (Carmichael 2017). Consistent with this, the Educational Support Partnership (2018) survey of over 1250 education professionals revealed that three quarters (75%) report experiencing physical and mental health issues in the last 2 years because of stress and their poor work-life balance. According to NASWUT (2019), 77% of teachers further feel that there is a widespread behaviour problem in schools, over one third suggesting they are not given appropriate training (i.e. 37%), information or advice (i.e. 33%) to help them deal with difficult pupil behaviour. Whilst the government has now started to make moves to address such issues (e.g. 200 K for mental-health first-aiders, Bloom 2017), teacher and pupil stress, combined with problematic pupil behaviour, are now endemic within the UK.

Perhaps unsurprisingly, competitive pressures have been highlighted as a major source for such pupil and staff difficulties in schools. Not dissimilar from the metricisation of HE, the introduction of open performance school league tables in the UK leads to prioritisation of student academic achievement above all else, for senior leaders, teachers and parents alike (see for example: https://www.gov.uk/school-performance-tables). However, there is mounting evidence that classrooms fostering social comparison and competitive self-interest, in contrast to cooperative and mutually supportive learning, are associated with increased occurrences of bullying (Di Stasio et al. 2016). Additional consequences of this 'academic results' focus include increasing self-focused competitive stress, fear of failure, shame and exclusion; all of which can undermine mental well-being and performance (Crocker et al. 2010; Irons and Gilbert 2005).

The Implementation of Compassion Based Initiatives in Primary and Secondary Educational Settings

Recognising the growing problems of competitive stress in schools, a growing number of well-being initiatives are beginning to primarily address well-being, transformative values and/or compassion.[3] More widely, Hanh and Weare (2017) provide educative and informative materials directed towards teachers (of all levels) to improve both their own and their pupils' well-being (see also Al-Ghabban 2018; Coles 2015; Lavelle et al. 2017). Considering CMT specifically, Welford and Langmead (2015) have developed 'Care to Achieve', a compassion based initiative which integrates core CMT tenets within a school-based setting. Results demonstrate that Care to Achieve has led to: an increase in staff well-being (via self-report and a decrease in sickness); an increase in parental engagement (measured by increased parental attendance in school for a range of activities); and a decrease in low level disruptive behaviour and fixed-term exclusions. Welford and Langmead (2015) acknowledge that the uptake of the approach, disseminated by word of mouth, highlights the potential credibility and attractiveness of compassion based initiatives in the UK. However, as declared by the authors themselves, there remains a need for further rigorous scientific evaluation of such approaches.

Taking this forward, Maratos et al. (submitted) have designed, progressed and scientifically evaluated a six module compassionate mind training initiative with the entire staffing population (n = 78) of a UK secondary school. Based upon the three core principles of CFT, this initial 'action research' included a blend of psychoeducation, imagery practices and group or dyadic based exercises. Whilst primarily a proof of concept study to investigate the feasibility and efficacy of CMT in UK school settings, the initiative was comprehensively evaluated using a mixed methods approach – with several positive results. For example, the CMT curriculum was well-received by staff, with the majority (over 90%) reporting that they would recommend the training to others. In terms of actual impact effectiveness, quantitative data revealed that those who practiced the CMT exercises demonstrated significant increases in self-compassion and significant decreases in self-criticism. Adding to this, qualitative exploration of the initiative revealed that staff were satisfied with the CMT activities, with a major theme emerging, i.e. 'The potentials of using CMT to deal with emotional difficulties'.

To sum, introducing secondary school teachers and staff to compassionate mind training (that has different elements of recognising emotions, mindfulness and developing compassion motivation for dealing with stress), proved very successful on a number of grounds. Thus, in evaluating this proof of concept research, Maratos et al. (submitted) argue that compassionate mind training may hold much promise

---

[3] e.g. 'The big picture' (Educational Endowment Foundation, https://educationendowmentfoundation.org.uk/school-themes); the Child Outcomes Research Consortium (https://www.corc.uk.net/) and the Mindfulness in Schools Project, University of Southampton (https://mindfulnessinschools.org/research/).

as a way of helping school staff (and especially teachers) counteract the current competitive nature of education and learn ways to counteract stress; especially that associated with self-criticism and anger rumination that contributes to burnout. However, what is now needed is a curricula suitable for mass roll-out both nationally and internationally, as well as pupil-friendly versions of the initiative, and, importantly, a curricula that is designed specifically for the challenges of students and staff within the HE sector. The need for such a bespoke HE curricula and steps being made towards this (e.g. the micro skills of compassion), are outlined below.

Promoting and Assessing Compassion in Higher Education

In addition to the adverse effects of education as a competitive process outlined above, a key contributor to the fatal distress amongst some HE students today is thought to be their low levels of social integration on campus, especially for black, ethnic minority and international (BME) students (UK National Union of Students (NUS) 2010).

It is in the class room, the NUS has concluded from its watershed study (2010), that FE and HE must work harder *"to promote social cohesion and better integrate their student bodies"* (p61). In particular, it looks to FE and HE to recognise that *"social inclusion"* and *"social cohesion"* (p61) *"could be achieved by increasing discussion and interactive work within the classroom"* (p61).

Academic staff and student led initiatives, increasingly in partnership, are trying to address this in many universities and Advance HE in the UK is encouraging co-operation and connection across UK universities in this regard. There are now a range of such partnerships that are focusing efforts on ungluing HE from its over reliance on 'the traditional lecture' and in particular, on the ubiquitous traditional written essay as a means of assessment. Both are too often linked to an inward-facing (Anglo/ethno-centric) curriculum that requires students to read texts that are predominantly written by white men. Lectures are derived from medieval times when a precious single text, possibly hand written, was the responsibility of the male university educator (or monk) to read aloud to male listening students – and students listened. This kind of approach and the kinds of material it often relies on hardly facilitates the ideation of multiple, alternative, innovative perspectives in student minds' (cf. University straplines) when they are thinking about the target subject. Thus, is it not only for the reasons pointed out above by the NUS that a growing number of university staff are trying to diversify their teaching and assessment practice to include team based learning and group work. It is academically appropriate for our times too and in shift-changing disciplines often a prerequisite of the regulatory body (e.g. for accreditation of Psychology degrees in the UK, the BPS specify *'The curriculum requirements … outline the need for practical work to cover a wide variety of methodologies … Students should … engage in practical work. Accredited programmes will be expected to demonstrate the ways in which they accommodate these expectations'* (BPS 2016, p21)). A delay to progress here, however, is that when (homogenous or diverse) students are required to work together, they have seldom been taught how to do this in ways that – at least where the science of compassion is concerned – are based on an empirical, up to date evidence base. Thus, while guidance may be given to students on referencing, citing and so on, there is no basic training or help with the cognitively demanding processes of group work management. This means that in terms of the universal psychosocial processes that can be experienced by individuals in a team, students are unsure about how to cope with the quiet member in the group who says (or contributes) little or nothing to group discussions, or the person who dominates (or monopolises) team discussions because of over enthusiasm, or anxiety (Yalom and Leszsz 2005), or individualistic competitiveness and private enterprise (Chickering 2010); or all of these. These are the very factors that come up again and again in student reports of what has undermined their group's social cohesion and hobbled its academic performance (Gilbert et al. 2018).

Businesses are urging universities to address this. The Hay Group (2015) report that in their study of business needs they found that: *"93% of businesses believe strong people skills deliver commercial impact* [whereas] *51% of graduates believe people skills get in the way of getting the job done"*. In similar research, the British Chamber of Commerce (2014) reported: *"Over half (57%) said that young people are lacking basic 'soft' skills, such as communication and team working, to succeed in the working world."* (HR Review 2014). Yet Google, which has recently spent US$5M on a study to identify the key defining feature of its highest performing teams (from a sample of 180 teams) found that the key, defining, shared feature was not ambition, a leader, a mix of skills or personalities, experience or qualifications. It was kindness (Duhigg 2016) and this is what appeared to raise the teams' collective intelligence. The company is joined by IBM, PcW and many other companies investing in ways to accelerate the nurturing of effective in-house team dynamics that attend to safeness in psychosocial processes (The Times Top 100 Graduate Employers.com). This trend is vital for 'business-facing' HE to pay attention to in relation to the rising levels of its key customers' distress and suicides once they try the HE business product. It is also vital to address if universities wish to pay proper attention to ensuring their graduates progress onto graduate positions (i.e. their DELHI statistics).

How is HE therefore, to catch up with businesses, with current research on compassion as a matter of intellectual honesty, and above all, how is it to catch up with its duty to its key customers: students? Its failures in all three areas is becoming increasingly transparent and public.

We argue here, that a vital component of the solution is that the science of compassion – being built now through the work of multiple disciplines – is a force to be reckoned with by HE on the institution's own terms, namely its pre-occupation with the measurement of student academic success. Indeed, it is becoming evident that there is a correlation between compassion on the HE curricula and statistically identified enhancements to academic performance, compared with control groups (Gilbert 2016; Doolan et al. submitted). Training of staff and students requires explanation and a little classroom practice – while on subject task – of the simple, observable 'micro skills of compassion' for *group/team work*. Where HE practitioners develop this kind of compassionate practice amongst their students as part of the in-class teaching and learning experience, increases are observed with respect to student engagement with each other, the subject area and their academic performances, as compared to controls (Gilbert 2016, 2017a, b, c; Doolan et al. submitted). It is on these terms that we can discuss how the training of students in the micro skills of compassion in their dealings with each other, regardless of level or subject, can be embedded into the curriculum and *made credit bearing* towards attainment of the modern university degree.

The University of Hertfordshire (UH) brands itself as 'An international business-facing university' (1st August, 2018) It is committed to working with local and other businesses in areas such as Knowledge Exchange, Research Partnerships with business, and has a strong emphasis on the development of graduate skills around employability. Its business school is the largest in the south east of England. The micro skills of compassion in group work – what they look like in action and their theoretical basis for use in group discussion work – has been researched and trialled in this school (as well as other schools in the university[4]). On some modules, students are supported by academic staff in their use of the easily taught micro skills of compassion during task-focussed, timed, face-to-face discussions in seminars and/or tutorials. Then, in final, end of module, filmed small group discussions, students are tutor-assessed individually for: research skills, critical/analytical thinking and, importantly, the use of the micro skills of compassion that they have been taught, and have practiced using in seminars and tutorials throughout the model (See Fig. 18.1 for assessment criteria for the micro skills of compassion). The use of these micro skills of compassion – including standing down monopolisers when necessary (not silencing them) and drawing in quieter members of the group – are credit bearing towards these students' degrees. With minor adaptions to assessment practice, this is the case on some degree programmes, post and under graduate, in the Schools (departments) of the Humanities, Computer Science and Business at the University of Hertfordshire where the research around this CfP has been developed. Staff from, currently, 36 other universities (UK, Canada, USA and Europe) are also now networked and engaging with this form of CfP.

To expand, the Compassionate Mind Foundation's model of compassion, as well as some of its core principles of CMT, have been combined with findings of research into the ethnography of university class room behaviours, with and (for control purposes) – without staff and student exposure to that model. This research included close attention to, and recording of, the often non-verbal, but nevertheless observable details of enactments of compassionate (or non-compassionate) behaviours of students for themselves and others in discussion group work. Here, certain compassionate actions were found again and again to intensify the group's focus on group social cohesion and criticality on task; in other words, inclusivity and intellectual risk taking. The micro skills that facilitated this in student groups in class, including

---

[4]Additionally, a further pilot is underway with students in the Life Sciences (i.e. Psychology) department of the University of Derby.

(Allocated 10% - 35% of marks in current HE practice)

Category of Assessment	Distinction (70% +)	Commendation 69-60%	Pass (59-50%)	Marginal fail F (49-40%)	Clear fail (below 40%) *
1. Research Skills ? ↓					
1.2 Criticality/ analytical thinking ?					
2.1 Compassionate group management	Excellent use of eye contact and inclusive body language; eliciting, encouraging and acknowledging the contributions of others; asking for clarity or elaboration; checking the understanding of the group.	Very good use of eye contact and inclusive body language; eliciting, encouraging and acknowledging the contributions of others; asking for clarity or elaboration; checking the understanding of the group.	Good use of eye contact and inclusive body language; eliciting, encouraging and acknowledging the contributions of others; asking for clarity or elaboration; checking the understanding of the group.	Body language signals little interest in what is said by others, or may focus on one or two other students only. Either monopolises or makes little contribution to discussion. Speaks too fast, or inaudibly.	Body language signals little or no interest in what is said by others, or may focus on one other student only. Either monopolises or makes little contribution to discussion. Speaks too fast, or inaudibly.

* A grade of 0-19% indicates that there is little or nothing of merit in the assignment.

Fig. 18.1 Core assessment/marking criteria for use of the micro skills of compassion in discussion group work. (Gilbert 2016 https://compassioninhe.wordpress.com/)

amongst relative strangers, were introduced in the first hour of the module, and thereafter embedded into routine class room discussion practice by staff and students. Thinking then of the HE focus on metricisation, a statistical analysis was made on a module of ethnically diverse business students (n = 38) to identify evidence of: (i) negative, positive or no impact of the teaching; and (ii) assessing of compassion (as above), on individual student academic performance – specifically in relation to critical thinking. In the essay assignment on the module, critical thinking percentage marks for each individual student clearly mirrored the UK HE sector's overall 14–15% achievement attainment gap between BME students (and also international students) and local white students. Yet for critical thinking in the context of compassion, as was possible in the discussion groups, no statistical evidence could be found of an attainment gap between white and BME students when all the essays and all the presentations were double marked by two senior business lecturers (Gilbert 2016). A similar study undertaken amongst (n = 220) computer science undergraduate students, compared to a control has had similar results (Doolan et al. submitted).

Thus this research, taken in the context of that evidenced throughout the education sector to date, demonstrates that developing most staff and students in their expert and astute use of the micro skills of compassion in group work, is not only a fast and easy endeavour, but a grounds to improve social-relating (an important transformative skill recognised in real-world settings). One further reason for this is the close-to-the surface appetite in students and staff to stand down from the relentless HE promotion of what Chickering (2010) describes as competitive individualism and private enterprise and promote learning instead. Here is the evidence based, theoretically underpinned component of compassion that can be added to assessment of many types of face to face, interactional group work.

Summary

To conclude, much research demonstrates that the cultivation of a compassion-based ethos, and associated practices, has important effects on mental states and well-being. Specifically, the positive effects of compassionate mind training are not only demonstrated in therapeutic based settings, but across both public and private sector settings, with recent evidence emerging of its utility in school-based settings. Added to this, Gilbert (2016, 2018a, b, et al. 2010) and Doolan et al. submitted) have revealed evidence of its many benefits in higher education, with the use of the micro skills of compassion in group work. This simple CMT based intervention has been found in studies so far (ibid) to equip and motivate students to seek out ways to enhance each other's social and learning experiences in task focussed groups to degrees they would not normally have been inclined to attempt. The impacts on academic achievement are now coming to light through quantitative data (ibid). Here, there is an alignment with the aims of universities that are striving to ensure students are fit for graduate employment, as well as able to cope with championing HE's remit to serve the public good through enhanced pro-social thinking processes in groups and communities. Schools and universities alike are more likely to meet their own stated aims if they attend with absolute attention to catching up with a now formidable body of evidence of the role of compassion in education. If this is done then their current aims (and values) may evolve too. This is why we resolutely argue for embedding compassion into school and HE environments. If UK institutes of learning truly embrace the core values they advertise, they will attend to the science of compassion to nurture and protect the health and well-being – and thus irreplaceable talents – of their staff and student bodies.

References

Al-Ghabban, A. (2018). A compassion framework: The role of compassion in schools in promoting well-being and supporting the social and emotional development of children and young people. *Pastoral Care in Education, 36*, 1–13.

Arch, J. J., Brown, K. W., Dean, D. J., Landy, L. N., Brown, K. D., & Laudenslager, M. L. (2014). Self-compassion training modulates alpha-amylase, heart rate variability, and subjective responses to social evaluative threat in women. *Psychoneuroendocrinology, 42*, 49–58.

Bloom, A. (2017). Government puts 200k behind plan for mental health first-aiders in every secondary. Retrieved from: https://www.tes.com/news/government-puts-ps200k-behind-plan-mental-health-first-aiders-every-secondary.

Carmichael, N. (2017). *Recruitment and retention of teachers.* Retrieved from: https://publications.parliament.uk/pa/cm201617/cmselect/cmeduc/199/199.pdf.

Chang, Q., Liu, R., & Shen, Z. (2013). Effects of slow breathing rate on blood pressure and heart rate variabilities. *International Journal of Cardiology, 169*(1), e6–e8.

Chickering, A. W. (2010). A retrospect on higher education's commitment to moral and civic education. *Journal of College and Character, 11*(3), 1–6.

Coles, M. I. (2015). *Towards the compassionate school. From golden rule to golden thread.* London: Institute of Education press.

Cowan, C. S. M., Callaghan, B. L., Kan, J. M., & Richardson, R. (2016). The lasting impact of early-life adversity on individuals and their descendants: Potential mechanisms and hope for intervention. *Genes, Brain and Behavior, 15*(1), 155–168.

Crocker, J., & Canevello, A. (2008). Creating and undermining social support in communal relationships: The role of compassionate and self-image goals. *Journal of Personality and Social Psychology, 95*, 555–575.

Crocker, J., & Canevello, A. (2012). Consequences of self-image and compassionate goals. In P. G. Devine & A. Plant (Eds.), *Advances in experimental social psychology* (pp. 229–277). New York: Elsevier.

Crocker, J., Canevello, A., Breines, J. G., & Flynn, H. (2010). Interpersonal goals and change in anxiety and dysphoria in first-semester college students. *Journal of Personality and Social Psychology, 98*, 1009–1024.

Destination of Higher Leavers. (2018). *Experts in UK higher education data and analysis, and the designated data body for England.* Retrieved from: https://www.hesa.ac.uk/.

Di Stasio, M. R., Savage, R., & Burgos, G. (2016). Social comparison, competition and teacher–student relationships in junior high school classrooms predicts bullying and victimisation. *Journal of Adolescence, 53*, 207–216.

Doolan, M., Gilbert, T., Beka, S., Spencer, N., Crotta, M., & Davari, S. (submitted). Compassion on university degree programmes at a UK University: The neuroscience of effective group work. Special issue: Neuroscience of learning and development: Implications for the design and evaluation of student learning and development. *Journal of Research in Innovative Teaching and Learning. Emerald Publishing.* ISSN: 2397–7604.

Duarte, J., McEwan, K., Barnes, C., Gilbert, P., & Maratos, F. A. (2015). Do therapeutic imagery practices affect physiological and emotional indicators of threat in high self-critics? *Psychology and Psychotherapy: Theory, Research and Practice, 88*(3), 270–284.

Duhigg, C. (2016). What Google learned from its quest to build the perfect team. *The New York Times Magazine.* Retrieved from: http://www.nytimes.com/2016/02/28/magazine/what-google-learned-from-its-quest-to-build-the-perfect-team.

Gilbert, P. (1989/2016). *Human nature and suffering.* London: Routledge.

Gilbert, P. (2009). Introducing compassion-focused therapy. *Advances in Psychiatric Treatment, 15*(3), 199–208.

Gilbert, P. (2010). *Compassion focused therapy: The CBT distinctive features series.* London: Routledge.

Gilbert, P. (2014). The origins and nature of compassion focused therapy. *British Journal of Clinical Psychology, 53*(1), 6–41.

Gilbert, T. (2016). Assess compassion in higher education? Why and how would we do that? *LINK, 2*(1). Available at: http://www.herts.ac.uk/link/volume-2,-issue-1/assess-compassion-in-higher-education-how-and-why-would-we-do-that/.

Gilbert, P. (2017a). *Compassion: Concepts, research and applications*. London: Routledge.

Gilbert, P. (2017b). Compassion as a social mentality: An evolutionary approach. In P. Gilbert (Ed.), *Compassion: Concepts, research and applications* (pp. 31–68). London: Routledge.

Gilbert, T. (2017). Chapter 13: When looking is allowed: What compassionate group work looks like in a UK university. In P. Gibbs (Ed.), *The pedagogy of compassion at the heart of higher education* (pp. 189–202). London: Springer.

Gilbert, P. (2018a). *Living like crazy*. York: Annwyn House.

Gilbert, T. (2018b). *Compassion-in-HE*. University of Hertfordshire. Available at: https://compassioninhe.wordpress.com/.

Gilbert, T., Doolan, N. T. F.,. M., Beka, S., Spencer, N., Crotta, M., & Davari, S. (2018). Compassion on university degree programmes at a UK university: The neuroscience of effective group work. *Journal of Research in Innovative Teaching & Learning, 11*(1), 4–21.

Gilbert, P., & Choden. (2013). *Mindful compassion. Using the power of mindfulness and compassion to transform our lives*. Little: Brown Book Group.

Grove, J. (2018). Half of UK academics 'suffer stress-linked mental health problems': Scholars at greater risk of stress-related illness than police, medics and local authority staff, research suggests. *Times Higher Education*. Retrieved from: https://www.timeshighereducation.com/news/half-uk-academics-suffer-stress-linked-mental-health-problems.

Gyimah, S. (2018). *Delivering value for money in the age of the student*. Speech: The universities minister calls for a better deal for students at the HEPI annual conference. Retrieved from: https://www.gov.uk/government/speeches/delivering-value-for-money-in-the-age-of-the-student.

Hanh, T. N., & Weare, K. (2017). *Happy teachers change the world*. London: Parallax Press.

Hamilton, T. K., & Schweitzer, R. D. (2000). The cost of being perfect: Perfectionism and suicide ideation in university students. *Australian and New Zealand Journal of Psychiatry, 34*(5), 829–835.

Hjeltnes, A., Binder, P. E., Moltu, C., & Dundas, I. (2015). Facing the fear of failure: An explorative qualitative study of client experiences in a mindfulness-based stress reduction program for university students with academic evaluation anxiety. *International Journal of Qualitative Studies on Health and Well-Being, 10*(1), 27990.

HR Review. (2014). 88% of businesses believe school leavers are unprepared for the world of work. Retrieved from: https://www.hrreview.co.uk/hr-news/l-d-news/school-leavers-are-unprepared-for-the-world-of-work/53791

Irons, C., & Gilbert, P. (2005). Evolved mechanisms in adolescent anxiety and depression. The role of attachment and social rank systems. *Journal of Adolescent, 28*, 325–341.

Kirby, J. N. (2017). Compassion interventions: The programmes, the evidence, and implications for research and practice. *Psychology and Psychotherapy: Theory, Research and Practice, 90*(3), 432–455.

Kirby, J., & Gilbert, P. (2017). The emergence of the compassion focused therapies. In *Compassion: Concepts, research and applications* (pp. 258–285). London: Routledge.

Kirby, J. N., Tellegen, C. L., & Steindl, S. (2017). A systematic review and meta-analysis of compassion-based interventions: Current state of knowledge and future directions. *Behavior Therapy*. https://doi.org/10.1016/j.beth.2017.06.003.

Knowledge Exchange Framework. (2018). Retrieved from http://www.hefce.ac.uk

Lavelle, B. D., Flook, L., & GhahremaniIn, D. G. (2017). A call for compassion and care in education: Toward a more comprehensive prosocial framework for the field. In E. M. Seppälä, E. Simon-Thomas, S. L. Brown, M. C. Worline, L. Cameron, & J. R. Doty (Eds.), *The Oxford handbook of compassion science* (pp. 475–483). New York: Oxford University Press.

Maratos, F. A. & Sheffield, D. (in preparation). *Brief compassion-focused imagery dampens pain responses*.

Maratos, F. A., Montague, J. Aziz, H., Welford, M., Wood, W., Barnes, C., Sheffield, D., Gilbert, P. (submitted). Evaluation of a compassionate mind training intervention with school teachers and support staff.

Matos, M., Duarte, C., Duarte, J., Pinto-Gouveia, J., Petrocchi, N., Basran, J., & Gilbert, P. (2017). Psychological and physiological effects of compassionate mind training: A pilot randomised controlled study. *Mindfulness, 8*(6), 1699–1712.

Matos, M., Duarte, J., Duarte, C., Gilbert, P., & Pinto-Gouveia, J. (2018). How one experiences and embodies compassionate mind training influences its effectiveness. *Mindfulness, 9*(4), 1224–1235.

Mayseless, O. (2016). *The caring motivation: An integrated theory.* Oxford: Oxford University Press.

Mental Health. (2016). *Fundamental factors about mental health 2016.* Retrieved from: https://www.mentalhealth.org.uk/sites/default/files/fundamental-facts-about-mental-health-2016.pdf.

Mikulincer, M., & Shaver, P. R. (2007). *Attachment in adulthood: Structure, dynamics, and change.* Guilford Press.

Mikulincer, M., & Shaver, P. R. (2016). *Attachment in adulthood: Structure, dynamics, and change* (2nd ed.). New York: Guilford Press.

Mitsui, N., Asakura, S., Inoue, T., Shimizu, Y., Fujii, Y., Kako, Y., Tenaka, T., Obe, K., Inoue, T., & Kusumi, I. (2013). Temperament and character profiles of Japanese university student suicide completers. *Comprehensive Psychiatry, 54*(5), 556–561. https://doi.org/10.1016/j.comppsych.2012.11.002.

NASWUT. (2019). *The Big Question Report (2018).* Retrieved from: https://www.nasuwt.org.uk/uploads/assets/uploaded/6c7508a4-9051-4d1d-8cdedb297ed7170a.pdf

National Union of Students. (2010). *Race for equality.* Retrieved from: https://www.nus.org.uk/en/news/race-for-equality/.

Office of National Statistics (GB). (2017). *Student suicides in those aged 18 and above, by sex and usual place of residence, deaths registered in England and Wales between 2001 and 2015.* Retrieved from: https://www.ons.gov.uk/peoplepopulationandcommunity/birthsdeathsandmarriages/deaths/adhocs/005991studentsuicidesinthoseaged18yearsandabovebysexandusualplaceofresidenceindicatordeathsregisteredinenglandandwalesbetween2001and2015.

Research Excellence Framework 2021. (2018). Retrieved from http://www.ref.ac.uk/.

Ricard, M. (2015). *Altruism. The power of compassion to change itself and the world.* London: Atlantic Books.

Richardson, M., McEwan, K., Maratos, F., & Sheffield, D. (2016). Joy and calm: How an evolutionary functional model of affect regulation informs positive emotions in nature. *Evolutionary Psychological Science, 2*(4), 308–320.

Rockliff, H., Gilbert, P., McEwan, K., Lightman, S., & Glover, D. (2008). A pilot exploration of heart rate variability and salivary cortisol responses to compassion-focused imagery. *Journal of Clinical Neuropsychiatry, 5*(3), 132–139.

Rodway, C., Tham, S. G., Ibrahim, S., Turnbull, P., Windfuhr, K., Shaw, J., & Appleby, L. (2016). Suicide in children and young people in England: A consecutive case series. *The Lancet Psychiatry, 3*(8), 751–759.

Seppälä, E. M., Simon-Thomas, E., Brown, S. L., Worline, M. C., Cameron, L., & Doty, J. R. (Eds.). (2017). *The Oxford handbook of compassion science.* New York: Oxford University Press.

Singer, T., & Bolz, M. (2012). *Compassion: Bridging practice and science.* Retrieved from: http://www.compassion-training.org/?lang=en&page=about.

Teaching Excellence Framework. (2018). Retrieved from .http://www.officeforstudents.org.uk/

The BPS, (2016). *Standards for the accreditation of undergraduate, conversion and integrated Masters programmes in psychology.* Retrieved from: https://www1.bps.org.uk/system/files/Public%20files/PaCT/Undergraduate%20Accreditation%202016_WEB.pdf.

HR Review (2014)*88% of businesses believe school leavers are unprepared for the world of work.* Retrieved from: http://www.britishchambers.org.uk/press-office/press-releases/young-people-need-more-support-to-make-transition-from-education-to-work,-says-bcc.html.

The Educational Support Partnership. (2018). Retrieved from: https://www.educationsupportpartnership.org.uk/.

The Key. (2017). *State of education survey report 2017*. Retrieved from: https://stateofed.thekey-support.com/.

The Times Top One Hundred Graduate Employers for 2017–2018. (n.d.). *The Times*. Retrieved from: http://www.top100graduateemployers.com/employers.

UCU. (2018). *Higher education branch access note*. Retrieved from http://www.ucu.org.uk/media/9311/UCUBANHE29/pdf/HE_Pay_claim_submitted.pdf.

Universities UK. (2016). *New programme to address mental health and wellbeing in universities*. Retrieved from: https://www.universitiesuk.ac.uk/news/Pages/New-programme-to-address-mental-health-and-wellbeing-in-universities.aspx.

Universities UK. (2018). *Regulation of higher education*. Retrieved from https://www.universitiesuk.ac.uk/policy-and-analysis/Pages/regulation.aspx

Wang, X., Cai, L., Qian, J., & Peng, J. (2014). Social support moderates stress effects on depression. *International Journal of Mental Health Systems, 8*, 41. (on line). https://doi.org/10.1186/1752-4458-8-41.

Welford, M., & Langmead, K. (2015). Compassion-based initiatives in educational settings. *Educational and Child Psychology, 32*(1), 71–80.

Weng, H. Y., Fox, A. S., Shackman, A. J., Stodola, D. E., Caldwell, J. Z., Olson, M. C., & Davidson, R. J. (2013). Compassion training alters altruism and neural responses to suffering. *Psychological Science, 24*(7), 1171–1180.

Weng, H. Y., Lapate, R. C., Stodola, D. E., Rogers, G. M., & Davidson, R. J. (2018). Visual attention to suffering after compassion training is associated with decreased amygdala responses. *Frontiers in Psychology, 9,* 771.

Wood, A. M., Froh, J. J., & Geraghty, A. W. (2010). Gratitude and well-being: A review and theoretical integration. *Clinical Psychology Review, 30*(7), 890–905.

Yalom, I., & Leszsz, M. (2005). *The theory and practice of group psychotherapy* (5th ed.). New York: Basic Books.

Chapter 19
Moving Beyond 'Homo Economicus' into Spaces for Kindness in Higher Education: The Critical Corridor Talk of Informal Higher Education Leadership

Jill Jameson

Abstract Dialogic spaces for kindness in higher education, located in the 'critical corridor talk' (CCT) of informal leaders positioned quietly in the background in many universities, are a form of moral resistance in an era excessively dominated by the values of some of the harsher exponents of economic rationalism. This is a secret language of dialogic resistance, to be found under the radar, tucked away in the blindspots of formally recognised communication. It stoically challenges an arguably unhealthy obsession with efficient management, marketisation and economic proficiency at any cost that is, in some institutions, promoted by the harder managerial taskmasters symbolically represented in the concept of 'homo economicus'. This chapter argues that such 'understage' dialogic spaces for kindness are emerging slowly but with progressively firm resistance to challenge unhealthy forms of managerial instrumentalism in some low trust situations in a stratified UK higher education system. The accumulation of such spaces is occurring almost invisibly, in a subtle, persistent manner, like a soft, repetitive reminder of the need for human values, gently but relentlessly aiming to compensate for and wash away the mistakes, confusion and suffering bound up in poor management. This theoretical chapter, informed by empirical data, discusses the need to recognise this quiet form of understated kindness as a pre-eminent but under-recognised quality, currently marginalised in a higher education system more overtly focused on self-promotion, targets, outputs and league tables than on the well-being of staff and students. Drawing from leadership data and auto-ethnographic observations (2005–2017), I argue that this informal, resistant academic critique is gradually questioning

---

An earlier version of this chapter with substantially differing data and commentary is published in: (Jameson 2018)

J. Jameson (✉)
University of Greenwich, London, UK
e-mail: j.jameson@greenwich.ac.uk

P. Gibbs et al. (eds.), *Values of the University in a Time of Uncertainty*,
https://doi.org/10.1007/978-3-030-15970-2_19

economically-driven 'command and control' managerialism. The Critical Corridor Talk model proposed here and elsewhere (Jameson J, Higher Educ Q 72:375–389, 2018) builds on Barnett's concept of 'critical being' (Higher education: a critical business. SRHE/Open University Press, Buckingham, 1997), to theorise the ways in which academic staff find relief from hard-nosed forms of management by sharing moments of truthful dialogic communication, kindness and empathy for colleagues in the 'critical corridor talk' of informal distributed leadership networks. 'Negative capability' is a form of self-reflexive resistance against the 'false necessity' of performative goals demanded by neoliberalist economic management. Resistant informal leadership challenges the manufactured performativity of higher education environments where some in power overstep the acceptable roles of good management. Yet to foster trust, such resistant leadership needs to ensure it continually practises both kindness and correct moral principles itself.

Keywords Critical corridor talk · Kindness · Leadership · Human values · Performative goals

Introduction

The capacity to withstand challenges effectively while remaining ethically resolute despite difficulties in times of oppression may be designated 'stoicism'. It may have an enigmatic quality, characterised by a depth of integrity that can remain largely unobserved, arguably too intangible in some cases to be pinned down completely in empirical observation. This chapter argues for the likely existence of a form of shared community stoicism amongst university staff, particularly those positioned at lower hierarchical levels of power. This seems to take place in the tacit knowledge exchange and kindly presence of a muted form of dialogue involving 'Critical Corridor Talk' (CCT, Jameson 2018), which usually, though not exclusively, occurs amongst non-managerial staff. It can be argued that this subterranean socio-cultural dialogic phenomenon is hidden beneath the iceberg of officially recognised forms of procedural knowledge in higher education, like a secret underground resistance movement, only visible to its participants.

To identify the phenomenon, this chapter puts forward a theoretical model of morally resistant distributed leadership, promoting the marginalised virtue of kindness, which, with some exceptions (Clegg and Rowland 2010; see also complementary chapters defining kindness in this volume) has been relatively neglected as a value in higher education. The chapter is overtly informed by prior literature on resistance (Lucas 2014; Ollin 2005; Trowler 1998), criticality and dialogic learning (Barnett 1997; Freire 1972; Renshaw 2004; Wegerif and Mercer 1997); managerialism and performativity (Ball 2003; Deem 1998; Leathwood and Read 2013; McNay 2005; Slaughter and Leslie 1997), and, in the background, by empirical data from interviews, electronic surveys, and a series of auto-ethnographic reflections on leadership as a participant-observer in 2005–2018, including several surveys carried out during 2008–2017 (Jameson 2012, 2018).

'*Homo Economicus*' and Moral Hazard: Managerialism Through Quantitative Measures

It seems clear that higher education management conducted through a stratified hierarchy of authority-led power relations, legitimised by quantitative marketised measures to meet the demands of '*homo economicus*' (Thaler 2000) in a regulatory state environment, is now a frequently manifested organisational form in UK higher education (Deem et al. 2007). This form of 'academic capitalism' as identified in the US (Slaughter and Leslie 1997; Slaughter and Rhoades 2004) also seems to be a key feature of the higher education landscape in numerous other countries, at least for the present, as captured in strategic management plans, key performance targets, metrics and learning analytics dashboards. To counter this trend, however, many researchers have pointed out that various challenges to managerialism may offer the kinds of reflective, complex and subtle responses that comprise an emerging informal moral resistance provided by critical academic leadership (Bacon 2014; Gill 2009; Leathwood and Read 2009; Ollin 2005). These are the kinds of 'understage' responses that shape the cultural underlife of an institution, as Trowler points out in relation to his discussion of institutional cultures in higher education as both constructed interactively and enacted (Trowler 1998:34).

Within this resistant trend, a critique of questionable forms of micromanagerial controlling behaviour, including bullying and excessive performance monitoring, thinly justified by economic rationalism, has emerged in extensive prior literature on managerialism and new public management in higher education and elsewhere in the public sector. For over three decades now in higher education research, this extensive critique has identified a problematic deprofessionalisation of academic staff (Clarke and Newman 1997; Deem 1998; Deem and Brehony 2005; Lea 2011; McNay 2005), as well as alternative forms of collective leadership (Bolden et al. 2008) and collegiality (Elton 2008; Tapper and Palfreyman 2002; Bacon 2014). These approaches can be depicted as either dichotomous or complementary alternatives in analysing the tensions between management and collegial academia (Tight 2014) and/or as different forms of academic rebellion against an audit culture (Leathwood and Read 2012).

A seemingly exhausted fragility emerges from related research on academic labour (Hall 2014), regarding the stressful levels of marginalisation, disempowerment and 'performativity' demands that academics increasingly face. As part of this trend, Gill (2009) is amongst those who have identified a combined 'punishing intensification of work' and disproportionately harsh governmentality of self-monitoring, which together are making academic work increasingly precarious (Gill 2009: 9; Hall 2018). This is particularly the case for those already marginalised for reasons of gender, ethnicity and socio-economic class. In Lea's view, there tends now to be within many higher education institutions a blind corporate trust of a 'managerial template … [that] … has become the normative model of the university'. Lea critiques the possible loss of critical academic insight and objectively questioning analysis within some corporate university management situations, with a concomitant increase in the 'moral hazard' (*ibid.*) that may emerge within corporations overly wedded to a marketised economically-focused corporate managerial model (Lea 2011:835–6). It is important to consider the potentially damaging nature of micromanagement in such environments and the ways in which some excessively controlling forms of higher education authority may be perceived by inappropriately 'micro-managed' staff and students as cruel and humiliating. Resultant feelings of alienation may negatively impact on academic staff well-being, happiness and success. A lack of empathy and understanding amongst those who ambitiously gravitate upwards towards ever greater power in institutions, seeking self-aggrandising authority and status, may result in staff lower down the hierarchy feeling bullied, overlooked and undermined by managers.

Kindness, Moral Resistance and Negative Capability

In the above context, this chapter was developed from the research questions: *'how and why do academic staff talk to each other with kindness to support mutual survival from experiences of poor management in higher education? Is this just gossip?'* This issue emerged spontaneously from selected data analysis of trust and leadership interviews and surveys and from extensive spontaneous observations of informal discussions experienced by the author over many years at gatherings involving academics from across the UK. These conversations are broadly classifiable as 'critical corridor talk' (Jameson 2018). This informal, spontaneously occurring 'talk' amongst academics is a form of persistent counter-discourse against the instrumentalist goal-driven rhetoric of managers in some institutions (Leach 1997). It could also be defined with reference to 'mass intellectuality' as a form of reciprocal dialogic liberation from the oppression of excessive, inappropriately enacted managerial control (Hall and Winn 2017). The identified form of talk is, in ideal situations, mutually respectful and egalitarian, engaging in a truthful, vulnerable and compassionate *'I-Thou'* dialogic exchange. This is in strong contrast to the painfully mechanistic and anonymised *'I-It'* environment of some corporatised institutions, in which staff feel undervalued as human beings (Buber 1958).

The ongoing critical talk identified, with its concomitant tensions, seemed to involve staff and students from many different institutions from across the UK, including management, academics, support staff and post-graduate students. It echoed the troublesome notes of 'displaced dissent' captured in the margins of the author's prior auto-ethnographic experiences (Jameson 2010; 2011a, b) from more than two decades of research and professional experience of higher education and was observed by the author to occur across many geographically dispersed institutions at various levels.

Methodological Considerations

However, such corridor talk was resistant to formal quantitative data collection and analysis, since, as soon as one tried to pin it down through quantitative methods, the phenomenon seemed mostly to disappear from sustained scrutiny, hence suggesting a need for qualitative data collection and the employment of reflective methods. Such elusive informal counter-discourse appeared to emerge spontaneously as soon as academics had a secure space in which they felt safe to talk privately together. This occurred, for example, in lunch or exercise breaks, in unofficial corridor chats, informal pre-meeting gatherings and in post-event drinks and journey talks, as a form of 'letting off steam' in resistance to the institutional formalities of never-ending metrics, monitoring, regulatory scrutiny, and the governmentality of performative self-monitoring (Ball 2003; Foucault 1991; Leathwood and Read 2009).

Paradoxically, it almost seemed as if, everywhere that the phenomenon could *not* officially be identified and recorded through research observation, there it was, strongly present again, whilst, for the most part, during official feedback and evaluation sessions, it seemed to vanish, instantly becoming more elusive, muted and circumspect. There were two main exceptions to this: in selected confidential, anonymised electronic surveys and in private interview settings, a good number of respondents, who indicated that there was little opportunity to voice these concerns otherwise in a safe way, expressed an unusual level of honesty and vulnerability in a sharp critique of the conditions under which they worked. Therefore, a need was identified to capture the ambiguity and subtlety of this 'critical corridor talk' through carefully chosen methods, such as confidential qualitative surveys and interviews where possible, and, where not, to reflect on and analyse what might be happening through informal observations of these exchanges. This chapter therefore gathers together reflections on the phenomenon to draw out a model for Critical Corridor Talk, building on related earlier analysis (Jameson 2018).

Reflections on Dialogic Spaces for Critical Moral Resistance

In the development of earlier definitions of 'negative capability' as non-formulaic responsiveness to uncertainty in collective academic leadership (Unger 2007; Jameson 2012, 2014), the author reflects here on the space for informal moral resistance that may be involved in these hidden dialogic exchanges, which are, arguably, a form of 'serious gossip' (Curren 2008; Leach *ibid.*). The stoical characteristics identified in Keats's elusive ideas on 'negative capability' (Scott 2005) demonstrate resilience in coping with emotional and intellectual trials, managing uncertainty through selective action, while pragmatically fulfilling essential tasks. When appropriately practised, this form of resistance appears to be a disciplined, finely balanced capability to suspend judgement and create space for reflection and exchange with others in resisting an impetuous rush either to impose a 'false necessity' via unnecessarily destructive changes or to retreat from engagement by blocking all new initiatives. It could be summarised briefly in a [modified] version of the popular idiom, 'look [and think, and check with others] before you leap'.

The author asserts that the relational functioning of critical moral resistance in dialogic spaces in higher education may be observable more within the *absences* of overt retaliatory behaviours than through any particularly discernible presence. In 'critical corridor talk', it is argued, a form of quiet alternative leadership may be operating that is to an extent deliberately unseen, may never be seen, and is arguably unknowable in its entirety, being hidden within spaces of silence and quiet dialogue. Reflecting on the literature on hidden cultures, corridor talk and silence (Leach 1997; Gill 2009), the author argues that distributed neo-collegial leadership, in its more effective manifestations, may operate almost invisibly. As Lao Tse (Laozi) allegedly asserted c. C4th BC, regarding the most effective form of leadership, 'as for the best leaders, the people do not know of their existence' (Laozi and Chen 1989). Such informal leadership, characterised by humility and grace, escapes reductively diminutive 'branding' via quantifiable metrics in the academy of knowledge, asserting in its own complex, subtle way a defiant, enduring adherence to the moral superiority of kindness as a value and a practice in higher education.

Kindness Within Informal Leadership

This widens out definitions of leadership to address the more informal, shared and quieter dimensions of leadership amongst the many definitional properties of the term. Assuming that one starts from Northouse's definition of leadership as '…a process whereby an individual influences a group of individuals to achieve a common goal' (2004, p.3), in the case of 'critical corridor talk', the process seems to be that of recovery from the trials of academic life as an *'It'* in an *'I-It'* relationship with management in a harsh environment (Buber 1958). The individuals and group comprise the academics involved, and the common goal is to achieve ongoing success, fulfilment and happiness in working life.

The distributed informal leadership of those engaged in 'critical corridor talk' is therefore like a resistance movement of those academics in higher education who do not particularly seek power for themselves, but instead seek to find alternative ways to redefine the values and meanings shaping peer group working relationships with others into more productive interactive cooperation in which differing voices are welcomed and respected. These academic staff place value on the multi-voiced dialogic experience of sharing the ways in which they define a good quality of working life in higher education, carrying out research and teaching *per se*, as a process and end in itself. They are therefore desirous of a better time, situation and place in which to work, and better values by which to live, rather than the acquisition of more personal power. They are demonstrating a form of moral quietude, the stoic virtues of temperance and moderate frugality: in the sense of 'having enough' in their current roles, rather than seeking ever greater self-aggrandisement. The dialogic aspect of this resides in its meaning-making sociocultural multi-voiced sense of agency (Wegerif and Mercer 1997) in cumulative and exploratory critical corridor talk.

The awareness and influence of this informal leadership is frequently demonstrated more by lower level or marginalised staff, who receive little high-status recognition or pay, but instead are subjected to negative criticism, control and scrutiny by managers who, ironically, are also dependent on the efforts of such staff to achieve overall institutional targets. A mainly unexpressed awareness of injustice and alienation operates here too, as a form of sustained 'silent silencing' of alienated criticism of the institution (Mathiesen 2005).

Taking place, in this context, in many ways underground, this process of 'hiding the light' of critical being in the quiet corridor talk of moral resistance struggles to uphold continuing ethical values, including particularly that of kindness, in a stoical internal determination against those that would, unthinkingly or not, capture and destroy it. On the surface, such alternative undercover leadership 'plays the game' of strategic compliance sufficiently well to survive and even thrive (Leathwood and Read 2013), without compromising the integrity of its adherents, negotiating sensible outcomes for the common good. Its proponents share resistant strategies about 'managing upwards', 'keeping your balance' and 'acting always as the adult' in their relationships with managers. To avoid becoming victims, these informal leaders tend to exercise their professional autonomy and critical judgement through the kinds of selective, ethical 'constructive subversions' identified by Ollin in her account of teachers' resistant struggles against government policy (2004).

The academics engaged in 'critical corridor talk' seem to participate in this talk and in selective 'constructive subversions' as a survival mechanism at a time of generalised uncertainty within the management of the institutions in which they work. They are also proactively resistant to the moral compromises involved in overtly adversarial power struggles within their higher education organisational environments. This response tends to shape itself in reaction to questionable behaviours amongst some of the managers in authority at the time. It can also shape itself against peer group and subordinate behaviours and indeed any difficult work situation. Yet, even in the most challenging circumstances, those practising informal distributed leadership within such 'corridor talk' recognise a continuing need for discerningly ethical self-scrutiny to avoid carelessly inappropriate over-reactions to authority from instinctively defiant subordinate positions.

Drawing on these observations, a theoretical model was designed (see also Jameson 2018) to try to capture the dynamic that seemed to be occurring across numerous institutions. Figure 19.1 demonstrates a theoretical model of the pressures that seemingly underpin and give rise to dialogic learning through the kindness of 'I-Thou' exchanges that may emerge in 'critical corridor talk'. Institutional management (IM) has key goals, targets and work demands that are identified as necessary for institutional success. Academic staff, being contractually obliged to

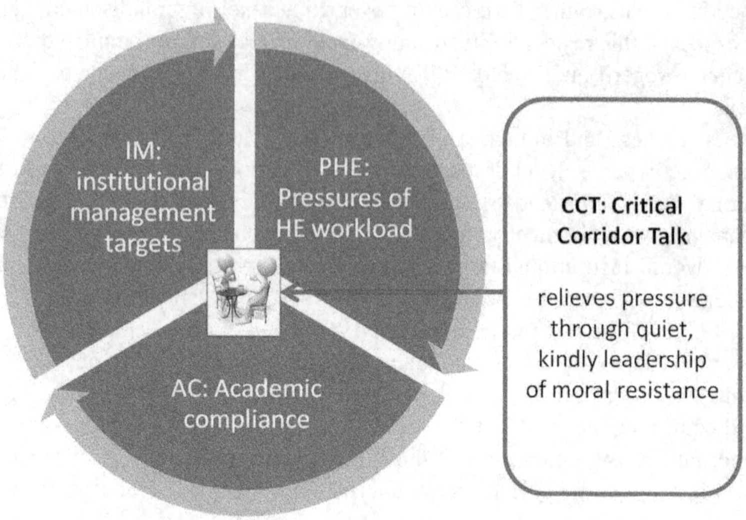

Fig. 19.1 Critical corridor talk: dialogic spaces for kindness in informal leadership

comply (AC), work towards the achievement of these goals, but numerous and increasing workload pressures in the environment (PHE) mean tension is built up, for which there is no formal release, given compliance (AC) and monitoring by both self and IM. Therefore, CCT emerges as a pressure release: an escape valve, in which both mutually respectful community engagement and dialogic learning can take place in the compassionate understanding of a proactively created safe space. The key institutional problem is that, while IM possesses the role-based authority and resources to direct status-driven power, these authorities are in some cases not acting as leaders but as goal-fixated transactional managers who have little awareness of the needs of their staff, combined with a lack of empathy. By contrast, informal leadership influence may sometimes be demonstrated by talented lower level staff who lack high-status recognition or pay but are authentically committed both to high quality work and the well-being of their fellow staff. Such emergent leaders, forming a potential threat to ineffective managers, may be ignored and side-lined from achieving any promotional opportunities. The irony of this, as indicated above, is that positional managers may be reliant on the very staff whose needs they are neglecting to meet key institutional performance goals. Hence, both institutional managers and staff, notably academics, but also others in administration and professional services, become locked into unhelpfully stressful patterns of behaviour in which the institutional environment becomes increasingly dysfunctional.

Collegial Spaces: Collective Academic Leadership

Expanding on the hypothetical model, this chapter argues that the institutional emphasis on managerialism as an arguably necessary approach to the management of large-scale higher education institutions has tended to overlook the relatively invisible collegial spaces in which emergent individual and collective academic leadership in English higher education already occurs in interactive dialogic exchange. Lea's corporate higher education 'managerial template' (Lea 2011) therefore omits to recognise this dynamic, which occurs in reaction to overt managerialism, sometimes spontaneously, frequently quietly, amongst the larger body of academic staff, regardless of status. The identification of this process recognises that the vast body of academic staffing is populated by highly intelligent, articulate, capable people who may have little official 'voice' in management (Bacon 2014; Parr 2013). Yet these staff continue, mainly in low key ways, and for the most part effectively, to lead the students, researchers, teaching sessions, research fields, subject groups, project teams, academic and enterprising initiatives that make up the greater proportion of work in higher education institutions, in what is one of the highest performing systems in the world (Hazelkorn 2015). The shared common purposes held by this wider group of academic staff, both larger than and sometimes also including relatively atypical academic managers, form a more or less 'invisible' collective form of stoic leadership, distributed extensively amongst staff, that continues to sustain and motivate higher education institutions, often without recognition or formal authority (Hickman and Sorenson 2013).

Negative Capability and 'Invisible' Leadership

The chapter argues that the complex quality of 'negative capability', including its self-reflexively critical approach, may be amongst the characteristics of the 'invisible' neo-collegial distributed academic leadership identified above that enable staff to cope with multiple contested agendas involved in responding to the supercomplexity of higher education environments (Barnett 2000). Negative capability is defined as a resiliently firm reflective capacity to resist making easy but wrong judgements in response to the 'false necessity' of performative 'quick fixes'. This reliable, somewhat understated quality insists on adhering to good practice and high standards of ethics to build long-term trust in coping proactively with ambiguity and change (Simpson and French 2006; Jameson 2012). However, the stoical aspect of this quality maintains a consistently self-questioning tolerance, combined with humility and flexibility, in its openness to innovation and change. Hence, it avoids the fixed stubborn arrogance of those who assume they are always right. The complex attribute of negative capability promotes more subtle ways of thinking about the motivations of academic leaders and managers than zero-sum conceptions of managerialism and collegiality (Tight 2014), while resisting the 'false necessity' of deterministic solutions, as Unger puts it:

> Negative capability – the power to act non-formulaically, in defiance of what rules and routines would predict, a power that may be inspired and strengthened, or discouraged and weakened ... the [mind's] power of recursive infinity and non-formulaic initiative... (Unger 2007: 134).

This chapter puts forward a model for negative capability with reference to self-reflexivity (McKenzie 2000) and non-formulaic responsiveness. Drawing on the above extensive data collected in long-term research on trust and leadership (2005–2018) amongst university staff in semi-structured interviews (n = 18), surveys (n = 140 and a focus group (n = 6) (Jameson 2012) successive findings from individual staff indicated that, paradoxically, 'less is sometimes more' regarding leadership and management visibility (see Fig. 19.2). Although 'strong' and 'visible' leadership in higher education management is frequently praised in government policy documents, it is argued here that quieter forms of relatively 'invisible' distributed leadership amongst the mass of staff may be, paradoxically, as much if not more effective in maintaining quality institutions than overt forms of corporate managerial authority.

The proposed model (see Fig. 19.2) demonstrates the stages involved in self-reflexive leadership responses to individual or organisational challenges. From (1) a resistance to the 'false necessity' of hasty conclusions/action, requiring emotional

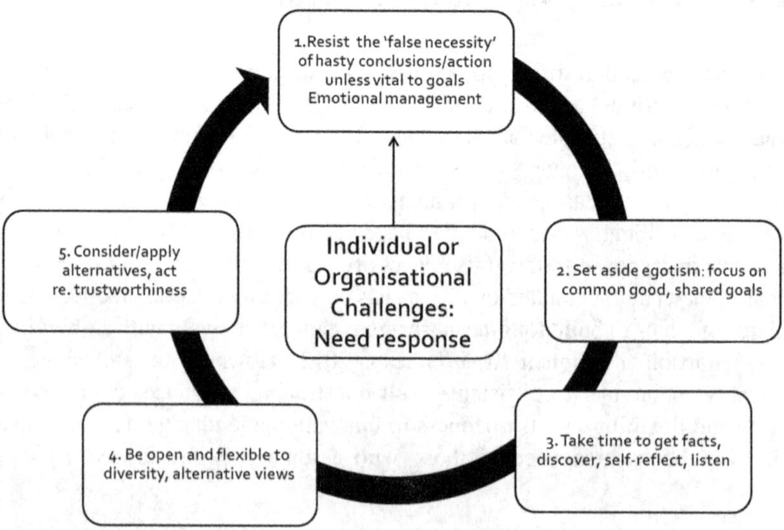

Fig. 19.2 Self-reflexive negative capability: invisible leadership in higher education

self-management, and (2) the ability to set aside egotism in focusing on the common good of shared goals, (3) time is taken to obtain facts, discover, self-reflect and listen, with (4) openness and flexibility regarding diversity of opinions, in order that (5) more considered solutions are achieved which result in continuously improved outcomes and action that fosters trustworthiness.

Creating Dialogic Spaces for Kindness

Within the critical corridor talk identified, therefore, a form of semi-invisible resistant mass leadership amongst academics in higher education is arguably taking place in the mutuality of dialogic exchange. It is this capacity for reflective awareness, negotiated within the strictures of performative academic environments, that is creating necessary spaces for kindness and compassion, protecting those who feel voiceless, marginalised and over-regulated within low trust academic environments. As an example of the type of situation reported in the empirical data, this respondent to one of the surveys on low trust situations noted the lack of compassion demonstrated by senior management to staff in his university, even to the unexpected death of a former staff member:

> Regarding lack of compassion, let me give an example. Last year, a much-liked head of department who had left the university died unexpectedly. There was no recognition among senior managers of the impact this may have had on staff, and the only concession to decency was an email sent by the senior manager's PA copying an email (incorrectly!) that another member of staff had posted (Survey respondent #20, UK university, 2015).

This senior lecturer academic respondent to the surveys was amongst a large minority of respondents who identified, either directly or implicitly, a need for more emotional intelligence, kindness and compassion in the institutional management of people working in higher education institutions. He commented of his institution that relationships between management and staff were: "Poor – staff are treated as expendable costs within the organisation" and that the institution was characterised by 'authority-compliance management – high concern for task, but low concern for people'. He recorded that he had a 'total lack of trust' in senior managers to look after the well-being of staff members (*ibid.*).

This kind of example from the data was replicated in the responses of many others who had no official voice to speak out about or change such issues. For example, in response to the survey question *Q23: "What kinds of leadership behaviours have built trust in your team and/or organisation generally? Can you give examples?"*, respondent #103, an older female administrative staff member in a post-1992 university in England, observed that there was a need for: "Openness; ability to synthesise evidence from a range of sources; intuition and empathy", while respondent #97, a white male aged 51–60 in a modern university in East England, felt that "Discussion and gaining a shared understanding" built trust, and respondent #91, a male head of department aged 41–50 in a higher and further education college in

London, said that trust was built by leaders who were: "Role models demonstrating integrity, confidentiality, loyalty and supporting staff in difficulties."

In response to the survey question *Q20: "Thinking about why you responded this way, can you say who you trust at work and who trusts you?"*, respondent #79, a white female senior lecturer from a university in the South East of England, said that she trusted:

> A group of colleagues [with] who[m] it has been possible to, over time, develop a shared sense of desire for a better working environment. Also two or three colleagues that I have intuitively accepted as being trustworthy ... There are pockets of staff trying to work professionally but no particular identifiable group. Many staff seek out other staff that they can communicate with on a higher level of trust; this frequently has no relationship to role or status. Many become insular in order to avoid unprofessional treatment or circumstances (Survey respondent #79, UK university).

The type of dialogic space for kindness and shared exchange identified by survey respondent #79 was deliberately created and nurtured by her as a form of survivalist strategic resistance to what she identified as her institution's highly incompetent, unprofessional senior staff. The managers she encountered in her workplace were, in her view, "blundering incompetent bullies" who "do not value staff; they are reported to frequently say discriminatory things and publicly criticise staff ... they show incompetence in their roles and display unprofessional behaviours". In order to cope in this dysfunctional working environment, in which she could neither complain nor radically change the management, she summed up her approach:

> "I work towards enabling staff to be trustworthy by setting an example and enforcing professional behaviours. When staff feel secure they feel more at ease. If the assumption is to trust, then that usually snowballs, if a member of staff fails to behave in an appropriate manner then that has to be dealt with firmly but fairly. If that is done, levels of trust tend to increase (Survey respondent #79, UK university).

Summing up the situation on values practised in higher education from her point of view, respondent #19, a part-time female lecturer in a university in the South East of England, identified sectoral level changes to institutional values demonstrated or not by senior leaders:

> Leadership in HE used to be about academic respect – a valuing of this kind of expertise but that also went with support that is no longer there. There is a lack of mindful thought, a desire to grab at promotion or to be a manager and these managers are not necessarily good academics. Conversely good academics do not necessarily make good leaders. I am concerned now that the values of leadership currently in place in HE demand accountability for others but not for self, seem frequently about rising up a ladder or getting monies/prestige rather than being about actually having genuine self-knowledge and awareness that nurtures others and supports creativity and success. This is not a caring environment to work in and that is something that needs to be created because although it is possible to do well, loyalty is in short supply (Survey respondent #19, UK university).

The need for a caring environment in which to work seemed to be a strong driver for such staff, who benefited from the dialogic spaces in which they were able to cultivate quiet reflection and mutual respect together. The mere act of responding to an anonymous research survey on trust and leadership therefore seemed to have had some appeal for these participants, as an outlet for the expression of instances of problematic concerns that might otherwise go unreported. For example, the following survey responses, gathered together to give a series of snapshots, were just 20 typical replies from those received within the 53 written comments in reply to the question, *'What kinds of leadership behaviours have reduced trust between staff in your team and/or organisation? Can you give examples?'* (Q24: Trust and Leadership survey 2011–2018, with each respondent's number in brackets) (Fig. 19.3).

In the above instances, the need for improved levels of concern for others, integrity, trustworthiness, generosity and honesty in the management of the institution is a vivid implicit demonstration of a lack of kindness operating within the institution. Respondents had a range of tactics to cope with deficient situations in which there was low trust.

What seems to be in evidence here is the kind of 'silent silencing' of this cultural underlife of counter-discourse into the overt and inert forms of cultural acquiescence that Mathiesen (2005) identifies, in which the respite offered by kindness to those who feel silenced from the expression of any critique resides in the quieter circles of the invisibilised informal leadership. A number of respondents directly addressed the fact that they did not feel confident either to criticise management or to speak of that voicelessness. Many alluded to the problematic gap between man-

- Very, very subtle ethnic differentiation (#1)
- Lack of communication (#2)
- Not delivering on promises and not making decisions about things that affect my future (#3)
- Decisions made behind my back (#5)
- Neo-liberal performativity. Measurement of performance by numbers and simplistic reading of data. Management forget what it is like to be at the other end. (#6)
- Withholding information different versions for different audiences (#7)
- Lack of communication, lack of transparency, lack of inclusivity, failure to hear messages (#8)
- Rushed decisions (#9)
- A clique being created: insiders /outsiders; lack of integrity; poor communication; limited (#10)
- Interference/micro-management and inconsistency. (#11)
- Divide and conquer from senior management. (#12)
- Falsehoods given by senior management, such as security of employment. (#13)
- Underhand ways of reorganising staffing - not being "straight" about unacceptable performance and using underhand ways of "getting rid" of staff (#14)
- Rushed decisions, occasional lapses in communication (#15)
- Making expedient decisions without due consultation or explanation. (#16)
- Self interest (#17)
- Managers here have no idea what the staff do they just want results and you never see them unless something has gone very wrong (#18)
- Constant restructures and pruning of capable staff. Lack of transparency about HR processes and decision making in general. (#19)
- Saying one thing and doing another. Showing complete distrust of staff by actions/behaviour or lack of action/behaviour. When staff give their time or make an extra effort, there is no acknowledgement or reward. Saying 'everyone' is getting a certain percentage bonus and top management taking significantly more than 'everyone'. Amending minutes and notes that go to Governors. (#20)

Fig. 19.3 Responses to survey question on leadership behaviours reducing trust

agement and staff, as in the example of respondent #11, a male lecturer aged 41–50 in a Russell Group university in London, who replied to *Q3: "How far is there a culture of trust? e.g. do staff trust senior managers and do senior managers trust staff?"*, by saying, "There is a culture of separating the two. The senior management makes decisions without even a pretence of consultation with staff." This respondent went on to say that losses to his university had occurred to cause this: "There are aftershocks following the loss of income (fees). Communications use the rhetoric of loss of income, impoverished institutions in order to implement radical changes at the expense of employees. Interestingly this applies to Russell Group wealthy universities as well." (ibid.)

Respondents' views on the need for understage critical dialogic spaces for kindness, reflection and mutual learning therefore seemed to be come from differing situations across many different types of higher education institutions in different geographical locations. Although the extent of spread and impact of this issue in higher education is not currently quantifiable from the limitations of this small, long-term theoretical, mixed method, mainly qualitative study, it provides useful information to follow up in future research.

Conclusion

In other words, a rather strange situation may be going on in some of the institutions in which respondents were (and in many cases still are) working. While managers are overtly in charge, collective informal distributed leadership, enacted in elusive forms of counter-discourse amongst some highly-functioning but often lower status academics, exerted hidden influence, 'upwards managing the managers' behind the scenes. The ways in which this seems to occur is not particularly visible anywhere, never being formally discussed, yet many, at various levels, seem to be aware of it, through the critical corridor talk that is secret between them. These conversations, exchanged amongst the mutually wounded, are about stoical forms of strategic survival, demonstrating morally resistant behavioural values of compassion, mutual understanding and kindly advice: academics swap stories of the good or bad, latest developments and tactics, give and are given advice in return. The secret informal knowledge transmitted does not officially exist in the organisation, although anecdotally it is recognised as instrumental in academic success, failure, survival and change.

As discussed in this chapter, negative capability is a stoic capacity (Curren 2008) to withstand difficulties in balancing uncertainties, underpinning the tacit knowledge and moral support for resistance shared between academics that is crucial for survival. Through the secret language of survival talk that is not just gossip but a creative form of dialogic counter-discourse exchanged with colleagues in critical corridor chats, important understandings are aired and swapped. What seems to distinguish this form of critical talk from mindless gossip is that it is a shared, mutually respectful series of truthful exchanges in which multi-voiced dialogic learning is taking place as academic identities are being healed and reformed. This occurs through the vulnerabilities of recounting deeply felt working difficulties in an *'I-Thou'* highly trusting relationship. In this, mutual survival tactics collectively discussed in the kindness and acceptance of behavioural integrity and compassion for the other is the aim. Such talk is therefore neither trivial nor superficial, though undoubtedly there may occur both lighter moments of playfulness and also forms of negotiated disputation. Further auto-ethnographic and mixed method research may explore and capture more of the ambiguous, subtle dynamics at play when the kindness of 'critical corridor talk' emerges to help academics cope with increasing pressures. However, the informal leadership involved needs to engage also with self-critical monitoring, always observing ethical principles, to foster trust when resisting the apparently manufactured performativity of some higher education environments in which some of those in power overstep the acceptable boundaries of good management.

References

Bacon, E. (2014). *Neo-collegiality: Restoring academic engagement in the managerial university.* London: The Leadership Foundation for Higher Education.

Ball, S. J. (2003). The teacher's soul and the terrors of performativity. *Journal of Education Policy, 18*(2), 215–228.

Barnett, R. (1997). *Higher education: A critical business.* Buckingham: SRHE/Open University Press.

Barnett, R. (2000). *Realizing the university in an age of supercomplexity.* Buckingham: Society for Research into Higher Education/Open University Press.

Bolden, R., Petrov, G., & Gosling, J. (2008). *Developing collective leadership in higher education.* London: Leadership Foundation for Higher Education.

Buber, M. (1958). *I and thou.* New York: Charles Scribner's Sons.

Clarke, J., & Newman, J. (1997). *The managerial state: Power, politics and ideology in the remaking of social welfare.* London: Sage.

Clegg, S., & Rowland, S. (2010). Kindness in pedagogical practice and academic life. *British Journal of Sociology of Education, 31*(6), 719–735.

Curren, R. (Ed.). (2008). *A companion to the philosophy of education. Blackwell companions to philosophy.* Oxford: Blackwell Publishing.

Daza, S. L. (2012). Complicity as infiltration: The (im)possibilities of research with/in nsf engineering grants in the age of neoliberal scientism. *Qualitative Inquiry, 18*(9), 773–786.

Deem, R. (1998). New managerialism in higher education: The management of performances and cultures in universities. *International Studies in Sociology of Education, 8*(1), 47–70.

Deem, R., & Brehony, K. J. (2005). Management as ideology: The case of 'new managerialism' in higher education. *Oxford Review of Education, 31*(2), 217–235.

Deem, R., Hillyard, S., & Reed, M. (2007). *Knowledge, higher education, and the new managerialism: The changing management of UK universities.* Oxford: Oxford University Press.

Elton, L. (2008). Collegiality and complexity: Humboldt's relevance to British universities today. *Higher Education Quarterly, 62,* 224–236.

Foucault, M. (1991). *The Foucault effect: Studies in governmentality.* Chicago: University of Chicago Press.

Freire, P. (1972) *Pedagogy of the oppressed* Myra Bergman Ramos, Trans.). New York: Herder.

Gill, R. (2009). Breaking the silence: The hidden injuries of neo-liberal academia. In R. Flood & R. Gill (Eds.), *Secrecy and silence in the research process: Feminist reflections.* London: Routledge.

Hall, R. (2014). On the abolition of academic labour: The relationship between intellectual workers and mass intellectuality. tripleC: Communication, capitalism & critique. *Open Access Journal for a Global Sustainable Information Society, 12*(2), 822–837.

Hall, R. (2018). On the alienation of academic labour and the possibilities for mass intellectuality. *tripleC: Communication, Capitalism & Critique. Open Access Journal for a Global Sustainable Information Society, 16*(1), 97–113.

Hall, R., & Winn, J. (Eds.). (2017). *Mass intellectuality and democratic leadership in higher education*. London: Bloomsbury Academic.

Hazelkorn, E. (2015). *Rankings and the reshaping of higher education: The battle for world-class excellence*. Basingstoke: Palgrave Macmillan.

Henkel, M. (1997). Shifting boundaries and the academic profession. In M. Kogan and U. Teichler (Eds.), *Key challenges to the academic profession* (pp. 191–204). Paris.

Hickman, G. R., & Sorenson, G. J. (2013). *The power of invisible leadership: How a compelling common purpose inspires exceptional leadership* (pp. 2–3). London: Sage.

Jameson, J. (2008). *Leadership: Professional communities of leadership practice in post-compulsory education*. Stirling University: ESCalate: Discussions in Education Series, The Higher Education Subject Centre for Education.

Jameson, J. (2010). Trust & leadership in post-compulsory education: Some snapshots of displaced dissent. *Power in Education Journal, 2*(2), 48–62. Accessed 19 Sept 2018: http://www.wwwords.co.uk/rss/abstract.asp?j=power&aid=4028.

Jameson, J. (2011a). Dance like a butterfly, sting like a bee: Moments of trust, power and heautogogic leadership in post-compulsory education. In J. Satterthwaite, H. Piper, P. Sikes, & S. Webster (Eds.), *Trust in education: Truth and values*. Stoke on Trent: Trentham Books.

Jameson, J. (2011b). *Trust, the visibility/invisibity leadership paradox, and a model for reflective negative capability in the academic management of english higher education*. Society for Research into Higher Education (SRHE) Annual conference. Accessed 19 Sept 2018. https://doi.org/10.13140/RG.2.1.1954.7605.

Jameson, J. (2012). Leadership values, trust and negative capability: Managing the uncertainties of future English higher education. *Higher Education Quarterly, 66*(4), 391–414.

Jameson, J. (2014). Why we need distributed, transformational e-leadership and Trust in the Fifth age of educational media and technology. In J. Viteli & M. Leikomaa (Eds.), *Proceedings of EdMedia 2014–world conference on educational media and technology* (pp. 14–28). Tampere, Finland: Association for the Advancement of Computing in Education (AACE). Retrieved March 27, 2019, https://www.learntechlib.org/p/148035/.

Jameson, J. (2018). Critical corridor talk: Just gossip or stoic resistance? Unrecognised informal higher education leadership. *Higher Education Quarterly, 72*(4), 375–389. https://onlinelibrary.wiley.com/doi/full/10.1111/hequ.12174.

Keats, J., in Scott, G. F. (Ed.) (2005). *Selected letters of John Keats: Based on the texts of Hyder Edward Rollins*. Boston: Harvard University Press.

Laozi, & Chen, E. M. (1989). *The Tao Te Ching: A new translation with commentary*. St. Paul: Paragon House.

Lea, D. R. (2011). The managerial university and the decline of modern thought. *Educational Philosophy and Theory, 43*(8), 816–837.

Leach, M. (1997). Feminist figurations: Gossip as a counter discourse. *International Journal of Qualitative Studies in Education, 10*(3), 305–314.

Leathwood, C., & Read, B. (2009). *Gender and the changing face of higher education: A feminised future? Maidenhead*. Surrey: Society for Research into Higher Education/ Open University Press.

Leathwood, C., & Read, B. (2012). *Assessing the impact of developments in research policy for research on higher education: An exploratory study. Research report*. London: Society for Research into Higher Education. Retrieved 27th March, 2019 from: https://www.srhe.ac.uk/downloads/Leathwood_Read_Final_Report_16_July_2012.pdf.

Leathwood, C., & Read, B. (2013). Research policy and academic performativity: Compliance, contestation and complicity. *Studies in Higher Education, 38*(8), 1162–1174.

Lucas, L. (2014). Academic resistance to quality assurance processes in higher education in the UK. *Policy and Society, 33*, 3.

Marginson, S. (2011). Higher education and public good. *Higher Education Quarterly, 65*(4), 411–433.

Mathiesen, T. (2005). *Silently silenced: Essays on the creation of acquiescence in modern society.* Hook: Waterside Press.

McKenzie, T. (2000). Supercomplexity and the need for a practice and scholarship of self-reflexiveness in university research and teaching. *Staff and Educational Development International, 4*(3), 205–216.

McNay, I. (2005). Managing institutions in a Mass HE system. In I. McNay (Ed.), *Beyond mass higher education: Building on experience.* Maidenhead: SRHE/Open University Press.

Ollin, R. (2005). Professionals, poachers or street level bureaucrats: Government policy, teaching identities and constructive subversions. In *Discourses of education in the age of imperialism* (pp. 151–162). Trentham Books.

Parr, C. (2013). The best University workplace survey: Staff unheard? *Times Higher Education, 15*(August), 51–62.

Renshaw, P. D. (2004). Dialogic learning teaching and instruction. In *Dialogic learning* (pp. 1–15). Dordrecht: Springer.

Simpson, P., & French, R. (2006). Negative capability and the capacity to think in the present moment: Some implications for leadership practice. *Leadership, 2*(2), 245–255.

Simpson, P., French, R., & Harvey, C. (2002). Leadership and negative capability. *Human Relations, 55*(10), 1209–1226.

Slaughter, S., & Leslie, L. (1997). *Academic capitalism: Politics, policies and the entrepreneurial university.* Baltimore: Johns Hopkins University Press.

Slaughter, S., & Rhoades, G. (2004). *Academic capitalism and the new economy: Markets, state, and higher education.* Baltimore: Johns Hopkins University Press.

Tapper, T., & Palfreyman, D. (2002). Understanding collegiality: The changing Oxbridge model. *Tertiary Education and Management, 8*(1), 47–63.

Thaler, R. H. (2000). From homo economicus to homo sapiens. *The Journal of Economic Perspectives, 14*(1), 133–141.

Thornton, M. (2009). Academic un-freedom in the new knowledge economy. In A. Brew & L. Lucas (Eds.), *Academic research and researchers* (pp. 19–34). Maidenhead: SRHE and Open University Press.

Tight, M. (2014). Collegiality and managerialism: A false dichotomy? Evidence from the higher education literature. *Tertiary Education and Management, 20*(4), 294–306.

Trowler, P. R. (1998). *Academics responding to change. New higher education frameworks and academic cultures.* London: Society for Research into Higher Education, Ltd. Open University Press Imprint.

UNESCO. (n.d.). Forum on Higher Education Research and Knowledge and the International Centre for Higher Education Research Kassel, INCHER-Kassel. http://portal.unesco.org/education/en/files/54977/11970234265Key_Challanges_Academic_Profession_REV.pdf/Key_Challanges_Academic_Profession_REV.pdf.

Unger, R. M. (2007). *The self awakened: Pragmatism unbound.* Cambridge, MA: Harvard University Press.

Wegerif, R., & Mercer, N. (1997). A dialogical framework for investigating talk. In R. Wegerif & P. Scrimshaw (Eds.), *Computers and talk in the primary classroom* (pp. 49–65). Clevedon: Multilingual Matters.

Author Biographies (in Order of Chapters)

Part One

David Scott is Professor of Curriculum, Pedagogy and Assessment at University College London, Institute of Education. His three most recent books are: (with B. Scott) Equalities and Inequalities in the English Education System, University College London, Institute of Education Press; (with C. Posner, C. Martin and E. Guzman) The Mexican Education System, University College London Press; and (with S. Leaton-Gray and P. Mehisto) Curriculum Reform in the European Schools: Towards a twenty-first century Vision, Palgrave MacMillan. His work can be positioned within some elements of critical realism.

Paul Gibbs is professor of Middlesex University, founder of the Centre for Education Research and Scholarship, a Distinguished Professor at the Open University in Hong Kong, visiting Professor at the University of Technology, Sydney and Visiting Fellow of the Centre for Higher Education Policy, New College, Oxford. He has published four books in the last 2 years: *Transdisciplinary Higher Education*; *Why Universities Should Seek Happiness and Contentment*, the *Pedagogy of Compassion at the Heart of Higher Education* and *Transdisciplinary Theory, Practice and Education: The Art of Collaborative Research and Collective Learning*. Paul has four more books in various stages of production and is also Series Editor of SpringerBriefs on Key Thinkers in Education and Debating Higher Education: Philosophical Perspectives for Springer Academic Press and Editor-in-Chief of Higher Education Quarterly. Paul is a founder board member of the Philosophy and Theory of Higher Education Association

© Springer Nature Switzerland AG 2019
P. Gibbs et al. (eds.), *Values of the University in a Time of Uncertainty*,
https://doi.org/10.1007/978-3-030-15970-2

Part Two

Ronald Barnett is Emeritus Professor of Higher Education, University College London Institute of Education. He has produced over 30 books on the philosophy of higher education, his latest sole-authored work being his idea of the university: *The Ecological University: A Feasible Utopia*. His books have been translated into several languages and many have won prizes. He has been described as 'one of the most eloquent defenders of the university of reason'. He is the inaugural recipient of the EAIR Award for 'Outstanding Contribution to Higher Education Research, Policy and Practice' and has been an invited keynote speaker in 40 countries.

Alex Elwick is a researcher at Middlesex University and a lecturer at UCL Institute of Education. His work is concerned with education policy and social justice at national/regional (government) and local (institutional) levels. He has published on topics including the Prevent policy in education; values and value statements in universities; and urban school system reform. His AHRC-funded doctorate explored learning in art galleries and he has been a British Research Council Fellow at the Kluge Center, Library of Congress, Washington DC.

Kate Maguire is Associate Professor of Professional Practice in the Faculty of Professional and Social Sciences at Middlesex University and head of its transdisciplinary research degree programmes. Her background is social anthropology of the Middle East and organisational psychology both as a researcher and practitioner. Coming into higher education from careers in journalism, political research and trauma studies she has engaged with anthropologically informed innovative research methodologies and research pedagogy relevant to professional practice research with particular interest in bridging difference, embracing complexity and theorising professional practice particularly ethics in practice to enhance professional learning and organisational change. She has led on field work design and implementation for a number of projects and innovations, journals and books and has lectured all over the world.

Ian McNay is Professor Emeritus, Higher Education and Management, University of Greenwich. He has run programmes on leadership, management and organisation culture in universities in over 20 countries. He approaches this from the bottom up, from the perspective of the led, the managed. Other research interests have been in widening participation and progression, and the impact of research quality assessment. His career started as an administrator and policy advisor in the UK and in Business Education in a Brussels-based European organisation and ESADE, Barcelona. He became an academic at age 35, joining the Open University, and he has also held a chair at the, now, Anglia Ruskin University.

Simon Robinson Rev. Professor Robinson, educated at Oxford and Edinburgh Universities, entered university chaplaincy and then lectured in Edinburgh and Leeds Universities. In 2004 he joined Leeds Beckett University as Professor of Applied and Professional Ethics. His books include: *Values in Higher Education; Islam and the West; Spirituality and the Practice of Healthcare; Spirituality, Ethics and Care; Leadership Responsibility; The Practice of Business Ethics;*

Co-Charismatic Leadership; The Practice of Integrity in Business; The Spirituality of Responsibility. Simon is Director of the Research Centre for Governance, Leadership and Global Responsibility, Leeds Business School, and Editor in Chief of the *Journal of Global Responsibility.*

Sabina Siebert is Professor of Management at the Adam Smith Business School, University of Glasgow UK. Her research interests include organisational trust and distrust, professions, and management in the creative industries. She employs a range of qualitative methodologies including discourse analysis, narrative analysis and organisational ethnography. Recently she has researched an ancient profession – Scottish advocates (a paper based on this study was published in the Academy of Management Journal). Currently, as an Academic Fellow of the UK Parliament, she is studying the institutional consequences of the proposed move of Parliament to a temporary location. In collaboration with Barbara Czarniawska, she is also researching the careers of secret service agents drawing on spies' biographies.

Carolina Guzmán-Valenzuela is an Associate Professor at the Institute of Education senior researcher at the Centre for Advanced Research in Education at the University of Chile. She has led competitive research projects on (i) academic identities, (ii) the role of universities in the twenty-first century and their links to the state and the knowledge economy, (iii) the relationships between teaching and learning in higher education; and (iv) the production of knowledge from a geopolitical perspective. She collaborates with various international research networks in higher education. She has published in leading journals and books. She is frequently invited to give seminars and contribute to international conferences.

Part Three

Victoria de Rilke: Dr. de Rijke is Associate Professor at Middlesex University, where she is Director of CERS, the Centre for Education Research and Scholarship. Her own research and publication is transdisciplinary, across the fields of literature and the arts, children's literature, play, pedagogy and animal studies, through the associations of metaphor. Examples of co-edited works include *Nose Book: Representations of the Nose in the Arts and Literature,* (2000) and *The Impossibility of Art Education,* (1999). *Playful research for DUCK (2008), SUPERTOYS: A User's Manual,* (2008) and *This Book is Intentionally Blank* (1990) also formed artworks exhibited at national and international galleries. *The A-Z of Dangerous Food* (2012) is an example of several artworks, publications and events co-produced with Rebecca Sinker at Tate Gallery, London, such as *"The Empty Box" Playground, PG4* (2015) and the *ART IS...PLAY event* (2016). Defence of playful learning and the arts is her life's work.

Martin G. Erikson is Associate Professor of Psychology at University of Borås, Sweden. He completed his PhD in Psychology in 2006 at Lund University, Sweden, with a thesis about the self in relation to motivation. His research is currently focused on various aspects of higher education, and the intersection between higher education and science studies. Recent publications have concerned practices and concepts of higher education, covering a wide scope from student motivation to critical thinking, including an interest in consequences of educational practice and academic values for educational policy and conceptions of educational quality. Erikson has also held an academic leadership position as Chair of the Research and Education Board at the University of Borås since 2012.

Jon Nixon is Honorary Professor within the Lifelong Learning Research and Development Centre of the Education University of Hong Kong and Visiting Professor within the School of Education and Health at Middlesex University, UK. He writes in the areas of intellectual history and the philosophy of higher education. His recently authored books include *Rosa Luxemburg and the Struggle for Democratic Renewal* (Pluto Press, 2018) and *Hannah Arendt and the Politics of Friendship* (Bloomsbury 2015). He has also recently edited *Higher Education in Austerity Europe* (Bloomsbury 2017).

Abdullah Sahin is a reader in Islamic education at the Centre for Education Studies (CES), University of Warwick, UK. Dr. Sahin is a member of the Warwick Religions and Education Research Unit at CES and the course leader for MA in Religions, Society and Education (Islamic Education Pathway). Dr. Sahin comes from an Islamic studies, theology, educational studies and social sciences background. He has conducted research on religious identity formation among British Muslim youth and his work aims to establish Islamic Education Studies as an interdisciplinary field of empirical research, scholarship and professional development. He has taught at the universities of Birmingham and Aberdeen and the Gulf University for Science and Technology (Kuwait). Dr. Sahin has produced numerous scholarly publications on Islam and education. His most recently published book is entitled New Directions in Islamic Education: Pedagogy and Identity Formation (Kube Academic, Leicester, Rev. Imprint 2014).

Alison Scott-Baumann is Professor of Society and Belief in the Centre of Islamic Studies in the Near and Middle East Department at SOAS and her work has two interrelated and also distinct research strands, social justice and philosophy. Her research has recently been recognised and rewarded by world-class research grants from Leverhulme (2012–2013), ESRC (2012–2013) and AHRC (2015–2018). Alison applies philosophy to social justice issues, regarding Islam, higher education and feminist debates. She is also known internationally for her philosophical research and was awarded a Leverhulme Fellowship for original research on Ricoeur, Kant and Sartre (2012–2013). She works extensively on Ricoeur and is an invited member of the Conseil Scientifique of the Fonds Ricoeur in Paris. She publishes regularly on Ricoeur and speaks frequently at international conferences in Europe and USA. She is a Visiting Researcher in the Politics, Philosophy and Religion Department at Lancaster University and a Visiting Researcher at VU Amsterdam University in the Centre for Islamic Theology.

Part Four

María Cristina Sierras-Davó is a PhD Candidate at the Faculty of Health Sciences, University of Alicante in Spain. Her research interests are focused on Healthcare Improvement Science and Quality Improvement in Practice contexts. Her PhD research is nowadays concentrating on developing an Improvement Science Evaluation Framework for Health Professions and Evaluation Tools for Healthcare Improvement Science Learning. She has a Master Degree in Nursing Research and recently, she also got her Master Degree in Business Administration. Nowadays she is working as a Clinical Trial Assistant at Janssen (Johnson&Johnson) and has previous experience as clinical nurse as well as Study Coordinator in Clinical Trials. Along her carreer she obtained two research grants associated to her participation as Assistant and Early Stage Researcher in the European Commission funded project named as ISTEW European Project.

Manuel Lillo-Crespo is an Associate Professor and International Mobility Coordinator at the Faculty of Health Sciences, University of Alicante in Spain. He is also part of the Management Team at Vistahermosa HLA Hospital in Alicante and recently appointed as Fellow of the Royal College of Surgeons in Ireland. He is a Phd in Health and Medical Anthropology with experience in: Clinical and Healthcare Management and Administration, Healthcare and Quality Improvement Science, Qualitative and Mixed Methods and Educational Research applied to Practice Healthcare Contexts. Nowadays, he is an active researcher and team lead on different International and European Commission funded Projects such as: ISTEW Project; Palliare Project, PPS Project, Multidimensional Analytical Training in Education, HEALINT Project and a DAPHNE Project. He has mentored over 10 PhD Dissertations, has more than 60 publications in scientific.

Kathryn Waddington's current research interests include emotion in organisations, and the practices that promote and sustain compassion in action. She began her professional career in nursing at Kings College Hospital in London and has a PhD in Psychology from the University of London where she investigated the characteristics and role of gossip in nursing and healthcare organisations. She has published widely including the research monograph *Gossip and Organisations* (2012), and numerous articles and chapters which examine the role of gossip in organisational culture and climate, and its value as an under-used but important early warning signal of organisational failure.

Frances Maratos is Associate Professor/Reader in Emotion Science at the University of Derby. Her research is centred on understanding psychological, neurological, cognitive and physiological correlates of emotional well-being, with a specific focus on understanding threat-processing and the use of compassion for emotion-regulation. She has published over 20 papers in these specific areas, as well as a number of book chapters. In recent years she has also become a key individual within the compassion in schools movement, helping initiate and progress associated international research programmes.

Paul Gilbert, FBPsS, PhD, OBE is Professor of Clinical Psychology at the University of Derby and honorary visiting Prof at the University of Queensland. Until his retirement (2016) he was also an NHS Consultant Clinical Psychologist. Paul's research focus includes evolutionary approaches to psychopathology including mood, shame and self-criticism from which he developed Compassion Focused Therapy. He is a Fellow of the British Psychological Society, president of the BABCP 2002–2004, and was awarded an OBE in 2011 for services to mental health. He has written/edited 21 books and over 250 papers/book chapters. In 2006 he established the Compassionate Mind Foundation.

Theo Gilbert is Associate Professor in Teaching and Learning, at the University of Hertfordshire. His research translates rich, current scholarship on the psychobiological model of compassion into evidence-based, practical micro-skills of compassion for group-work that can be taught, supported and assessed (i.e. credit-bearing) on the modern University degree. He trains HE educators from both STEM and social sciences in this approach, and is networking and supporting staff in, so far, 35 universities. He is creator of the Compassion in HE website of practical resources for compassion-focused educators: https://compassioninhe.wordpress.com/. His research is published in a number of journals and book chapters.

Jill Jameson is Professor of Education and Chair/Director, Centre for Leadership and Enterprise, Faculty of Education and Health, University of Greenwich, a Visiting Fellow (2018) and Associate (2018–2021) of Lucy Cavendish College, University of Cambridge and an Associate Member, Cambridge Educational Dialogues Research Group, Faculty of Education, University of Cambridge. Chair of the Society for Research into Higher Education (2012–2017), and Convenor for the Post-Compulsory and Lifelong Learning SIG, British Educational Research Association (BERA, 2011–2013), Jill has published widely in education and is Editor of a forthcoming book on *Global Leadership in Higher Education* (Routledge) for the OXCHEPs Series: International Studies on Higher Education, New College, University of Oxford.

Index

CPSIA information can be obtained
at www.ICGtesting.com
Printed in the USA
LVHW080900300619
622769LV00013B/267/P